The Political Economy of Development

Political Economy and Development

Published in association with the International Initiative for Promoting Political Economy (IIPPE)

Edited by
Ben Fine (SOAS, University of London)
Dimitris Milonakis (University of Crete)

Political economy and the theory of economic and social development have long been fellow travellers, sharing an interdisciplinary and multidimensional character. Over the last 50 years, mainstream economics has become totally formalistic, attaching itself to increasingly narrow methods and techniques at the expense of other approaches. Despite this narrowness, neoclassical economics has expanded its domain of application to other social sciences, but has shown itself incapable of addressing social phenomena and coming to terms with current developments in the world economy.

With world financial crises no longer a distant memory, and neo-liberalism and postmodernism in retreat, prospects for political economy have strengthened. It allows constructive liaison between the dismal and other social sciences and rich potential in charting and explaining combined and uneven development.

The objective of this series is to support the revival and renewal of political economy, both in itself and in dialogue with other social sciences. Drawing on rich traditions, we invite contributions that constructively engage with heterodox economics, critically assess mainstream economics, address contemporary developments, and offer alternative policy prescriptions.

Also available:

Theories of Social Capital: Researchers Behaving Badly
Ben Fine

THE POLITICAL ECONOMY OF DEVELOPMENT

The World Bank, Neoliberalism and
Development Research

Edited by
Kate Bayliss, Ben Fine and Elisa Van Waeyenberge

PlutoPress
www.plutobooks.com

First published 2011 by Pluto Press
345 Archway Road, London N6 5AA

www.plutobooks.com

Distributed in the United States of America exclusively by
Palgrave Macmillan, a division of St. Martin's Press LLC,
175 Fifth Avenue, New York, NY 10010

British Library Cataloguing in Publication Data
A catalogue record for this book is available from the British Library

ISBN   978 0 7453 3104 1   Hardback
ISBN   978 0 7453 3103 4   Paperback

Library of Congress Cataloging in Publication Data applied for

This book is printed on paper suitable for recycling and made from fully managed
and sustained forest sources. Logging, pulping and manufacturing processes are
expected to conform to the environmental standards of the country of origin.

10   9   8   7   6   5   4   3   2   1

Designed and produced for Pluto Press by Chase Publishing Services Ltd
Typeset from disk by Stanford DTP Services, Northampton, England
Simultaneously printed digitally by CPI Antony Rowe, Chippenham, UK and
Edwards Bros in the United States of America

Contents

PART III   CONTINUITY OR CHANGE?

Acronyms and Abbreviations

AAA	Analytical and Advisory Activities
AICD	Africa Infrastructure Country Diagnostic
AIDS	Acquired Immune Deficiency Syndrome
ANDS	Afghanistan National Development Strategy
ARD	Agriculture and Rural Development
AREU	Afghan Research and Evaluation Unit
ART	Anti-Retroviral Therapies
BalAEF	Baltic American Enterprise Fund
BBI	Bringing Back In
BIS	Bank for International Settlements
CBO	Community-Based Organisation
CDF	Comprehensive Development Framework
CEE	Central and Eastern European
CIS	Commonwealth of Independent States
CN	Counter Narcotics
CND	Counter Narcotics Directorate
CPAU	Cooperation for Peace and Unity
CPIA	Country Policy and Institutional Assessment
DEC	Development Economics Department of the World Bank
DECRG	Development Economics Research Group
DfID	Department for International Development
DIA	Defense Intelligence Agency
ECB	European Central Bank
ESW	Economic and Sector Work
FAO	Food and Agriculture Organisation
FCR	Full Cost Recovery
GDF	Global Development Finance
GDP	Gross Domestic Product
GFRP	Global Food Crisis Response Program
GNI	Gross National Income
HIV	Human Immunodeficiency Virus
I-ANDS	Interim Afghanistan National Development Strategy
IBNET	International Benchmarking Network
IBRD	International Bank for Reconstruction and Development

ICF	Infrastructure Crisis Facility
IDA	International Development Association
IEG	Independent Evaluation Group
IFAD	International Fund for Agricultural Development
IFC	International Finance Corporation
IFI	International Financial Institution
IFPRI	International Food Policy Research Institute
ILO	International Labour Organisation
IMF	International Monetary Fund
INFRA	Infrastructure Recovery and Assets
IPG	International Public Good
LDC	Less Developed Country
LIDC	London International Development Centre
MDG	Millennium Development Goal
MIGA	Multilateral Investment Guarantee Agency
MIT	Massachusetts Institute of Technology
MNC	Multinational Company
NCNP	Neoclassical Neo-Populist
NGO	Non-Governmental Organisation
NIC	Newly Industrialising Country
NIE	New Institutional Economics
NORAD	Norwegian Agency for Development Cooperation
ODA	Official Development Assistance
OECD	Organisation for Economic Cooperation and Development
PBA	Performance Based Aid
PPIAF	Public Private Infrastructure Advisory Facility
PPP	Public–Private Partnership
PRR	Policy Research Report
PRSP	Poverty Reduction Strategy Papers
PRWP	Policy Research Working Paper
PSD	Private Sector Development
PSP	Private Sector Participation
PWC	Post-Washington Consensus
SCP	Structure Conduct and Performance
SDH	Social Determinants of Health
SME	Small and Medium Enterprises
SOE	State-Owned Enterprise
SSA	Sub-Saharan Africa
SSR	Security Sector Reform
STI	Sexually Transmitted Infections
TVE	Township and Village Enterprises

UNDP   United Nations Development Programme
WBG   World Bank Group
WDR   World Development Report
WSS   Water Supply and Sanitation
WTO   World Trade Organisation

Preface

Late in 2006, the World Bank issued a report (Deaton et al. 2006) of the findings of an independent evaluation of research activities carried out by the Bank between 1998 and 2005 by a group of eminent economists chaired by Angus Deaton. However, it was with mixed feelings that in early 2007 a small group of us consulted the evaluation report. As longstanding critics of the Bank, such a review was most welcome to us. But we had doubts over the extent to which a review commissioned by the Bank itself would be sufficiently independent and critical and whether it would, in any case, have any impact. On balance, we were more than pleasantly surprised with the strength of criticism within the Deaton Report, which is a positive reflection upon the intellectual integrity of those who were involved in its production. In our view, it was imperative that the report's findings regarding the deficiencies of World Bank research should be widely broadcast, especially the Bank's blatant use and abuse of research for unjustified advocacy purposes. Such criticisms were not new, even from within the Bank itself, but the claim could no longer be made that the critics were dissidents of some sort or were without establishment credentials and status. The report seemed to offer the platform from which to strengthen calls for reform of the Bank's research, advocacy and, ultimately, policy.

Nevertheless, we found the deliberations of the Deaton Report to be limited in scope and depth – not least in the questions asked, the ways in which answers were constructed and the substance of those answers. This was largely by virtue of the deep commitment to mainstream economics of those involved in producing the report. For this reason, we organised a seminar series through the London International Development Centre (LIDC) with the purpose of bringing wider attention to the Deaton Report itself. The aim was to offer the Deaton evaluation as a critical point of departure for a more extensive assessment of the role of the World Bank in research on development and to explore alternative approaches.

The papers from that seminar series form the basis for this book. But the Deaton Report, whilst serving as the initial prompt and remaining as a critical reference point throughout the contributions, has occupied a considerably lesser prominence than originally anticipated. This is for two reasons. First, to our surprise and great disappointment, the Deaton Report has scarcely been acknowledged by the development community (including, though this is less surprising, the Bank itself). Casual conversation with many leading scholars, practitioners and donors suggests that its existence has scarcely registered, let alone has its content been understood and absorbed.

In retrospect, this reflects our own optimism regarding the power of 'independent' peer review. With hindsight, the critical nature of some of the observations of the report may be the reason that it has attracted so little attention. As this volume documents again and again, and as the Deaton Report itself might have anticipated if it had paid sufficient attention to similar exercises in the past, its unwelcome deliberations from the Bank's perspective sealed its fate as far as wide dissemination and debate have been concerned. Accordingly, our volume could not assume that the Deaton critical assessments were common knowledge. Hence, the Deaton Report can only loosely be the basis from which we can probe for deeper reasons for the poverty of Bank research, advocacy and policy as well as making an assessment of the implications of, and alternatives to, such weaknesses. Thus, whilst as an intellectual exercise the Deaton Report is an excellent starting point, in practice it is something of a roundabout way of getting to our ultimate goals.

In addition, our efforts were unavoidably influenced by the maxim 'stuff happens'. Any assessment of World Bank research now needs to take account of the global crisis that broke at the end of 2007, and for a number of different reasons. First, and most important, the crisis sheds light on the realities of contemporary capitalism, including the past patterns of development as well as the prospects for the future. Second, no one can doubt, at least in principle, that mainstream economics has been rocked, if not wrecked, by the crisis and the form it has taken; this is especially so of the Bank's past research, so wedded has this been to the promotion of market forces in general and of those of finance in particular. The crisis provides substantial evidence to justify a reassessment of the Bank's activities as well as a re-evaluation of the contributions from its critics. Third, and paradoxically given that the Bank has been complicit with, if not a contributory causal factor in, the current crisis, its role alongside that of the IMF, has been strengthened in the wake of the crisis. Attention has turned to the International Financial Institutions as desperate attempts are made to find saviours and relieve the impact of the crisis in the developing world. This opens up the need for critical assessment of the responses in research, policy and advocacy of the Bank as the crisis has unfolded. In general, we find the impact of the crisis upon the Bank has been one of business as usual, only more so.

While the substance of the crisis rested outside the Deaton deliberations that concluded prior to its onset, the value of our earlier starting point with Deaton has been to identify exactly what is business and what is usual for the Bank. It has also allowed us to strengthen our commitment to alternatives which will not now appear as unusual or radical as they might have previously. In the wake of the crisis, hitherto unimaginable economic policies have been not only imagined but adopted in the attempt to restore stability through that major instrument of instability, the global financial system and its national components. Furthermore, as events around the world illustrate the failings of traditional orthodoxy, the papers presented in this volume are a timely pointer to alternative perspectives.

Part I
Preliminaries and Principles

The birth in 1998 of the post-Washington Consensus (PWC), launched by Joe Stiglitz (1998a) as chief economist at the World Bank, appeared at the time to be a dramatic event in signalling potential departure from the Washington Consensus, not least in scholarship. Nonetheless, it prompted two extreme reactions, possibly caricatured here, at opposite ends of the spectrum. One was to see this as another ideological shift in the continuing subordination of the Bank to developed-country (especially US) interests, with neo-liberal policies set to continue to be adopted. The other was to view this as a genuine shift in direction, enabling much greater potential through progressive engagement with the Bank.

In a volume that in many respects can be seen as a predecessor of this, a more nuanced position was adopted (Fine, Lapavitsas and Pincus 2001). It sought to unpick the PWC across its different dimensions, focusing on scholarship, but also on policy in practice and the Bank's ideological shift from being dogmatically pro-market to, let us say, not being anti-state. It also demonstrated that the impact of the PWC across different topics was uneven and differentiated. The limitations of the PWC were also exposed in terms of an exclusive reliance upon the market-imperfections approach of mainstream neoclassical economics for which Stiglitz was renowned, if more widely applied than for (the new) development economics alone.

The present volume, with Jomo and Fine (eds) (2006) as something of an intermediate state-of-the-art stepping stone, continues to put flesh on the bones provided by these themes. But, as covered in this first part, it also adds to them in the following ways. First, it locates the impact of the PWC in the context of the continuing evolution of neo-liberalism, emphasising how much (as sharply revealed by the global crisis) it has been underpinned by what has been termed 'financialisation'. In many respects, the PWC can be seen as a more moderate and tempered version of neo-liberalism, seeking to pursue financialisation by means other than shock therapy. Making markets work, in other words; but the markets working, or advancing, most over the period of the PWC have been those of finance. Second, this part charts the rise of the Bank as a self-proclaimed knowledge bank, albeit one with a somewhat more limited range of assets and derivatives than its real world counterpart. The rise of the knowledge bank is indicative of the increasing and deliberate command that the Bank exercises over development discourse, for both economic and social policy, projecting influence and control from its base within orthodox economics. It does so despite what, as exposed by the Deaton Report (Deaton et al. 2006), is poor-quality research by the standards of that economics. And despite, as we argue throughout the rest of this book, the impoverished capacity of such economics to address adequately the issues of economic, let alone social, development.

Since the launch of the PWC, there has been a considerable volume of excellent scholarly contributions exposing the limitations of the World Bank's research, of which, of course, the Deaton Report is one. Throughout this volume, we have drawn upon this research for both its critical substance and its offer of alternatives. What we have also sought to do, however, is to locate such research both in the wider role of the Bank itself and in its interaction with broader material and intellectual developments. This allows for such themes to be picked up in the case-study chapters that follow in Part II, finessing general developments and their interaction across particular fields of study.

1
The World Bank, Neo-Liberalism and Development Research

Elisa Van Waeyenberge, Ben Fine and Kate Bayliss

1.1 PRELUDE: A TALE OF THREE RESIGNATIONS

In the autumn of 2006, one week after its Annual Meetings, the findings were released of an external evaluation of World Bank research that had been undertaken between 1998 and 2006 (Deaton et al. 2006). The evaluation had been commissioned by the Bank and was carried out by a panel of four distinguished development economists, with Angus Deaton acting as chair.[1]

The period covered by the review had revealed itself to be particularly tumultuous in the history of Bank research. Joe Stiglitz, at the time vice president and chief economist, had opened 1998 with a bang. At the WIDER annual lecture, he delivered his now much-celebrated address, 'More Instruments and Broader Goals: Moving towards the Post-Washington Consensus' (Stiglitz 1998a). As indicated by the title, Stiglitz called for an urgent reorientation of the Bank's development paradigm, beyond what he perceived as the excessively narrow bias that was the basis of the Washington Consensus that had steered Bank policies during the 1980s and early 1990s. For Stiglitz, the Washington Consensus had been 'at best incomplete and at worst misguided' (p.3). A more 'holistic' and 'broad-based' approach to development was to be pursued through a broader set of policy instruments than those traditionally associated with the Washington Consensus – itself shorthand for macroeconomic 'stabilisation', i.e. fiscal austerity, trade liberalisation, privatisation, and so on. In the autumn of the same year, Stiglitz (1998b) issued another urgent call from a public platform for a new development paradigm to be promoted by the Bank. One year later, he was forced to resign from his job as chief economist.

Meanwhile the drafting of the 2000/01 World Development Report (WDR) was under way. 'Attacking Poverty' was important for the Bank (World Bank 2001a). As a World Development Report, it summed up and publicly advertised Bank ideas in a particular area. Further, it was part of a longer-term exercise that sought, over a period of ten years, to reformulate Bank analysis and policy on poverty – with poverty reduction sitting at the heart of the Bank's proclaimed mission. Ravi Kanbur, another distinguished development economist, known to be broadly in tune with the more comprehensive and 'holistic' approach advocated by Stiglitz and the then Bank president James Wolfensohn, had been tasked with leading the team writing the report. Yet by mid 2000, soon after drafts of the report had been circulated for comment to representatives of the Bank's member governments and to researchers in and outside the Bank, Kanbur had departed his post.

Within the Bank's main research department, the Development Economics Research Group (DECRG), led between 1998 and 2003 by Paul Collier, another drama was about to unfold. William Easterly, a senior advisor in the Macroeconomics and Growth division of DECRG since 1989, had received clearance from the Bank to write a book on some of his research findings regarding the causes of growth. After authoring an op-ed piece in the *Financial Times* summarising some of his findings, he found himself the subject of a misconduct investigation. He too had left his job at the Bank before the end of 2001.[2]

To the extent that the postures adopted by these three high-level Bank staff diverged from the official line espoused by the Bank, their positions became compromised and unacceptable. The resignations forced to the fore a set of tensions between scholarly efforts at the Bank, its advocacy role and the specific policy imperatives the institution was seeking to promote and, where necessary, defend.

This book seeks to assess critically the Bank's development research both in how it affects particular debates and policies about development and through a closer look at the role it plays for the Bank itself, with particular attention to the shifting contradictions within and across Bank scholarship, its advocacy, and the policies the institution promotes. The Deaton evaluation provides a critical lens through which this endeavour is approached. The report sought to assess the extent to which Bank research contributed to its two main stated objectives: the generation of new knowledge on development and the broadening of the understanding of development policy. This was broached across nine fields of enquiry: macroeconomics and growth; fiscal policy, public sector management and governance; trade and international economics; poverty and social welfare; human development; finance and private sector development; agriculture and rural development; infrastructure and urban development; and the environment. Running to 165 pages, it came out in favour of a formal 'knowledge' role for the Bank, but denounced a set of fundamental shortcomings regarding the way in which the Bank discharged itself of its intellectual responsibilities.

The failure of the report, however, to situate the Bank's research effort within a set of broader political–economic pressures bearing upon the Bank's scholarly activity, and the absence of any exploration of how the relationship between Bank research, rhetoric and policy priorities is mediated, were striking (see Chapter 2). The way the Deaton Report dealt with (or avoided) the resignations mentioned above serves as an illustration. For example, the book that sat at the heart of Easterly's resignation, *The Elusive Quest for Growth*, Easterly (2001a), was hailed by Deaton et al. (2006, p.50) as 'perhaps the most cited and influential of all of the Bank's research output' – without a hint of the controversy the book had ignited within the Bank. Further, Deaton et al. (p.11) put forward the fact that one of the Bank's former chief economists, the unnamed Stiglitz, was a Nobel laureate as evidence of the Bank's alleged leading edge in development research. But there was no mention of the forced departure of Stiglitz from the Bank. Nor was there any mention of Kanbur's resignation, while a later (and more sober and less self-constrained) Deaton (2009a, p.107) highlighted the shenanigans surrounding the 2000/01 WDR for 'the internal disarray that it revealed within the Bank, particularly on the role of growth in poverty reduction'.

These yawning gaps in the Deaton evaluation may have been the consequence of a naive, sophisticated or complicit panel, or some mix of all three, as hope sprung eternal that some limited but positive influence on the Bank's research might prevail in the wake of the panel's extensive deliberations. What stands out is how the Deaton Report was committed to a particular, as it were 'neutral', appraisal of the Bank's knowledge role (by way of standard of scholarship and suitability as such for advocacy), without seeking to situate this more broadly vis-à-vis the Bank's role as lender and advocate of a particular interpretative and policy order.

This failure, or at least self-limitation, serves as point of departure for a more critical and deeper assessment of the Bank's development research over the last decade across the select set of research topics covered in this book. Such an assessment acquires significance in the context of the Bank's formal emphasis on its role as a knowledge bank since the late 1990s. This role was adopted against the backdrop of a formal transition from Washington to post-Washington Consensus as the Bank's legitimacy as an agent of development came under doubt. Further, critical assessment of the role of knowledge bank is all the more urgent in the context of the global crisis at the time of writing, through which the failure of the Bank's analytical and policy frameworks is (once more) dramatically exposed.

As an introduction, this chapter recounts briefly the trajectory of the rhetorical and policy paradigms that have prevailed at the Bank since the early 1980s. This allows the Bank's role in the promulgation of a 'neo-liberal' order to be situated as well as to examine the shifting nature of that order. The crisis not only sheds light on the poverty of the Bank's research in the past, but also reveals the inadequacies of its responses to the crisis as a result of continuities inherited from its pre-crisis configuration of advocacy, scholarship and policy in practice. This volume, then, uncovers the nature and role of the Bank's research as it has been. This allows us to offer alternative perspectives for the future, not least on the stances of the Bank – whose status has been enhanced, rather than shattered, even though the consequences of the policies with which it has at least been complicit continue to unfold (see below).

1.2 FROM WASHINGTON CONSENSUS TO WHAT CRISIS?

The Bank was instrumental in promoting the neo-liberal perspectives on development that came to dominate the agenda of many international development actors during the 1980s. Summed up as the Washington Consensus (Williamson 1990), these perspectives displaced a short-lived focus on poverty reduction that had emerged during the 1970s and had been combined with a generally favourable appraisal of the need for the state to intervene to promote development (Fine 2009c). The Washington Consensus aimed at economic policy reform, with the purpose of eliminating all obstacles to a 'perfect market' as the presumed optimal path to growth. This implied an emphasis on 'fiscal discipline', curtailment of government subsidies, interest rate liberalisation, trade liberalisation, privatisation and deregulation.

By the early 1990s, however, the pernicious implications of the reform packages promoted under the Washington Consensus became increasingly apparent and the Bank's half-century anniversary was marked by vocal campaigns that 50 years had been enough. Aware of the urgent need to restyle the Bank and address the serious challenges presented by the various pressures bearing upon the institution, attempts were instigated to reassert the Bank's central role as a 'development institution seeking to fight poverty' and to move beyond the 'technical' and 'narrow' approach that had characterised the Washington Consensus. This entailed calls for a more 'comprehensive' approach to development (Wolfensohn 1999), accompanying the arguments for a post-Washington Consensus (PWC) put forward by Joe Stiglitz.

The new agenda tried, at least in principle (or at the rhetorical level), to move beyond the reductionist conception of the development process as exclusively reliant upon market forces which was implied by the Washington Consensus. It, further, sought to project a different view of state–society interactions. The presumed antagonism between state and society/market gave way to a notion of 'partnership': the private and public sectors were now understood to be intimately 'entwined' (Stiglitz 1998a, p.41). In this approach, the persistence of market failures and missing markets was increasingly recognised, and the PWC tentatively provided a rationale for piecemeal and discretionary intervention on a wider scale, where previously such a rationale was denied in principle if not, it should be emphasised, in practice. The underlying logic remained one, however, of promoting the market through state intervention as necessary.[3]

To some extent, the move from Washington Consensus to, or towards, PWC created collective confusion over the shifting postures of the Bank. At one extreme, the hardest critics simply portrayed the PWC as a rhetorical device to sustain neo-liberal policies; at the other, the PWC was perceived to herald a fundamental departure from neo-liberalism. Meanwhile, doubt was also being expressed about the nature of neo-liberalism itself, whether it had any conceptual purchase upon a world in which its supposed all-pervasive influence could lead to such a wide range of diverse policies and outcomes across time, place and issue (see Fine 2009a, 2009d–f and 2011, and Fine and Hall 2011).

Our own view is that the PWC has been indicative of a new phase of neo-liberalism rather than a break with it. This requires, though, a refined understanding of neo-liberalism itself, for conundrums associated with its diversity can and must be addressed if the shifting postures of the World Bank (and of neo-liberalism itself more generally) are to be satisfactorily understood, especially in the wake of the crisis, in which the levels of state intervention to rescue the financial system have been unprecedented. Does this signal the end of neo-liberalism across ideology, scholarship (the efficient market hypothesis for financial markets is surely dead and buried) and policy in practice? (Are we all Keynesians once more?)

This points to an enduring feature of neo-liberalism as it emerged from the global crises of the 1970s – that it has always been a contradictory and shifting amalgam of ideology, scholarship and policy in practice. In particular, neo-liberalism has never been short of state intervention. Indeed, it has positively deployed it to promote not so much the amorphous market as the interests of private capital.

In this respect, of course, at least in principle, it is no different from the 'Keynesian' period that preceded it. But what has distinguished the era of neo-liberalism is the extent to which such intervention has been driven by, if not reduced to, what has become termed 'financialisation'.[4] The last three decades has witnessed an extraordinary expansion of finance, a proliferation of asset types, their attachment to speculation, their extension into ever more areas of economic and social life (not least subprime housing), and distributional gains (and losses) that have enriched the few. Neo-liberalism has been first and foremost about underpinning such financialisation, whether directly through deregulation and liberalisation of finance itself, or indirectly through the conduits created for it, most notably with privatisation for example. In short, neo-liberalism has been about the state promotion of private capital in general and of finance in particular.

But, in addition, neo-liberalism has experienced two broadly delineated phases of roughly equal length. The first, associated with Reaganism and Thatcherism, is appropriately dubbed shock therapy, although of earlier origin and wider application than the transition economies of eastern Europe – as Latin American experience in the 1980s can testify, for example. This phase was certainly not one of withdrawal of the market, but was aimed at promoting private capital through the state, not least through privatisation, deregulation, commercialisation, fiscal austerity and so on. By contrast, the second phase of neo-liberalism (more attuned to the sensibilities of the social market, Third Wayism or, in the developmental context, the PWC) has broadly drawn upon two elements. One has been to temper and respond to the dysfunctions of the first phase given the extent to which the promotion of private capital has created tensions in economic and social reproduction. The other, more significant and in a sense acutely revealed by response to the current crisis, has been more overtly and broadly to deploy the state to sustain the promotion of private capital in general and finance in particular. To put it crudely, once you have done as much privatisation as the system will bear under the neo-liberal rhetoric of withdrawal of state intervention, then the time has come to use the state to correct market imperfections and to improve its workings, as in public–private partnerships, for example. As beautifully put by Stiglitz (2008, p.2), defining the new 'left' precisely in these terms, '[t]he left now understands markets, and the role they can and should play in the economy ... the new left is trying to make markets work'. But where we see 'markets', we should read 'capital in general', and where we see 'capital in general' we should read 'finance in particular'.

In this light, then, the shift from Washington Consensus to PWC corresponds more broadly to a transition from the one phase of neo-liberalism – where the sole emphasis was on extending the role of markets – to another, where the state is called upon to abet the original project as the manifold contradictions it generated erupted (see Fine 2009a and d–f). Even when compared with the pre-Washington Consensus, McNamara era, the PWC appeared as a 'regression', in contrast with the former's tolerance (and support) for state-controlled development enterprises (Fine 2001b, p.15). The rhetoric and scholarship of the PWC is unambiguously one that shifts towards being more state and poverty friendly, permissive of piecemeal interventions 'to make markets work', although the timing and nature of the shifts in rhetoric and scholarship remain diverse. Why, for example, did it take five years or more for its impact to be felt on amending the dogmatic policy in favour of privatisation, unless to get as much of it in hand as possible before requiring the state to strengthen support for the insertion of the private sector into the provision of economic and social infrastructure (Bayliss and Fine (eds) 2008)?

For the shifts from Washington Consensus to PWC coincided with important (operational) changes within the World Bank Group (WBG) that primarily belied the rhetorical and scholarly shifts in stance. Early in 2002, the institution's board of directors endorsed the Bank's Private Sector Development Strategy as its corporate blueprint (World Bank 2002c). The strategy projected two main objectives: to extend the reach of markets through investment-climate reform with a special focus on measures that help micro-, small and medium enterprises ('opportunity'); and to improve access to basic infrastructure and social services through private participation ('empowerment'). The broad claim of the strategy was to shift performance risks of operations from domestic taxpayers in developing countries to private parties, where these were deemed better able to bear or manage risk.[5]

With the fast-growing commitment to the agenda of Private Sector Development (PSD) at the heart of WBG activities, the scope for synergies between the private and public sector arms of the WBG took on special importance. This accommodated and dovetailed with an existing trend. For, with the fast expansion of private international capital flows that had characterised the late 1990s (collapsing at the turn of the century after a series of international financial crises, only to pick up again very rapidly after 2002), the Bank's traditional activities as a public finance institution had started to decline.[6] However, disbursements of the WBG's private sector affiliate, the International Finance Corporation (IFC), and the activities of the Multilateral Investment Guarantee Agency (MIGA), provider of non-commercial risk guarantees to the private sector, grew rapidly. PSD as a mission fitted well with these institutional changes. The Bank's 2007 'Long Term Strategic Exercise' (World Bank 2007c, p.8) explained:

> With the increased focus in the development community on the private sector, and with the strong positioning of IFC and MIGA and the investment climate operations within IDA and IBRD activities, the World Bank Group is particularly well positioned to contribute further to the development of the private sector. This raises the issue of how best to align the Group focus on the private sector at the corporate and subsequently at the regional and country levels. A stronger focus on private sector development is important to better and stronger synergy across the World Bank Group.

The search for complementarities between its private and public sector arms implied that the former, the IFC, would focus on mobilising private finance for development projects, while the public sector arms, the IBRD and the IDA, would support institution- and capacity-building activities to aid the expansion of the private sector, including its participation in a host of non-traditional areas such as health and education (see IFC 2007). In line with such a direction, the composition of IBRD/IDA infrastructural loans, between the 1980s and 2000, in the telecommunications and power sectors, for instance, changed from being dominated by the (public sector) construction of facilities to a main concern with policy reform, privatisation and private entry (World Bank 2002c, p.22).

The different arms of the WBG would hence work together ('exploit their synergies') to promote the market (and thus private, and often foreign, enterprise), with a recognition of the need for the state to advance the latter. This was very much in line with the PWC and was reflected in the capacity/institution building programmes of the official (or public sector) arms of the institution. Such an altered operational configuration of the WBG implied that private firms rapidly increased as a proportion of its clients.[7] This stood in sharp contrast to its official mission to be a public financial institution seeking to promote development and combat poverty.

These corporate realignments were accompanied by an emphasis on the Bank's unique position as knowledge gatherer and disseminator (see Chapter 2). The knowledge mission highlighted the Bank's supposedly unique ability to share (as opposed to dominate and filter) decades of learning about economic development with clients around the world. Such an emphasis did not necessarily repair the disconnection between the Bank's projected purpose, to be a public financial institution seeking to promote development and combat poverty, and the reality implied by the underlying shifts between its official and private lending arms. Nevertheless, it could serve to draw attention away from the Bank's traditional (public) financing role, now increasingly focused on the private sector. The 2007 'Long Term Strategic Exercise' stressed that 'the World Bank Group will succeed *only* if it retains and improves its role as the development community's "knowledge bank", especially with its purely financial value-added [role] likely to decline' (World Bank 2007c, p.11, emphasis added).

But in mid 2007, the drive of fast-expanding private capital flows, both those promoted by the Bank and those upon which its activities had been reconfigured, came to an abrupt halt. What originated as a crisis in a particular segment of the US credit market soon transformed into a global financial and economic crisis with global output and global trade falling, respectively, by over 2 and nearly 12 per cent in 2009. This amounts to the sharpest downturn in the global economy over the last 60 years (see Addison and Tarp 2009). The number of jobless worldwide has increased by 34 million (since 2007), reaching an estimated 212 million in 2009 (ILO 2010). The repercussions in the developing world have been no less dramatic. Output in the developing world grew very slowly, by 1.2 per cent in 2009, translating into a fall of 2.2 per cent once India and China are excluded (World Bank 2010b, p.3). Sub-Saharan Africa (SSA) will have lost around 7 per cent of its output by the end of 2010, as compared with pre-crisis forecasts. These trends imply that, by the end of 2010, an estimated additional 64 million people will be living in extreme poverty (below US$ 1.25 a day). Substantial losses with regard to progress towards the Millennium Development Goals will be incurred (IMF/World Bank 2010).

The global financial and economic crisis has had important repercussions for development finance. Private investment flows to developing countries – which had peaked in 2007 – fell by more than 40 per cent in 2008, as access to international debt markets dried up and portfolio equity nearly ceased (World Bank 2009g). Emerging market borrowers also faced increased competition from developed countries as the latter started expanding government deficit debt financing as well as government-guaranteed bank debt issuance. Further, aid flows came under threat in view of the fiscal pressures in the donor countries triggered by the crisis. And workers' remittances, which had become as important a source of foreign exchange for developing countries as official aid itself, were projected to decline as employment conditions worsened in the North and South, and the most vulnerable workers were the first to lose their jobs.

Apart from the dramatic effects in the real economy, the crisis threw into disarray the model of development that had been so heavily promoted by the International Financial Institutions (IFIs), not least in its emphasis on financial openness and deregulation. Across various countries in the industrialised world, governments intervened with enormous rescue packages for the financial sector, initiated counter-cyclical policies of various kinds, and provided comprehensive guarantee programmes for the banking industry (see Hall 2008), policies traditionally abhorred by the IFIs.

Whether such actions are likely to induce a fundamental rethink of the policy order traditionally promoted by the IFIs remains to be seen. First indications, however, do not point towards radical departures (across scholarship, rhetoric or practice). Indeed, a strong asymmetry, or 'mental dichotomy' (Ocampo, in Gallagher 2009, p.29), seems to persist. While developed countries undertake counter-cyclical policies, developing and transition economies are 'encouraged' to undertake pro-cyclical policies. And where counter-cyclical policy or other interventions by government are necessary to avoid excessive costs to society, these should not be interpreted as 'permanent deviations from well-established policy positions'

(Demirgüç-Kunt and Servén 2009, p.45).[8] A policy brief produced by the Bank in late 2008 (Brahmbhatt et al. 2008, p.17), surveying the possible policy responses to the financial crisis, explains:

Addressing the crisis will change incentives and constraints faced by decision makers, in some cases threatening sustainable reform efforts, in others creating new opportunities. It will be particularly important for policymakers to ensure that short term measures aimed at addressing immediate macroeconomic and social pressures do not jeopardise longer term growth and development prospects, for example, by creating costly new distortions that become difficult to remove because they have come to be supported by powerful vested interests.

In a more recent document outlining the contours of what the World Bank Group would like in a post-crisis world, the Bank insists (World Bank 2010a, p.5) that:

a preliminary assessment of possible lessons from the crisis does not point toward a revolution in policy. Instead, the crisis may help accelerate the shift toward a more pragmatic policy framework which continues to give primacy to a competitive private sector and a dynamic export sector as drivers of growth, employment and productivity.

Further, the initial relative resilience of certain countries in the South to the economic and financial crisis, due, among other things, to these countries' large reserve holdings, has been claimed by the IFIs to be the result of their policy advice, rather than that the original need for such large reserves is linked to the policies of openness promoted by the IFIs (and the increased volatility risk attached to these) and that the cost of holding such large reserves for development, both domestically and abroad, is accounted for (see Chapter 10). Indeed, and paradoxically, the presence of such reserves is not evidence of lack of financialisation in the developing world, but indicates the form it has taken. Apart from the implications for limiting the scope for economic policy in the past, no less than for developed countries, this is also indicative of the extent to which domestic interests and elites aligned to financial returns have evolved and/or been strengthened, with corresponding implications for more dismal future prospects for reorienting policy, even if promotion of finance in and of itself has been discredited (see Robinson 2010 and Ashman et al. 2010) in the case of South Africa.

As such, while the Bank's response to the crisis needs unpicking for specific areas, with due attention to the way in which rhetorical and/or scholarly shifts, if any, relate to operational realities, little intent has as yet transpired to reconsider generally and radically the prevailing paradigm. At the level of discourse, the current president of the Bank has been referring to 'modernising multilateralism' (Zoellick 2008) and 'responsible globalisation' (Zoellick 2009). The talk is of private capital and markets to remain the 'drivers of growth', with private capital still understood as 'the critical factor in building infrastructure, supplying energy, financing businesses and trade, and fostering regional integration within an open global economy' (Zoellick 2008). The Bank will, further, assist the private sector 'to assume the critical handoff from the government's crisis response actions' (Zoellick 2009). A 'pick and mix' from the various analytical openings offered intellectually by the 'imperfect markets' paradigm of the PWC, now through reference to the 'facilitating state', as Lin (currently chief economist) puts it (Lin and Chang 2009), may be as good as it gets (see Chapter 11). In short, policies risk being characterised by marked and strengthened continuities.

This has been particularly striking in the Bank's response to the implications of the global crisis for infrastructure finance (see also Chapter 4). The Bank's reaction to the fall in infrastructure investment as a result of the crisis has, from the start, been characterised by continued (opportunistic) support for the private sector. This has entailed: support for governments in strengthening the environment for public–private partnerships; direct leveraging of private sector financing (through the IBRD/IDA, IFC and MIGA); and scaling up of support for new financing and partnerships. The 2009 *World Bank Annual Report* (World Bank 2009c, p.21, emphasis added) highlights how:

> [t]he new INFRA [Infrastructure Recovery and Asset] Platform, developed as part of the Bank's Vulnerability Fund, will work in tandem with IFC's new Infrastructure Crisis Facility to provide developing countries with a set of technical and financial assistance proposals that enable them to maintain or expand infrastructure investments during global economic downturns ... These infrastructure investments, expected to reach $15 billion a year over fiscal 2009–11, *will leverage and support private sector initiatives in the field.*

Despite the vulnerability of developing-country governments to international private infrastructure investment (see Chapter 4), the crisis has served to perpetuate the Bank's support for private capital in the sector. The combined use of World Bank Group instruments – including guarantees, risk mitigation instruments and financing – in support of the leveraging of private flows aims to assure such a direction in infrastructure investments. Paradoxically, the failure of the private sector as revealed by the crisis has, despite its heavy promotion in the past by the World Bank, meant that the latter has more funds and leverage available, certainly in relative terms, to pursue the agenda of private sector participation in traditionally public sector activities.

Indeed, more generally, the crisis has provided an opportunity for the Bank to *strengthen* itself as an institution, along the priorities charted since the early 2000s. In 2010, the IBRD received its first general capital increase for 20 years to over US$86 billion. This followed the rapid expansion of IBRD lending in 2009, which nearly tripled and exceeded 32 billion (commitments) in that year.[9] IBRD lending is projected to range between US$40 and US$50 billion in 2010, after a period of stagnation and decline in demand for IBRD resources since the turn of the century, with net disbursements (grants/loans minus repayments) persistently negative between 2002 and 2008. The IFC also benefited from a capital increase (US$200 million), while planning to raise additional capital through a (hybrid) bond issuance and from retained earnings. This follows the very rapid expansion of IFC activities as its (net) investments (loans, equity and debt securities) doubled between 2005 and 2009 and remained high, at just over US$22 billion, in 2009 – with its activities explicitly targeted at bridging the crisis-induced financing gap for private or public–private partnerships for infrastructure projects (through the IFC Infrastructure Crisis Facility), apart from guaranteeing the continuation of trade credit and bank recapitalisations (World Bank 2009c).

With such strengthened resources, the World Bank sees a particular role for itself in building its 'new multilateralism' in the post-crisis era, a vision set out in recently disclosed documents (World Bank 2010a, 2010d). Apart from reasserting an important role in financing, the post-crisis vision remains strongly committed to a projected 'knowledge role' for the Bank, with knowledge understood as the Bank's 'core strategic asset'. For the World Bank president the institution remains 'a repository of global best practice in development, combining implementation experience, research and learning, drawing on both public and private sectors' (Zoellick 2009).

This brings us back to the themes and rationale for this book: the Bank's role as an intellectual actor in development, although this is never detached from its policy and ideological roles. 'Knowledge' has been a recurring theme in Bank reinventions since the mid 1990s, and its meaning and purpose for the Bank, and beyond, need to be assessed fully and critically. This is done across a number of areas in the remainder of this book, an endeavour which aims to situate Bank research vis-à-vis broader development scholarship, as well as changing advocacy and policy positions, not least in the context of the current crisis. Such an endeavour is particularly compelling, more so as the crisis seems to have offered significant opportunity to the Bank to strengthen its role in development. For the Bank itself understands the failures of previous frameworks in accounting for the current economic crisis as evidence of an even greater need for its own analytical activity: 'The global financial crisis and the associated questioning of conventional wisdom will create *more* demand for the Bank's knowledge services over the coming years, underscoring the critical need for the Bank to strengthen its knowledge base' (World Bank 2009c, p.19, emphasis added).

From our perspective, this is an invitation to observe the law that to each and every action there should be an equal and opposite reaction; although our resources, and those of others, to deliver such a reaction are so much more confined than those of the Bank itself and its camp of followers. What we have been able to achieve in this volume is outlined in the following section.

1.3   OVERVIEW OF THE CHAPTERS

Chapter 2 critically examines the idea of the 'knowledge bank' as it has been heavily promoted by the Bank since the mid 1990s. The Bank's own arguments for such a role are surveyed and are confronted with an existing critical scholarship on the way the Bank exercises its intellectual role. Crucially, the Bank's projection of its knowledge as being neutral, technical and apolitical is debunked, and attention is drawn to the political–economic and disciplinary environments within which Bank knowledge takes form and is propagated. The chapter then uses these broad observations as the starting point to review the main findings of the Deaton evaluation of Bank research. This allows the charting of a set of themes regarding the Deaton Report and Bank research which recur through the subsequent chapters in the book. These include: the report's strong denunciation of the Bank's use of poor scholarship for advocacy purposes, combined with its failure to situate this tendency more broadly in the policy imperatives that prevail upon (and are promoted by) the Bank; the unfortunate disciplinary bias in the make-up of the evaluation panel, which is dominated by (mainstream) economists; the apparent disconnect between the severity of the criticisms uttered in the report and the mild nature of the recommendations which focus on organisational rather than systemic and institutional issues; the absence of any consideration within the report of the existing critical literature on Bank performance and research; and a technical predilection in assessing Bank research without any indication of how development itself is understood by the evaluators or the Bank.

Chapter 3 takes a closer look at the aid scholarship and practices of the Bank. The Bank has been a leader in the aid community, at least since its promotion of structural adjustment programmes. Since the late 1990s it has been a keen supporter of a shift towards an ex post form of conditionality, where aid flows are conditioned on the state of the policy and institutional environment. This practice of performance-based aid (PBA) has been strongly supported by a set of analytical contributions emanating from the Bank seeking to promote the argument that aid only affects growth positively when a core set of 'good' policies and institutions are already in place. These traditionally refer to low inflation, a budget surplus and trade openness, but also extend to include a host of 'good governance' features.

The Deaton Report took particular issue with this aid-effectiveness research, denouncing its failure to satisfy standard criteria of good scholarship. Further, the Bank was admonished for the strong advocacy purpose to which this very poor research had been put. The Deaton Report, nevertheless, failed to engage with the broader dynamics within which the Bank's aid practices take form and which condition the mediation between its research and policy in practice, here in the context of aid. Chapter 3 seeks to fill this gap by taking a closer look at the particular policy order the aid practice of PBAs seeks to protect. This is done on the basis of a detailed deconstruction of the Bank's mechanism through which PBA allocations are determined. Furthermore, attention is drawn to the role of the Bank's applied knowledge exercise, in terms of its production of numerous country and sector reports, in ensuring the continuation of a set of policy priorities within policymaking in the poor countries of the South, even when apparent changes in the aid-allocation mechanism seem to indicate a trend to the contrary.

Chapter 4 considers the evidence in support of water privatisation and the relationship between this and advocacy and policy. The chapter discusses empirical research in this sector in terms of two phases – the first in the early 2000s when privatisation of infrastructure was gaining momentum, and the second in the late 2000s where support was waning in light of the challenges with implementation. A common thread running through much of this research has been an often unduly positive interpretation of the findings of the impact of privatisation.

The chapter goes on to consider the elements that are missing from mainstream evaluation of water-sector policy. These include unequal initial conditions, and 'non-economic' factors in relation to access to water, such as community arrangements, as well as power and politics. While there are many challenges in water delivery in SSA, these are not likely to be overcome by privatisation. It is clear that decades of neo-liberal reforms have generated little improvement in terms of water access in the region. However, the recent crisis has strengthened commitment to private sector involvement, with the World Bank providing support to protect private investment in infrastructure. The private sector is still seen as the ticket to greater efficiency – which continues to be the overriding objective for World Bank policy. The author concludes by demonstrating that the continued preoccupation with a handful of largely economic indicators will not stimulate greater access and may even be a disincentive to serving poor households. An alternative approach is required, with universal coverage as a starting point.

Chapter 5 charts the meteoric rise – and fall – of social capital at the World Bank. It was a key concept through which the PWC enhanced its scholarly legitimacy by incorporating non-economists, inter-disciplinarity, the acknowledgement of market imperfections, and the role of the social or non-economic, whilst allowing neo-liberal anti-statism to flourish to a large degree in principle and practice in deference to an amorphous, self-help civil society as its surrogate. Whilst proponents of social capital at the Bank perceived themselves as some sort of valiant intellectual knights civilising an economics and economists in distress, the reality is that they offered a conduit through which broader internal critique of the non-economic aspects of the Bank's (intellectual) activities could be muted whilst the even more critical weaknesses of its economics were scarcely addressed. Having served this legitimising role within and for the Bank, social capital declined in its presence there in the noughties as rapidly as it had risen in the last years of the millennium.

But its effects, and the impetus behind them derived from the Bank's fanatical if temporary support, live on in developmental discourse and more widely. Despite what have been devastating criticisms of the concept and its application, it has continued to prosper across an ever expanding range of topics and disciplines, although its direct presence in policymaking has been negligble other than as an ideological rationale. In particular, the chapter illustrates the use of social capital in the literature on the social determinants of health, where, as in other applications, it has been seen as something of, almost literally, a wonder medicine. You can be healthier the more social capital you have, just as, in its favoured period, the Bank (in)famously saw social capital as the 'missing link' in development. At best, such use of social capital in addressing health places a smokescreen around fundamental social determinants of health such as levels and incidence of provision of basic needs, including primary and preventative health services provided through the public sector, free at the point of delivery (as opposed to the now increasingly discredited user charges). At worst, appeal to social capital positively undermines policy designed to promote public provision, as continues to be the case in Bank policy towards health (and other elements of economic and social welfare). In short, social capital offers a remarkable example of the opportunism of World Bank research and its dismal influence on the research and policy communities to which it is more or less directly attached.

Chapter 6 critically assesses two aspects of World Bank research into HIV/AIDS and consequent policies: micro-behaviour modelling and the impact of macro-level factors. The first element focuses on the behaviour and decision making of the individual and suggests that higher income levels for women will reduce prevalence. However, this is based on flawed research methods and is inconsistent with evidence of higher prevalence among more wealthy households. The use of such models is mis-focused; they are unable to encompass the wider social and economic factors of relevance.

The chapter then goes on to consider the World Bank's attempt to incorporate these broader parameters by indentifying the relationship between HIV prevalence and a wider set of economic and social factors. These attempts are shown to be similarly lacking, with structural factors incorporated simplistically and erroneously.

The idea that higher income levels will lead to lower prevalence does not fit with evidence from SSA that the highest prevalence rates occur in the countries with the highest regional income (South Africa, Botswana, Namibia). Furthermore the Bank approach ignores intra-country diversity and important contributions from HIV/AIDS specialists in other fields – such as epidemiologists, gender specialists and political economists. The chapter proposes alternative approaches to addressing the HIV/AIDS pandemic based around public health delivery and cites evidence in support of government-led initiatives, for example in Uganda and Senegal. Highlighted is the diversity across countries and the need for clearer socio-economic profiles of the pandemic in each country as the basis for policy.

Chapter 7 addresses the World Bank's evolving approach to agriculture and rural development (ARD), covering research (scholarship), rhetoric (advocacy) and policy. The chapter demonstrates that the Bank's position has shifted over the years, with a tendency towards adding on new issues as they come into Bank general policy, leading effectively to a shopping list of agendas without a sense of what is central and what is tangential. However, despite changes in the approach over time, there have been two permanent features throughout its evolution: the use of neoclassical economics for theoretical and methodological choices in research, and the entrenchment of pro-market/neo-liberal ideology in policy.

This preoccupation with market-oriented frameworks has led to the glossing over of inherent contradictions and tensions, replacing these with simplistic assumptions. In addition, both research and lending are spread thinly and thus diluted over many micro areas with an emphasis on 'win–win' solutions. These limitations are discussed with specific reference to the 2008 World Development Report (WDR 2008), and in relation to the Bank's response to the 2007–2008 food crisis. The chapter concludes with recommendations for an alternative perspective: that a large development organisation such as the World Bank needs to focus on bigger issues, such as what drives or hinders capitalist development in agriculture, incorporating a historically grounded theory of uneven capitalist development, structural relations of inequality (class, gender, ethnicity), inter-sectoral linkages and the corresponding institutionalised forms taken by conflict, power and 'governance'.

Chapter 8 explores World Bank research and policy in financial-sector liberalisation with specific reference to the entry of foreign banks into domestic banking in developing countries. Such policies were, according to World Bank publications, expected to increase competition and stimulate financial development. The chapter provides a critical assessment of Bank research in this field, showing how use has been made of an analytical framework the limitations of which were long-established and understood, even by Bank staff. Furthermore there has been no engagement with evidence of predatory behaviour on the part of foreign banks. The Bank's flawed research was used widely in support of policy. For, as a broader push for foreign-bank entry started to emerge with the launch of the 1986 Uruguay Round, in which US negotiators started to insist on the liberalisation of financial services, so did literature arguing the potential benefits for foreign banks in developing countries.

Foreign bank entry then grew rapidly in Latin American and East European countries. The result was a major shift in the structure of lending away from domestic enterprises and towards individuals. Lending behaviour by foreign banks created vulnerabilities in host economies around the world. The Bank response to this phenomenon was to avoid meaningful engagement with evidence that questioned their policy. Rather they argued that the problems stemmed from the incomplete nature of the entry, calling for *greater* liberalisation. The Bank has also produced research to counter claims that foreign-bank entry has reduced access to credit; but all research that reaches such conclusions comes from Bank sources. The continued failure of Bank research at least to question the analytical foundations of its arguments in the face of the current economic crisis suggests a scientific process compromised by prior policy aims.

Chapter 9 examines the analysis of violent conflict, highlighting some of the features of the relationships between policy and research or evidence. It is shown how debates around conflict have incorporated soft opinion and a narrow evidence base that lays claim to hard science. There is strong pressure for standardisation of policy measures and formulaic solutions. Where these use sophisticated statistical methods, they convey the false impression of certainty and evidence-based truth. Corresponding flaws in such accounts are highlighted by the authors in a review of World Bank research into civil war, where extensive empirical methods have reached apparently firm conclusions, showing that greed is more important than grievance in explaining the onset of civil war; and that, shortly after conflict, countries face a 50 per cent risk of renewed conflict within the next five years. These findings are widely cited as if well-established, whereas the original research was less than conclusive.

The analytical approach is dominated by economics, while inputs from other experts – historians, anthropologists – are dismissed.

The chapter then looks in detail at research on Afghanistan, starting with the lack of reliable data. Data collection is a relatively new activity and much data, though collected by foreigners, is analysed and written up in English. In addition, research is driven by a need to sell a success story to support international geopolitical (particularly US) interests. Stories of complexity that generate findings that are difficult to operationalise are quietly left to one side. This is demonstrated in a review of policy responses to opium production, which in recent years, with US and UK support, have moved towards eradication through counter-narcotics (CN) strategies. This policy response is justified by three main policy discourses, each of which is widely questioned by available evidence. Reasons to account for the continued adherence to policy based on flawed research include the mix and range of function that mainstream policy narratives perform for a diverse set of actors. CN is an industry in itself, and policies are the result of complex negotiations and interests that inform them, with distant attachment to implementation and outcomes on the ground. Significantly, whilst there have been healthy contributions and debate in some aspects of Bank research, when it comes to 'conflict resolution', problems of the simple lack of sufficient evidence are compounded by the sorting, packaging and selling of what evidence is available.

Chapter 10 provides a discussion of a particularly thorny issue for the World Bank – the economic success of China despite the country's failure to follow orthodox transition policies. The chapter assesses two propositions put forward to account for China's success. The first is based on institutions: the state machinery has created two types of institutions – those that support the market and those that supplant it – and achievements are attributed to market-like reforms while problems are ascribed to supplanting elements. The author shows that the evidence to support this proposition is weak, and the Chinese experience indicates that the principles of individualistic property rights are neither necessary nor sufficient for generating rapid growth. A second proposition is thus required. According to this, China's growth is the result of its low level of industrialisation at the start of its reforms which has allowed it to postpone those that are most painful. However, it is argued here that China developed in spite of, rather than because of, its initial state of development.

The chapter demonstrates how dramatically the country's performance has diverged from that of other transition economies and considers alternative interpretations of China's success. The Chinese experience differs fundamentally from other emerging economies in the way that the state is engaged in economic and political affairs, and this has been crucial for the country's economic success. Where the country did experiment with Washington Consensus-style policies in the mid 1990s, these were quickly reversed after a downturn in economic activity ensued. The country's experience of the financial crisis has been shaped by its development of a financial sector designed to support economic activity rather than the other way round. China is now an important world economic power, particularly through its symbiosis with the USA, and presents a potential challenge both to the dominance of the international trading and financial systems by the dollar (and the corresponding US trade and balance-of-payments deficits) and certainly, symbolically, to subservience to financialisation itself.

Chapter 11, in conclusion, draws lessons from across the individual chapters taken as a whole. Those concerning the poverty of scholarship, even by the Bank's own standards, as well as the shifting and inconsistent relations between such scholarship, ideology and policy in practice, cannot be emphasised too much. We also point to the continued absence of, or failure to address and debate, certain topics and frameworks, such as that associated with the developmental state paradigm from the past, and financialisation as a newly emerging concept for understanding the systemic roles of global finance. Whilst our own coverage in this volume is far from complete, owing to limitations of time, space and expertise, with explicit attention to poverty research at the Bank being a major omission, the Bank itself has no excuse for failing to engage with more or less well-established topics and approaches, other than its own discomfort should it do so. And we look to the future of World Bank research in the light of the global crisis – or should that be crises (of food, energy and climate)? – at time of writing, as the World Bank redefines itself as a knowledge bank in changed circumstances. Close attention to the Bank's own stated renewal of research directions promises little other than more of the same, as market and institutional imperfection economics rules the way and allows for wide, if directed, discretion for policy in practice on ever wider fronts (see Fine 2009c, in which this is understood as 'zombieconomics' within development studies). Prospects for health, as in the past, especially in Africa, are shown to be driven by pushing for private sector participation. And, on the newer terrain of climate change, the Bank has simultaneously been promoting large-scale projects that are pollution intensive *and* positioning itself to take the lead in commanding the development finance to be made available for ameliorating global warming. At least in this area, campaigning has fully exposed the contradictions in the Bank's role – situated as it is between promoting both development and developed-country (especially US) interests – to the verge of breaking point. Only if the latter interests can be overcome, in this as in other areas, will there be any prospect of a healthier contribution by the Bank to research and its attachment to policy in practice. In the meantime, we hope to have strengthened and updated critique of the Bank as agent of both 'development' and development discourse and to have pointed to alternative banks of knowledge in doing so.

NOTES

1. Bank researchers and their consultants produced around 4,000 papers, books and reports during the period that spans the Deaton review. The Deaton evaluation pursued two routes in its attempt to appraise this research output: the panel members conducted interviews with a wide range of people in and outside the Bank, and a group of co-evaluators was drawn in to comment on a sample of nearly 200 research projects. The co-evaluators were selected by the panel on the basis of their perceived expertise in a particular field, and this determined the nature of the research projects assigned to them. The findings from the various evaluators' reports and interviews are summed up in 'An Evaluation of World Bank Research, 1998–2005', Deaton et al. (2006), referred to here as the Deaton Report. The individual evaluators' reports are available at: http://econ.worldbank.org/WBSITE/EXTERNAL/EXTDEC/EXTRESEARCH/0,,contentMDK:21165468~menuPK:598503~pagePK:64165401~piPK:64165026~theSitePK:469382,00.html

2. After his resignation as Chief Economist, Stiglitz stayed on as then-President James Wolfensohn's special advisor until April 2000, when he was also forced out of that role. See Wade (2002) for a good account of the events leading up to Stiglitz's and Kanbur's resignations; see Kanbur (2001a) for his own account of the events leading up to his departure; and, see the World Bank Group Staff Association Newsletter November/December (2001) on Easterly's resignation, http://www.brettonwoodsproject.org/topic/knowledgebank/sanews.pdf

3. See Broad and Cavanagh (2009) for a creative account of the trajectories of, and various permutations to, the Washington Consensus over the last three decades.

4. See Fine (2007d, 2010e and 2011) for some discussion of the rapidly growing literature on financialisation.

5. See Bayliss and Hall (2001) for a comprehensive critique.

6. Two institutions within the WBG traditionally include the official, public sector as their clients, the International Bank for Reconstruction and Development (IBRD)

which provides loans at near-market rates, and the International Development Association (IDA) which provides concessional finance.

7. In 2008, IFC lending surpassed the total of IBRD lending and IDA assistance.

8. The authors continue: 'Neither monetary policy nor capital controls can substitute for well designed prudential regulation ... Public ownership or too aggressive regulation would simply hamper financial development and growth.'

9. Disbursements nearly doubled during that same period.

2
A Knowledge Bank?

Elisa Van Waeyenberge and Ben Fine

2.1 INTRODUCTION

The Deaton Report (Deaton et al. 2006) opens by introducing the World Bank as one of the most important centres of research in development today, if not the most important. It draws attention (p.12) to an ongoing effort

> to reposition the World Bank as the 'Knowledge Bank,' with lending operations playing a reduced role, and the Bank playing a more important role as a source of policy knowledge. In many ways this is responding to the changing demand for the Bank's services. We already see that a number of middle income countries ... or even countries approaching middle income ... either do not really need the Bank as a lender or are moving in that direction ... Moreover, even in the case of the poorest countries, where access to IDA loans ... remains economically important, there is now an on-going discussion of whether the Bank ought to move to a model where it is less a lender and more a helping hand, dispensing grants and advice.

The knowledge idea, of course, is not new. The Bank has aspired to a leadership role in the intellectual realm of development at least since the Robert McNamara or pre-Washington Consensus era (1968–1981). The Bank's capacity to exercise a leadership role in this respect has, however, varied with the broader environment in which it operates; it has been affected by the general availability of resources for development finance, the ideological climate in its main shareholder, and the nature of the assistance it provides (project versus programme aid). The 1980s saw a conjunction of events that promoted the intellectual role of the Bank and, by the early 1990s, it had attained leadership in the (intellectual and policy) world of development framed around its identified priorities. The knowledge mission became formally celebrated as James Wolfensohn took on the role of president of the Bank in the mid 1990s, and, since the onset of the global financial and economic crisis, 'Bank knowledge' has been re-emphasised, with the Bank continuing to perceive itself as 'well placed to link research, policy analysis and practitioners' knowledge and apply these to real-world operational problems' (World Bank 2010c, p.iv). For the World Bank, '[t]he new global economic and financial architecture that will emerge from the crisis will influence the development progress of developing countries, and calls for renewed efforts to provide appropriate *knowledge and policy* expertise to developing countries' (2010a, p.18, original emphasis).

The next section situates the notion of the 'knowledge bank' as promoted by the Bank and subjects to critical scrutiny the way the Bank understands this role. This is followed in Section 3 by a general overview of what the Deaton Report achieved and an account of its pervasive shortcomings. This allows for the charting of a set of themes that recur throughout the subsequent chapters, which examine, across a set of areas, the nature and implications of the Bank's knowledge role, its shifting relationship to Bank advocacy and policy, and the Bank's response (or lack of it) in the context of the latest financial and economic crisis.

2.2 BANKING ON KNOWLEDGE OR KNOWLEDGE ON THE BANK

With the arrival of James Wolfensohn as president of the Bank in 1995, the knowledge idea was put squarely at the centre of his renewal programme for the institution. The Bank was to become, in effect, a knowledge bank (Wolfensohn 1996a, p.7). This reflected an awareness that the Bank's financial weight might, if anything, be on the decline (see Chapter 1). Gilbert and Vines (2000, p.29), staunch supporters of the knowledge turn, argued that '[t]he Bank's knowledge and cumulated experience of the development process provides the justification for a continuing role for the World Bank in an era where international capital markets appear overliquid rather than underliquid'.

Although Wolfensohn's emphasis on knowledge originally drew on the corporate practice of knowledge management and aimed at organisational aspects of the institution, with the purpose of improving internal learning and efficiency (see King and McGrath 2004), the paradigm rapidly broadened to encompass a wide-ranging definition of a knowledge mission for the Bank. In this way, the

Bank's strategy for knowledge sharing quickly expanded, with the objective of making its know-how and experience accessible not only internally to Bank staff, but also externally to clients, 'partners' and 'stakeholders' around the world. In the process, the Bank sought to reach those who as yet had little or no access to the organisation's expertise. The *1997 Annual Report* (World Bank 1997c, p.7) explained:

> The Bank is made up of an unmatched repository of experience and understanding about development issues, which too often has been underused ... To meet client needs more effectively and better equip Bank staff, work began on developing a knowledge management system in fiscal 1997 to disseminate and apply lessons of experience among staff and clients. Through this system, complex information is distilled into usable formats for delivery to those who need it: policymakers, parliamentarians, NGOs and journalists, in ways that build vital understandings in member countries.

Thus, with the Bank now formally identified as a source of 'global knowledge', it would seek to strengthen the knowledge base for all development partners (IDA 2004, p.9). It would concentrate on becoming the world's premier development institution, forging a common agenda on major issues and being in the 'forefront of development as a learning exercise' (Bergesen 1999, p.190).[1] While the transfer of knowledge had always been a dimension of the Bank's role, the newly formed knowledge initiative sought to 'broaden the scope and raise the profile of this function' (World Bank 2003b, p. viii), creating a 'world-class knowledge management system' and 'improving and expanding the sharing of knowledge with its clients and partners' (p.xi). This conveniently combined with the increased emphasis on performance-based allocations of aid, which put 'policy learning' at the centre of aid practices (see Chapter 3).

Since the onset of the global and financial crisis, knowledge remains at the centre of the Bank's mission: 'Today more than ever, development knowledge helps to define the Bank's comparative advantage' (World Bank 2010c, p.1). For the Bank 'is uniquely placed to link research, policy analysis, and practitioners' knowledge globally through rigorous analysis, learning services, implementation support, and convening power. Leveraging these core strengths offers a tremendous opportunity to enhance the Bank's effectiveness' (World Bank 2010c, p.1).

Indeed, the Bank discerns a distinct role for itself in 'helping formulate the international community's post-crisis development paradigms' (p.2). Defined as the Bank's 'core strategic asset', the 2010 Knowledge Strategy charts three necessary courses of action to guarantee its knowledge advantage (World Bank 2010c, p. iii):

> improve the Bank's ability to capture, create and deliver knowledge to its clients through global technical practices; make the vast amount of knowledge produced by the Bank more impact driven; and strengthen the Bank's global connector role, linking country practitioners and policy makers to sources and centers of knowledge and innovation dispersed across the world.

For the World Bank, '[g]lobal development knowledge is key to our future relevance and effectiveness. The Bank's distinctive knowledge comes from our combination of presence and experience on the ground, and world class analytics and leadership on development thinking' (World Bank 2010d, p.8).

The Bank's knowledge mission is operationalised in various ways. These include academic research taking place in its research department (DEC); the applied analytical services supplied through the operational departments undertaking what the Bank refers to as 'economic and sector work'; the training programme undertaken by the World Bank Institute; and a host of 'global knowledge networks', including the Global Development Gateway, the Global Development Network and the Researchers Alliance for Development.[2] The resources available across these various knowledge activities dwarf any university department or research institute working on development and imply that the Bank is not just one among a number of equal actors in the world of development (see also Stern and Ferreira 1997).

Between 2006 and 2008, the Bank spent US$32 million annually on research and related activities (includes dissemination of research findings) (World Bank 2009b, p.15). During this period, Bank staff and consultants produced around 7,000 publications, including 430 books, over 2,000 scholarly articles in peer-reviewed journals and 1,000 policy research working papers. Bank researchers also produced 2,000 other papers, such as discussion and technical papers (p.17). The Bank has its own academic journals, the *World Bank Economic Review* and the *World Bank Research Observer*, produces a quarterly newsletter, the *Research Digest*, to inform development practitioners about its research findings, and distributes a monthly Research E-Newsletter. In 2008, the Bank's research department's website received 16.58 million page hits, a 12 per cent increase over the previous year (p.34). Apart from the research taking place in its research department, the Bank undertakes a vast number of country-driven 'analytical and advisory activities' (AAA). These represent the bulk of the Bank's formal 'knowledge portfolio', and expenditure on such activities amounted to US$285 million in 2008 (see also Chapter 3).

Bank research is organised around the following themes, with the thematic distribution in terms of share of research projects for 2008 between brackets: finance and private sector development (15 per cent); human development and public services (22 per cent); macroeconomics and growth (14 per cent); poverty and inequality (12 per cent); sustainable rural and urban development (18 per cent); trade and international integration (11 per cent); and other – including dissemination and outreach projects – accounting for the rest (p.18).

For the Bank, its knowledge role is akin to that of a 'clearinghouse for knowledge about development', a corporate 'memory bank' of best practices, and a collector and disseminator of the best development knowledge from outside organisations (World Bank 1998b, p.140). In its arguments, the creation and dissemination of its knowledge fulfil the function of an international public good (Stigtlitz 1999a and Squire 2000). The supply of such a public good will be deficient without active public support, and this gives rise to a crucial role for the Bank (Stiglitz 1999c, Squire 2000, Gilbert, Powell and Vines 1999 and World Bank 1998a and 1998b). Stiglitz (1999c, p.590, emphasis added) elucidated:

> The accumulation, processing, and dissemination of knowledge in development, as well as working more broadly to close the knowledge gap, is the *special* responsibility of the World Bank. The two activities of the Bank are complementary. Knowledge, particularly knowledge about the institutions and policies that make market economies work better, leads to higher returns and better allocation of capital ... The World Bank has a role to play in providing such advice that extends beyond the public-good nature of knowledge. It is, and is widely perceived to be, an honest broker.

This applies both to the knowledge created in the Bank's research department and to the much broader knowledge exercise in its operational departments: 'A great deal of the Bank's analytical work, which in several cases is carried out jointly with other development partners, can be regarded as a "public good" for both the client country and the development community' (IDA 2004, p.24).[3]

In these accounts, the Bank is characterised by economies of scale and scope in policy or development knowledge and, concomitantly, has a unique capacity to analyse, codify and disseminate development experience around the world (Wolfensohn 1996b, Stern and Ferreira 1997, Gilbert, Powell and Vines 1999, Squire 2000 and Picciotto 2002). This combines with an argument regarding the difficulties of structuring incentives in order for outside research institutes to deliver the kind of research the World Bank seeks to promote. Squire (2000, p.109) asserts that:

> without an in-house capacity, integrating the results of research into the World Bank's everyday operations and making those results available to policy-makers in developing countries does not happen. This usually requires an in-house champion, and the best champion is almost always the researcher. This then supplies the primary rationale for an in-house research capacity at the World Bank.

And, while for Squire the influence of research on operations provides the basis for the argument in favour of in-house research at the Bank, Gilbert and Vines (2000) emphasise the alleged neutral and professional character of Bank research:[4] 'The Bank is in a position to give advice which is more disinterested than that provided by professional consultants, more professional than that provided by academics and more comprehensive than that provided by NGOs' (p.29).

This goal of explicitly attaining a central role for knowledge within the Bank's activities is presented as being strictly beneficial for development. As such, it is prone to a set of serious misgivings. First, the discourse around the knowledge bank, projecting the notion that (its) knowledge is objective and value-neutral, implies a dramatic disregard for the socio-historical, political and economic context within which knowledge – including Bank knowledge – is produced, as well as for the socio-political or economic functions knowledge might fulfil. Mehta (1999),[5] however, reminds us that 'knowledge is plural, perspectival and largely socially constructed ... knowledge is created in and contingent on specific socio-historical, political and economic contexts, the study of which is almost as important as the study of knowledge itself' (p.153).

Second, this is not some point of general postmodernist critical discourse, for critical commentaries on the construction of the Bank's knowledge abound on the basis of more mundane grounds. These have drawn attention to the following: the shareholder realities of the Bank and, in particular, the role of the United States as major donor and influence; the implications of the embedded relationship of the Bank to the financial markets; and the prevalence of economics as the Bank's 'high scholarly discipline' (see Gwin 1994, Wade 1996 and 2002, Kapur, Lewis and Webb 1997, Mehta 1999 and 2001, Standing 2000, Fine 2001a, Samoff and Stromquist 2001, Kapur 2002 and Peet 2003).

Third, these broad governance features have a set of concrete implications. Broad (2006, p.397) identifies what she describes as a form of 'soft law', unstated and sometimes at the expense of formal procedures, which establishes 'a de facto series of incentives that make it clear – all along the DEC hierarchy – what kind of research is being encouraged'. Through a closer look at the particular hiring and promotion practices, the selective enforcement of rules, the specific ways in which dissonant discourse is discouraged, data are manipulated, and the way in which research findings are projected outside the Bank, the mechanisms of 'paradigm maintenance' operating in the Bank's Development Economics Vice-Presidency (DEC) are uncovered. Through these, individuals and work 'resonating' with neo-liberal ideology are privileged.

This, of course, does not imply that research staff at the Bank are characterised by universally shared understandings on all aspects of development, but that 'dissonant discourse', if tolerated, is neither encouraged nor promoted (see also Samoff 1992, p.65). In addition, the External Affairs Department of the Bank, whose stature grew rapidly during the Wolfensohn presidency, plays a special role in the amplification of a particular discourse within and beyond the Bank (see Ellerman 2001 and Broad 2006).

Fourth, and as a result, Bank research tends to be characterised by a set of shortcomings. Fine (2001a, p.205) sums these up as follows:[6]

> poor quality, poor engagement with alternatives (Americanisation), excessive dissemination at the expense of independent research capacity building (ditto), poor coherence and integration in how research is used in choice, design, monitoring and assessment of activities, overgeneralisation in order to rationalise loans and

leave room for discretion despite need for country and issue specificity, and limited engagement in self-criticism and assessment even when there are sea-changes in approach.

Fifth is a bias in favour of economics in the Bank's research and analysis and the resulting reductionist character of Bank knowledge, notwithstanding an increase in the appointment of non-economist social scientists as research staff in the Bank (albeit *outside* its research department) (see Bebbington et al. 2004). The staff at DEC is dominated by economists who are mainly the product of the graduate economics departments of English-speaking but, especially, US universities (Kapur, Lewis and Webb 1997 and Stern and Ferreira 1997). A former programme director for knowledge management at the Bank, Denning (2001, p.143) notes:

> There is still only one sociologist on the entire research staff, with significant risks to the distortion of knowledge generated, which is obviously multidisciplinary in nature. One can imagine what would happen to a piece of research showing that the problems of development are non-economic in origin and that a wider array of disciplines are needed. It is barely conceivable that such a piece of work would be proposed (who would propose it?), or carried out (who would do it?), or if carried out, that it would be regarded seriously by economists whose careers are linked to preserving the economic orientation of the research department.

Nevertheless, as the intellectual contribution of the Bank is not confined to its research department, the particular skill mix of the operational departments and the changes therein could have bearing on the nature of the knowledge produced by the Bank. Yet non-economists employed within the Bank have tended to leave core economic issues unchallenged, trying to peg their own concerns onto an otherwise undisturbed economic agenda (see Fine 2001a and Chapter 5).[7] Leiteritz and Weaver (2005, p.382) observe:

> The quantitative shift in the staff skills mix towards the new 'priority' sectors may have countered the physical dominance of economists in the Bank and may eventually lead to meaningful transformation in how 'the Bank' as a collective set of actors 'think' about development, but this has not spontaneously disrupted the economics orthodoxy within the Bank's development approach. Several interviews with Bank staff confirm that non-economic

social scientists within the organisation feel compelled to adapt their ideas to the theoretical and methodological language of the prevailing economic theory, whether it is neoclassical economics prominent in the 1980s or the current fashion of institutional economics, in order to influence conceptual and operational reality in the Bank. The observation by M. Cernea that non-economic social scientists (especially sociologists and anthropologists) hired in the mid 1990s 'did not land in an intellectual vacuum' but rather 'landed onto an in-house culture unfamiliar and resistant to this new socio-cultural knowledge and expertise' is echoed in many commentaries on the fate of new development ideas within the Bank.

Sixth, within the confines of a framework of knowledge creation as an international public good, how to prioritise between different types of knowledge remains an unaddressed issue. The point has been made, in particular, with respect to social science research versus crop or vaccine research (see Kanbur 2001b and Kapur 2003 and 2006). Kapur (2006) ponders:[8] 'If the Bank were to cut its Analytical and Advisory Activities (AAA) expenditures ... shifting its focus from the social sciences to funding research in the health sciences, would the global welfare of the poor increase or decline?' (p.160). Kapur also draws attention to the relatively expensive nature of in-house Bank research – even when compared to universities in the United States, let alone those in developing countries – and argues that the Bank's research activities should be like a National Science Foundation funding activity rather than in-house research (and levels of intellectual and ideological control would be lessened).

Seventh, in counterpoint to the observation by Gilbert and Vines (2000, p.29) quoted earlier regarding the 'disinterested' nature of Bank advice, Kapur (2003, p.13) emphasises how Bank research is undermined by 'its lack of independence, real or perceived, and without this independence the Bank's research will always be found wanting as a global public good'. Kanbur (2002, p.22) insists that:

the Bank as a whole cannot possibly be viewed as an independent arbiter of social science research. It is owned by the rich countries, and it has operational policies that need to be defended. These features mean that social science research done by the Bank itself cannot fully lay claim to the mantle of an IPG [International Public Good].

A conflict of interest clearly underlies the Bank's joint role as an analyst and lender (see also Wade 2002 and Debt Relief International 2002). The potential problems of combining the provision of funds with engaging in authoritative claims about development as well as of the institutionalisation of a funding agency as a provider of development advisory services are manifold. Samoff and Bidemi (2003, p.32) observe that:

> what is deemed valid and legitimate information ('knowledge') will become increasingly centralised in the North; information that is collected in the South will be shaped and framed by its interpreters ... That powerful role in determining what is and what is not knowledge will be obscured by the mystique of science and scientific method. The centralisation of the determination of what is knowledge entrenches the role of the elite education and research institutions in the world, nearly all located in the most affluent countries. What is deemed to be the important knowledge is likely to become more technical and less humanistic and critical ... Overall, information databases created and maintained by authoritative institutions in the North with substantial economic leverage and ideological influence are most likely to reinforce existing power relations, both within and across countries.

In sum, the Bank's knowledge exercise, rather than resembling a neutral, politically impartial or technical enterprise, needs to be understood within its political–economic–disciplinary contexts. These have important implications for the particular ideas favoured by the Bank at specific moments in time and across a range of topics. They need to be teased out, and the nature of the impact of Bank discourse, scholarship and rhetoric on the terms of various debates in development revealed.

It is argued in the following section that the Deaton Report both pointed in the direction of a set of tensions bearing upon the Bank's knowledge exercise and, at the same time, failed to pursue these tensions to their origins and situate them more broadly in the context of the particular political–economic and disciplinary constellations within which Bank knowledge takes form and is promoted. This fundamental failing of the Deaton exercise provides the backdrop against which a more critical assessment of the Bank's role in development research across a range of areas is undertaken in the rest of the book. The following section reviews the main findings from the evaluation and considers some of the limitations in the evaluation process, demonstrating how these reflect the structural and intellectual constraints of the institution itself.

2.3   THE DEATON REPORT

The Deaton Report (Deaton et al. 2006) provides us with what at first sight appears to be a critical reading of the Bank's research. After brief praise of it as 'of very high quality ... directed towards issues that are of great importance to the Bank, and ... executed to the highest standards of the profession' (p.37), the Deaton Report quickly moves on to 'a number of deficiencies'. A great deal of Bank research is 'undistinguished' and 'not well-directed either to academic or policy concerns' (p.38). 'The quality of execution does not always match the importance and the relevance of the topic, and is often unacceptably far behind the best-practice methods' (p.38). Further, some prominent Bank research is 'technically flawed' and 'in some cases strong policy positions have been supported by such (non) evidence' (p.38).

Indeed, a striking feature of the Deaton Report is not only its emphasis on the extent of poor scholarship but also the use of such scholarship for purposes of 'advocacy' and worse. Thus (p.6):

> the panel has substantial criticisms of the way that this research was used to proselytise on behalf of Bank policy, often without expressing appropriate scepticism. Internal research that was favorable to Bank positions was given greater prominence, and unfavorable research ignored ... balance was lost in favor of advocacy ... there was a serious failure of the checks and balances that should separate advocacy and research.

These themes around advocacy, proselytising and balance recur. For (p.38):

> putting too much weight on preliminary or flawed work could [why not 'does'?] expose the Bank to charges that its research is tailored or selected to support its predetermined positions, and the panel believes that, in some cases, the Bank proselytised selected new work in major policy speeches and publications, without appropriate caveats on its reliability ... this happened with some of the Bank's work on aid effectiveness.[9]

More generally, '[o]ne criticism that was made repeatedly [by assessors] is that research tended to jump to policy conclusions that were not well-supported by the evidence' (p.40). And, of course (p.84):

it is very difficult to be fully objective about the results of your pet project ... There is much selection of evidence, with obscure, sometimes unpublished, studies with the 'right' message given prominence over better and better-known studies that come to the 'wrong' conclusion'.

Indeed, this is all so bad that (p.149):

[t]he panel is particularly concerned with finding a way to fund Bank research that protects its independence, and guarantees that Bank research does not degenerate into pure advocacy of the type that has become all too prevalent in the global poverty debate.

In summary (p.161),

[m]anagers of research at the Bank need to maintain checks and balances that preserve the credibility of its research. In particular, it needs to resist the temptation to make strong claims about preliminary and controversial research that appears to support policies that the Bank has historically supported.

In view of this, we are ultimately offered what might be thought to be the epitome of understatement: 'Nevertheless, over the review period, we are concerned that the independence of Bank research may have *frayed at the edges*' (p.156, emphasis added).

These comments combine with the report's denunciation of the scant use of country-specific knowledge available within the institution, as well as the limited collaboration with researchers from the developing world (p.39). The evaluation also points to the lack of external critical engagement, debate and self-reflection (p.73):

Evaluators also noted that a high proportion of the citations in this group of [less distinguished] papers are to other Bank papers, many of them unpublished. In some cases, where groups are almost entirely inward looking, the degree of self-reference rises almost to the level of parody.

In addition, the report reproduces the comment from a Bank researcher (p.125):

> Research ... is essentially a form of rhetoric. It is often not about doing research to discover new knowledge but to justify some previously determined policy. It is not unusual to be told that 'we should do an evaluation to prove that X program works,' for instance. Or 'we have to run some regressions to show that Y agenda matters for growth otherwise we will not have Bank buy-in.' Peer reviewing is often fixed by appointing cronies as reviewers who are not in a position to make critical comments.

Further, another interviewee, active as a researcher in the Bank, observes: 'There was an enormous amount of interference by the PR people, especially after Wolfensohn became president; research was not supposed to offend NGOs, nor to provide them with material they could use to criticize the Bank' (p.127). And, for another, 'the WDRs (and PRRs [Policy Research Reports]) were a prime example of research where the conclusions are "either predetermined or negotiated in advance" ... This stuff is largely worthless' (p.129).

In light of these problems of advocacy bias, scant use of developing-country researchers, nearly grotesque self-referential habits and other failings, the Deaton Report seeks to put much of this right through a number of recommendations. There appears to be something of a disconnect between the severity of the criticisms and the mild nature of the recommendations. For Deaton et al., the shortcomings are, in essence, the result of an administrative budget squeeze and stem from a set of imbalances characterising the Bank's research exercise. The latter crop up, among others, in the domain of rigour versus relevance; responsiveness and independence; policy relevance and academic distinction; and advocacy of 'good' policies versus the production of new policy ideas. The Bank's comparative research advantage remains understood in terms of economies of scale and scope in knowledge generation, unique opportunities generated by the conjunction of research and policymaking, and the breadth of the Bank's country involvement – much in line with the Bank's own account of its knowledge advantage documented above (pp.14–18).

In such an account, the deficiencies in the Bank's exercise of its knowledge role can best be addressed by securing an endowment for Bank research, which would guarantee both financial continuity and greater independence of research, and by altering the incentives and structures steering research. The latter would involve: improved cost accounting; a change in the structure for allocating and planning research; the design of better quality control mechanisms; and a strengthening of interactions with academics. Following Deaton et al., the matter is then one of incentives and systems, without any acknowledgment that the dull weight of such mundane research serves as a highly functional defence against engaging better scholars, and criticism, from outside the Bank, let alone from within. The Deaton Report's illustrations of the Bank's persistent research failures, nevertheless, speak volumes about the institutional culture in which the Bank undertakes its research, and presume that both institution and culture would need to be reformed.

Endemic dynamics emerging from, among other things, the Bank's shareholder realities, the specific nature of its relationship to the financial markets, or the general state of its 'highly scholarly discipline' (Kapur, Lewis and Webb 1997), economics, remain firmly beyond the report's horizon. This failure to recognise the broader, political–economic dimensions to the Bank's knowledge role, amply commented upon in existing critical commentary on the Bank (see above) – itself completely ignored in the Deaton Report – is striking. The only time we encounter an indication of possible implications of the Bank's shareholder realities for its research, incidentally also the only reference to an existing appraisal of the Bank as 'intellectual actor', is by way of an assessment of Bank research during the 1980s on debt rescheduling by a former chief economist and a then employee of DEC (Stern and Ferreira 1997). Still, the report treads cautiously (p.20):

> *They* suggest that the reasons why Bank research lagged behind research outside which had already turned against forcing developing countries to pay everything they owed, is that the Bank's major shareholders were worried about hurting the banks in their own countries. (emphasis added)

But if research performs an advocacy role – as repeatedly highlighted in the report – what informs the nature and direction of that role? The report refers to 'Bank positions' (p.6), but what are these? Where do they come from? How do they evolve? What imperatives do they obey? How is the relationship between these 'positions' and research brokered? How do they translate into Bank practice? And how does Bank scholarship (or is it 'advocacy'?)

mediate between these positions and Bank practices? The report provides no answers.

Indeed, the report's understanding of the relationship between scholarship, advocacy/proselytising/rhetoric/ideology, and policy is remarkably limited. These three elements are not necessarily mutually consistent with one another; but nor are they independent of one another; and they have a shifting relationship between one another over time and place and across issues.[10] Significantly, the Deaton Report more or less neglects policy (of the Bank) in practice and sees the relationship between scholarship and advocacy as a simple dualism of making them more compatible with one another, inevitably closing the gap towards scholarship and against advocacy.

This is unfortunate, especially as the report observes, in a rare example of insight on these issues, that the Bank is in a position to address 'the "big" questions, such issues as how to reduce poverty, how to help Africa grow faster, how to balance social sectors like health and education with more narrowly economic investments, or whether and under what circumstances aid works'. Not surprisingly, then, 'Bank researchers almost certainly have more influence on Bank operations *indirectly*, through their influence on the broad community, as *directly*, through their advice on particular programs and projects' (p.14).

As a result of failing to pursue this further, the report is seriously deficient in its framework of analysis, for two major reasons. First is the failure to see the strained relationship between scholarship and advocacy (and policy) as longstanding (if not unchanging in substance), endemic, institutionalised and functional for the discretion and control of the Bank in the development arena. The heavy hand of advocacy and policy over scholarship has so frequently been emphasised by critics of the Bank, especially under the Washington Consensus. For, in changing the debate about development, the Bank has generally set a limited agenda, within narrow limits, precluding and failing to engage with many alternatives, and has deployed its resources and influence to manage debate. Indeed, when the Bank purportedly shifts debate, as in its discussion of the East Asian Miracle for example, it often sees itself as raising a new issue and being original when, in effect, what is happening is to wipe the slate clean of what is generally more radical and insightful scholarship and proceed as if it never existed. In short, paradigm and issue shift at the Bank is not the consequence of scholarship. On the contrary, in general, it is shifts in scholarship that are the servant of other goals and pressures.[11]

Second, in a parody of the report's own critique of the Bank's introspection, is the total absence of any consideration of the voluminous critical literature that already exists on these aspects of the Bank's performance. Every critic of the Bank, and most of its practitioners and supporters, know that it seeks to suppress criticism and, where this fails, it certainly does not engage with it other than to seek to manage it (see above).

In this light, the Deaton evaluation has effectively reinvented the wheel in pointing to the deep deficiencies in World Bank research, although it has squared off the wheel in not engaging with earlier, fuller and more wide-ranging accounts and in not identifying in what direction the putative wheel is rolling. Despite its most welcome, wide-ranging, and relatively rare assessment from its own perspective, it may well have confined itself to yet another telling but archived critique of Bank output and process. It is observed that (p.8):

> Bank research has not been monitored and evaluated as often as is desirable. The fact that our evaluation is the first in seven years is not unrelated to some of the problems we have found. More regular evaluations would permit early termination of bad projects, and would help limit the long tail of undistinguished work.

Yet, there is no assessment of how evaluations, within the Bank or otherwise, are responded to, if at all, and this is certainly more important than a greater frequency of (ignored) evaluations. In this respect, the shelf-gathering-dust experience of the Deaton Report itself is of telling significance.

These failings are hardly surprising in view of other critical weaknesses of the Deaton process. First, the analytical framework is adopted exclusively from within mainstream economics and, in general, is at the forefront of the discipline, at least in some respects, as it is currently. This involves a general predisposition towards both mathematical models as theory and methodological individualism. But there is a departure from exclusive reliance upon the idea that markets work perfectly, and there is also inclusion of non-market factors. Particular emphasis is based upon econometrics, as evidence-based research for the purposes of policymaking.[12]

The Deaton approach is certainly more than sufficient to address World Bank research on its own terms and from the perspective of mainstream economics, and to give it a considerable going over. But it is extremely narrow in its economic theory; and it is totally lacking in interdisciplinarity. For the latter, in particular, we have a critique of the Deaton Report by Rao and Woolcock (2007a and b) for failing to have engaged any non-economists amongst the assessors.[13] They point to the disciplinary monopoly of economics in the Bank's research, and in Deaton's assessment, at the expense of other disciplines. They overlook, however, that this monopoly holds equally within economics as well, excluding alternatives that are open to interdisciplinarity other than on the terms of economics imperialism (adding non-economic variables to the economic) (Fine and Milonakis 2009). Thus, when the report suggests that '[c]urrently, there is very little frontline academic work being done *by economists* in such important areas as urban economics, transportation, climate change, and infrastructure' (p.15, emphasis added), the implication is that no economic analysis is being done, despite these topics being of central importance to other disciplines as well, including specialised journals for the purpose.[14]

Significantly, then, the criterion that comes to the fore in assessing the quality of World Bank research is by refereeing for an economics journal. There is a bias towards 'the three top general interest journals', such as the *American Economic Review*, *Journal of Political Economy*, and *Quarterly Journal of Economics*, as well as *Econometrica* and *Journal of Finance* (p.37). These are notable for their narrowness in theory and method and, of necessity, not being attuned to development. There is also a tension in accepting this criterion of top journals and, yet, remaining critical of its consequences. For '[i]n spite of having been published in the *American Economic Review*, the Burnside and Dollar paper is unconvincing' (p.54). And (p.55):

> the Bank did not appear to recognise the weakness of this evidence. Not only did it form the basis for the PRR *Assessing Aid*, but its results were built upon in a series of papers by Collier and Dollar that were published between 2001 and 2004 in the *Economic Journal*, in the *European Economic Review*, and in *World Development*.

Further, while Deaton et al. assess Bank research through an economic (and often econometric) and technical prism of orthodoxy, the assessment remains, in general, separate from any projected understanding regarding development. In the report, 'scholarship' becomes akin to 'advocacy' when the former fails to pass a certain technical threshold, without any investigation of the specific ideas regarding development embedded in this 'scholarship' (now 'advocacy'). As much as Bank research, for Deaton et al., is a matter of incentives, it is also judged on the basis of its technical merits, rather than such an assessment involving critical engagement with content beyond this narrow horizon. The question, however, remains of how the Deaton process would have judged embedded ideas regarding development if it had explicitly addressed them. The report gives no indication of how development may be understood, let alone of how this would compare to the various (and evolving) frameworks that have steered the Bank's understanding of development, themselves barely deserving of mention in the report.

This failure to judge the quality of World Bank research from any sort of perspective on the major issues of concern is striking. There is little to learn from the report on development itself or the development literature, quite apart from the debates that these have inspired within orthodoxy around the Bank's unquestioned agenda. The preoccupation with technique implies that the report offers little of substance other than a judgement of quality detached from substance.

Significantly, the term 'Washington Consensus' only appears once in the report, and 'post-Washington Consensus' not at all. But surely the dominance of World Bank research by the Washington Consensus, and its displacement just as the research period covered by the Deaton evaluation is beginning, is the key to any assessment of research activity and its reform? To spell it out, was the Washington Consensus justified? If not, has its influence on research been remedied by the post-Washington Consensus? Questions such as these are imperative to any assessment of the nature, dynamic and impact of World Bank research, unless reduced to fence-sitting on technique. And, finally, almost unbelievably, the Deaton Report makes no reference whatsoever to Poverty Reduction Strategy Papers (PRSPs), in acronym or otherwise. The term 'Millennium Development Goal' (or 'MDG') appears only three times in the Deaton Report. And the same neglect applies to the Comprehensive Development Framework. Like the Washington Consensus that preceded it, it too only warrants a single citation throughout the report: 'Issues are seen through the lens of current Bank policies, even when not obviously appropriate. The WDR on *Entering the 21st Century* is burdened with having to mount a sustained defense of the Comprehensive Development Strategy' (p.81).

So, whilst policy relevance is offered by the Deaton Report as a criterion for judging research, it fails to mention either the Bank's organising conceptual framework or its policy framework for the period under review, other than in passing.

2.4 CONCLUDING REMARKS

As already indicated in our Preface, the impact of the Deaton Report on development practice and the development community (from where do its ideas derive?) was far less than might have been warranted given the extent of the exercise (an assessment of all World Bank research outputs over the period 1998 to 2005) and the eminence of the assessors (a panel consisting of Angus Deaton (chair), Princeton University; Kenneth Rogoff, Harvard University; Abhijit Banerjee, M.I.T.; and Nora Lustig, Director of the Poverty Group at UNDP; they in turn recruited 24 thematic evaluators, including the current World Bank chief economist, Justin Lin). This lack of impact is all the more surprising and disappointing given the severity and nature of the criticisms levelled at Bank research practice, which have already been outlined in some detail. Within the Bank itself, the findings of the report were understood as an endorsement of the Bank's research capacity, if accompanied by a small slap on the wrists for excessive proselytism in a limited number of research areas (World Bank 2009b, p.75). Pushing the argument a bit further, Dethier (2007, p.475), an ardent DEC staffer, accused Deaton et al. of failing 'to provide objective evidence that the Bank's research "tail" is longer than that of other leading institutions'.

Disillusion with the limited purpose to which his evaluation was put may have subsequently prompted Deaton to declare (not least given his piece's title) that 'the development expertise that is the centre of the World Bank's mission may not exist in useful form or, at the least, needs to be fundamentally rethought and restricted' (2009a, pp.113–14). Elsewhere, he has observed that 'there is great frustration with aid organisations, particularly the World Bank, for allegedly failing to learn from its projects and to build up a systematic catalogue of what works and what does not' (2009b, p.3).[15] In personal correspondence on these points, Deaton confesses that his views (to the extent that they could be expressed within the confines of the report process) have hardened, whilst also expressing concerns over how World Bank research has been adopted or placed in academic institutions other than itself.

It is, of course, a shame that such ex post considerations did, possibly could, not inform the assessment ex ante, at least as factors in investigating and explaining the shifting context, content, motivation and impact of Bank research. And the context itself has already moved on as a result of the financial crisis that post-dated the evaluation. Consequently, the essays that follow have confronted a twofold task in assessing the role of the World Bank as knowledge bank – one is to expose its deficiencies in research in general, the other is to do so in light of the crisis in particular. In these respects, there is a striking feature of World Bank research as contributing to the research community more generally. The Bank's contributions are often so weak and unacceptable that serious scholars are simply dismissive without engagement. On the other hand, the 'knowledge' stance of the Bank is so extensive that it does command engagement in an uneven, unevenly controlled and selective manner, to such an excess that it can set the agenda and methods of debate. What the Deaton process demonstrates is the limited effect of critique of the Bank's scholarship when expressed within its own frame of reference. Our own, more widely cast contributions are liable to stretch beyond the horizon of the Bank's knowledge. This should be so not only in substance but also in process. For the hopes for more progressive and more satisfactorily grounded research depend upon *activism* against the Bank's roles in advocacy, scholarship and policy. It is insufficient simply to inform of more appropriate analytical frameworks and content, as has so often been demonstrated in the past by the treatment, through incorporation, neglect or peremptory dismissal, of even the mildest critics.

NOTES

1. See also Gavin and Rodrik (1995), Ryrie (1995), Krueger (1998), Gilbert, Powell and Vines (1999) and Squire (2000).
2. See Stone (2000) on the Global Development Network; King and McGrath (2004) on the Global Development Gateway and Van Waeyenberge (2007, pp.106–8) on the Researchers Alliance for Development.
3. See also Chapter 3.
4. Fine (2002b, p.131) parodies Squire (2000):

    > it is reported that World Bank research has a marginal product of twelve to fifteen times its cost, p.124. On this basis, if the Bank did give me a job, I could work this little known and appreciated fact into a model of endogenous growth. It would show, other things being equal, that if World Bank staff and remuneration were doubled over the next four years (salaries to act as screening device to improve quality even more ...), world GDP could be tripled by the end of the decade.

5. See also Caddell (1999), Nustad and Sending (2000), Standing (2000), Samoff and Stromquist (2001), Torres (2001) and Stone (2003).
6. See also Ranis (2003) and below.

7. See Stone (2007) on how the Bank's tendency towards 'disciplinary monopoly' permeates the various knowledge networks that have emerged from the Bank.
8. See Fine (2009c, p.895) who observes how the Bank *and* its critics, and their corresponding debates, have focused on the theory as opposed to the material practices of development:

> The World Bank has both increased its influence on the social science of development and the influence of such social science (and economics within it) on development thinking. This has been at the expense of practitioners on the ground, in the sense of those with technical expertise who deliver development policy, unless these be social scientists. Policy debate has increasingly been about ideas, the knowledge bank, as opposed to delivery.

9. This research is the focus of Chapter 3.
10. Fine (2001a), Fine, Lapavitsas and Pincus (2001), Jomo and Fine (eds) (2006), and Bayliss and Fine (eds) (2008).
11. See Wade (1996) on the East Asian Miracle, and Fine, Lapavitsas and Pincus (eds) (2001) and Jomo and Fine (eds) (2006) for the shift from the Washington to the post-Washington Consensus. More recently, on PRSPs etc., see Fraser (2005), Tan (2007) and Van Waeyenberge (2007).
12. It is surely no accident that Deaton himself is one of the world's leading econometricians (his own modest claims to the contrary) rather than a development economist (if orthodoxy allows the difference these days).
13. The report itself opines, 'we find it hard to imagine a group of evaluators who would be more distinguished or more qualified to evaluate the quality of development research' (p.41); and, '[o]ur evaluators represent the very best in contemporary research in development, and they did what the databases [of citations] cannot do, which is to read the work' (p.45).
14. Note that the quotation continues (pp.15–16):

> A prime example of the second kind of failure [to provide intellectual public goods], research that is unlikely to be done by top academics[,] is replication and testing ... [W]ithin academia replicating what someone has already done, although widely practiced, is not done systematically, and it is perceived as derivative and unoriginal, and not highly valued.

No evidence is offered for the later assertions, and they might be thought to be contradicted by mainstream economics itself, and certainly by social capital.

15. Note that his contribution is also highly critical of the new research mantra across development economics, randomised controlled trials (RCT), which also was being strongly promoted by some of the Deaton assessors.

Part II
Research in Practice

The contributions to this part are, first and foremost, indicative of the huge range over which World Bank research roams. It was not always thus. Under the Washington Consensus, with its emphasis upon leaving everything to the market, there was less incentive to offer widely cast research other than to demonstrate the efficacy of the market and inefficacy of the state. For the pre-Washington Consensus, as it were, the Bank had only relatively recently, and reluctantly, been drawn into funding social development as opposed to physical infrastructure. The culture of the Bank, and its ethos as a hard-nosed user of its funds required its loans and investments to be real in some sense (Benjamin 2007). That culture has now, in the era of the PWC, been transformed beyond recognition, not only with the exploding breadth of policy interventions (with corresponding attention to research and advocacy) but also in a correspondingly soft role as purveyor of knowledge.

Second, although the core framework derived from neoclassical economics is common across the vast majority of World Bank research (with potential for market and institutional imperfections under the PWC), it is sufficiently flexible to allow for considerable diversity across different areas of research, in part in response to the different demands of advocacy and policy in practice (whether research meets, or is consistent with these or not). Collectively, these chapters tease out these differences, whilst searching out the considerable flaws in the methods deployed in World Bank research, as well as within the application of those methods.

Third, in particular, and crudely oversimplifying, Chapters 3 (on the allocation of aid in practice) and 9 (on violence and conflict) point to the dissonances between research and policy with, respectively, aid allocation tightening on Washington Consensus principles in the age of the PWC, and what is often excellent empirical research on the political economy of opium production in Afghanistan being set aside in deference to the dictates of justifying the military interventions there. Chapters 4, 6 and 8, on water privatisation, HIV/AIDS, and the liberalisation of (personal) banking to allow the entry of foreign firms, offer stunning illustrations of flawed research on their own terms, by virtue of the absolute neglect of broader literature and factors, with the presumption that Bank research has been designed to support preconceived policy prescriptions. Chapter 5 (on social capital) highlights the promotion by the World Bank of a concept that has offered little or no influence over policy. Rather it has played a legitimising role for research on the non-economic without questioning the economic. And it has provided an ideological rationale for a softly–softly approach in allowing for a renewal of the role of the state in deference to amorphous civil society participation as harbinger of development. Chapter 7 (on agriculture) reveals a remarkable hotchpotch of neo-populism and neoclassical economics – ranging across land reform for redistribution in favour of small-scale farmers to secure property rights as a means to promoting investment and productivity on the land – in an area that has been sorely neglected by the Bank, despite its significance for the majority of the population in the poorest countries. Neglect for entirely different reasons has been the fate of China, as revealed in Chapter 10, since the country's success stands out as the most powerful of empirical refutations of the prognostications of the Bank in the age of the PWC, just as the east Asian NICs contradicted the Washington Consensus.

In such broad terms, these analyses indicate the complexity of World Bank research by topic. This places great demands upon the (critical) researcher in commanding the materials that the Bank offers, especially in deconstructing its content, context and evolving dynamics, and in offering alternatives from more radical traditions within the study of development. Consequently, the latter are losing their hold as parts of conventional wisdom as the knowledge bank develops a universal network of branches across topics and disciplines. We certainly do not consider that these case studies are the last word on the topics covered, not least because the Bank's postures can evolve rapidly alongside the diversity of material conditions they putatively seek to address. And our coverage by topic is desperately limited relative to the range now covered by the Bank. At the very least, we hope that the reader, researcher or activist, will be convinced of the need to sustain such perspectives and will even find some lessons on how to go about adding to them.

3
Understanding Aid at the Bank

Elisa Van Waeyenberge

3.1 INTRODUCTION

The World Bank has been a leader in aid, not least through its role in promoting structural adjustment programmes across the developing world since the early 1980s. For almost a decade now, the Bank has, further, sought to redefine aid and conditionality practices, with a greater emphasis on a priori assessments of a country's policy and institutional environment when allocating aid through 'selectivity' or performance-based aid allocations, rather than conditioning aid flows on the promise of future reforms. The selective allocation of its aid proceeds on the basis of Bank staff assessments of countries' policies and institutions. These are embedded in the Bank's Country Policy and Institutional Assessment (CPIA).

The insistence on attention to the nature of existing policies and institutions, rather than promises for reform, as the basis on which to ration aid, was propelled forward by the Bank's aid-effectiveness research (Burnside and Dollar 1997 and 2000, Collier and Dollar 1999, 2001 and 2002, and World Bank 1998a). This research quickly rose to prominence and came to occupy centre stage in the debate on aid. The Deaton evaluation took particular issue with it, singling out the research as a prime example of the poor scholarship that can be undertaken at, and vigorously proselytised by, the Bank. Yet, somewhat paradoxically, the failings of the Deaton evaluation, highlighted in Chapter 2, singularly stood out where its critique sought to be at its most forceful. As argued earlier, the Deaton evaluation was, in general, oblivious to institutional dynamics characterising Bank research that are related to the broader setting within which both Bank policies and research come about and take effect. Further, the evaluation displayed a strong bias in favour of technique over substance. These shortcomings had strong implications for the report's assessment of the Bank's aid-effectiveness research, where the policy–scholarship–rhetoric conundrum, which the Deaton evaluation was at pains to ignore, imposed itself very starkly.

This chapter seeks to move beyond the Deaton critique in an assessment of the Bank's aid research. This involves an investigation into the nature of the aid scholarship promoted by the Bank and its effect on the broader debate regarding aid impact. It further necessitates a closer look into the *aid practice* that the particular scholarship has sought to defend, i.e. performance-based aid allocations on the basis of the CPIA. The investigation into the Bank's aid-allocation mechanism, further, draws attention to a dimension of the Bank's interaction with its clients that has often been overlooked, namely the applied analytical work (Analytical and Advisory Activities, or AAA) taking place in the Bank's operational departments. This analytical work, not covered as part of the remit of the Deaton Report, has important implications for the way in which policy is designed in developing countries, as it easily crowds out other research capacity and policy advice. Finally, the global financial crisis has highlighted the persistent (and worsened) funding requirements in much of the developing world, and thrown old certainties into disarray. There is little indication, however, that the Bank has seized this dramatic moment to alter the way it understands (and prescribes policies for) aid and development.

The chapter proceeds as follows. First, the main arguments of the Bank's aid research are documented. This is followed, second, by their critical examination, with the concerns highlighted in the Deaton Report serving as starting points. Third, the limits of the Deaton critique are exposed, taking us to the heart of the research–policy–advocacy conundrum. Fourth, the operational practice promoted through the aid research (and ignored in the Deaton Report) is documented, unveiling an operational perspective on the rationale for the Bank's aid research. This brings us, fifth, to a brief account of the way in which the Bank exercises its knowledge role in its interaction with its low-income clients, with particular attention on its 'economic and sector work' (ESW), and the implications of this for the conditioning of the policy space in these countries. This reverberates with the broader knowledge theme, eagerly espoused by the Bank over the last decade (see Chapter 1). The chapter concludes with a brief assessment of the nature of the Bank's aid response to the current global financial and economic crisis.

3.2   UNDERSTANDING AID AT THE BANK

The late 1990s saw a vigorous re-engagement with the macroeconomics of aid. This was prompted by a set of World Bank contributions which sought to provide scholarly support for the increasingly popular practice of performance-based aid allocations (or 'selectivity'). The Bank's aid research centred around: a paper by Burnside and Dollar (2000), 'Aid, Policies and Growth', first circulated as a World Bank Working Paper (Burnside and Dollar 1997); a Policy Research Report, 'Assessing Aid' (World Bank 1998a), built on Burnside and Dollar's central premise of conditional aid effectiveness; and a set of later contributions by Collier and Dollar (1999, 2001, 2002) that extended the Burnside and Dollar premise into a prescriptive model for 'poverty-efficient' aid allocations.[1] 'A Case for Aid' (World Bank 2002a) summed up the Bank's position at the United Nations Monterrey Conference and further built on these core references, and Collier and Dollar (2004) restated the basic arguments in a special issue of the *Economic Journal*. Finally, another flagship report, 'Aid and Reform in Africa' (World Bank 2001b), brought together a set of case studies on aid, conditionality and reform, framed by the general Burnside and Dollar message.

It was argued across these various contributions that aid only positively affected the growth rate of a recipient country if a certain set of policies/institutions was characteristic of the country. Further, aid did not affect the policy/institutional environment of a country. Hence, aid should be (re)allocated towards those countries characterised by a 'good' policy and institutional environment. The latter broadly reflected the Bank's CPIA, on which more below, or, more narrowly, focused on the 'core' macroeconomic policy stance of budget surplus, low inflation and trade openness. Under such a performance-based allocation of aid, or selectivity, the conditionality accompanying (or now preceding) aid no longer reflected the flow of reforms, but the state of the policy and institutional environment. Conditions would relate to past rather than future actions.

This idea of making loans/grants conditional on what had already been achieved in terms of policy/institutional reform combined with an emphasis on a more advisory role for donors. A country not yet characterised by an 'appropriate' environment was to be a recipient of 'aid skills', or advice, rather than of 'aid money'. 'Assessing Aid' (World Bank 1998a, p.4) elucidated: 'Aid can nurture reform even in the most distorted environments – but it requires patience and a focus on ideas, not money.'

Aid's two dimensions ('financial' versus 'ideational') became distinct and separate. Selectivity meant channelling financial aid to countries with 'appropriate' policy environments and using non-lending services more strategically to support the emergence of a set of policies/institutions. The 'pedagogical' role of the donor community, and of the World Bank in particular, received special emphasis. Collier (2000a, p.307) explained:

> By abandoning the notion of aid as a 'reward' for policy improvement, donors move to a model of partnership. However with those governments which adopt really poor policies, partnerships are not beneficial. Engagement with those governments and with their societies in the battle of ideas is the means by which donors can best hope to influence policy.

These ideas were put forward by a few well-known development economists, employed at the time in the Bank's research department (Development Economics Research Group, or DECRG). As the Director of DECRG between April 1998 and April 2003, Paul Collier played a steering role in the endeavour. The position gave him occasion to develop further a set of ideas regarding aid and conditionality he had started to explore previously (see Collier et al. 1997, Collier 1997a and b). The other major player in the aid-effectiveness research was David Dollar, a much celebrated Bank researcher who had persistently demonstrated his faculty for providing 'scholarly' support for the neo-liberal paradigm – most famously in Dollar and Kraay (2002) (also subjected to strong critique in the Deaton Report), the development of the Dollar index of trade openness, and the aid-effectiveness research.[2] Whilst engaging in the aid-effectiveness research, David Dollar was a research manager in DECRG. He subsequently became director of development policy within the Bank's research department and was finally promoted to country director for China and Mongolia, a much coveted job at the Bank.[3]

3.3 AID, POLICIES, GROWTH ... AND THE DEATON REPORT

The Deaton Report's assessment of the Bank's aid-effectiveness research started by recognising the enormous influence the Bank's research on aid had on the debate (Deaton et al. 2006, p.52). This was indeed the case, both in academic and policy terms. In the context of the latter, Doornbos (2000, p.103) observed:

the 'Dollar-report' ... in putting forward the research finding that 'good' performers are 'best' able to absorb and utilise aid funds effectively, has come to provide a policy rationale for this new approach. Through reference to 'scientific' evidence presented in this report, 'selectivity' can be advocated and rationalised as being the most cost-effective and results-oriented donor strategy. Hence the keen interest with which this report has been taken up for discussion in various donor circuits.

Dollar himself (2001, p.1044) attributed alleged improvements in the growth performance of aid to his (and his collaborators') research efforts:

> It is always difficult to measure the impact of research. The fact that aid allocation has improved dramatically during the 1990s can be attributed to a number of factors, such as the end of the Cold War and the reform of aid agencies. But surely research results indicating how to make aid more effective played some role as well ... The first version of 'Aid, policies and growth' was circulated in 1996; this paper showed that aid in fact did affect growth, but that its impact depended on the quality of policies. Many of the changes in the second half of the 1990s have been consistent with the argumentation developed in aid effectiveness research. Suppose we attribute to research one percent of the credit for improved aid allocation ... The efficiency of aid improved by 200 percent over the decade, so we are basically ascribing to research a 2 percent improvement in the efficiency of aid. Was the money spent on research a good investment? Starting from the 1990 level of efficiency, a one-time 2 percent improvement in the efficiency of aid would lift an additional 120,000 people out of poverty in the first year. The World Bank spent about $1 million on all of its aid effectiveness research, including the publication of Assessing Aid and worldwide dissemination. The efficiency of ODA [Official Development Assistance] in 1990 was about 100 people lifted out of poverty per million dollars. Thus, the return on research in the first year was 120,000 percent of the return on the typical aid dollar of 1990. And of course one of the special features of knowledge creation is that it can be used year after year with no additional knowledge generation costs. So, the productivity of research would actually be many times the rough estimate produced above.

Academically, a large literature emerged critical of the core Burnside–Dollar result of conditional aid effectiveness.[4] This literature focused on issues of model specification, econometric technique and data selection. It exposed how the Bank-promoted paradigm was based on a biased research effort and poor theoretical and econometric practice and was not representative of the broader findings of the aid-impact literature. We are guarded against the simplistic understanding of the processes of aid, reform, growth and poverty reduction that underlie the Bank's propositions. It was often concluded that the policies embedded in the original Burnside–Dollar–Collier exercise were neither necessary nor sufficient for aid effectiveness, thus undermining the (scholarly) rationale for the Bank's policy stance of selective or performance-based aid allocations (see also below).

The Bank aid research was, further, characterised by excessive insularity and a failure to engage with criticism, even when it remained within the remit of frameworks readily understandable by Bank researchers. As one commentator observed (Morrissey 2000, p.373):

> Assessing Aid does not adequately take stock of what is known and what is not known about the macroeconomic impacts of aid. Important elements of what was and is known ... are not mentioned. Sometimes this results in a tendency to reinvent the wheel ... but other times the tendency is to misrepresent the evidence, as in whether aid effectiveness is conditional on good policy. It is right that the Bank should contribute to the debate. If it is to do so, it is only reasonable to expect that its researchers keep abreast of what is being done outside Washington, and perhaps most saliently, outside of the US.

Finally, the Bank's aid-effectiveness research was a good illustration of the way in which country-specific analysis and contributions from the developing world, when integrated, could so easily be put in the service of a set of predetermined ideas. The Bank's aid-effectiveness research was complemented by an edited volume of case studies, *Aid and Reform in Africa* (World Bank 2001b), which sought to bring together accounts of the experience of aid and policy reform in ten African countries.[5]

The various case studies compiled in *Aid and Reform in Africa* frequently drew a picture that portrayed a reality which was, at a minimum, more complex than implied by the Burnside–Collier–

Dollar propositions regarding aid, policy reform and growth. Nevertheless, the Bank's editorial team, in the overview of the book, framed the findings of the various chapters to the neglect of the specificities revealed in them (see also Tarp 2001). Indeed, whereas the case studies brimmed with evidence of the significance of financial aid for both the direction of a country's policy reform and its economic performance, Dollar, Devarajan and Holmgren (2001, p.28) summed up as follows:

> large-scale finance has, if anything, a negative effect, reducing the need to reform; and conditionality has typically failed in the absence of a serious movement for change. Technical assistance and policy dialogue, on the other hand, have helped governments and their civil societies learn about policy from neighbours and from their own experimentation.

This gross misrepresentation by the editors of the lessons projected by the various cases revealed the ease with which case study material, when undertaken, could be put in the service of a general policy position, and indicated how participation of non-Bank and regionally based researchers could be reduced to little more than a token attempt to draw on perceived local expertise, with the revealed ultimate purpose of further bestowing legitimacy on a predetermined policy agenda. This was unfortunate, given the potential often ascribed to the Word Bank to complement the inevitable shortcomings of statistical analysis with qualitative studies of individual countries.

The Deaton Report took issue with similar, if more select, problems. Apart from a comment regarding the fact that two of the 'policy measures' in Burnside and Dollar's policy index were measures of outcomes rather than policies (inflation and budget surplus), the focus is on econometric matters pertaining to the robustness of the results and the instrumental variable technique deployed in an attempt to deal with the well-known problem of endogeneity in aid regressions (aid is both a determinant of economic performance and determined by it) (Deaton et al. 2006, pp.54–5). These shortcomings are exacerbated, according to the report, by the serious abuse of the capacity of the 'scholarship' to support specific policies. The World Bank is admonished for the heavy advocacy use to which its 'scholarship' has been put and for its failure to correct itself at any point in this regard:[6]

Much of this line of research appears to have such deep flaws that, at present, the results cannot be regarded as remotely reliable, much as one might want to believe the results. There is a deeper problem here than simply a wrong assessment of provocative new research results. The problem is that in major Bank policy speeches and publications, it proselytized the new work without appropriate caveats on its reliability ... it is ... clear that the Bank seriously over-reached in prematurely putting its globalization, aid and poverty publications on a pedestal. Nor has it corrected itself to this day. (p.53)

Indeed, in the context of the latter, the Bank has developed a particular technique according to which it can make reference to various critiques levelled at its propositions, while at the same time safeguarding the essential policy messages embedded in these. The 2003 Annual Review of Development Effectiveness (World Bank 2004a) provides a good illustration. In its first chapter, three premises upon which the Bank's strategy for poverty reduction rests were set out. These included the by now familiar mantras, first, that aid is more effective in promoting poverty reduction and growth in 'good' policy/institutional environments; secondly, that aid is neither necessary nor sufficient for 'good' policy and cannot substitute for the crucial factor, 'ownership', although it can foster and reinforce 'ownership'; and, thirdly, that what works well in one country may not work in another, and that donors have a crucial role in the dissemination of knowledge about various experiences with the reform process. The review then pointed to the exposed weaknesses, mainly of the Dollar–Burnside findings, yet proceeded, unencumbered by these various critiques, with the original premise of the need to allocate aid flows selectively on the basis of the CPIA (see below) and to foster 'ownership' in line with the prescribed policies and institutions.

With regard to the Deaton Report, the reply of the Bank's then chief economist, François Bourguignon, to the report's contentions with the Bank's aid research, in less than 100 words, simply argued that the report's critique focused exclusively on cross-country technique, apparently a minor attribute of its aid research. Bourguignon (2006, p.7) defended the research on the basis that it had 'stimulated a useful debate within academia and development agencies that goes on to this day'. He interestingly added that the findings reported in 'Assessing Aid' did not provide justification for Bank policy – as implied by the Deaton critique – 'but in fact were critical of Bank policy of the time', an observation to which we return below.

3.4 THE PERSISTENCE OF THE SCHOLARSHIP–ADVOCACY–POLICY CONUNDRUM

Yet, though much of the Deaton Report cast a critical eye on the Bank's aid research, its comments were interlaced with two important qualifications. First, the Bank's research on aid effectiveness was said to be no weaker than most of the literature on aid effectiveness (pp.55–56). Second, the report emphatically emphasised that the Bank results had great intuitive appeal (p.53):

> We wish to emphasize that we, too, believe that countries with good policies and institutions are far more likely to benefit from aid than, say, countries with deep corruption and poor governance where aid can delay reform rather than enhancing it. There is a strong theoretical presumption in favour of this commonsense dictum.

These observations are revealing and go to the heart of the inadequacies of the Deaton evaluation.

First, then, in the matter of poor scholarship one could not agree more with the Deaton Report. Indeed, most of the aid-effectiveness research is bad, although the Burnside and Dollar contributions rank with the worst of it. But *why* is this so? Could it be in any manner related to the reality that more than one-third of all aid-effectiveness research is financed by donors, with the Bank playing a major role in that respect. Samoff (1992) refers to the 'financial–intellectual complex', denouncing the implications of the conjunction of development assistance and research for the scope and nature of the research effort, both directly through funding and indirectly through impact on the terms of the debate. Research undertaken under such an aegis can be narrow and easily takes the 'existing patterns of economic, political and social organisation as givens' (p.60). The process of knowledge creation is often obscured and the power relations embedded in the research, and the programmes it supports, mystified. Particular understandings are privileged and attention is diverted away from alternative perspectives.[7]

In the context of aid, an area of research particularly affected by this complex, this has implied a restricted conceptualisation of the analytical realm, being predicated on a common acceptance of the donor-projected purposes of aid, to the neglect of the broader international political, economic and financial context within which aid outcomes take form. An inadequate understanding of what aid is, has, further, been exacerbated by deficient accounts of economic mechanisms in line with mainstream understandings of growth and resource allocation, and by futile attempts to overcome these by recourse to econometric 'proof'. The aid-impact literature has failed, in general, to provide adequate insights into the dynamics of aid outcomes. It has been characterised by a persistent incapacity to take the specific and defining features of aid and development in particular country settings into account. Little consideration has been given to the reality that the causes and outcomes of aid are complex, uncertain and vary across different donor–recipient situations, rendering a general theory essentially inappropriate.

As the debate evolved, drawing on manifold innovations in mainstream economic theory, alleged increased levels of sophistication in the analysis failed to improve the understanding of the mechanisms of aid impact or allow for clear-cut conclusions. Indeed, this seemed a futile exercise in the context of inadequate analytical categories and behavioural assumptions, with any particular conclusion regarding aid effectiveness easily countered by mere manipulation of models and/or data. The debate became reduced to quibbles regarding the significance of a coefficient in aid-growth regressions and continuously circumvented serious reflection on the first principles of theorising and model building.

The extent to which the various dimensions and institutions of aid manage to restructure the recipient or debtor economies has easily been downplayed, and the role of aid in the broader political–economic–financial setting misunderstood. These shortcomings are dramatic with Burnside and Dollar, who ignore the structural relations within which aid outcomes come about and the broader non-aid features affecting these. The key for aid effectiveness becomes entirely located at the level of the debtor economy, to the complete disregard of the structural features of the environment in which aid and its various policies take form and effect. This includes the politico-economic, commercial and financial relations between donor and recipient, which typically involve trade, debt, foreign investment, migration or military aid and which have important implications for access to aid, the form aid takes, and the continuity of and command over aid.

So, the financial–intellectual complex has important consequences for the aid-impact literature, and this is aggravated by the analytical habit of mainstream economics to consider what are perceived to be the politics of aid – touching upon who gives aid, why and to whom – as distinct from the economics of aid. Further, the reach of the complex seems to extend to the Deaton Report itself. The evaluation is heavily encumbered both by its institutional context and also by its disciplinary make-up, with mainstream economists predominating. This has particular consequences, including the absence of an acknowledgement of the politics in the scholarship, advocacy or practices of the Bank, or of any critical examination of the relationship between these (see Chapter 1).

Second, the Deaton Report emphasises the 'intuitive appeal' of the aid practice attached to the Burnside and Dollar findings (see quote above). But what is to be made of this? Does it mean that if only the technique used to support the policy conclusions embedded in Burnside and Dollar had been more solid, the Bank could have legitimately drawn upon the research to support the core *practice* that aid should be allocated selectively to 'good' performers, while poor performers would benefit from ideas or knowledge? Is this all simply that 'a serious failure in the checks and balances within the system … has led the Bank to repeatedly trumpet these early empirical results without recognizing their fragile and tentative nature' (p.53), i.e. a matter of structures and incentives related to research matters *only*? Or do the operational imperatives defended on the basis of a particular research endeavour now also matter?

By emphasising the alleged intuitive appeal of the Bank's aid-effectiveness premise, the Deaton Report expresses sympathy for a particular aid *practice* whilst, at the same time, remaining highly critical of the way in which this practice had come to be supported through specific *scholarship*, with the latter threatening the credibility and utility of Bank research in general (p.57). Whereas, throughout, the report is at pains to avoid the scholarship–advocacy–practice conundrum, this 'intuitive' slip propels it straight into it.

But then, how is this aid practice understood or assessed in the report, and how is it situated vis-à-vis the Bank's former aid practices – not least the infamous structural adjustment programmes – and the scholarship and rhetoric attached to these? Spelling it out more clearly, what has happened to structural adjustment and the Washington Consensus? How do selectivity or performance-based aid, the post-Washington Consensus and 'Assessing Aid' relate to these and to each other? Given that the Deaton Report specifies neither the policy context within which Burnside and Dollar emerged, nor refers to the shift, at least at the level of discourse, from Washington to post-Washington Consensus, is it a surprise that Bourguignon (2006), then chief economist of the Bank, quoted above, countered the report's findings with the argument that 'Assessing Aid' was indeed *critical* of Bank policy at the time, rather than supportive of it, as implied in the Deaton Report? Ultimately, the importance of 'Assessing Aid' for the Bank – and hence its heavy use for advocacy purposes – can be understood only by situating it vis-à-vis both operational and rhetorical realities of the Bank pertaining to aid, and the changes in them. This brings us to the next section.

3.5   ASSESSING AID IN POLICY PERSPECTIVE

As mentioned earlier, from the early 1980s, the Bank became engaged in structural adjustment programmes, through which aid was disbursed in return for policy reform. The policy reform imposed through such conditionality embodied a set of neo-liberal measures which sought to open, privatise and deregulate the economy (see Chapter 1).

Fifteen years on from the initiation of structural adjustment, and in light of a mainly negative experience, the view emerged within the Bank, evident in its report 'Adjustment in Africa' (World Bank 1994), that while adjustment had promoted 'sound' policies, it had not necessarily produced strong results in terms of growth and poverty reduction. For the Bank, poor economic performance was due to poor implementation. Better 'local ownership' of its reform programmes was projected as a precondition for success. Following this, the ambition to exercise greater selectivity in the allocation of aid flows gained currency. An update report on adjustment lending in sub-Saharan Africa (World Bank 1997a) stated:

> Increased selectivity is required, to stop financing delays in the adoption of needed reforms. The poor results from the past show that lack of selectivity resulted in financing too many cases of low growth and increased indebtedness. This was an unanticipated effect of excessive willingness to support weak programs and/or reluctant reformers.

Instead of imposing conditions to be achieved in response to the receipt of loans, loans were to become conditional on what had been achieved beforehand.

The critical feature of the selectivity approach is the mechanism along which suitability of countries to receive aid flows is determined. Today, the Bank's performance-based allocation system is founded on the CPIA. The CPIA involves staff assessments of a country's institutional and policy environment that feed into the Bank's aid-allocation formula. The formal link between staff assessment of the performance of aid recipients' economies and aid allocation by the Bank dates back to 1977. Originally, however, this assessment exercise was mainly concerned with economic performance indicators of aid recipients (including growth and savings rates), and the assessments remained strictly confidential. The definition of the criteria upon which countries were assessed, their relative importance, and the rating and disclosure policies were subject to important changes over the years. Significantly, the emphasis moved to an exclusive concern with policy inputs. The 1998 redesign of the criteria was particularly important as it set out to reconfigure the Bank's performance rating process, now renamed the CPIA, in a manner that sought to reflect the findings of 'Assessing Aid', with its emphasis on specific policies and institutions as preconditions for aid effectiveness.

In the early 2000s, the disclosure procedures governing the CPIA process were overhauled. CPIA scores and their justification were now shared with country counterparts; CPIA questionnaires were made publicly available; and an annual quintile ranking of aid-eligible countries was produced on the basis of their scores, though the latter remained undisclosed. In 2006, the numerical scores of the previous year's rating exercise were fully disclosed, for the first time, to the Bank's aid clients. The official reason for disclosure referred to the Bank's aspiration to operate in a more transparent way. The disclosure of CPIA scores, nevertheless, also indicated a Bank keen to strengthen its function as a norm-setter in the broader development community. For disclosure allowed the Bank to promote the CPIA, not just as a rationing device in the allocation of aid, but also as an advocacy tool, a normative benchmark, at both country level and in the broader donor community.[8]

Currently, the CPIA involves the attribution by Bank staff of a score on a scale from one to six for 16 criteria in a particular policy matrix for each country eligible for Bank aid through its 'soft window', the International Development Association (IDA). The average of these, the CPIA score, feeds into a resource-allocation formula for Bank aid resources that is 16 times more sensitive to changes in policy/institutional variables than to changes in income per capita (as a proxy for poverty).

According to Bank staff, the CPIA criteria include 'a wide range of what is generally accepted as important for development' (Gelb, Ngo and Ye 2004, p.19). They encompass an economic core touching upon macroeconomic and structural policies, which is augmented with concerns for governance and social inclusion or equity. Closer scrutiny of the CPIA, however, reveals how it is built around the following precepts: low inflation; an implicit preference for a surplus budgetary position; minimal restrictions on trade and capital flows; 'flexible' goods, labour and land markets; market-determined interest rates; prohibition of directed credit; competition policies guaranteeing equal treatment of foreign and domestic investors ('national treatment'); 'virtually' complete capital-account convertibility; protection of shareholder rights ('good corporate governance'); and no restrictions on public sector procurement.

As such, the CPIA perpetuates the traditional biases of the Washington Consensus: a monetarist preoccupation with inflation in the context of monetary and exchange-rate policy; a fiscal stance dominated by concerns of crowding out; a bias against trade intervention; a bias against interventions in the commodity and labour markets; a bias in favour of private-property rights structures; imposition of Anglo-American corporate governance principles; and a preoccupation with corruption as a source of (static) welfare loss. Social and institutional concerns are added to this predetermined set of imperatives (see Van Waeyenberge 2009).

The move towards increased selectivity in Bank practice and the promotion of the CPIA procedure beyond the Bank, with the CPIA anchored on an essentially unchanged ambition to promote a fundamental set of neo-liberal policies, happened against the backdrop of a revival of the Bank rhetoric on poverty reduction ('our dream is a world free of poverty') and a high-profile purported move *beyond* the Washington Consensus, of which the Bank's then chief economist Joe Stiglitz's call for a post-Washington Consensus in 1998, and then president James Wolfensohn's proposal for a Comprehensive Development Framework, were emblematic (see Chapter 1).

The formal 'scholarly' support for the selectivity practice, in the guise of the analytical and empirical arguments provided, in the late 1990s, by Burnside and colleagues, then, glosses over possible disjunctures emerging from a continued commitment to a particular Bank agenda in practice – selectivity on the basis of an assessment tool heavily infused by the Washington Consensus – and discursive shifts beyond the Washington Consensus. Further, Collier and Dollar (1999, 2001 and 2002) *explicitly* bring the selectivity notion into the service of the Bank's renewed emphasis on poverty reduction. Finally, the emphasis on Bank ideas or knowledge embedded in the selectivity notion – countries characterised by 'poor' policy/ institutional environments should benefit from 'aid skills' or 'advice' rather than aid finance – conveniently gelled with the vigorous promotion by Wolfensohn of an explicit knowledge role for the Bank (see Chapter 2 and below).

As such, the 'scholarship' of Burnside and colleagues contributed to the rationalisation of two distinct but related imperatives defining Bank practices in the late 1990s: the increasingly selective allocation of aid flows (on the basis of an agenda that remained driven by the Washington Consensus) and the heavy emphasis on the importance of the Bank's knowledge in interaction with its clients. These two aspects of Bank interaction with its aid clients – funding and 'ideas' – were, further, brought together in the particular way in which the CPIA exercise came to be practised.

3.6   AID AND AAA

When aid flows are allocated selectively on the basis of the CPIA, Bank staff subject the relevant countries to the CPIA assessment exercise. This is done on the basis of narrative guidelines describing which policy/institutional environment merits what kind of scores as well as through reference to a set of diagnostic reports to be consulted by Bank staff when exercising their judgement in the attribution of CPIA scores.[9] The use of diagnostic reports in the CPIA exercise draws attention to the Bank's analytical effort in steering its interaction with clients. Indeed, as the Bank understands it, the two dimensions of its role in the 'global development architecture', namely 'resources flows and policy dialogue', come together in the form of the Bank's performance-based allocation system (IDA 2007, p.1). Yet, to appreciate the full extent to which the Bank exercises influence over a country's policy design, the Bank's applied analytical work, or Analytical and Advisory Activities (AAA), requires scrutiny beyond the role it performs in supporting the Bank's aid allocation procedure. Indeed, for the Bank's former president, James Wolfensohn, AAA constituted the more important source of development knowledge generated by the Bank compared to the output generated by its research department. For AAA plays an important role in Bank–country interaction, since it allows general policy imperatives to be translated into specific country contexts and, in the absence of sufficiently powerful alternative 'knowledge' providers, commands strong policy purchase.

Economic and sector work (ESW) has been the main component of AAA. This seeks, for specific country or sector contexts, to operationalise the general policy direction that emerges from the Bank's research department, with the explicit intent of influencing client countries' policies and programmes (World Bank 2003c). While it was originally justified as necessary to ensure that Bank resources are put to proper use, its purpose has significantly broadened, and ESW outputs have come to span a wide range of policy issues, far beyond what can strictly be considered fiduciary concerns. This has resulted in the Bank currently attributing five different objectives to its ESW. These include, in order of imputed importance (IDA 2006, pp.19–20): to inform government policy; to inform lending; to inform and stimulate public debate; to build client analytic capacity; and to influence the development community. When the Bank measures the extent to which these objectives have been attained, a set of result indicators is assigned to each objective. These are instructive. For the first objective, it is assessed if the particular country to which the specific ESW pertains has adopted new legislation – if a government decree has been issued or if a new government strategy has been adopted. For the second objective, the result indicators are straightforward: has a lending programme been agreed or is a new loan under preparation or implementation? For the third objective, results are reflected in whether the media in the relevant country widely reports Bank analysis, and whether major local stakeholders and academic publications give Bank views due attention. For the fourth objective, results are measured on the basis of whether the client makes a major analytic contribution to the ESW, and whether the client is learning to produce output 'independently'. For the last objective, an assessment is made of whether additional resources were mobilised as a result of the ESW and whether there was a shift in donor policy or priorities (IDA 2006). A strong and explicit advocacy role for ESW clearly transpires.

Four trends have characterised ESW activity over the last few years. First, there has been a fast expansion in ESW, with expenditures on ESW reaching over US$280 million in 2008 (compared to a budget for the Bank's research department of just over US$30 million) (World Bank 2009b, p.41). This follows a decline and stagnation of resources allocated to ESW previously, with ESW expenditure reaching just below US$80 million in 2001 (World Bank 2004b, p.29).

Secondly, ESW has been characterised by attempts to bring about greater 'client participation'. The Bank sees ESW as an important instrument for building institutional capacity, 'ownership' and consensus for reform efforts. The Bank, however, understands the purpose of participatory ESW as follows. It is an important means of transmitting information and building consensus, crucial to the effective internalisation of the policy advice embodied in its analytical work, and a way to create a constituency for policy 'innovation' – rather than a means through which a locally anchored or informed understanding of a particular policy context could be incorporated.

Thirdly, ESW has become much more broadly disseminated through the Bank's website, through government offices, workshops and conferences, and the Bank's External Affairs department plays an important role in this effort (IDA 2006). Samoff and Bidemi (2003, p.40) observe that:

> Formerly, many of the World Bank's documents remained confidential, available only to its staff and a small circle of others. More recently, more of its publications are broadly circulated, many now instantly accessible on its massive website … Even resource starved African university libraries and bare shelf bookshops may have an ample supply of World Bank publications.

The authors point to the dual edge of such a proliferation. On the one hand, it is desirable that Bank analysis is widely available, as it allows the tracing of its thinking. On the other, however, the profusion of documents and their authoritative character makes the Bank

> the centre and focus of discussion and often the term-setter, manager, and arbiter of the discussion itself. The World Bank is not, however, a neutral discussion organiser but rather an institution with a strong agenda. Notwithstanding the plethora of publications, those mixed roles do not assure transparency or accountability or even equitable access to a debate in which issues are fully aired and critics have effective time at the microphone.

Finally, the Bank has encouraged greater collaboration with other development agencies in undertaking analytical work, in an attempt to pool knowledge and harmonise approaches across donors. These efforts are reflected in a growing body of joint ESW products delivered mainly to IDA clients, including those focused on poverty, financial management, private sector development and the environment (IDA 2003, pp.3–4).[10] These 'partnerships' with other donor agencies enable the Bank to leverage its effort and to have greater impact, as other aid agencies increasingly use the Bank's diagnostic results and findings in their own country programmes (IMF/World Bank 2004, p.6).

In sum, while ESW was originally justified on the basis of fiduciary concerns, it has increasingly assumed an advocacy role – spanning a broad range of issues, often undertaken under alleged participatory guise, and benefiting from a substantial dissemination exercise. The Bank also explicitly refers to its ESW as 'global public goods', to be used to 'motivate reforms through cross-country comparisons and benchmarking' (World Bank 2005b, p.30). Indeed, in the two instances in which the Deaton Report refers to this type of analytical and advisory activity, the 'Doing Business' reports and the 'Investment Climate' surveys, these are commended for the benchmarking role they might fulfil (Deaton et al. 2006, p.49) – without any indication of the particular policy matrix often promoted through these reports or its repercussions for development; such omissions are much in line with the weaknesses of the Deaton Report identified in Chapter 2.

Further, the proliferation of these reports (and hence the Bank's projected influence over a country's policy space through the exercise of its 'knowledge' role) needs to be seen in the context of a set of factors that have severely affected domestic capacity for policy analysis in low-income countries. First, there has been a sustained erosion and undermining of state capacity for policy analysis in developing countries that have been engaged in far-reaching structural adjustment exercises (see Bangura 2000 and Mkandawire 2002). This has been the result of a number of factors, including fiscal stringency imposed upon states, a heavy reliance on expatriate technical staff by donor agencies, and the particular way in which ownership has been understood by donors: in the words of Mkandawire (2002, p.155), 'capacity-building' exercises have more the character of cloning than the production of people with critical analytical skills.

This has been compounded, secondly, by a sustained erosion of the university sector as a centre of knowledge in many low-income countries (see King 2001a). A complex set of factors has contributed to such a state of affairs, some of which relate to donor policies.[11] In the context of the latter, the 1980s and most of the 1990s were marked by an emphasis on support for primary education and away from higher education. Such a shift was inspired by rates-of-return analysis on education, mainly advocated by World Bank economists, who promoted the idea that the highest private and social rates of return to education were at the primary level. In addition, the notion prevailed that subsidisation of higher education did not benefit the poor. The effect of the shift away from higher education was particularly severe in sub-Saharan Africa, where Bank support plunged dramatically in the 1980s (see Bangura 2000 and Samoff and Bidemi 2003). This effect was compounded by donors' support for a consultancy culture, where think tanks rather than universities tended to be favoured as sites of policy analysis (Vaa 2003 and Samoff and Bidemi 2003).

The knowledge discourse (and endogenous growth theory) has, nevertheless, led to the re-emergence of higher education on the donor agenda (Mundy 2002 and King and McGrath 2004). However, and thirdly, this has happened against the backdrop of the rapid privatisation and internationalisation of the market in education and policy services – developments in which the Bank has played an important role, and which are reflected in a rapid increase in involvement of the International Finance Corporation in the education sector (IFC 2001 and Salmi 2002).[12] For King (2001b, p.18):

> The new preoccupation with Knowledge Management in the North must be situated in the context of the brave new world of the internationalisation of the trade in educational services. It must also take account of the aggressive internationalisation of higher education in the North and the continuing challenges to the sustainability of research knowledge in the South.

The internationalisation of higher education has significant implications for the development of higher education in developing and transition countries. National institutions are likely to be faced with increasingly intense competition from foreign providers which, without appropriate protective measures by the institutions themselves or by governments, could seriously affect their status and survival in the medium to long term (Bennell and Pearce 1998, p.24, and King 2001a). This may have further implications for in-country capacity to contribute to the conceptualisation of the policy space in accordance with the specificities of the country.

Finally, these developments need to be situated in the context of the fast expansion of the Bank's own training programme. Through the World Bank Institute, the Bank trained approximately 39,500 participants in 2008 (World Bank Institute 2009, p.60). This is up dramatically from 7,000 in 1996, but down from the peak of 110,000 reached in 2005. And, whereas traditionally the World Bank Institute focused on government cadres or local policymakers for its training programmes, it has increasingly targeted a broader audience, now also including, apart from government officials (50 per cent of its clientele), academics (16 per cent) and representatives from the private (20 per cent) and non-governmental sectors (10 per cent) (World Bank Institute 2009, p.11).

3.7 CONCLUSION

In the late 1990s, the Bank became a strong promoter of the practice to allocate aid flows selectively on the basis of a predetermined policy/institutional matrix. This shift came about in response to the poor results of its adjustment packages and the particular understanding attached to such results – with projected implementation failures dominating programme failures. Selectivity or performance-based aid allocations reflected an ambition to tighten the way in which policy reform could be enforced in recipient countries. Together with the increased popularity of such an aid-allocation mechanism, the Bank expanded its country-specific analytical work. Such work became part and parcel of Bank–recipient interaction, with the assessment exercise upon which aid flows are allocated heavily informed by it. The increased use of country-specific analysis in Bank–recipient interaction could be understood, in light of the PWC, to reflect greater recognition of the need for country specificity in designing and negotiating reforms. Yet the rise in prominence of the Bank's AAA occurred against the backdrop of a sustained erosion of the capacity to formulate alternatives in the South, with serious concomitant risks for crowding out of the policy space in specific countries.

Parallel to these developments, a particular research effort took place in the Bank's research department. This sought to illustrate how aid effectiveness was conditional on the prevalence of a set of policies and institutions. The exercise was severely flawed. It was, nevertheless, successful in setting the terms of a debate that mainly produced variations on its premise, often in an attempt to counter the policy proposition of the need for policy-selective aid allocations. The Deaton Report took issue with a set of deficiencies characterising the Bank's aid research, but failed to situate this more broadly within the relevant policy context, leaving a glaring gap in explaining why the Bank should have sought to promote so vigorously such an obviously weak research endeavour, other than to offer support in advocacy to equally unexplained policy perspectives.

Finally, in the wake of the recent economic and financial crisis, the Bank has put in place a set of ad hoc measures to protect core spending (in health, education, safety nets, agriculture and infrastructure, underpinned by private sector participation; see Chapter 4) in those countries that have been strongly affected by the crisis. It has, however, been slow to disburse much-needed assistance to low-income countries. Actual disbursements through the Bank's low-income assistance window remained at the same level in 2009 as the year before, and disbursements to sub-Saharan Africa were down by $500 million (World Bank 2009c). This is in contrast to the fast expansion of disbursements to its middle-income clients. With this recent dramatic reversal of fate for its middle-income business, documented in Chapter 1, the Bank's aid activities may become less significant as compared to the trends that had confronted the institution during the last ten years, when the fast decline in demand for loans from its middle-income clients had forced it to emphasise its role both in aid and in 'knowledge'. This trend may be worsened as donor governments in the North reduce their aid budgets under general conditions of fiscal tightening.

Further, there is little indication that the crisis will be used to rethink the Bank's general aid and conditionality practices. On the contrary. The CPIA remains at the centre of the IDA's usual allocation mechanism without having been subjected to any change.[13] This implies that the fundamental policy matrix projected as necessary for growth (and aid effectiveness) remains unaltered. This is despite the Bank's own admission that those low-income countries that suffered a higher impact during the recent crisis also had higher average CPIA scores compared to countries which were less affected by the crisis (IDA 2009, p.16). Further, as this chapter was put into final draft, a leaked copy of an internal evaluation of the CPIA by the Bank's Independent Evaluation Group (IEG) became available.[14] The IEG had been tasked in 2008 with undertaking a review of the CPIA, with the results of its evaluation to be presented to the board and subsequently to be made public in September 2009. For reasons that remain unclear, this did not happen. The report remained undisclosed for six months past its projected publication date. A look at the evaluation's findings fuels suspicions that disclosure was deliberately delayed. Indeed, the criticisms levelled at the CPIA in the report provide sceptics within and beyond the Bank with much-needed armoury to strengthen demands for a full review of the procedure. For, while the main tenet of the evaluation is sufficiently conservative, its critical tenor cannot but be noticed. The evaluation concedes that the existing (mainstream) literature

> offers only mixed evidence regarding the relevance of the content of the CPIA for aid effectiveness broadly defined – that is, that it represents the policies and institutions important for aid to lead to growth … (I)t is difficult to establish an empirical link between the CPIA and growth outcomes. (IEG 2009, p.viii)

It is recommended that a 'thorough review of the adequacy of each criterion' is undertaken which needs to 'reflect the latest thinking on development and lessons learned', and for the CPIA to be revised as necessary (p.viii). Specifically, the CPIA criteria 'should reflect an appropriate balance between liberalisation and regulation'. Further,

> (b)ased on … the lack of consensus in the literature on the conditions under which aid has an impact on growth, it can be surmised that the way the CPIA enters the formula for the allocation of IDA funds is driven much more by fiduciary and possibly other concerns of donors than by the objectives of achieving growth and poverty reduction. (p.viii)

The purpose to which these findings will be put remains uncertain. Much will probably depend on the conditions under which the Bank's aid funds will be replenished in the future, and the delay in releasing the findings of the evaluation may have been an attempt on the part of Bank management to keep these firmly out of bounds over the course of the imminent aid-fund replenishment exercise. The evaluation, however, provides important material for various actors, including low-income borrowers, who wish to engage the Bank on its own terms, now even more urgently, as the crisis exposes the dramatic failings of the neo-liberal precepts traditionally peddled by the Bank.

NOTES

1. The three papers by Collier and Dollar (1999, 2001 and 2002) convey the same argument, but the two later versions sought to remedy technical mistakes that had cropped up in the 1999 paper. For a good account, see Beynon (2001).
2. For a critique of Dollar and Kraay (2002) see Weisbrot et al. (2000) and Lubker, Smith and Weeks (2002). For a critique of the Dollar trade index, see Rodriguez and Rodrik (2000) and Subasat (2003).
3. As mentioned in Chapter 1, William Easterly was forced out of the Bank during Dollar and Collier's heyday in the Bank's research department. As a senior economist in the Bank's research department, Easterly had called for a slightly more prudent reading of the Dollar–Collier results (Easterly 2003 and Easterly, Levine and Roodman 2003), but had not otherwise fundamentally challenged the more general Bank outlook regarding aid and growth (Dollar and Easterly 1999, Easterly 2002).
4. For a brief overview, see McGillivray et al. (2006).
5. The research hypotheses to be examined in the various cases, much in line with the Burnside–Dollar–Collier thesis, were as follows (Dollar, Devarajan and Holmgren 2001): first, countries choose to reform independent of aid; second, non-financial aid (technical assistance, advisory services and analytical work) has a better impact than financial aid on the generation of policy reform in 'bad' policy environments; third, financial aid works when policy reforms and institution building are under way.
6. See also: 'it should have been clear form the outset that the evidence could not bear the weight that was placed by it in the argument about, and justification for, Bank policy' (p.54). Indeed, the results 'would require an unusually generous suspension of disbelief' (p.55). And (p.56): 'We think that the Bank was unwise to place so much weight on one paper whose evidence is so unconvincing ... the Bank reports ... used it selectively to support an advocacy position'. Or (p.55): 'we *are* arguing that its [the Burnside and Dollar paper] results provide only the weakest of evidence for their central contention, that aid is effective when policies are sound'.
7. See also Mehta (2006) for a denunciation of the pervasiveness of the 'aid industry' for determining the directions within research on development; and Mosse (2006) for an account of the hazards confronted by an anthropologist who drew on his experience in the pay of a bilateral donor agency, here the British aid agency, to author a book critical of international development policies and practices.
8. As a result of active promotion by the Bank of the CPIA across the broader donor community, other development agencies have started to model their aid practices on it. Today, the African and Asian Development Funds use the Bank's CPIA questionnaire to allocate their aid, while the allocation processes of Dutch and British aid draw formally on the Bank's CPIA scores. Although not strictly based on the CPIA, the USA's millennium challenge account selects countries on the basis of their demonstrated commitment to a set of policies and institutions reflecting the selectivity practice. Further, the latest debt sustainability framework proposed by the international financial institutions relies on the CPIA to determine debt distress thresholds.
9. See Van Waeyenberge (2009) for an elaborate account.

10. See www.countryanalyticwork.net, a joint donor website which compiles country analytic work by various organisations.

11. On the various reasons for the decline of higher education and research institutions in crisis-stricken countries, see Rasheed (1994), Mkandawire (1997), Bangura (2000), Mkandawire (2000), Samoff and Bidemi (2003) and Vaa (2003).

12. For critical commentary on this trend, see Norrag News (1998), Norrag News (2000), Coraggio (2001), King (2001a) and Scherrer (2005).

13. This is in contrast to the calls by the UN Commission of Experts, under the leadership of Joe Stiglitz, for the repudiation of governance indicators, like the CPIA, in determining aid allocations (UN 2009a, p.84).

14. See http://www.ifiwatchnet.org/?q=en/node/33039.

4
A Cup Half Full: The World Bank's Assessment of Water Privatisation

Kate Bayliss

4.1 INTRODUCTION

Privatisation has featured in the World Bank's public sector reform strategy since the early 1990s and has formed the cornerstone of infrastructure policy (Bayliss and Fine 2008). While the Bank's position has shifted over the years, this has been largely as a pragmatic response to the practical challenges of implementation rather than a reflection of any fundamental departure from the institution's persistent commitment to the private sector. For, as argued in Chapter 1, the transition from the Washington Consensus to the post-Washington Consensus (PWC), often perceived as a softening of a strong pro-market position, promotes the idea that the state is needed to create the right conditions for *further* participation of private capital. The underlying support for privatisation continues much as before (see also Bayliss 2006).

It has become clear, however, that privatisation, when it comes to infrastructure, is not the golden ticket it was once thought and proclaimed to be. Rather than bringing efficiency gains and investment finance, the private sector has proved to be more fickle than was originally promised. The profit motive, expected to be the key to improving poorly performing utilities in developing countries, has in practice led to private investors avoiding what they perceive to be risky investments. Further, where contracts have been signed with the private sector, these have been difficult to maintain. This has been particularly so for the water sector and in sub-Saharan Africa (SSA).

The essence of the World Bank response to the challenges has been as follows. First, attempts have been made to minimise the risk to which private firms are exposed and, thereby, to continue with privatisation in some shape or form. This has meant sector restructuring to allow relatively low-risk private sector participation

(PSP) as well as a proliferation of financial mechanisms to underwrite private sector risk (Bayliss 2009). Second, expectations have been cut back. It has been recognised that it may have been too much to expect the private sector to bring finance, but privatisation is still promoted as a means to achieve efficiency (Marin 2009). Third, given the lack of interest by the international private sector, attention has turned to the domestic private sector with its perceived dynamic and entrepreneurial qualities (Kariuki and Schwartz 2005). Finally, when recognising that full-scale privatisation is unlikely to be achieved in the near future, a grudging tolerance of the state has (re-) emerged. However, the emphasis is on moulding the institutional framework to make the state more like the private sector, for example with widespread corporatisation and a focus on 'efficiency'. Such an approach is effectively a means to mimic the private sector and obliterates any alternative models based on public sector ethos and solidarity. In addition, by creating a private sector-like state provider, the foundations are laid for future privatisation.

Privatisation policies are implemented typically with a view to increasing efficiency and bringing investment, but what evidence is there that this is achieved? This chapter explores the empirical evidence presented by the World Bank to support privatisation policies, with particular reference to water and to SSA. Research and policy in this area fall broadly into two phases. The first arose from an initial ideological commitment to privatisation for which empirical backing was sought. The second phase demonstrates a renewed, if slightly more measured, effort to provide evidence of the benefits in response to the clear failures of privatisation to deliver as promised. This review shows that, even with questionable methodology and dubious data, Bank researchers have placed an unduly positive spin on their results to conclude that privatisation is beneficial. That they continue to do so in the face of evident failings demonstrates the persistent bias characterising their research.

The chapter is organised as follows. The following two sections look at the first and second phases of privatisation empirical literature. Section 4.4 explores some of the wider issues that are neglected in orthodox analysis. Section 4.5 considers the track record of privatisation-oriented reforms in SSA before section 4.6 concludes.

4.2   POLICY-BASED EVIDENCE

The initial push for privatisation in developing countries was not founded on theoretical and empirical analysis but on a perception of public sector inefficiency and private sector superiority, combined with an international ideological wave of support emanating from the United Kingdom. The evolution of the World Bank's promotion of this policy has been documented elsewhere. Bayliss and Fine (2008) show how privatisation gained momentum and its remit was extended during the 1990s to encompass not just competitive industries but monopolistic infrastructure utilities as well. With the end of the Cold War, there was a sense of urgency arising from the perceived transitory nature of the political change. According to Stiglitz (1998a, p.20) 'no one knew how long the reform window would stay open'. Involvement of the private sector in the delivery of water supply and sanitation goes back to the early 1990s and was a feature of the World Bank's 1993 water policy (Prasad 2007). Empirical research came only later.

The main challenge in an empirical assessment of the impact of privatisation is determining what would have happened if privatisation had not taken place. Two methodological approaches have been to the fore. One option is to create a hypothetical model of what would have happened in the absence of privatisation. The alternative is to compare private with public utilities and attempt to control for other influences. Both approaches have their limitations. Where a hypothetical model is derived, this is inevitably based on more or less arbitrary assumptions about what influences are modelled and how. Where public and private utilities are compared, it is difficult to ensure that the cases in the two categories are sufficiently similar or that differences between them are sufficiently accounted for.

The use of a hypothetical counterfactual in the assessment of privatisation was pioneered by Galal et al. (1994). It was applied to the water sector in a series of case studies edited by Mary Shirley (2002) of the World Bank. The studies in this compilation were influential for other Bank outputs (such as Kessides 2004) and were part of the research sample that was evaluated by the Deaton assessors (see Chapter 2). Shirley compiles case studies of six cities (Buenos Aires, Mexico City, Lima, Santiago, Abidjan and Conakry). Only two of these (Buenos Aires and Conakry), however, allow the effect of privatisation to be assessed. Based on an assumed counterfactual, the authors derive a numerical per capita value for the welfare effects of privatisation. They find, for instance, that in Buenos Aires, water privatisation created welfare gains that were equivalent to US$150 per capita while in Conakry, the amount was US$12.

Overall the Deaton evaluation of this research was positive. Galiani (2006) commented that – unlike some of the other findings from the Deaton process – the policy recommendations were commensurate with the research findings, and commends Shirley (2002) for not presenting privatisation as a panacea, but for also highlighting privatisation's shortcomings and unfulfilled promises. In line with the PWC, the study finds that the benefits of contracting out water services to private operation seem larger for countries with weaker public sector institutions.

As part of the Deaton evaluation process, Morduch reviews one of the component cases of the Shirley volume – the analysis of the water privatisation in Conakry, Guinea by Menard and Clarke (2002) – generally in favourable terms, highlighting, in particular, the openness of the authors in discussing both the successes and failures of private sector involvement, but finds the conclusions 'surprisingly booster-ish' (Morduch 2006, p.51). The Conakry paper finds a number of negative effects from privatisation – prices rose very steeply, unaccounted-for-water remained high, and there was little expansion in connections. Yet the authors conclude that the policy was a success. According to Morduch, 'The introduction and conclusion read as if the message was spun to accentuate the positives. Perhaps it was not deliberate, but the moments of advocacy are unnecessary' (p.51).

Yet these studies face a set of fundamental problems. First, a key difficulty with such assessments is the reliability of the data. The researchers examining the privatisation in Conakry point out that they had to use as a baseline pre-privatisation data, which were of questionable quality (Menard and Clarke 2002). Second, as stated above, these studies evaluate privatisation (or reform) on the basis of an artificially constructed counterfactual in which authors attempt to determine what would have happened in its absence. Such an exercise necessitates a set of assumptions. Typical is that, without privatisation, service provision would have continued along its former trajectory. Thus, privatisation is presented as the only option for reform to shift performance. Third, certain outcomes are accounted for in terms of benefits from the privatisation process, although the link may be somewhat dubious. In Guinea, for example, water privatisation was a precondition for the disbursement of aid funds. The assessment of privatisation found that it was beneficial largely because of the significant increase in investment, financed by donors and which would not have been forthcoming otherwise (Menard and Clarke 2002). As a result, it is wrong to suggest that privatisation per se was the cause of this inflow of funds as opposed to its being an ex post reward for having privatised. It was not the involvement of the private sector, but the conditions set by donors, that gave rise to the financial inflow following privatisation, and funds could equally have been provided to the public sector.

Thus, the counterfactual might at least have been along the lines of comparison with what the public sector would have achieved with levels of funding from donors that were similar to those offered in the wake of privatisation. On the other hand, of course, dogmatic privatisers could equally argue on the basis of realpolitik that privatisation is the way to attract donor funding. But, then, donor funding should be seen as the source of success and not privatisation as such. In short, deploying counterfactuals should, at least in principle, take a very subtle and wide-ranging assessment of causal factors rather than relying upon a before and after comparison of impact data, since reasons for change have to be explained and not simply measured. Whilst the latter can be suggestive – look, privatisation improved things – immediate impressions can also be misleading since the privatisation as such may only be a minor part of the story. Such considerations apply equally to Buenos Aires, see below. Unless, for example, improved sources of investment are identified in privatisation studies, the precision of imputed US$ gains in per capita welfare are entirely spurious.

A fourth problem with the privatisations evaluated in the Shirley volume is the short span of time over which they were considered, not least because they have since collapsed, raising questions about sustainability. The privatisation in Conakry has been the subject of the World Bank's own project evaluation (World Bank 2006) and has been rated as 'unsatisfactory', a major factor being the withdrawal of the private operator, which is attributed to global circumstances (p.8):

> One important external factor was the progressive worldwide disengagement of international operators from the water supply sector. Although this trend has been more obvious in concessions than in lease contracts, there is no doubt that, by the turn of the century, international operators became more and more selective and did not hesitate to withdraw from less promising markets.

This highlights the vulnerability of infrastructure policies based on the international private sector.

A subsequent empirical study of the impact of water privatisation adopted econometric techniques to compare privatised with public provision. Galiani, Gertler and Schargrodsky (2005) examined public and private service delivery in Argentina and this receives special mention from a reviewer for the Deaton Report.[1] Argentina implemented a major privatisation programme in the 1990s which included the privatisation of local water companies for about 30 per cent of the country's municipalities, covering around 60 per cent of the population. In their evaluation, Galiani, Gertler and Schargrodsky find a strong positive effect of this privatisation programme. They compare mortality rates in privatised with those of non-privatised utilities and conclude that child mortality fell by 8 per cent in the areas where water was privatised, and that the effect was largest (26 per cent) in the poorest areas where expansion of the network was greatest (p.85). This, then, on the surface, presents compelling evidence in support of privatisation of water.

The authors prove 'unequivocally' that it was privatisation and nothing else that caused the reductions in child mortality. They test for other factors that might have had an influence, including, for example, that there was some kind of political or economic feature of the municipalities that were privatised, that they had higher income levels or spent more on healthcare with their privatisation revenues. The authors find no evidence for these hypotheses and conclude 'the newly privatised water firms were more efficient, invested more in physical infrastructure and provided better service quality than their previous public incarnations' (p.113).

While this study offers a detailed econometric analysis to establish a connection between mortality and privatisation, the authors fail to identify the processes by which such benefits are achieved, neglecting the impact of all other relevant variables, such as housing conditions, sewerage and inequality. More research would be required to understand the mechanisms by which ownership of water is translated into health effects, as simply privatising or even providing connections does not necessarily make people healthier (see Bayliss and Fine 2008).[2]

Galiani, Gertler and Schargrodsky suggest that privatised utilities increased the numbers of connections to the water and sewerage networks, and that this led to the reductions in mortality. What the authors have established, then, is that privatisation, in this case, has been associated with an increase in infrastructure spending and higher numbers of connections which have led to reductions in child mortality. So a key question is why and how did these contracts lead to more connections? In common with the research presented by Shirley and others above, this analysis of privatisation in Argentina fails to indicate how access expansion was financed. Was this the result of effectively regulated contractual obligations imposed on private firms, was the investment financed by donors, or was it end-users that paid for connections? Their econometrics does not address these questions. Moreover, privatisation in the water sector is not normally associated with investment, except where this has been funded by donors for whom privatisation was a prerequisite for the release of funds (Hall and Lobina 2006).

The study by Galiani, Gertler and Schargrodsky does attempt to isolate 'pathways' by which privatisation generates improvements that lead to reductions in mortality. They do this by focusing on the case of the privatisation of water in Buenos Aires to Aguas Argentinas (a subsidiary of the French firm Suez), where there was a considerable increase in the number of households connected to piped water. However, in this case, the extensive investment in the water sector was largely financed by the World Bank's International Finance Corporation (IFC) and other development banks. The Buenos Aires water privatisation was a flagship project for both the government and the World Bank and so benefited from financial support as well as from pressure from government and donors for it to succeed. It would appear, then, that it is donor financial support rather than efficiency gains that gave rise to increased investment and mortality reductions. In addition, the arrangement subsequently collapsed in Buenos Aires with the onset of the financial crisis, and Suez withdrew from this contract (and others in Argentina), failing to meet sustainability criteria.

In a study of elsewhere in Latin America, another World Bank publication (not covered in the Deaton process) found that water privatisation was also associated with an increase in connections, but this was no greater than the increase in connections in utilities that had not been privatised (Clarke, Kosec and Wallsten 2009). In an attempt to portray findings in a positive light, the research found no evidence of a negative distributional impact of privatisation, which leads the researchers to conclude that at least privatisation did not penalise poor households.

Yet, during the 2000s, it became increasingly clear that water-sector privatisation in the form of long-term concessions was not going to materialise. Contracts were running into difficulties and there was little interest from the international private sector. It began to appear as if a more measured approach was being adopted, at least in terms of scholarship and advocacy. For example, the World Bank flagship report on infrastructure (Kessides 2004), while incorporating the findings by Shirley, is cautious in its interpretation of these, and emphasises the need for more information and greater attention to low-income households. In addition, the report describes privatisation as 'oversold and misunderstood' (p.6). Whilst it might have seemed that support for privatisation was in decline, it was entering a new phase.

4.3   A RENAISSANCE FOR WATER PRIVATISATION?

According to a World Bank paper in 2006 the 'investment boom' in developing-country water of the late 1990s was followed by declining investment and the cancellation of several high-profile projects. As a result, 'enthusiasm has been replaced by doubts' (Marin and Izaguirre 2006, p.1). However, while it might be concluded that privatisation has not been successful, Marin and Izaguirre prefer to look on the bright side. Earlier expectations were, it seems, over-egged, although the authors are also at pains to point out that, while there have been a number of high profile failures, a number of contracts are still in place. Their view is that privatisation is entering a new phase, with private activity focusing on smaller projects, new players entering the market, and contractual arrangements that combine private operation with public financing. The late 2000s have seen a resurgence of empirical support for infrastructure privatisation underpinned by a number of publications from the World Bank and associated agencies. There is a sense that these are attempting to present the definitive position on the effects of privatisation and are intended to renew support for waning privatisation policies. This is explored below with reference to water in SSA.

In similar vein to the papers discussed above, a 2009 World Bank study attempts to assess the effects of privatisation of water and electricity by comparing the performance of privatised enterprises with that of a sample of public utilities (Gassner, Popov and Pushak 2009). The study addresses the impact of privatisation 'as rigorously as possible' (p.2), claiming to use a database covering 'as comprehensively as possible, all the electricity distribution and water and sanitation that experienced PSP between the beginning of the 1990s and 2002' (p.2). This amounts to more than 1,200 utilities in 71 developing and transition economies, including 301 utilities with PSP and 926 state-owned enterprises (SOEs) over more than a decade of operation. This research is widely promoted and is the subject of a briefing paper (Gridlines – a free download publication produced by Public Private Infrastructure Advisory Facility (PPIAF), which is described as a multi-donor technical-assistance facility, housed at the World Bank) and is available as a downloadable book.

The research attempts to compare 'like with like' by identifying public and private utilities with similar attributes which can then be 'matched'. The ideal is to find pairs that operate in the same sector in the same country and that are otherwise sufficiently alike that any variation in performance can be closely linked to the difference in ownership (p.17). Use is then made of a 'dual estimation strategy'. This means that the first set of results compares all utilities with PSP with SOEs generally, while the second dataset compares utilities with PSP with SOEs that have been 'matched'.

The study finds (and the following text is widely cited in publicity for the book) that '[t]he private sector delivers on expectations of higher labor productivity and operational efficiency, convincingly outperforming a set of comparable companies that remained state owned and operated' (p.3). In water and sanitation, the study finds that privatisation is associated with a 12 per cent increase in residential connections, a 54 per cent increase in residential connections per worker, a 19 per cent increase in residential coverage for sanitation services, a 19 per cent increase in water sold per worker (following the introduction of concession contracts), and a 41 per cent increase in the number of hours of daily water service. The clear suggestion, from the book itself and from the summary versions that accompany it, is that privatisation is beneficial.

There are two downsides according to the authors. The research finds that, following PSP, employment falls by 22 per cent in water – although this is not really a downside for those interested in efficiency as measured by labour productivity. In addition, there is no conclusive evidence of increased investment with PSP. The authors, however, also point to a parallel lack of investment in public networks.

There are a number of concerns with this research and its inter-pretation. First, it is not clear that the authors do compare like with like (one aspect of the counterfactual problem). This is difficult to achieve as it is typically the better performing utilities that are privatised. These are most attractive to investors and equally the ones that are more likely to remain privatised. In common with the study by Galiani, Gertler and Schargrodsky, cited above, Gassner,

Popov and Pushak (2009) attempt to address the problem that privatised utilities may have particularly advantageous attributes that could affect the results. The authors statistically identify characteristics that make PSP more likely – more residential connections, unemployment, GDP per capita and inflation are all included in the variable mix. They conclude that governments do not introduce PSP randomly (p.31). They fail to mention, however, that privatisation is also about the decision of investors who are interested in low-risk investments – i.e. the more stable, well-performing utilities, with supportive governments. The worst-performing utilities are more likely to remain in the public sector, so the benefits of privatisation are likely to be overstated.

Second, this is a static analysis, while privatisation is more of a process than a specific one-off event. As discussed above, two of the water privatisations that were initially regarded as successful have since collapsed (Buenos Aires and Conakry). Furthermore, achieving privatisation itself is extremely demanding, particularly in water and particularly in SSA. It is often a long and tortuous experience which takes several years and sometimes comes to nothing. Some countries have spent years trying to privatise (Bayliss and Fine 2008, p.100). The costs of privatising itself – lump-sum in achieving it and recurrent in regulating it, for example – are overlooked and/ or taken as freely provided by the state. This raises issues of the demands placed upon the state's assets and its institutional capacities that might be better used for other purposes than promoting the private sector.

Third, the sample is heavily biased towards Latin America, and it is not clear that the findings are relevant to other regions. The implication from Gassner, Popov and Pushak (2009) is that privatising can generate similar benefits elsewhere. Yet, of the entire sample of 977 water utilities, 836 are state-owned and 141 are classified as incorporating PSP. Of these 141, just three are from SSA, and the econometric results did not hold for this region, although this was not mentioned in the published study as it was not considered to affect the validity and applicability of the findings. Looking in more detail at the three private utilities from SSA, one, from Uganda, had a short-term management contract with a private firm and is now widely celebrated as an example of a successful *public* utility (see discussion on Marin 2009, below). Another utility, the electricity and water operator in Mali, was renationalised in 2005 when the contract collapsed. The third, in Côte d'Ivoire, is something of an anomaly as it was privatised in 1960, some 30 years before any of the others. The diversity of these three cases challenges the notion that an econometric exercise of this scale can generate results with universal relevance. In addition, a review of empirical literature into the impact of privatisation in other sectors suggests that findings from elsewhere may not apply to SSA straightforwardly (Bayliss and Fine 2008, p.36).

Fourth, a curious finding from the research is that privatisation is associated with an increase in connections and yet not with an increase in investment. The question is how are these connections financed? In common with the work of Galiani, Gertler and Schargrodsky, the study fails to provide any indication of the link between privatisation and donors. The suggestion is that privatising per se generates such results, while often, to repeat, privatisation is associated with, or is a precondition for, donor funding, and it is the latter which leads to increases in connections. In SSA at least, water sector investment is heavily aid-dependent and has received very little funding from the private sector. The authors acknowledge that the data used do not allow them to distinguish between sources of capital.[3]

Finally, the paper illustrates how empirical research and neo-liberal policies are mutually self-supporting. The dependent variables are all about efficiency, with little reference to equity. Thus the study shows how privatisation affects the number of residential connections (but not how these are distributed), collection rate (but not the rate of disconnections), water sold per worker (but not labour conditions), number of employees (but not casual workers), and investment per worker (but not what proportion of this is funded by donors).

A further couple of publications emerged in 2009 from the PPIAF and the World Bank, focusing specifically on water. A report by World Bank water and sanitation specialist Philippe Marin (2009), presents an overview of developments with Public–Private Partnerships (PPPs)[4] in the delivery of water, documenting the demise of large MNCs in such arrangements and growing activity from smaller companies based in the South. Bearing in mind the limitations of both econometric and case study approaches, this study opts to pursue the 'middle ground' (p.40). This means that the research aims to present an advance on the case study approach by including a large number of studies, but also to look in more detail at individual projects and so provide greater depth than econometric exercises.

The study reviews the performance of more than 65 urban water PPP projects. By population, they cover around 80 per cent of the water PPP projects that were awarded before 2003. The study focuses on the net improvements achieved under these PPPs. These are assessed according to the following criteria – access and coverage expansion, quality of service, operational efficiency and tariff levels. The first key finding of the study is that water PPPs are a viable option in developing countries (p.6). The author claims that privatisation (or PPPs) have stood the test of time and that '[o]verall the performance of water PPPs is more positive than is commonly believed' (p.10).

The same data could be used to reach negative conclusions regarding the impact of PPPs in the delivery of water. Out of 65 developing countries that embarked on water PPPs during the past two decades, at least 41 still had private water operators (Marin 2009, p.6). However, this equally indicates that 24 countries (over a third) had reverted to public management. The paper further asserts that a total of 205 million people in developing countries have been served by water PPP projects at some point during the past 15 years. At the end of 2007, about 160 million of those were still being served by PPPs while 45 million had seen their PPPs terminated or not renewed at expiration (p.6). Of these 160 million, about 50 million are served by PPP projects that can be classified as broadly successful. For the author, the population served by mixed or disappointing PPPs is about 20 million with the remaining 90 million served under PPP projects that had not been reviewed. So, Marin can only claim that 50 million out of 205 million people are receiving water from PPP projects that are considered successful. That is less than a quarter and might be construed as lying on the low side.

Later in the contribution, Marin is more appropriately circumspect (p.121):

This overall review shows that the track record of water PPPs in developing countries has been very diverse, with good, mixed, and poor projects. Such diversity in outcomes is well-illustrated by the experiences in Latin America and Sub-Saharan Africa. In these two regions, documented successful projects account for 20 million and 25 million people, respectively, compared with 16 million and 20 million people for terminated and expired projects.

Indeed, in SSA approximately half of the PPPs awarded have either been terminated early or have expired, with a return to public management. This is described as 'a high rate that can be linked to a challenging environment for reforms' (p.28). Note, then, that PPP is not considered an inappropriate policy – it is the *environment* that is challenging.

Further, in a departure from the studies previously cited, some reference is made to sources of investment finance, very little of which seems to come from the private sector. Virtually all investment is from donors, the public sector or from revenue from the utility activities. This, however, is not considered to be a failing of privatisation. It simply requires an adjustment of expectations. It transpires that the focus on private operators as potential providers of finance was misplaced. The biggest improvements that private water operators can make are in operational efficiency and service quality (p.8):

> A new approach is emerging for maximizing the potential contribution of private water operators in the developing world. The focus of PPP should be on using private operators to improve operational efficiency and quality of service instead of primarily trying to attract private financing. A new generation of water PPP projects already has been gradually emerging, as these elements were being internalized by the market ... More and more countries are adopting a PPP model in which investment is largely funded by public money with the private operator focusing on improving service and operational efficiency.

This approach attempts to separate finance (provided by the public sector) from efficiency, which is to be generated by the private sector; but the two are closely connected. Investment in infrastructure is often crucial to bringing about the supposed efficiency benefits of PPP. Improvements in billing and revenue collection are often only possible when accompanied by improvements in regularity of service as the result of investment. Similarly, water quality improvements typically require capital investment. Increased access also stems from investment. It is hence misleading to attribute these outcomes simply to the involvement of the private sector when they stem from donor and public funds. These two issues cannot be separated. The benefits of PPP are overstated as a result.

So, privatisation is now only to be encouraged to bring improvements in efficiency. The study stretches to include a 'sense of competition' as a further possible benefit: 'the actual contribution of water PPPs may be greater than that achieved in specific projects – through the introduction of a much needed sense of competition and accountability in an erstwhile monopolistic sector' (p.10).

But the contribution of the private sector may be much less than apparently achieved if efficiency gains are the result of public sector financed investment. The study points to a blurring of the traditional boundaries between public and private sectors with different contractual frameworks. It argues that this will foster 'a more buoyant and competitive market and more choices for decision makers in government'. This suggests that what is needed is a broader concept of partnership. Such benefits all seem rather tenuous, given that all we can expect is greater 'efficiency' which is in large part dependent on public sector investment and a 'sense of competition'. Next to these meagre gains we need to weigh the huge amount of resources that go into implementing privatisation, for example, in terms of lawyers and consultants, as well as the neglect of alternatives.

This paper goes further than others in acknowledging the downsides of privatisation. Unlike earlier studies, Marin accepts that PPPs do not always deliver and that there are examples of good public utilities, citing Burkina Faso and Uganda (which is classified as a case of PSP in the study by Gassner, Popov and Pushak discussed above). He also points to the importance of social and political factors. The report finds that PPPs do not generate equity and desired trickle-down will not accrue (p.134). However, the model of PPP is not questioned. Rather, what is required is to establish social priorities, work out the cost of these ('after accounting for the expected efficiency savings', p.135) and then the government needs to step in with additional funding. What the study reveals is that the terms of PPPs are typically ones of transfers of capital from the public to the private sector in return for improvements in efficiency in the narrowest of senses. Overall, the information presented could be used to offer a damning critique of PPP in water, with improvements largely financed by donors and governments and a relatively high rate of failure even out of the advantaged privatisations that have been achieved. Instead the picture presented is of a policy that is more challenging than first thought, but, nevertheless, one that can bring substantial benefits: 'the private sector has much to offer and in many forms' (p.148). The favourable interpretation is designed to encourage further PPPs.

A parallel report, also published in 2009, contains a review of 15 PPP contracts in West and Central Africa (Fall et al. 2009). Of these contracts, five are considered successful, five are deemed unsuccessful, three have a mixed outcome and, for two, it is too early to draw firm conclusions. This is, again, a fairly high failure rate. The authors attempt to document the reasons for success – most notably in Côte d'Ivoire, Senegal and Burkina Faso. The analysis is almost entirely in terms of the strength of the contractual arrangements, although some reference is made to the support of the respective governments.

The paper neglects to mention that the utilities in Senegal and Burkina Faso were both performing relatively well before the arrival of the private sector (see Bayliss 2003 for discussion on Senegal and World Bank 2008c for details on Burkina Faso). An alternative interpretation would be that a strong public utility is better able to make effective use of private sector expertise, while a weak public utility cannot be made strong by a private operator. The other case study (Côte d'Ivoire) showed marked improvements after 1988. Water has, however, been managed privately in Côte d'Ivoire since 1960. Clearly, it is not PSP per se that is responsible for such a performance. In addition, Senegal and Burkina Faso benefited from donor finance.

These recent papers have represented a resurgence of privatisation spin. They offer not only a positive portrayal but the incorporation of the private sector as a desirable goal. A reversion to the public sector is subtly depicted as a failure, and the thrust is to push those measures needed to make privatisation possible. Discussion skirts around alternative interpretations, such as that successful reform requires a strong public sector and extensive investment – neither of which emerge from PPP. In common with the evaluation of the papers reviewed in the Deaton process, these overstate the positives and no alternative options are considered.

Such World Bank research is not out of step with other research, as there is very little empirical privatisation literature on water provision in SSA.[5] The field is dominated by the Bank. Another output of the World Bank in this area has attracted considerably less attention. Estache and Kouassi (2002) use a different methodology to estimate a production frontier for the water sector in Africa based on an assessment of the efficiency levels of 21 utilities. The authors are not looking to assess the effect of ownership directly, but to consider the factors that affect utility performance. Their findings indicate a great heterogeneity in the performance of the utilities, with a wide range of efficiency outcomes. They conclude that driving factors of performance in each firm are the institutional capacity and governance quality of the country. One of the results from their analysis is that privatisation has a significant positive effect on performance. This, say the authors, is in contrast with research for Asia (Estache and Rossi 2002), which found no significant difference between the performance of public and private utilities. This paper presents a marked contrast with the above studies in the interpretation of findings. Despite a positive significant effect of privatisation on efficiency, the authors put this in context when they conclude: 'The main challenges are however not in the water sector. Governance issues and the weakness of institutions have been and continue to contribute to explain a large share of excess costs' (Estache and Kouassi 2002, p.17).

4.4 PRIVATISATION POLICY CONTEXT

Empirical research starts with privatisation as a fait accompli. However, it is not always clear where exactly privatisation begins. The actual transfer of ownership and/or responsibility to the private sector is the culmination of a rickety process which may or may not achieve the desired end result. Privatisation is typically preceded by some form of corporatisation or commercialisation legislation to set the utility at 'arm's length' from the government, and revisions to pricing policies to achieve cost recovery. Public utilities are reformed and assessed according to private sector criteria. Such measures pave the way for future privatisation.

This approach is manifest in the use of performance evaluation criteria that are based largely on terms of 'efficiency'. The International Benchmarking Network for Water and Sanitation Utilities (IBNET, www.ib-net.org), launched in 2005 and funded by DfID, the World Bank and the Water and Sanitation Programme (WSP), provides a database of indicators of water utility performance. These indicators include service coverage, efficiency, reliability, financial sustainability, environmental sustainability, and affordability (which provides data on price, relating it to GNI per capita). The emphasis is on reducing costs (particularly labour costs) and increasing revenue. Notably absent are indicators of social outcomes, such as labour conditions or access for poor households. Other dimensions to systems of delivery are ignored and these are discussed below.

First, non-economic factors in the allocation of water resources, such as those that might be found in an anthropological perspective, are omitted. For example, Mosse (2008) describes the World Bank approach as one that is narrowly 'management', an approach which – along with that of engineering – has dominated expert discourses on water. Instead, Mosse points out that water systems are products of history and are not only shaped by, but also themselves shape, social and political relations. There is a two-way relationship between water and society. State–citizen relationships are framed and challenged around water. Economics and econometrics have come to dominate water management and evaluation. But the rules around water, such as pricing, are the result of cultural and political processes rather than an equilibrium outcome from competition or market principles (Mosse 2008). Similarly, Fine (2009d) has put forward a public sector systems of provision approach to social policy and infrastructural provision which incorporates specificity and diversity to identify and incorporate all relevant elements in the process of provision, investigating how they interact and situating them in relation to more general systemic functioning (see also Bayliss and Fine 2008 for discussion in relation to water and electricity).

Second, pre-existing delivery systems are ignored. In a discussion on Latin America, Boelens (2009) demonstrates how neo-liberalism paradoxically gives the impression of incorporating multiculturalism and indigenous systems, but, in practice, tramples them under the premise of equality. Thus, notions of collectivism and community are replaced with the rights of the individual. Where there are traditional or alternative systems of water access, imposing a formal western model of pursuit of self-interest may not be appropriate. Furthermore, the neo-liberal state fails actively to balance societal injustice, since everyone is treated as equal with, for example, rural peasants presumed to compete for access to water on an equal footing with MNCs and owners of large farm holdings. The conceptual framework is not redistributive and ignores initial conditions of historical inequality. Inequitable water delivery systems in SSA have their roots in colonial structures where fully reticulated water services were provided for a small elite while the majority of the population had a lower standard of service with private or communal standpipes, and this discriminatory framework persists (Kjellen 2006). Without specific measures to address entrenched inequalities, imposing commercialisation will continue to reproduce this duality of service.

Third, neo-liberal policies in the water sector have failed to address the core underlying problems that account for the lack of access for many. Poor service delivery stems from many factors including weak capacity, lack of investment and low incomes of end users. Policies adopted have been a mix of efforts to increase efficiency and financial sustainability, to the detriment of a more comprehensive approach. Policy sequencing has been random, as have linkages with other sectors such as health. So, for example, there has been considerable emphasis on price increases, a concern reflective of covering costs. But price increases have often preceded investment (as they were supposed to generate the revenue to finance investment), with the result that people have been charged more for a poor and unimproved service (as, for example, following water privatisation in Tanzania, discussed in Bayliss and Fine 2008). Not surprisingly, such an approach has led to resentment rather than financial sustainability. In addition, price increases can drive people to alternative water sources, with ambiguous implications for the impact on overall revenue. Furthermore, the full cost recovery (FCR) approach is far from scientific. For example, many water utilities with ageing infrastructure have high rates of leakage. Should these costs be covered in FCR pricing policies?

Finally, despite the Dublin Principles,[6] water is not simply some other economic commodity. For example, increases in the price of key inputs have led to upward pressure on prices. Unlike other commodities, this has led to serious health risks. In Kenya, for example, where the 2002 Water Act paved the way for the formation of private water companies, a sharp increase in the price of electricity (a key input into the distribution of water) led to a 50 per cent increase in the price charged for water by the privatised water companies. The price hike, instead of increasing funds, led to lower revenue levels and rising costs as consumers looked for alternative sources of water, thereby threatening private water companies' financial sustainability. As debts to the electricity company mounted, the supply was disconnected to some water treatment plants, creating acute water shortages and in some places resulting in cholera outbreaks (Oirere 2009). Thus, commercialisation and privatisation have failed to address the core constraints of weak capacity and lack of finance in a fragile sector structure. This case shows that a basic service such as water cannot be considered as a normal marketed commodity, as an increase in the price of a key input – electricity – can easily generate a major public health risk.

4.5   AFRICA WATER: A SECTOR IN CRISIS

The World Bank research discussed above is narrowly focused on comparisons of different types of utilities. Even then, the support for privatisation is not strong; but researchers have tried to look for a silver lining. As the previous section highlights, many contextual factors are neglected in the Bank's approach. In SSA, water privatisation has not been simply about a contractual arrangement with the private sector, but represents a major shift in the legal and constitutional framework, with sector policy based around attracting the private sector. It would be difficult to capture fully the impact of this changing landscape over the past two decades, and a comprehensive empirical assessment is beyond the scope of this chapter. This section reviews the track record of water provision in SSA in the context of donor-led reforms. This is a region in which a number of countries rely extensively on foreign aid and where many governments have been closely wedded to the World Bank neo-liberal approach in the water sector, adopting commercialisation and some achieving privatisation, although this was often short-lived (see Bayliss 2008 for more details on success and failures in privatisation implementation in SSA).

The region is not on track to meet its Millennium Development Goal (MDG) target for water, and even this is a paltry 75 per cent rate of access by 2015 (JMP 2008). Between 1990 and 2006 (a period when neo-liberal policies were widely adopted), the number of people with access to safe water increased by 39 per cent, but this failed to keep up with population growth. The number of people without access to safe water increased over the same period by around 66 million – an increase of 25 per cent. In 2006, 331 million people still did not have access to an improved drinking water source.[7] The challenges are particularly acute in urban areas (JMP 2008 and see discussion in Adam and Bayliss 2011).

Donor funding is more important in SSA than in other regions. Official Development Assistance (ODA) is responsible for around 27 per cent of capital investment in the sector in SSA (Foster and Briceño-Garmendia 2010), although the figure rises to nearer 48 per cent for low-income countries and in some cases is even higher. Donors provide more than 90 per cent of funding for the Water Supply and Sanitation (WSS) sector in Ghana and 62 per cent in Kenya (WSP 2006, pp.27 and 35). The private sector has brought virtually no investment outside resource-rich countries in the region. Average tariffs in SSA are high by developing-country standards at around US$0.67 per m^3, which is considered to be around two-thirds of the cost recovery tariff. In OECD countries average water tariffs are around US$1 per m^3 (Foster and Briceño-Garmendia 2010). To get to cost recovery tariffs in SSA, these then need to increase to levels approaching those of OECD countries, despite the vast difference in incomes. Large amounts of finance are required to get the region on track to achieve the MDGs.

Thus, after almost two decades of neo-liberal reforms, the sector is in crisis, with chronic underfunding, growing numbers without access (especially in urban areas) and prices at levels beyond affordability for many. In addition, in this context of low levels of coverage and insufficient funding, the world has gone into recession. Africa's economic growth has been slashed as a result, falling from an average of 6 per cent in the three years before the recession to 2.3 per cent in 2009. The main transmission channels have been the collapse in commodity prices and fall in export volumes. Other channels of transmission include a decline in workers' remittances and in foreign direct investment, although aid levels have been maintained during the crisis.[8]

There are concerns that the crisis will lead to reductions in domestic welfare consumption of water and sanitation and that governments will be unable to sustain essential expenditure. Crisis-induced fiscal austerity is often disproportionately biased against growth-promoting public expenditure such as investment in infrastructure (World Bank 2008d). The picture is particularly bleak for the water sector. Falling incomes will reduce ability to pay, while other costs, such as for energy, will put upward pressure on prices and incomes (Saghir 2009). According to Katherine Sierra, vice president for sustainable development at the World Bank: 'The global financial crisis comes to a water sector that is chronically under-funded. It comes when even larger investments are needed to cope with new challenges produced by increasing urbanisation and demographic growth' (Sierra 2009). In addition, past crises indicate that spending on water infrastructure bears a disproportionate share of the decline in public investments.[9] Thus the sector, which was already weak, is set to suffer further in the wake of the financial crisis.

The World Bank response to the crisis with regard to infrastructure has been to encourage counter-cyclical public spending. According to the chief economist of the World Bank: 'Aggressive government spending worldwide on infrastructure and other public projects is likely to be more effective than broad tax cuts in supporting global economic growth'.[10] However, not many governments have the means to do this in the poorest countries – which make up much of SSA.[11] To mitigate the effects of the crisis the World Bank launched two initiatives in April 2009, the Infrastructure Recovery and Assets Platform (INFRA) and the Infrastructure Crisis Facility (ICF), to provide stimulus packages with a significant infrastructure component.

INFRA is to provide US$45 billion in infrastructure lending over the next three years, an increase of US$15 billion over the three years preceding the crisis.[12] INFRA is intended to help governments to respond to the negative effects of the global crisis on their infrastructure services and investment programmes. It will provide advice and policy options to governments to minimise the impact 'while limiting market distortions' (INFRA 2009, p.2). In addition INFRA will provide technical and financial support for both public and private activity in infrastructure (INFRA 2010a). A key social objective of the INFRA programme is that infrastructure investments are designed to maximise employment opportunities (INFRA 2010b, p.2). The response from the World Bank therefore appears to be supportive of public investment, but the Bank also wants to soften the impact of the crisis on the private sector.

PPPs are clearly still desirable according to INFRA, and some of their supposed advantages for governments are listed as: 'the transfer of key risks to the private sector, expansion of the scope and quality of the Government's infrastructure investment program, stimulation of private sector activity, and access to the (often greater) efficiency and innovation of the private sector' (INFRA 2009, p.14). Note that the transfer of risk is considered to be a benefit from PPPs. Earlier the same document sets out some recommended measures to ensure that PPPs are not casualties of the crisis, suggesting a strong moral imperative because low-income households could be the losers if this were to be the case (INFRA 2009, p.8):

> [T]he drop in the economic value of the PPP threatens it with significant delay or even cancellation. The impact could be particularly great on poor communities who are highly dependent upon basic infrastructure (especially utilities) but are the least able to pay for such services.

Thus PPPs are still considered to be important and beneficial to poor households and need to be supported through the global financial crisis.

The options presented by INFRA to support PPPs are: to restructure the project; provide funded support to the PPP; and/ or to provide contingent support to the PPP. The crisis may deter the private sector, so greater compensation may be needed: 'In this higher risk environment, private investors may need a higher expected return, a reduction in transferred risk – or both' (INFRA 2009, p.8). Restructuring measures mostly involve reducing the burden on the private sector (extending the project deadlines, lowering technical requirements, or increasing the revenue stream – for example, by increasing the tariff), thereby shifting more risk onto the government. Thus, while a positive feature of the private sector is considered to be that it absorbs government risk, the same document calls on governments to take on risks to protect the private sector. INFRA offers the range of World Bank financial products to minimise private sector risk, which is typically transferred to the government (Bayliss 2009).

The other World Bank crisis support facility, the ICF, is entirely about cushioning the private sector and it is managed by the IFC. It was established to provide support to the private sector to protect private investment in infrastructure. The facility will provide rollover financing and help to recapitalise viable private or public–private funded infrastructure projects facing financial distress. Over the next three years, IFC intends to contribute up to $300 million in equity, with other sources expected to bring in at least $2 billion.[13]

Thus, a large element of the Bank's crisis response is not targeted towards public investment, but aims to prop up private sector investments, and privatisation in infrastructure remains a key objective. The nuances in research discussed above have clearly escaped policymaking. The Bank's crisis response will be to provide funds and policy advice to find ways to maintain private sector returns and reduce private sector risks by ensuring that these are taken on by developing-country governments. Despite the vulnerability of developing-country governments to international private infrastructure investment, as the cases discussed earlier in this paper demonstrate, the crisis has been used to provide greater legitimacy for the World Bank to support private capital (see also Chapter 1).

Moreover, looking in greater depth at some of the responses of Bank officials, it is clear that the crisis – as well as the weak state of infrastructure that preceded it – is found to be reason, and opportunity, to strengthen neo-liberal positions. Saghir (2009) makes it clear that the World Bank will continue to support the activities of the private sector in the delivery of water, as this is considered central to achieving efficiency, which in turn is a prerequisite for financial sustainability. The major emphasis is on the fact that the crisis could affect efficiency and payment for water rather than that many more could shift into water poverty. The World Bank's keynote address to the World Water Forum in 2009 voices concern that, after all the effort to get people to pay for water, it may all unravel as incomes fall. Payment rates are already reported to be falling. Data from more than 2,000 water utilities show that the ratio of revenue to operating cost went down significantly in 2007. Anecdotal evidence reportedly indicates that this trend is continuing (Sierra 2009).

With specific reference to SSA, the extensive review of African infrastructure carried out by the Africa Infrastructure Country Diagnostic (AICD) research programme has drawn attention to the fragility of African infrastructure. The flagship report from a detailed assessment by Foster and Briceño-Garmendia (2010) widens the policy agenda a little, with mention now of the governing structure of water provision and of the households who are outside the networked supply, but the essence of the policy response is still the same – higher cost recovery and greater efficiency. In the absence of an obvious source of finance, the authors discuss improving outcomes within the existing 'resource envelope' (p.304) stating that serious inefficiencies cost the region US$2.7 billion a year. These 'inefficiencies' include underpricing (i.e. below full capital-cost recovery) as well as 'operational inefficiencies', which include under-collection of revenues and distribution losses (p.299). Thus the only solution proposed for persistent lack of finance is to tighten further the financial reins.

While, undoubtedly, there are inefficiencies in the public sector delivery of water in SSA, there is little evidence that these will be improved by bringing in the private sector. Furthermore, this relentless drive for efficiency needs to be considered in context. It is not an end in itself. Some types of inefficiency (such as excess labour) may be less troublesome than others (such as high leakage rates). Some types of inefficiency may be more easily addressed than others. This obsession with productive efficiency has dominated policy for the past 20 years. The myth continues that by making utilities more efficient, there will be more money to finance extension of access and quality of service. It must now be clear that this will not happen. The existing infrastructure is in desperate need of finance, so that extending access to low income households is far beyond the financial reach of utilities.

The underlying presumption is that a more efficient utility will have more funds to achieve social objectives; but there is no incentive for a utility to pursue social objectives when performance is measured in financial terms. There is, however, every incentive to serve high-volume consumers that are regular payers since the cost of serving these is lower than trying to reach poor households that have low consumption. The assumed homogeneity of end-users means that performance will appear to be better, according to typically used indicators, if a utility supplies the factories of large corporations at lower cost rather than slum communities. Continuing along this narrow path will result in further inequality. Rather than calling for belt tightening, the onset of the crisis should be an opportunity for a radical rethink in how to use donor and government spending to alleviate the conditions of the poorest. Spronk (2010), for example, discusses the notion of 'social efficiency'. That properly funded public provision of water ahead of the crisis would have been the best safeguard against its effects is simply policy on another planet (although, it seems, it is easier to search for water on Mars that it is to provide it on earth).[14]

4.6 CONCLUSION

The preceding discussion has highlighted both the challenges in estimating the effects of privatisation and the ease with which its benefits can be exaggerated. The account reveals the extent of artistic, or advocacy, licence in terms of choice of variables and data. However, give or take a dubious result of statistical significance or not, privatisation as policy has yet to prove itself to be of major economic significance in the delivery of water in SSA. Despite slow and slowing rates of privatisation in practice, there has been a preoccupation with the policy – and where privatisation is not achieved, with commercialisation – across the region, even and especially in the wake of the economic crisis.

It is important to emphasise that the analysis presented here is not intended to obscure the poor performance of some public sector utilities in the SSA region. However, poor governance in the water sector is likely to be reflected throughout the state sector and be the result of systemic issues. The point is that these are not overcome by privatisation. The World Bank in both its analysis and policy is aware of the importance of politics in the delivery of basic services. But privatisation cannot overcome or dismiss such considerations. Rather, if a private company is to survive in a politically charged context, they themselves need to play the political game. As a result, successful privatisations tend to occur where there has been strong political support and where there was already an effective public provider. What we do not see is a private operator stepping in and transforming a weak utility.

An alternative approach is needed in terms of policy and research. To date these have been mutually reinforcing dimensions of the neo-liberal paradigm. But a static examination of a handful of market-oriented indicators is not sufficient. The wider context is important, and water delivery incorporates complex social issues, such as custom, history and equity. For effective policy, detailed country-level research is required. This would mean an assessment of how water is provided and analysis of the specific constraints. Bland generalisations about the appropriateness or otherwise of PSPs need to be reconsidered. The underlying assumptions need to be critically assessed. All end-users are not the same. In many parts of the SSA, urban water is characterised by dual circuits of supply, with wealthy consumers connected to cheap, piped networks while poor households pay a higher price for low quality water. This will continue for as long as the policy focus is on utility efficiency and privatisation. Eradication of water poverty needs to be the central and immediate policy goal. It is not enough to wait until such time as utilities are efficient before extension and low-income access become achievable.

The dominance of privatisation as first port of call and ultimate goal needs to be dismantled. There has been a confusion of ends and means, with the private sector dogmatically regarded as superior when the focus should be on universal coverage with commensurate health benefits. 'Efficiency' is not an end in itself if it means only serving a wealthy minority. The details of success stories need to be carefully analysed and treated with suspicion. In addition, policy options that provide greater scrutiny of the utility as well as support for civil society to hold service providers to account need to be explored. While the costs of water have to be met, it is not simply an economic good. The knock-on effects from effective access for health and education are well-documented. A narrow focus on a set of neo-liberal goals will not achieve this.

NOTES

1. One Deaton evaluator, Michael Kremer, decided not to reach a decision on the quality of World Bank research on the basis of his allocated sample of work, but instead opted to comment on what he considers to be good research in infrastructure, and he takes the Galiani case study on water privatisation in Argentina to make his point. He highlights this paper because, in his view, not only does it constitute good and careful research about a policy-relevant issue

in infrastructure in developing countries, but also because it provides strong evidence against a widely perceived view: in this case, that water privatisation is bad for social outcomes (Kremer 2006).

2. See Deaton himself (2009b) for a swingeing attack on the weakness of research that identifies only outcomes and not processes.

3. Personal communication with authors of the study.

4. There seems to be no difference between Private Sector Participation (PSP) and Public–Private Partnerships (PPPs), as the same cases fall into both categories.

5. Other research outside the World Bank has not found a positive effect from privatisation (Kirkpatrick, Parker and Zhang 2004).

6. The Dublin Statement on Water and Sustainable Development, adopted by the UN in January 1992. Principle 4: Water has an economic value in all its competing uses and should be recognised as an economic good.

7. Even these figures are likely to be understated. Research into the accuracy of JMP data in countries of the former Soviet Union indicate that while they show an increase in the proportion of households with piped water, deterioration in infrastructure has led to poor quality of water received due to leakage and infiltration (OECD 2006).

8. http://www.africaneconomicoutlook.org/en/outlook/.

9. This is referred to (but without source) by Katherine Sierra (1999).

10. Justin Lin, chief economist, World Bank, *Business Times*, Singapore, 13 November 2008.

11. 'Infrastructure Recovery and Assets (INFRA) Platform: A Response to Support Infrastructure during the Crisis', April 2009, http://siteresources.worldbank.org/INTSDNETWORK/Resources/WBG_INFRA_apr09.pdf.

12. 'World Bank to Invest $45 billion in Infrastructure to Help Create Jobs and Speed Crisis Recovery', World Bank Press Release, April 2009.

13. IFC Issue Brief, 'Infrastructure Crisis Facility', December 2008.

14. http://www.timesonline.co.uk/tol/news/science/space/article6849802.ece.

5
Social Capital and Health

Ben Fine

5.1   INTRODUCTION

Over the past two decades, social capital has witnessed an astonishing rise to prominence across the social sciences. Before the mini-research industry to discover the contrary in the 1990s, it effectively did not exist in its present form at all.[1] In its modern reincarnation, it was first associated with the radical sociology of Pierre Bourdieu, but its intellectual life was soon shifted to more moderate, even conservative, US traditions, variously (mis) interpreted,[2] emphasising the enormous significance of civil society to economic and social functioning. The idea was rapidly and fully adopted and promoted by the World Bank in the second half of the 1990s as the 'missing link' in focusing upon the sources of development.[3] But by the early years of the new millennium, its most prominent proponents at the Bank had already confessed to the weakness of the idea and that it had served its purpose in converting its economists to a more rounded approach in their deliberations (Bebbington et al. 2004 and 2006).[4] As a result, or otherwise (see below), social capital experienced just as rapid a decline at the World Bank over the last half of the first decade of the new millennium. Nonetheless, in part prompted by the World Bank's support, but also benefiting from a momentum of its own, social capital has continued to thrive across the social sciences.

It would appear, then, that social capital would offer an ideal topic for examining the dynamic, quality and impact of World Bank research. Yet the Deaton review of its research over the period 1998 to 2005 (Deaton et al. 2006) scarcely mentions social capital and is peremptorily damning. This might be a consequence of the random choice of work to be reviewed, supplemented for review by targeted selections of best practice research by the Bank itself, but after the decline of social capital. Even so, the failure to address social capital is indicative of broader weaknesses of the Deaton Report process, as

previously laid out in Chapter 2 in terms of a lack of interdisciplinarity and heterodoxy in perspective as well as a failure to address
the major issues and concerns around development. There is also a
failure to go further in exploring the reasons for the divide between
scholarship and advocacy, and their interaction with policy itself.
In this light, the (lack of) treatment of social capital in the Deaton
Report is critically assessed in Section 5.2.

Following that, Section 5.3 offers a wide-ranging critical
assessment of social capital and the role it has played within the
World Bank and more widely. It is suggested that it represents the
degradation (or 'McDonaldisation') of social theory and that its
adoption and promulgation by the Bank represents a particular
relationship between scholarship, rhetoric and policy (with little
impact upon the latter despite exaggerated claims). And a rather
different view is taken of the role of social capital at the Bank,
where it is seen as representing the strengthening and broadening
of influence of its economists as opposed to their being civilised into
taking other social science and scientists seriously.

Whatever the life of social capital at the World Bank, it has
become increasingly prolific in study of the social determinants of
health (SDH). As revealed in section 5.4, as with other applications
of social capital across the social sciences, it has become a universal
analytical fix, but one that tends to leave aside issues of class,
power, conflict, race and gender, although these are increasingly
being brought back in as a more or less token corrective. What also
stands out in the SDH literature, though, is the strength of voiced
opposition to social capital, a result of its relative radical origins
and of more careful attention to empirical evidence – in constructing
measures, identifying mechanisms, and distinguishing correlation
from causation.

The concluding remarks observe that the World Bank has been
responsible, then, for popularising social capital far beyond the
development community. As a result, the rise and fall of social
capital at the Bank is indicative both of the poverty and of the
influence of its research and advocacy. Whilst the direct impact
of social capital on policy has been extraordinarily limited, it has
played a legitimising role for policy rather than being an instrument
for it. Its crowding out of other intellectual assets has been the
most significant influence that it has exerted, with a far from
subtle introduction of the role of civil society, both to enhance the
working of the market at the expense of the role of the state and

to distract attention from conditionalities that have remained tied to Washington Consensus precepts.

5.2   DEATON AND SOCIAL CAPITAL

As indicated in Chapter 2, the major contextual framing of research at the World Bank, represented by the shift to MDGs, PRSPs, PWC, CDF, etc., scarcely warrants any attention in the Deaton Report. It might be presumed, with some justification, that this oversight is deliberate, in that such framing is irrelevant or even negative for research quality, as is explicitly observed in the report's being 'burdened with having to mount a sustained defense of the Comprehensive Development Strategy' (Deaton et al. 2006, p.81). Interestingly, this simple derogatory reference to the CDF is immediately followed by the only mention of social capital in the body of the Deaton Report itself: 'There is much political correctness including mindless cheerleading for cultural touchstones such as women, trees, and social capital, as in "women are an important engine of growth".' Leaving aside what this does for women and trees, social capital is not just contemptuously dismissed within the Deaton Report; it is otherwise completely ignored. This is a serious deficiency given the high profile played by social capital in the World Bank's research over the period covered by the Deaton Report and the lessons that might be learnt from it, whether in terms of cultural touchstones, political correctness, mindless cheerleading or otherwise.

In the evaluators' reports, social capital has marginally more mention and status. It arises in the assessment of 'Sample 150' by Acemoglu (2006).[5] This is the article by Collier and Gunning (1999), 'Explaining African Economic Performance'. It appeared in the *Journal of Economic Literature*, one of the leading economics journals, especially for surveys, and it is widely used for teaching purposes. At best, the assessment is faint in its praise, to the point of damning. The assessment of the piece mentions social capital three times. First, in response to the question, 'Are the conclusions consistent with the research findings?', it offers the answer, 'No. The paper jumps to conclusions about social capital, while there is nothing in previous research or even in this paper that suggests that social capital is a major factor.' And it adds and answers another question: 'If applicable, are policy recommendations commensurate with the findings? No. The evidence does not support social capital and the related policy recommendations.'

This is a reasonable assessment, although it should be added that Collier and Gunning mention social capital in their piece over 30 times, confining it to its impact on enforcement and learning and, otherwise, monotonously repeating the lack of social capital as a reason for poor economic performance in Africa. If genuinely and fully concerned with the role of World Bank research, the Deaton Report might reasonably have asked why such a prominent piece, in such a prominent journal and emanating from such prominent authors, should have appeared at all with such superficial analysis to the fore. And this is neither accidental nor marginal, as Collier not only served as director of the Development Research Group at the World Bank from 1998 to 2003, but is also director of the Centre for the Study of African Economies at Oxford University, which has played a major role in training African economists in line with World Bank thinking. Further, the main Deaton Report is scathing, as already revealed, over the work with which Collier is heavily associated concerning the impact of aid, and offers mixed support for his work on civil war and violence.[6] In short, particularly but not exclusively given his more recent high profile role through promotion of his latest book (Collier 2007), the example of his work, whether engaging social capital or otherwise, is evidence of the endemic nature of dissonance across scholarship, advocacy and policy at the World Bank from the highest levels down (chief economists excepted perhaps?).

As evaluator, Duflo (2006, p.1) is more upbeat, at least in passing, over the significance of social capital, placing it on a par with culture and poverty: 'The research I was asked to evaluate is arguably all on important issues for developing countries (culture, social capital, poverty)'. Otherwise, there is reference to a project with title, 'Social Capital'. This engages in participatory econometrics, 'a methodological theme that is not necessarily linked to work on social capital' (p.7). In addition, 'a theoretical paper on the possible impacts of different forms of social capital on health' is one 'which I did not find illuminating', and it would have been better to have 'put some of these ideas to the test' (p.8). Last, on a project with the title 'Social Exclusion and Poverty', the chapters from the World Development Report for 2000 'leave a little bit of a feeling of concluding that "good things are good" (i.e. social capital is good, but not when it excludes the poor)' (p.12).

The only other reference to social capital in the reports comes from Galiani (2006, p.30) in assessing the paper by Alatas, Pritchett and Wetterberg (2002) on local governance in Indonesia. It is observed that 'the authors seem knowledgeable of previous research on social capital, from various disciplines. They also show a deep familiarity with the history and present of Indonesia'. Indeed, they do. It leads them to be most cautious about drawing 'good is good' or policy conclusions. Galiani reports that (pp.31–2):

> [t]he findings of the paper do not directly suggest any policy recommendations, as the authors point out … Relatively little is known about how to use 'knowledge about the existing empirical associations between social activities and governance to engineer improvements in local governance through deliberate … policy actions'[7]

Such caution represents a relatively sophisticated take on social capital by the authors.

Overall, they are clearly aware that social capital is hard to define. Early on, they caution: 'We are self-consciously avoiding for now the obvious, but loaded and imprecise, term 'social capital' and are first just reporting on the empirical outcome of a survey' (p.6). And, equally, social capital is hard to measure, and hard to locate theoretically, empirically and policy-wise. As a result (p.42),

> [o]n a broader level this empirical work extends the literature on 'social capital' by demonstrating conclusively that not all local organizations are created equal. Depending on who is doing the organizing, and why, increased participation in local organizations can either be exclusionary and reinforce existing decision making powers and structures … or can widen the base of voice, information, and participation and increase the responsiveness of local government.

In other words, social capital is useless for advocacy unless these somewhat major stumbling blocks over definition, measurement and analytical and policy location are overlooked, as is so for the piece by Collier and Gunning and by the World Bank more generally, albeit for other purposes.

5.3   SOCIAL CAPITAL AND THE WORLD BANK

In earlier work over the last decade or more, I have been the fiercest critic of social capital, arguing that it should be rejected.[8] Whilst for this I have been variously accused of being extreme, a Marxist and an economist, the leading reason offered for doing away with social capital is that it represents and promotes the dumbing down and degradation of social science. In brief, this is because: it has evolved from rational-choice origins, which it conceals rather than escapes; it is universally and chaotically defined and applied across multitudes of applications that have little or no connection with one another; it overlooks or subordinates standard variables in social theory such as class, power, and conflict; it claims to complement the economic with the social and to take civil society seriously, whereas at most it uncritically accepts the market imperfection version of economics and parasitically appropriates, misrepresents, and reduces the understanding of both the social and civil society, elevating the significance of the latter at the expense of the state; and this all leads it to promote self-help at the collective level without challenging the root causes of deprivation and oppression. In addition, it has fuelled opportunism in academia in research, funding and popularisation. With few exceptions, the laying down of these criticisms, by others as well as myself, has remained unanswered – another unfortunate characteristic of the literature as critique is distorted and only partially absorbed by way of legitimising continuing use (see below).

As a result of its continuing evolution across the social sciences, I have recently dubbed social capital the McDonaldisation of social theory.[9] The leading social capitalist, Robert Putnam, is the Ronald McDonald of the approach, having been the single most cited author across the social sciences in the 1990s. Almost every article on social capital cites his work, and probably at least half of them contain explicit or implicit criticism, of one sort or another, of his approach, his methods, his results, their significance, his interpretation, their generality, his inconsistencies, and so on. He has answered none of these and, in his latest work, arguing that diverse ethnicity is associated with low social capital, he ignores relevant literature to construct his own self-critique to sustain the view that building bridging social capital is the way to respond in ethnically diverse communities (Putnam 2007). This is a significant descent into clowning, going even beyond the ideas, as posited by Putnam, that absence of social capital prevented the south of Italy developing from the twelfth century onwards, and the golden age of civil America declined over a generation because of people's dedication to watching television.

Over the past decade, the notion of social capital has grown without apparent limit across both what it is and what it can do.

How this has been achieved is in part apparent from its status as a middle-range theory, and social capital is notable for offering little or no innovation at a grander level. The mode of expansion in its scope is set out in the figures below. Figure 5.1 has given way to Figures 5.2 and 5.3, once imposed upon one another, with social capital fragmented into any number of variables (Figure 5.2), potentially with positive, negative or reverse causation (Figures 5.2 and 5.3, without reverse arrows), and able to be situated alongside conditioning or causal variables *A* and *B* (Figure 5.3), or even for these to be incorporated within the definition of social capital itself.

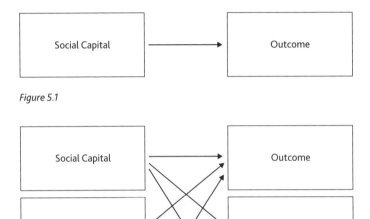

Figure 5.1

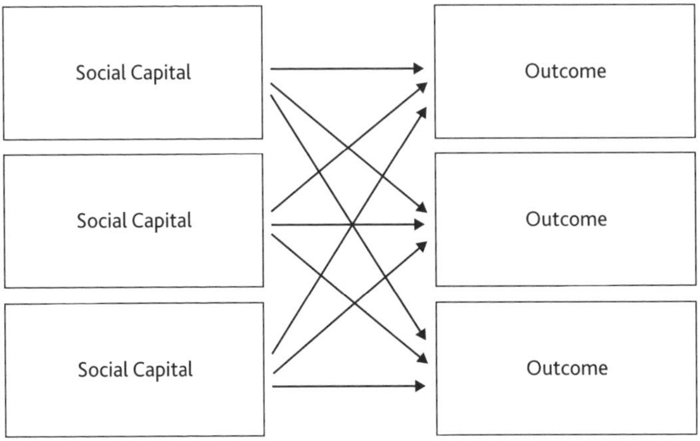

Figure 5.2

This has involved what I have termed 'bringing back in' (BBI) any number of those variables that were previously excluded. But it creates enormous problems for social capital. First, it has become definitionally chaotic, with each and every application potentially refining or redefining what is meant by social capital. Second, insofar as the definition of social capital and its impact depend upon variables *A* and *B*, then each and every social capital is different from one case to the next, and there is no reason to presume there are either comparative implications or that one social capital is the same as any other. Third, there is the danger of social capital becoming little more than a descriptive tautology, being present and positive in its effects whenever outcomes are deemed to be better than if it were not present.

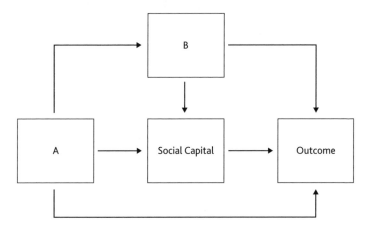

Figure 5.3

To a large extent, these conundrums have been, unsatisfactorily, addressed by seeking to disaggregate social capital into lower-level but still broad categories. These have been the cognitive, the relational and the network, for example, as well as bonding (within groups), bridging (across groups) and linking (variously across hierarchies and from civil society to the state). The problem is that such fixes are simply shattered by the equally broad but far less analytically neutral categories such as class, gender, ethnicity and race. But the strategy of BBI missing elements is wonderfully illustrated by Simon Szreter (2002a and b), one of Putnam's counterparts in the United Kingdom, if of lesser prominence, ably complemented by Halpern (2005), who served in a research capacity in the office of Tony Blair, then UK prime minister. Szreter seeks to rescue social capital from criticism by BBI class, power, politics, ideology, mass unemployment, globalisation, inequality, hierarchy, the state, and history, alongside a whole array of other analytical fragments.[10] And the motivation and goals for this exercise are offered with crystal clarity (Szreter 2002b, p.580):

It is implicit in this reading of social capital theory that there is an optimal dynamic balance of bonding, bridging, and linking social capital, which simultaneously facilitates democratic governance, economic efficiency and widely-dispersed human welfare, capabilities and functioning.

If class, power, and conflict, etc., are to be brought back in, it will be in a relatively tame version.

Such considerations set the context within which the World Bank heavily promoted social capital over the first half of the period covered by the Deaton Report. Its first major, relatively high-profile study suggested that joining a burial society in a Tanzanian village was more effective for the individual concerned, as well as for the rest of the village, than female education in reducing poverty (Narayan and Pritchett 1997). This was followed by a major research programme, including ten or more well-funded projects, one addressing differential mortality, health and well-being in post-transition Russia as a consequence of incidence of social capital (see Fine 2001a for a full account).

As I recognised at an early stage (Fine 1999),[11] and as was apparent from earlier discussion, social capital offered an ideal conduit for the transition between the Washington and the post-Washington Consensus. But, much more than this, as also anticipated at the time, the marginalised and small minority of non-economists at the Bank saw it as an opportunity to promote their own status and way of thinking within the Bank, and as a means of civilising economists into taking the contributions of non-economists, and the social, more seriously. This is now all accepted in retrospect (Bebbington et al. 2004 and 2006, and Fine 2007b, 2008b and 2010a for critique), an acceptance that is accompanied by the highly questionable judgement that the strategy was a success and was worth the compromises that had to be made. By the early years of the millennium, the World Bank's social capitalists were already abandoning social capital as a lever within the Bank, and they were able to move on to other issues such as governance and empowerment.

The paper by Bebbington et al. (2004), drafted by the Bank's leading social capitalists as an explanation for using and then dropping (or not, see below) a flawed concept, was already appearing in first drafts in 2002. It is remarkable, almost unique, in revealing some of the inner workings of the Bank and the motivation of its (dissident) staff given the proscription and penalties imposed by the Bank for going public (see Chapter 2). It is all anomalous, especially for the free rein given to the authors by the Bank (unlike Stiglitz, Kanbur and Easterly, they suffered no ill effects) and in light of the later commentary by Rao and Woolcock (2007a)[12] on the Deaton Report, in which the complaint is made of the continuing marginalisation of non-economists (see below). In addition, the timing embodied in the strategic confessions – that social capital was known to be flawed but an effective, if temporary, instrument for civilising economists – is problematic given the continuing momentum behind social capital displayed by the Bank's social capitalists (in publications, etc.), not least in the debate over social capital and health, covered in Section 5.4.

Part of an explanation for the unprecedented confessions and explanations by the World Bank's social capitalists must lie somewhere within the boundaries of retrospective self-delusion, self-justification, self-promotion and, to be frank, deceit, when such a disposition is both admitted and rationalised as a way of bringing about progressive change within the Bank to the advantage of the impoverished without. For an alternative reading of the rise and fall of social capital at the World Bank is that it offered an ideal concept for the economists to appropriate the 'non-economic', on their own terms, deflecting criticism for their deficiencies in economic and social analysis, and themselves moving on once social capital had served its purpose.

These might be thought to be unduly harsh and inappropriate judgements in a scholarly environment. But this is no more than descending to the level of individuals within the Bank, rather than leaving the gap between advocacy and scholarship, emphasised by the Deaton Report, at the institutional level. After all, the gap has to be the result of either poor or deceitful scholarship, or some combination of the two (alongside advocacy to persuade economists). And Bebbington et al. do justify their account of the promotion of social capital in terms of inner workings and motives within the Bank, to which they alone had privileged access and responsibility.[13] These considerations aside, it is more appropriate to perceive their strategy of reforming the thinking and practice of the Bank to have failed on its own terms, even more so if considered on a broader basis than for implications within the Bank alone.

For, first, economists at the Bank hardly needed to be persuaded to incorporate non-economic variables into their analysis in light of freakonomics imperialism and its application to development. As discussed above in the case of Collier, and on a much broader terrain of subject matter and individuals, the promotion of social capital had the perverse effect not only of legitimising the role of economists within the Bank but also of allowing that role to be extended to the non-economic.

Second, the goal of elevating the status of non-economists has hardly been achieved, and certainly not through the medium of social capital. Ironically, the Deaton Report could not be more scathing about social capital, where it does not ignore its contribution to research within the Bank. And Rao and Woolcock (2007a) feel compelled to reiterate, after the social capital deluge within the Bank, that non-economists are so marginalised that the Deaton Report does not even consider using an assessor of research who is not an economist.[14]

Third, irrespective of whether social capital had the effect of adding the social in some form to the economic within the Bank, what it did not do is to change the economic itself. The economics of the Bank is sorely deficient in content and scope, at most stretching to the boundaries allowed by the post-Washington Consensus in scholarship, rhetoric and policy. Indeed, even those limits proved to be unacceptable to the Bank, as evidenced by the departure of Stiglitz. The social capitalists within the Bank were and have remained remarkably quiet over this episode, even though their own prospects of socialising economists within the Bank surely depended upon both a more favourable economics and its more favourable marriage with the social.[15]

Fourth, one of the most striking but only occasionally observed features of social capital is that it has had practically no (overt and established) impact upon policymaking. Where are the studies, within the Bank or otherwise, which report that 'we set out to create social capital to bring about this outcome, and we succeeded'? Even Bebbington et al. (2006) rely upon limited evidence, without independent assessment. Amazingly, the Bank's website for social capital has a link for 'Social Capital and Policy',[16] but it is non-functional; indeed the overall website itself began to die from early 2000.

Fifth, even more significant are the policy shifts that were occurring within the Bank over which social capital had no purchase and made no comment. In particular, despite a rhetoric of retreat from dogmatic support for privatisation, the Bank has set about shifting support for infrastructural provision from the public to the private sector. However much social capital may have improved given project performance, the shifting composition of project funding was not addressed, even though the impact upon 'social capital' itself may be considered to have been far from negligible with the introduction of private in place of public provision.

Sixth, the preoccupation with promoting social capital within the Bank was complemented by an extraordinary degree of external promotion, incorporating far more progressive donor agencies and the development community more widely. This had the effect of undermining the potential for more external pressure on the Bank, in deference to the putative internal force for change deriving from social capital.

Seventh, the manoeuvrings of the social capitalists at the Bank are indicative of the McDonaldisation of social theory, not least in being academically deceitful. Over the time that social capital was being promoted within the Bank, there was no engagement with external criticism, although there was heavy promotion of social capital. Once it was decided that social capital had done its job within the Bank, all the criticisms that had been made of it were essentially accepted. The implications for the status of scholarship within the Bank, let alone in engaging in debate, are staggering, especially for a knowledge bank.

Last, following its rise and fall within the Bank, the status quo ex ante has not been restored as far as social capital is concerned. For the Bank played a major role in promoting the concept within development and more broadly, although it had an independent momentum of its own, not least through the Putnam phenomenon (and vice versa, Putnam having played an initiating role at the Bank as well). Casual observation does suggest that there was a dip in the popularity of social capital across the social sciences as the World Bank withdrew its support. But it has now regathered lost momentum, both within the Bank and much more broadly, not least in the field of health.

5.4 SOCIAL CAPITAL AND HEALTH

Although within the Bank social capital has fallen from grace (or has been withdrawn, as its proponents would have it), its impact more broadly has continued to be felt, with uncertain but significant influence arising out of the momentum delivered from the Bank. This is so whether for issues involving development or not, and with or without the continuing contributions of the Bank's own social capitalists, whose subsequent stances have become ambivalent, if not inconsistent. This section will demonstrate how social capital has muscled its way onto the health scene, where it was neither wanted nor needed, and, to an astonishing degree, at the expense of more traditional, progressive and well-founded approaches – although, commendably, the latter have fought back.

For, as will be seen, and as with other applications, the study of the social determinants of health (SDH) was well-established long before social capital appeared on the scene.[17] At that time, the field was heavily influenced by the idea that (income) inequality is a major source of ill health as a result of material and stress-induced relative deprivation. This approach has the benefit of moving away from medicalised and individualised accounts, with inequality potentially serving as a proxy for oppressive social relations, practices and conditions in general. Nonetheless, there is a weakness in establishing the mechanisms through which inequality translates into health outcomes,[18] and a neglect of the broader determinants of inequality itself and their more immediate and direct impact on health, giving rise to the so-called political-economy approach to the SDH (see Navarro (ed.) 2007, for example). Social capital offered the opportunity for the inequality approach opportunistically to support its position with the benefit of what appeared to be a well-established concept from across the social sciences.

Even so, as late as the volume of Marmot and Wilkinson (eds) (1999), from two of the leading British scholars, social capital scarcely warrants a mention. Kawachi and Wamala (eds) (2007) only contains a few passing references to social capital, none in the three contributions of Kawachi himself![19] This is despite Kawachi being one of the leading academics on SDH in the United States and a heavy promoter of social capital (see Kawachi et al. 1997 for a relatively early contribution). His own social capital is notable in this respect. He moderated the World Bank's electronic social capital newsletter, and with Putnam he co-authored an article on social capital and firearm ownership across the United States (Hemenway et al. 2001). This regresses individuals' firearm ownership against the number of times in the previous year they went bowling, played cards, entertained at home, sent greeting cards, and attended dinner parties. It accepts that issues such as race, urbanisation and poverty were omitted, and that correlation and causation have not been distinguished.[20] The National Riflemen's Association does not warrant a mention (although going to church is found, if insignificantly, to raise possession).[21]

This is just the unacceptable tip of the iceberg of standard empiricist fare as far as application of social capital to health is concerned.

Other studies,[22] using various measures and methods, have covered smoking and binge drinking (within a putative Bourdieu framework: Carpiano 2006 and 2007), the impact in Finland of speaking Swedish (higher status) or Finnish (Nyqvist et al. 2008 and Hyyppä and Mäki 2003), mental health (Almedom 2005, Lofors and Sundquist 2007, de Silva et al. 2007 and Miller et al. 2006), coronary heart disease (Sundquist 2004 and Sundquist, Johansson and Yang 2006), self-reported health, either with ethnic discrimination (Kavanagh, Turrell and Subramanian 2006, Lindström 2008 and Sundquist and Yang 2007) or without it (Mansyur et al. 2008), teen pregnancy and 'risky' and pre-marital sexual activity (Crosby and Holtgrave 2006, Crosby et al. 2003, Gold et al. 2002 and Djamba 2003), employee health at work (Oksanen et al. 2008), cancer and crime (Islam et al. 2008), life satisfaction and well-being (Yamaoka 2008), being overweight (Wakefield and Poland 2005), drug addiction and treatment (Cheung and Cheung 2003 and Mooney 2005), depressed mothers of young children (Mulvaney and Kendrick 2005), cannabis smoking (Lindström 2004), low birth weight, accidents and suicide (Folland 2007), suicide (Haynie, South and Bose 2006), indigenous health (Morrissey 2006), fatalism (Lindström 2006), alcohol consumption (Lindström 2005 and Bischof et al. 2003), children's health (Drukker et al. 2003), violence (Galea, Karpati and Kennedy 2002), volunteering (Blakely et al. 2006), kidney donation (Morgan et al. 2006), keeping of pets (Wood et al. 2005 and 2007) and dental caries (Pattussi et al. 2006).[23]

As a result, the proliferation of studies such as these has conformed to the McDonaldisation of the study of the SDH, with similar character and dynamic, especially of definitional and operational chaos (with limited policy implications) and BBI what has previously been omitted. At a relatively early stage, Macinko and Starfield (2001) offer genuine insight into the impact of social capital on the study of SDH, despite, or even because of, treating social capital as an element in a production function for health. From the literature, they identify four ways in which social capital affects health: through pathways; through networks; as a mediator in health policy and reform; and through elements of social deprivation. Based on a literature review, they also offer seven elements for a research agenda. These include: clarify the concept; explore pathways or mechanisms and distinguish from material conditions; develop a core set of social capital variables with internal consistency and psychometric testing (otherwise it is better to rely upon interpersonal trust, membership in groups, etc., individually rather than grouping these together in a single index); explore different aspects of health across different groups; sort out the effects of gender, class, region, etc.; identify the origins of social capital; draw out implications for policy from creating social capital; and identify cause and effect. Not unreasonably, with little or no prospect of this wish list being addressed, as opposed to undermined, they conclude: 'the concept has been stretched, modified, and extrapolated to cover so many types of relationships at so many levels of individual, group, institutional, and state analysis that the term has lost all heuristic value' (p.394). Equally, it has gained chaotic value.

Similarly, Muntaner, Lynch and Davey Smith (2001, p.213) are able to report: 'we have witnessed the rapid appearance of the concept of social capital in public health discourse'. They point, following the earlier survey of Hawe and Shiell (2000),[24] to the use of social capital as all that is good in a community, but at least allowing for non-individualised approaches to SDH to be adopted, albeit along the lines of mobilising society to put the sick Humpty Dumpty back together. For

> [i]n social epidemiology, more specifically, social capital presents a model of the social determinants of health that excludes any analysis of structural inequalities (e.g., class, gender, or racial/ethnic relations) in favour of a horizontal view of social relations based on distributive inequalities in income. As a consequence, political movements based on class, race/ethnicity, or gender are also ignored as explanations for reducing social inequalities in health.

This, in a sense, is an invitation, whether intended or not, to BBI all of those omitted factors – one that has been enthusiastically embraced in the subsequent literature, further adding to definitional chaos, as in other applications of social capital.

But, as I have emphasised when considering the invasion by social capital of other fields, each case has its own peculiarities, reflecting the nature of the subject matter and the traditions within which it has been addressed (as well as the timing of the incursion and even the personalities involved).[25] For SDH, this has meant a more than normally active opposition. In part, this is based upon a closer preoccupation with mechanisms and causation, given that the end result of (individual) ill health is unavoidable. As Leeder (1998, p.7) puts it:

for social capital to be useful for public health, there is a need to link it to epidemiological inquiry, with its irritating restrictions and ineradicable connection to reductionist science ... Classical epidemiology has in fact served us astonishingly well, and to discard it in favour of something less defined, more spiritual and social-elitist, would be a major mistake ... especially so if, as a substitute, vague descriptions of social phenomena, such as social capital, are proposed.

Even Kawachi (2001, p.32), not for the first time, confesses that 'the precise mechanisms underlying the connection between social capital and health still remain to be uncovered, but a great deal of evidence from epidemiology suggests that social support is an important determinant of longevity and quality of life'. In addition, social epidemiology has given birth to a strong strand of radical scholarship in identifying SDH, in opposition to more medicalised and individualised approaches that are unduly undersocialised. Scholars in this vein have reasonably viewed with dismay the displacement of race, class, gender, the imperatives of capitalism, and so on, by the amorphous and bland notion of social capital.

Even more distinctive overall in the social capital contributions to study of the SDH is the level of both systemic and individual honesty and integrity in empirical work. On casual observation, across the various case studies reported, something like a third report no impact of social capital on health. I suspect this to be unusual across the social sciences in any field. There is a very strong bias, especially within economics, to solicit and report positive results in a statistical sense. Individuals search and manipulate until they find them, and outlets publish accordingly. But health is different, possibly because of its attachment to medicine and treatment, with a tradition of placebos and drug and treatment trials.

For similar reasons, a further substantial proportion of case studies suggest that, even though social capital has an effect, it is much less important than other factors, with access to material resources to the fore. In addition, more than normal attention is paid to the traditional cautions attached to statistical work.[26] These include not confusing correlation with causation. The following is typical in its conclusion, and endearing in its content. Miller et al. (2006, p.1085) find that 'an increase by one standard deviation (measured at the village level) in social capital is associated with a decreased propensity to report feeling sad of 2 percent points, a 14 percent decline from the mean level'.[27] Most important seem to be the presence of a pharmacy garden and family planner's acceptance groups.

> This may not be surprising given that both group activities/forms of social capital are health-related. While one cannot interpret our estimates as the causal impact of social capital on health, our findings are suggestive that a research design able to delineate the causal relationships would be worthwhile. (p.1096)

Also more care than is normally found across the social capital literature is given to the definition and measurement of social capital, the relations between micro- and macro-effects, and the mechanisms, or health pathways, by which social capital might be deemed to function (see Milyo and Mellor 2003, Almedom 2005, Taylor et al. 2006, de Silva et al. 2006, Stephens 2008 and Veenstra et al. 2005 for some telling and varied contributions).

Of crucial significance in these respects are the extremely diverse and unavoidable causes, consequences and mechanisms relating health to social, material and individual circumstances. As a result, not least in light of the diagrams offered previously and the more than normally careful degree of empirical investigation and qualification attached to case studies, the majority of these heavily emphasise the extent to which, if there is a social capital effect, it is highly conditioned by the presence or not of other factors. Inevitably, this raises doubts about the universal applicability of a notion of social capital and the prospective dangers of relying upon it whilst setting aside those conditioning factors.

In light of the major conceptual failings outlined above as well as the weaknesses of empirical support, it is hardly surprising that the *International Journal of Epidemiology* should hold a fiercely contested debate over social capital, significantly introduced by Ebrahim (2004) as 'Social Capital: Everything or Nothing?'. It is striking that the case in favour should have been made by Szreter and Woolcock (2004a and b), the latter having been possibly the leading social capitalist at the Bank,[28] ably supported by Putnam (2004) and Kawachi et al. (2004). McDonaldisation was out in force.[29] Their contributions are remarkable for their inconsistencies, misrepresentations, errors and emptiness. Thus, Szreter and Woolcock (2004b, p.700) ambitiously locate social capital in the grand scheme of social science: 'The broad dialectical challenge in social theory is (or should be) addressing the structure–agency problem (also known as the micro–macro problem) – that is, unpacking the interactions and interconnections between individual choices and larger institutional forces.' Social capital is perceived to address this challenge in the wake of its neglect under the influence of postmodernism and rational choice.[30] It also offers a synthesis of the three traditional approaches to SDH – the radical political economy approach (its potential opponent), the inequality approach (in which relative deprivation causes stress and ill health, and which is most closely associated with Wilkinson, who is already on board), and the social support approach (its most natural ally).

How is this defence of social capital as a synthesis and addition to what has gone before to be mounted? First, with considerable honesty and, one suspects, to Putnam's dismay,[31] Szreter and Woolcock (2004a, p.653) observe of social capital that '[n]either Robert Putnam (and his Harvard colleagues) nor Richard Wilkinson … have undertaken fundamental theoretical work on the concept'. They rectify this by the simple expedient of positing bonding, bridging and linking social capital. Yet, the result, by their own confession, is relatively modest (2004b, p.702, emphasis added):

> [T]he compelling point being argued by proponents of the social capital perspective is that, without taking into account the *independent* effects of the workings of all three forms of social capital, our understanding remains incomplete. The crucial point about social capital is not that it provides a complete explanation for anything, but that most explanations are incomplete without it.

This quotation is crucial, revealing and slippery. For it falsely implies that rejection of social capital means omission of influences that are essential if not exhaustive. Indeed, this leads Szreter and Woolcock erroneously and scathingly to dismiss 'political economy' critics as reductionist to class, in part by grand appeal to more rounded Marxists such as Eric Hobsbawm and E.P. Thompson (p.703). But the political economy approach is much more nuanced than this in questioning the *independent* effect of whatever is deemed to be social capital (see below). Such social relations are not seen as reducible to class or whatever but, what is an entirely different matter, they are not allowed to be independent of it (any more, it might be added, than health is deemed by Szreter and Woolcock to be dependent upon social capital).[32]

Second, then, at least implicit in the theory of Szreter and Woolcock is that social capital is an independent causal factor. This is made explicit in Putnam's contribution (p.670), in which a causal mapping is provided with inequality, social capital and the state/political economy as the three mutually interdependent base factors determining health outcomes. And this is correctly acknowledged to be necessary by both Putnam and Szreter and Woolcock, for otherwise, if social capital attaches to the state, the theory becomes a tautology. Social capital has both to range over some but not all social relations, and those it does incorporate have to exert some sort of independent effect of their own. Ellaway (2004, p.681), in the same special issue, succinctly poses the conundrums involved in such analytical acrobatics:

> Their definition of social capital makes it difficult to measure empirically. However, this difficulty is further complicated by the issue that social capital is likely to be a *product* of class position and intersects with other social categories such as gender and ethnicity. Different levels of networks and variations in equality in interactions with powerful groups have long been noted as a feature of class position, and measures of social stratification. This makes social capital difficult to test in statistical models with health as an outcome since controlling for social factors does not adequately remove their influence.

In addition, the more radical political-economy approach is, with good reason, suspicious (in terms both of social capital's origins and of its content and dynamic in practice) that the claim to BBI class, race, gender, other structural determinants, and so on, is merely token – in the sense that it downplays their significance as causal factors. For Navarro (2004, p.673):[33]

> The key determinants of power in a society are the class (and race and gender) power relations that shape both civil society and political societies. Class relations (including class struggle) traverse and shape all dimensions of society – the state and the major institutions, including the major institutions of the knowledge and practice of health and medical care. There is no such thing as the 'state' separate from civil society. There are state power relations that reproduce the class, race, and gender relations dominant in civil society. Szreter and Woolcock's seeming unawareness of this also explains their lack of attention to the political context in which such power relations are reproduced ... both civil society and political society respond to the same class forces.

Further, as is easily recognised, the elevation of both the status and independence of social capital as a causal variable is suggestive that policy can be effective independent of other causes, although these are confessed to be potentially if not more, important: 'we are *not* arguing that social capital, however conceived, is or should be the sole or even the primary variable used to explain all public health outcomes' (Szreter and Woolcock 2004b, p.704).

In practice, their own policy prescriptions go little beyond appealing to the building of cooperative relations for a common purpose. This might be thought to border on the embarrassing when they seek solutions to the HIV/AIDS crisis in Africa and elsewhere. For

> [i]f social capital's key insight is that social relationships *really* matter, the focus in policy debates needs to unpack the black box of process to appreciate just how crucial are on-going face-to-face relationships to the delivery of key public health services, especially in developing countries. (2004b, p.704)

This is all seen as a complementary step to 'efforts to lower the costs of producing and disseminating anti-retroviral drugs ... [and] reducing the enormous stigmas (and misunderstandings) that still surround the disease'. Who could disagree? But the analytical issue is not just how to lower costs, but how the (health and pharmaceutical) systems to which they are attached constrain and influence both black box and stigma. For Szreter and Woolcock, this is all reduced to 'relationships within communities – that is linking social capital – that will, in turn, give them the credibility and leverage to help facilitate a long process of social change' (p.704). How the latter is to be achieved in the absence of the considerations posed by the political economy approach to health remains a mystery, except that those now wedded to the social capital approach are advised not to neglect the linking. For, they continue, '[o]n policy issues and in contexts such as this, a social capital conceptual arsenal restricted to a dichotomous "bonding" and "bridging" distinction is rendered needlessly tepid' (p.704).

This is indicative of the work that must be done by linking social capital, both analytically and strategically. The substance and limitations are beautifully and ironically summarised by Ellaway (2004, p.681):

A related problem with subtle refinements is that, given the popularity of the concept, decision makers of all political hues will have their own ideas and agendas. As the Taioseach (Prime Minister) for the Republic of Ireland, stated in a speech, 'We all know that the level and nature of interaction between people and groups is crucial to public well-being. But social capital could, at one extreme, be seen as so general and aspirational as to be irrelevant: at the other extreme it could easily fall into being merely another way of promising old-style ideologies ... I know that Prime Minister Blair has also shown a lot of interest in Professor Putnam's work. Indeed, it is an indication of its quality, that both President Clinton and his successor President Bush have been influenced by it.'

Earlier work has already indicated the much neglected neo-liberal roots of social capital in rational choice sociology and social capital's own promotion of neo-liberalism at an early stage (Fine 2010a). This is a tradition that emphasises that both market relations, and the non-market relations to support them, are best left to individuals. It sees the spontaneous creation of social capital as an argument *against* state economic and social intervention, even where the market works imperfectly. Significantly, in its modern reincarnation, Meadowcroft and Pennington (2007) see themselves as 'Rescuing Social Capital from Social Democracy' and for neo-liberalism. For New Labour and Third Wayism have become its natural home, as explicitly promoted by Szreter (2002a) himself,[34] although there is now a burgeoning literature demonstrating how social capital has had little impact on policy as such, but has rather been used as a rhetorical device to impose central control, devolve responsibility without resources, and manage dissent.

Third, in promoting social capital against these obstacles, Szreter and Woolcock simply ignore those criticisms, already laid out, that would appear to be impossible for them to answer. But they do respond when they can. Their original contribution offered an account of the role of erstwhile Liberal, Joseph Chamberlain, in promoting mortality decline in nineteenth-century Birmingham. The rejoinder of Smith and Lynch (2004), that Chamberlain later became a racist imperialist, is dismissed as irrelevant for being after the event (although this might bring into question the beneficial fluidity of social capital once it leaves the Birmingham bond and bridge). When Szreter (2004 and 2005) does respond, in the latter case to Razzell and Spence (2005), it becomes clear that social capital as an explanatory factor is hanging on by its fingernails, given that any account for mortality decline must address timing, age- and gender-specific rates, and the major influence of changes in child labour, real wages, nutrition, working mothers, family size, and housing, etc., against which social capital might be thought to decline into insignificance.

The final, and weakest, argument in favour of social capital is offered, despite its limitations, by most of its proponents and, occasionally, by its critics. This is that at least social capital puts the appropriate issues on the agenda and seeks to reconcile competing views. This is, however, reminiscent of (the errors of) the Deaton Report on the Bank's shifting of the development agenda. This is never a neutral exercise in terms of content, limits and focal point as observed by critics across the entire social capital enterprise, with more radical and penetrating scholarship tending to be precluded or, if it is incorporated, degraded.

Ultimately, Kawachi et al. (2004, p.689) accept that

> [u]nbridled enthusiasm for the adoption of social capital in public health has generated a backlash ... Some of the criticisms – for example, the perception that social capital is a 'cheap' solution for solving public health problems, or the tendency to view social capital as a panacea whilst ignoring its negative aspects – are justified.

But, irrespective of this 'and the formidable conceptual and methodological obstacles that remain', they close by concluding these must be tackled, 'because for better or for worse (in terms of population health and outcomes), social capital is here to stay'.[35] I wonder if they would have said the same of social eugenics, in view of its impressive array of popular and academic support!

Nor, when we consider the policy implications, is this merely some cheap jibe, once we substitute the more acceptable social capital-inspired social engineering for social eugenics. When social capital is measured by participation in local elections and is seen to be negatively correlated to mental ill health, this can be used as a rationale for the location of mental institutions (Lofors and Sundquist 2007). Ferguson (2006, p.8) argues that

> [e]mpirical precedents suggest that families with high levels of family social capital have a two-parent family structure, with the presence of a paternal figure ... Lastly, there is some evidence

that regular attendance by families and parochial education at Catholic schools for children are also positively correlated with high levels of community social capital.[36]

Indeed, 'of all the predictive factors associated with children's well-being, social capital – second only to poverty – has the highest influence on children's development and attainment of future outcomes' (p.9). The lack of social capital as a cause of crime and as a result of ethnic diversity attends us from our childhoods to our earlier graves.

The policy implications are mind-boggling once engaged in these terms, with Walters (2002) pointing to social capital as 're-imagining politics'. With its being located at both individual and collective (cultural) levels, 'social capital assesses politics in terms of social norms of performance rather than ideological legitimacy' (p.386), not least because 'a key presupposition of social capital theory is of the actor as a self-interested maximizing individual'. In the context of a state–society duality, social capital also holds out the promise of self-governance, as opposed to 'an image of politics as a system defined by the poles of elites and the governed. With social capital this stark polarization gives way to an image of the polity as a much more *horizontal* space of multiple communities' (p.388). This involves a shift from a 'bio-politics' – governing health, education and welfare in all its aspects – to ethopolitics, that of the population's trust, civility, volunteering, communalism, etc., which become manageable aspects of the system. 'Social capital brings the ambition of positivity and calculability to ethopolitical discourses … it offers a quantitative rendering of the ethical field, all the better to enhance its governability. It purports to make trust and civility measurable' (p.390) – rendering a field day of critical opportunities for those trained in the tradition of Foucault.

The result is that a new division can be added to the traditional ones between normal and pathological, sane and insane, social and anti-social, employed and unemployable, and excluded and included. It is the civic and the uncivic (p.392). But, unlike previous political theory and its notions of modernisation, 'with social capital, this stagist, developmental trajectory is not evident. Across space and time, all societies are analysable in terms of social capital' (p.395). Consequently, for the World Bank and other international agencies, 'it could be that social capital will offer them another way to express concern for social injustices, but in such a way that they are not required to address the thorny matter of economic exploitation' (p.394).

5.5 CONCLUDING REMARKS

In the event, with or without health, social capital has moved off the World Bank's agenda. But its influence on health studies, in part prompted by the Bank's erstwhile social capitalists, continues to grow apace, not least with a flush of government surveys to assess the relationship between social capital and health.[37] This raises the strategic issue of whether social capital can be reformed or whether it should be rejected. For, despite its legion deficiencies, amply documented within the literature both for health and more generally, there is always the prospect of enhancing social capital, by BBI and/or compromising to gain leverage and influence, as most obviously attempted by the World Bank social capitalists in relation to their economist colleagues.

With global warming, we have been advised that malaria may return to Italy. This reminds us of how the condition got its name – bad air. This is a totally wrong diagnosis, but it is certainly conceivable that efforts to improve air quality may have inadvertently diminished the incidence of malaria. Could the same be true of social capital, a 'benaria' for social theory?[38] And, if not in general, could social capital not be beneficial for the study of the SDH in particular?

As I have argued for other applications, attempts to reform social capital have been primarily marked by failure, despite what are occasionally excellent criticisms and case studies, but with the latter more often than not critically accepting the language of social capital, whilst otherwise rejecting it in its general practice (Fine 2010a). Such studies generally take the form of BBI, and especially BBI Bourdieu, to incorporate class, race, and gender (see Campbell and McLean 2002 and Stephens 2008, for example). Inevitably, following Bourdieu, this involves the BBI of context, not only in the sense of taking full account of complementary causes and conditioning variables, but also in terms of the construction of the meaning of health to practitioners themselves. Thus, Kreuter and Lezin (2002, p.251) accept that 'failure to take *social and political context* into account is a major barrier to the effective evaluation of community-based health promotion', and they appropriately close with the observation that

there are different ways of knowing, and different interpretations of 'reality' ... an epidemiologist, an anthropologist, a health
educator, and a layperson are likely to view a given problem
through different lenses. More importantly, each is quite likely
to detect a glimpse of reality that others may miss. All ... need
to seriously explore how their various views of reality can be
combined to give us new knowledge.

Thus, even though the social capital and SDH literature has been
unusually, if not absolutely diligent in qualifying the results of case
studies, it still remains liable to overgeneralise and homogenise across
what are different contexts, both in circumstance and meaning.
To this must be added the inclination to omit underlying causal
factors associated with power, conflict and material deprivation. As
a result, one can only be pessimistic about the prospects of turning
social capital into something more acceptable as an analytical tool.
In principle, its diverse appeals to social relations presumes an
illegitimate commonality across different case studies – one social
capital is not the same as another, and one has no comparative
lessons to draw from another. In practice, more nuanced studies in
the BBI vein merely serve to legitimise, even to fuel, the continuing
weight and momentum of standard social capital fare, offering more
variables to the concept's definitional lexicon.

In short, the rise and fall of social capital at the Bank is indicative
of many of the themes highlighted throughout this volume: the
dominance within the Bank of a narrow mainstream economics
with designs for hegemony over social, as well as economic, theory
and policy; the tensions between scholarship and advocacy (and
policy, see below); negotiating the passage from the Washington
to the post-Washington Consensus, whilst retaining considerable
antipathy towards the state; the confinement of intellectual
opposition and dissent to within the Bank; the undue influence of
the Bank's scholarship and research agenda on the wider intellectual
and donor community; and the failure of the putative knowledge
bank to debate fully and honestly with its critics. In addition, social
capital has displayed peculiar features of its own: the more or less
total irrelevance of the concept for policy and, thereby, its serving
primarily as a legitimising device in advocacy and scholarship (thus
emphasising the role of civil society, whilst policy strengthened its
orientation towards supporting private capital); and the capacity,
in these circumstances, for the Bank to tolerate, even publicly, the
most limited and ineffective of dissent, since this touched upon
neither its economics nor its policies.

NOTES

1. As established in Fine (2010a), earlier uses of social capital were totally differently focused – upon the systemic properties of capitalism and the effects of the total economic capital in aggregate. See also Fine (2009b) and Fine (2007c), in debate with Farr (2004 and 2007).
2. For Putnam's McDonaldisation of de Tocqueville and more, see McLean, Schultz and Steger (2002).
3. A phrase infamously deployed by Grootaert (1997), a leading social capital *economist* at the Bank; this is indicative of the all-purpose role social capital could play for the Bank's economists.
4. Michael Woolcock, Scott Guggenheim, Elizabeth Olson and Anthony Bebbington might be dubbed the major social capitalists at the Bank, serving as employees or consultants. See also Bebbington (2004, 2007 and 2008); but also Fine (2008b and 2010a).
5. It would be intriguing to know whether this piece was selected randomly for review or backfired, as '[w]e also asked the Bank's research director to nominate a group of "must read" outstanding papers or books from DEC' (p.41).
6. 'Acemoglu also strongly criticized the work for its lack of an appropriate conceptual and empirical framework. As a result, the regression analyses in these studies cannot be used to support the conclusions that they ostensibly reach' (p.64).
7. Quote taken by Galiani from Alatas, Pritchett and Wetterberg (2002, p.41).
8. See especially Fine (2001a and 2010a).
9. Fine (2007a), in a plenary address to the Critical Management Studies Conference, inspired by the presence of originator of the McDonaldisation thesis, George Ritzer, as fellow plenary speaker.
10. Note that the social capital literature has also begun to BBI Bourdieu (BBBI) and context, although these are inevitably reduced relative to the original, especially in Bourdieu's emphasis upon the diverse social construction of the meaning of social capital from one application to another.
11. See Fine (2001a) for fuller account, and also Fine (2003 and 2010a).
12. See also Rao and Woolcock (2007b). Note that they potentially misread the highly criticised report from Duflo (amongst a group of scholars, Sen and Douglas are judged to be senior, without Duflo necessarily implying all others in the mix are unknown, as Rao and Woolcock suggest). For the topic of culture addressed by these scholars, Duflo judges:

    > We are now in the presence of serious scholarship. The overall topic is relevant for the World Bank's poverty reduction strategy. Still, this is a difficult subject, and I sometimes have the sense that the World Bank's economists are stepping outside their comfort zone when they discuss it. (p.6).

    This seems to go at least as far as Rao and Woolcock's critique!
13. This leads to an unwittingly ironic appeal to critical discourse and institutional change as a rationale for their role within the Bank, even though such an approach has always been used to criticise, as well as to explain, the Bank's unacceptable postures.
14. Interestingly, as co-author, Bebbington is complaining of the same dominance of economists (over geographers) in the World Development Report for 2009 (an uncritical homage to the new economic geography), Rigg et al. (2009). And the

wish to finesse the new economic history by Woolcock, Szreter and Rao (2009) represents another addition to an apparently expanding academic niche for the civilising of economists across the social sciences, but from a position that is far from broad or deep, through the prism of a more radical stance within social theory and political economy.

15. Presumably, to his credit, Stiglitz seems to have borne no grudges for an apparent lack of overt support from the Bank's social capitalists in his hour of need. The leading non-economist social capitalist, Michael Woolcock, is now Director of Research at the Brooks World Poverty Institute, University of Manchester, which is headed by Stiglitz. This is a nice bit of social capital but, on this and other casual evidence, suggests a potentially worrying and increasing fluidity between Bank and academic postings, further consolidating the agenda-setting monopoly of the knowledge bank.

16. See http://web.worldbank.org/WBSITE/EXTERNAL/TOPICS/ EXTSOCIALDEVELOPMENT/EXTTSOCIALCAPITAL/0,,contentMDK:2018 6552~menuPK:418214~pagePK:148956~piPK:216618~theSitePK:401015,00. html.

17. See also Baum (2008) who demonstrates that study of the SDH can do without social capital after the event also (p.458):

> The Commission [on the Social Determinants of Health] was launched by the World Health Organisation in 2005 and its final report released in August 2008 ... The report makes three overarching recommendations which concern the importance of:
>
> (1) improving daily living conditions in which people are born, grow, live, work and age;
> (2) tackling the inequitable distribution of power, money and resources – the structural drivers of daily living conditions – globally, nationally and locally; and
> (3) measuring and understanding the problem of health inequities and assessing the impact of action.

18. See Deaton (2003) for the idea that inequality of income is not in and of itself a determinant of health outcomes, although it is accepted that it may be correlated and attached to other important determinants.

19. The book is entitled *Globalization and Health*, indicative of a dualism between globalisation and social capital, the latter especially confined to the level of the community in health studies. See the *Reader in Promoting Public Health* of Douglas, Earle and Handsley (2007), where social capital appears primarily within Part 5, 'Promoting Public Health at a Local Level', with public health through public policy and the impact of globalisation covered in the previous section.

20. Would you play cards with, invite to dinner, etc., someone with a gun?

21. Firearm ownership aside, Kunitz (2004, p.70) implicitly observes the impact of social capital through 'the destruction of President Clinton's plan for health care reform by a coalition of voluntary associations including the National Rifle Association, the Christian Coalition, the National Federation of Independent Businesses and the Health Insurance Association of America'. Muntaner (2004, p.675) appropriately suggests that if social capital had been dubbed social anarchy in view of its potentially negative effects (or social socialism because it is beneficial), it would have received short shrift – even though, it should be

added, reference might be made to negative social anarchy (or socialism). At the time of writing, Obama's plans await dilution.

22. This long list of references is included in order to confirm that the putative role of social capital as a wonder drug is not fanciful.

23. Note that for health, as with the application of social capital in other fields, particular factors seem to exert a strong influence on its presence (Scandinavia has provided numerous case studies and authors; for examples of these, in the case of SDH, see *Social Science and Medicine*). As Fulkerson and Thompson (2008, p.546) report:

> Using the *Sociological Abstracts* online database, we identify a total of 1,218 articles published across 450 journals that had the keyword 'social capital' in the title or abstract from 1988 through 2006 ... The highest producing journals of social capital articles are *Social Science and Medicine* (84), *Social Forces* (24), ... The highest producing journal, *Social Science and Medicine*, is alone responsible for 6.9 percent of the total number of social capital articles.

24. For other surveys, see Almedom (2005), Hawe and Shiell (2000), Szreter and Woolcock (2004a) and Kawachi et al. (2004), for example, and also www.socialcapitalgateway.org/NV-eng-health.htm.

25. It is unfortunate, but not necessary, for example, that Wilkinson, Kawachi and others should have jumped on the social capital bandwagon.

26. As Forbes and Wainwright (2001, p.811) observe,

> as with most health inequalities research these theorists do not describe the philosophical approach of their work. However, from the implicit metaphysical and epistemology positions adopted, their approach can be largely located within the positivist tradition, which is about constructing 'objective' realities or prototypes based on observable phenomena.

27. Apart from sadness, they also examine impact upon insomnia, anxiety and short temper.

28. Before attaching himself to social capital, Szreter was writing about SDH without its benefit. The term does not appear in Szreter and Mooney (1998) at all. Reminiscent of Putnam's (1993) Italian study, in which social capital only appears at the end, Szreter's (1997) first reference to it is within his conclusion – the lag to appear in print for the former contribution may have been longer than for the latter. Note that Labonté and Schrecker (2007a, p.2) can interpret Szreter's contributions as appealing for the formation of effective political coalitions for health provision without reference to social capital. Subsequently, Szreter (2002a and b) jumps the social capital bandwagon and ties it to New Labour politics, but the substantive dependence of his analyses on social capital as such is limited. By contrast, Woolcock has already abandoned social capital by the time his contributions with Szreter are appearing. It is far from clear how writing about social capital in the *International Journal of Epidemiology* brings about an influence upon the World Bank's economists, especially in view of the timing involved. Note also that Woolcock's (1998) first appearance as a social capitalist is in critical as much as synthetic vein. But this is before he is incorporated into the employ of the Bank.

29. Smith and Lynch (2004, p.691) note that whilst, in 1993, Putnam 'explicitly states that health should not be considered an outcome of social capital', seven years later 'he had dramatically reversed his opinion'. Muntaner and Lynch

(2002, p.262) highlight Putnam's ludicrous website claim that '[i]f you smoke and belong to no groups, it's a toss-up statistically whether you should stop smoking or start joining'. They tartly observe: 'We are unaware of any study that has shown that the act of joining a group conferred the same health protective effect as not smoking'.

30. Putnam (2004, p.667) also sees the social capital initiative as responding to 'several decades of intellectual and political hegemony on the part of an individualistic philosophy that claimed that "there is no such thing as society"'.

31. Putnam (2004, p.670) observes: 'In short, I agree with Szreter and Woolcock that the state (or public policy) must be embraced in any understanding of how social capital influences well-being, including health, while being slightly bemused by the claim that this view is novel'. It is surely truly astonishing that there should be even a tame dispute over the significance of the state for health in the context of any variable, social capital or otherwise.

32. In one response in the debate, Szreter (2004, p.708) closes with the assertion that

> [t]hinking in terms of social capital explains what went so wrong in the 1830s and why the 1850s represented only an alleviation of those problems, not a solution, whereas the 1870s constitutes the birth of something very new – a practical programme engendered by a new configuration and imagination of the social and political relationship between classes composing a city – new forms of social capital.

This might be thought to out-reduce class reductionism!

33. See also Navarro (2005).

34. See also Bridgen (2006, p.43) for a positive gloss on social capital, New Labour and health, 'an opportunity, rather than a threat' – at least the alternatives are recognised! See also Muntaner, Lynch and Davey Smith (2001).

35. This, too, is reminiscent of the contribution to the World Bank's email discussion group on social capital in which it is suggested that the social capital

> calves are out of the barn and into green pastures and not likely to return soon. The term social capital is now firmly entrenched in the language of social scientists. Thus, for now and for some considerable time in the future, the term 'social capital', will be in common use amongst social scientists if not economists'. (Fine 2001a, pp.241–2)

36. In an empirically flawed study, omitting levels of resourcing, etc., Coleman argued that Catholics did better at school for being better endowed with familial social capital.

37. And the World Bank's social capital assessment tool, SOCAT, is still available at http://siteresources.worldbank.org/INTSOCIALCAPITAL/Resources/Social-Capital-Assessment-Tool--SOCAT-/annex1.pdf.

38. And it will come as no surprise that social capital is deemed to be important for addressing malaria (see Mozumder and Marathe 2007, for example).

6
World Bank Research on HIV/AIDS: Praise Where It's Due?[1]

Deborah Johnston

6.1 AN INTRODUCTION TO WORLD BANK RESEARCH ON HIV AND AIDS

While initial analyses of the global economic crisis focused on the impacts on finance, jobs and growth, it has become increasingly clear that there will be a range of wider social impacts. Newspaper reports about cutbacks in donor and government expenditure on HIV/AIDS programmes (Palitza 2009, for example) have found support in a World Bank survey (2009e) which shows that many of the poorest countries expect to run rapidly into resource constraints on these programmes. Carried out in March 2009, the survey found that most countries expected the crisis to have a negative impact on AIDS treatment programmes as Less Developed Country (LDC) governments and international donors find their resources constrained – with one third anticipating that the impact would be felt quickly: '[w]hile only nine of 69 countries surveyed report that there has already been an impact on treatment, 33 percent of countries – home to 61 percent of people on treatment – expect some impact over the year, with concern highest in Sub-Saharan Africa' (World Bank 2009e, p.42). This prompted an announcement from the World Bank, on 24 April 2009, that it would spend US$3.1 billion on health financing for poor countries in 2009, tripling previous annual expenditure. If these funds are channelled into HIV/ AIDS programmes, this would have the effect both of boosting the low percentage of total Bank spending in this area and of increasing the Bank's role in international expenditure on the pandemic.[2]

In light of this, it is relevant to ask how sound the Bank's own research and practice will be as a guide to its expenditure. While the Deaton evaluation of World Bank research was positive about the Bank's research on HIV and AIDS, this chapter is far less optimistic. I show that the evidence base for World Bank work on HIV and AIDS is small and weak, and the methodology of its studies is inadequate. Concepts such as social class, social power and uneven economic development, which have been so important in heterodox work on the pandemic, are absent from the Bank's approach. Despite the weaknesses of Bank research, its results are presented as useful to policymakers in coming to critical decisions. Yet the results are inevitably liable to be inappropriate and over-simplified in seeking to formulate policy to combat HIV and AIDS.

Readers of this volume will be aware that the Deaton evaluation report was critical of many areas of World Bank research (see Chapter 2). However, it was decidedly positive about the Bank's research on HIV and AIDS. The overview report concluded that '[t]here has also been important Bank work on HIV/AIDS' (Deaton et al. 200, p.113) and that the 1997 World Bank report 'Confronting Aids' was one of the Bank's best policy reports (p.123). One of the evaluators, Christopher Udry, describes the Bank's HIV/AIDS work as being one of the Bank's 'significant contributions' and 'important research' (Udry 2006, p.1).

Interestingly, this positive assessment of World Bank research on HIV/AIDS, all of it constructed with the tools of mainstream economics, is at odds with the wider assessment of a degree of failure by mainstream economics to contribute to our understanding of the pandemic. It is generally agreed that there has been little economic research on HIV/AIDS. For example, in 2006, well-known health economists Scott McDonald and Jennifer Roberts (2006, p.229) asserted that there has been a surprising lack of economic work on the impact of AIDS. A second failing is that the economic research that exists does not elicit great confidence. In 2003, the United Nations argued that the true impact of HIV/AIDS may be 'more serious than most economic estimates suggest' (UN 2003, p.89), while individual economists have sometimes been taken aback with the results of their own methodology. For example, an IMF assessment found that AIDS was likely to have little impact on economic growth in Botswana, with its authors, Maitland MacFarlan and Silvia Sgherri (2001, p.11), agreeing that it was 'surprising that output and incomes continue growing at all when one-third to one-half of the current working age population is expected to die within about ten years'. It seems relevant then to ask whether the Deaton evaluators were correct in their positive assessment of World Bank research in this area, particularly if it influences the crisis-induced increase in Bank expenditure.

To investigate this, I will focus on World Bank research into HIV prevalence. This exists in two forms: a fashionable microeconomic approach, focusing on the drivers of individual behaviour; and a slightly older approach that looks at the way prevalence is affected by macro-level factors. The Deaton evaluation looked at the former type of research when assessing the work by Nancy Luke (2006), of Brown University, who received funding from the Bank. The second type of research was exemplified by the 1997 'Confronting Aids' report (World Bank 1997b), which is mentioned in the Deaton report, but not evaluated, as the study predated the evaluation's time span.

6.2   HIV PREVENTION AND MODELS OF INDIVIDUAL BEHAVIOUR

The vast majority of World Bank funding for HIV/AIDS has been spent on capacity-building of government, non-governmental organisations (NGOs) and community-based organisations (CBOs) to develop policies and projects that lead to behavioural change.[3] This focus on changing individual-level behaviour (through AIDS education and condom distribution) is the defining characteristic of the public health approach to the pandemic (Stillwaggon 2006 and Katz 2009). It provides fertile ground for the development of microeconomic models of decision making, best exemplified by Philipson and Posner (1995).[4] These model the way individuals develop an 'optimal' level of exposure to HIV, based on the cost of condoms, knowledge of transmission mechanisms and the likely impact on their life expectancy.

Models of this type, along with the general public health approach to HIV, have been criticised for envisaging sexual interactions as though they were the result of free, informed decisions. This assumption is particularly inappropriate in describing the sexual choices of women, who are constrained in making decisions over sex by gender-based social norms and practices. This is best exemplified by a quote from a UNAIDS publication that explains the inadequacies of the standard ABC approach ('practise Abstinence, Be faithful, use Condoms') (UNAIDS, UNFPA and UNIFEM 2004, p.16):[5]

[A]bstinence is meaningless to girls and women who are coerced or forced into sexual activity. Faithfulness offers little protection to wives whose husbands have several partners or were infected before they were married. Condoms require the cooperation of men, who may refuse to use them.

The Bank-sponsored paper by Nancy Luke (2006), mentioned above, speaks directly to this debate about individual-level decision making, utilising a microeconomic model of behaviour to show that women do make clear choices over sex. This paper was very positively reviewed by the member of the Deaton evaluation team assigned to it.[6] At the heart of the paper is a survey of a randomly selected sample of 1,028 men aged between 21 and 45 in the Kenyan town of Kisumu who reported having non-marital, non-commercial sexual partners (i.e. not wives or sex-workers). Luke then focuses on the determinants of risky sex between these men and their girlfriends. She argues that there is a clear relationship between condom use and transfers (or gifts) from a man to a woman, such that the greater the value of the transfers, the more likely that there will be unprotected sex. This research seems to restore power to the micro-modelling approach and to policymakers focused on individual decision makers. Luke asserts strongly that her results show that women are not vulnerable victims and instead are making 'conscious trade-offs between the risks and the benefits of informal exchange relationships' (p.345). She finds that a small change in transfers from men to women gives rise to a substantial decrease in condom use, with the policy conclusion being that improvements in the economic opportunities for women could change 'the terms of trade in the sexual marketplace significantly' (p.345). A secondary finding concerns the protective impact of male education: with every year of education, men are 3.5 per cent more likely to use a condom (p.338).

While Luke's work appears to be a convincing reassertion of the usefulness of individual-level behavioural modelling, it is vulnerable to criticisms on grounds of both data and methodology. One problem is the use of self-reported behaviour. Studying data for a number of African countries, de Walque (2007), a researcher based at the World Bank, finds a number of anomalies and concludes that self-reports of sexual behaviour are unreliable and that both research and policy should 'avoid relying exclusively on self-reported behaviour' (p.519). More damaging still for Luke's analysis (and her conclusion about the protective effects of education) is Bujra's (2006) class-based analysis of self-reported data in Tanzania. She analysed the 2003/04 Tanzanian HIV/AIDS Indicator Survey and compared prevalence data with the responses to behavioural questions. She found that the higher the wealth quintile, the more likely respondents would be to report few sexual partners and high use of condoms in risky sexual encounters (p.122). However, these results were at odds with the far higher prevalence rates found among higher-wealth quintiles in the 2003/04 survey (of which, more below), and Bujra suggests that the self-reported behaviour of richer or more educated individuals should not be taken entirely at face value, as 'such respondents would have been more likely to know what answers were expected and more articulate in asserting their moral standing' (p.122).

The criticisms of self-reported behavioural data do then present a serious empirical challenge to Luke's results, especially those regarding the protective effects of education. This aside, there are important questions over the assumptions and methodology of the model – not least whether the trade-offs she identifies for women can be included under the intellectually loaded term 'choice'.[7] Indeed, her work suggests large differences in bargaining power between men and women in her survey area, with women being far poorer and lacking income-earning opportunities. To what extent can these women be seen as making fully informed, free choices, given the asymmetries of economic and social power? Luke's model suggests that risky behaviour (and hence HIV risk) would be reduced if women had higher income, as higher-income women are seen as being more able to resist men's attempts to use transfers to persuade them to engage in unsafe sex. However, this conclusion is not supported by a systematic review of 35 or so studies, which finds mixed evidence on the link between female socio-economic status and HIV infection (Wojcicki 2005). Wojcicki reports that most studies find women with higher socio-economic status to have higher rates of infection and suggests that 'there is some indication that access to increased funds for women may put them at increased risk for HIV infection – potentially by giving them access to more partners or opportunities for travel' (p.19). Open to question, then, is the simplistic relationship drawn between poverty and HIV risk for women. The issue is more complex and we need to consider the kinds of lifestyles and power relationships faced by women.

Second, is it really possible to isolate decisions over HIV risk and money from other factors? For example, women not only run the risk of HIV if they have sex without condoms, they also risk pregnancy, which some may actively desire. Are women weighing up their options about the former or the latter? This may seem like splitting hairs – but the application of microeconomic modelling only makes sense if we think that we can isolate the decision-making processes made in practice. The model's construction around clear-cut, fully informed individual choices over a risky sex act is inappropriate. We might instead want to understand more about the role of condom use in different kinds of sexual relationship, where non-use of condoms may also be related to desires for pregnancy and signalling of trust. This would put far more emphasis on questions such as the duration of the relationship and its character than is allowed by the blanket categorisation employed by Luke.

More than that, Luke does not show how this model bears on the central relationships involved. Is risky, casual sex the relevant driver for high HIV prevalence in Kisumu? She needs to justify why she omitted commercial sexual transactions, coerced sex or sex between husband and wife. Similarly Luke considers the factors that affect the demand for condoms, but without reference to supply, i.e. simply presuming that condoms are accessible at a reasonable cost. On these points, her model has taken no account of the social epidemiology literature, worthy of review in some detail here.

First, attention should be drawn to the literature about which sexual activities drive high HIV levels. The results of local-level studies have generated a range of interpretations about the link between self-reported sexual activity and prevalence within a single community.[8] When the analysis moves to comparisons at either the regional or global level, it has proved difficult to draw conclusions about the relationship between patterns of sexual activity and HIV prevalence that can be agreed by epidemiologists. Wellings et al. (2006) find no relationship between sexual behaviour and sexual health from data for 59 countries. Individuals in industrialised countries tend to have more partners over their lifetime and engage in sex from an earlier age, but do not have higher HIV prevalence. Wellings et al. do find lower rates of reported condom use among people from poor countries compared to industrialised countries (pp.1714 and 1719), and they remain concerned about condom access and cost (p.1723). However, the rates of condom use that they report do not correspond neatly to HIV prevalence, as the lowest rates were for low-prevalence Latin American countries.

Similarly, identifying the factors leading to high HIV prevalence in African countries is difficult, although Wellings et al. do note that there is evidence to suggest a greater prevalence and duration of concurrent (i.e. overlapping) sexual relationships in some African countries than elsewhere (p.1714). Concurrency has then become the most promising avenue for investigation in the explanation for

HIV levels. However, the empirical evidence is not all clear-cut. For example, Lagarde et al. (2001) studied the link between concurrent sexual activity and HIV prevalence in five African cities and did not find a clear relationship between the two. In a related study of four African cities (UNAIDS 1999), no relationship could be found between HIV prevalence and a range of risky behaviours: high rates of partner change, contacts with sex workers, and concurrent sexual partnerships. While in high-prevalence areas girls become sexually active at a younger age, and men and women first married at a younger age, the researchers find that this cannot explain the extent of the difference in HIV prevalence. This debate has called into question the adequacy of the data that epidemiologists are forced to use, as it is not clear how well concurrency or other forms of what epidemiologists call 'sexual networks' can be captured by standard empirical approaches. For epidemiologists then, patterns of sexual networks are important in explaining how HIV risks are raised, rather than high numbers of partners or casual sex per se.

In addition, the studies above have identified other factors as increasing the risk of HIV acquisition. The UNAIDS (1999) study of four African cities found a link between HIV prevalence and two factors likely to increase HIV transmission during sexual contact: presence of untreated sexually transmitted infections (STIs) and low levels of male circumcision. These factors clearly affected the infectivity of HIV for any given sexual act, making transmission much easier. However, they are also factors that are determined by sociocultural attitudes (both towards male circumcision and the take-up of STI treatment) and the cost and availability of public health services.

Critical voices from outside epidemiology, such as Stillwaggon (2006) and Katz (2009), have suggested that the infectivity of the HIV virus in African countries may be higher because of malnutrition and parasitic illnesses, as these increase vulnerability to HIV infection as well as making HIV more infectious once it has been acquired. As Nattrass (2009) notes, the evidence for this is mixed, but it places greater attention on the wider role of health in explaining the infectiousness of HIV in any one place. Both Stillwaggon and Katz also point to a range of social and economic factors that may increase HIV prevalence because of their impact on the pattern of sexual networks. These include the extent of labour migration, border delays, gender power imbalances and population movements due to conflict. These concerns, together with those of the epidemiology literature, suggest that high HIV prevalence may be driven not only by individual decision making but also by a host of other factors. These might be artificially forced into an individualistic decision making framework, although, as already demonstrated, commitment to such an approach tends to narrow attention to those factors most directly attached to individualistic choice that are amenable to both modelling and data availability.

By contrast, and more specifically, the nature of the public health system will determine, for example, access to condoms and the extent of untreated STIs, as well as general ill health. Sociocultural attitudes by different classes will affect the degree of male circumcision and shape sexual networks. The nature of conflict and labour migration will also impact on patterns of sexual networking and affect the acceptability of particular practices. Clearly Luke's (2006) model, with its focus on individuals making choices about whether or not to use condoms in discrete acts of casual sex, is misfocused and unable to encompass the wider social and economic factors of relevance. These factors are often termed 'structural' in the social epidemiology literature because they cannot be understood at the level of individuals (e.g. Gupta et al. 2008). However, the World Bank has sponsored other work that seeks to identify the relationship between HIV prevalence and a wider set of economic and social factors. I now assess these.

6.3   WORLD BANK ANALYSIS AND STRUCTURAL FACTORS

As indicated, the World Bank research report 'Confronting Aids' (1997b) received praise in the Deaton evaluation. This work eschews the analysis of individual behaviour to consider instead the relationship between HIV prevalence and wider social and economic factors. It puts forward several hypotheses about the relationship between HIV prevalence, poverty and inequality. The following paragraph encapsulates them well (p.27):

> [P]overty and gender inequality make a society more vulnerable to HIV because a woman who is poor, either absolutely or relative to men, will find it harder to insist that her sex partner abstain from sex with other partners or use a condom … Poverty may also make a man more prone to having multiple casual partners, by preventing him from attracting a wife or by causing him to leave home in search of work.

The report goes on to test these hypotheses using national-level data and multi-country regression analysis, across 72 countries. Using 1994 data on GNP per capita and 1995 data on urban adult HIV prevalence, the authors find a strong association between low-income and HIV prevalence rates.

The report suggests that a US$2,000 increase in per capita income is associated with a reduction of about 4 percentage points in HIV prevalence (p.28). Similar findings are made for vertical inequality and gender inequality, i.e. a strong correlation exists between macro-level measures and HIV prevalence rates. The overall conclusion is that (pp.29–30):

> a country that improves per capita income and reduces inequality, for example, by implementing investment policies that generate jobs and raise economic growth, will reduce its risk of suffering an AIDS epidemic ... If, in addition, the country acts to close the literacy and urban employment gaps between men and women, HIV would have even more difficulty spreading.

These policy recommendations are congruent with the policies enshrined in the Millennium Development Goals, and the assumption is that the wider development agenda will also form the bedrock of the HIV/AIDS policy agenda. However, the 'Confronting Aids' report is open to empirical and methodological criticisms.

Several problems exist with the empirical basis for the multiple regression methodology employed by 'Confronting Aids'. Firstly, the data are of prevalence rather than incidence, which is not entirely suitable for assessing current HIV risk.[9] Furthermore, there are important weaknesses in the data on prevalence used in the report. While UNAIDS provides official data on HIV prevalence, its data are extrapolated from surveys of pregnant women at selected antenatal clinics. This has raised criticisms about both the choice of sample of antenatal clinics, particularly that there may be a bias towards urban sites or sites with high prevalence, and also the manner in which the results for pregnant women are then converted to rates for the population as a whole (Bennell 2004). The debate over UNAIDS prevalence data has been further fuelled by the divergent findings of population-based samples (such as demographic and health surveys and AIDS indicator surveys) (Bennell 2004).[10] This has, more recently, led UNAIDS to be more open about statistical errors in prevalence estimates and, on occasion, to revise their estimates in the light of those emerging from other sources. At the time 'Confronting Aids' was published, competing prevalence estimates were just beginning to emerge, and so it might have been understandable to rely heavily on the UNAIDS prevalence data. However, the report is completely unconcerned with the quality and source of prevalence data, despite the sensitivity of the results of the cross-country regression to the biases that are introduced.

Aside from the weakness of the data, there are important methodological drawbacks to the use of cross-country multiple regression analysis. It assumes a neat linear relationship between HIV prevalence and income, even though the intra-regional picture is clearly more complex. Within Africa, the highest prevalence rates occur in those countries with the *highest* regional income per capita, such as South Africa, Botswana and Namibia. Prevalence levels are lower in many African countries with far lower incomes, such as Mali, Burundi and Rwanda. In recent work, Nattrass (2009) has carried out multiple regression analysis using a dummy variable to indicate whether or not a country is Southern African and found that HIV prevalence is 8.3 times higher for countries in Southern Africa than might be expected given their levels of income per capita, nutrition and gender inequality in labour force participation. This is problematic for the cross-country multiple regression approach of 'Confronting Aids', which has an underlying assumption of universalism, i.e. that all countries experience the same relationship between HIV prevalence, poverty and inequality. Marks' (2007) review of work on Southern Africa suggests that high levels of prevalence are the result of the type of aggressive HIV subtype found in the region, socio-sexual dynamics, which involve significant levels of violence towards women, and the history of the region, which has promoted widespread male migration and deep-seated suspicion of the discourses of western medicine.

A further damaging aspect of 'Confronting Aids' is that it looks at national averages of HIV prevalence. This obscures the intra-country diversity in prevalence that can invalidate such regressions, and conceals a great deal about the way in which structural factors affect risk. Mishra et al. (2007) show that HIV prevalence is not distributed uniformly within populations. Using data from population-based surveys for Kenya, Ghana, Burkina Faso, Cameroon, Tanzania, Lesotho, Malawi and Uganda, they find that, in all eight countries, wealthier men and women tend to have higher prevalence of HIV than poorer ones. For women there is a clear linear relationship between wealth and HIV prevalence in all countries. However, for men, there was a clear linear relationship except in Lesotho and

Ghana, where there was an inverted-U relationship (i.e. those men in the middle wealth groups had the highest prevalence) (Mishra et al. 2007, p.33).[11] Data from the 2003/04 Tanzanian HIV/AIDS Indicator Survey illustrate this intra-country diversity further (DHS 2005). For both men and women, HIV prevalence increases with education. Adults with secondary or higher education are almost 50 per cent more likely to be infected with HIV than those with no education. HIV prevalence also increases with wealth, with infection rates three times higher among those in the highest wealth quintile than those in the lowest wealth quintile. Bujra's (2006) analysis suggests that this pattern of prevalence reflects underlying class dynamics and specific patterns of sexual networking associated with each class. She sees the greater wealth of educated elites, in particular the freedom of elite men from traditional social constraints, as allowing greater sexual networking and mobility in Tanzania. As a result they have a higher risk of HIV.

Whilst, then, the report allows for structural factors, it does so simplistically and erroneously. Structural factors operate with an important element of specificity. Further, intra-country patterns of prevalence are complex, with two implications. First, it is inappropriate to use national averages in large statistical investigations, given the lack of uniform patterns of prevalence. Second, attention to lack of intra-country patterns shows, in many African studies, that prevalence can rise with education and wealth. So, a simple story of education or wealth being protective against HIV is far too simplistic.

6.4   IMPLICATIONS FOR WORLD BANK POLICY ON HIV TRANSMISSION

As indicated, World Bank literature has evolved in two distinct streams. One is entirely focused on the individual and assumes that changing individual behaviour is the key to reducing HIV prevalence. This ignores the evidence on the complexity of sexual behaviour, as well as evidence for other structural factors that lead to high HIV prevalence. The second stream of research ties the HIV agenda to that of general development. Specifically, policies to reduce poverty and gender inequality will reduce HIV levels. However, this ignores the evidence that shows that wealth and education do not always protect against HIV and that there is a great deal of specificity in the way that HIV prevalence is related to wider structural factors. In both cases, World Bank stories about

HIV transmission have found it hard to explain the empirical patterns of HIV prevalence. Furthermore, they have generally failed to incorporate factors that appear important in the work of others writing about prevalence levels, such as epidemiologists, gender specialists and political economists.

What are the implications of this for policy to reduce HIV prevalence? The insights above broadly suggest that policies aiming to impact on class-based social norms and sexual networking patterns, geographic mobility and access to health care can have an important role in reducing HIV prevalence. These insights suggest that the present policy focus on individual behaviour change should be widened. As Jones (2004, p.399–400) argues: 'This is not to imply that individuals should be absolved from all responsibilities but, rather, that the "vulnerability" of specific individuals, groups and regions to HIV/AIDS should be situated within a more thorough analysis', one which considers the interaction of social, economic and historical contingencies of place.[12] The inclusion of structural factors in explanations of risk would make the public health approach to HIV/AIDS more like that for other infectious diseases. Katz (2009) argues that the public health perspective for other infectious diseases routinely considers population-wide vulnerabilities as well as individual risk. However, for HIV, while some more far-thinking policy bodies do consider some structural factors, they tend to choose those surrounding sexual and drugs behaviour (as opposed to general health status or social dislocation). Furthermore, Stillwaggon (2006) argues that even when social and economic factors are identified as being important in driving high HIV prevalence levels, the solutions remain focused on residual preventative action at the level of the individual. She provides the example of the USAID Corridors of Hope programme, which focused on the role that border delays play in the development of a market for commercial sex for truckers. Rather than changing the economic, bureaucratic or political factors that lead to these delays, Stillwaggon reports that the programme targeted behaviour change, communication and condom distribution at the borders.

What would 'structural' policies look like? Additional spending on broad programmes of public health, clean water and adequate food are likely to improve general biological susceptibility towards infection as well as specific susceptibility through untreated sexually transmitted infections (Stillwaggon 2006). In this light, it is worrying that progress on these areas has generally been slow and uneven, as seen in the latest Millennium Development Goal report (UN 2009b).

These are areas where the World Bank and other international financial institutions have a wider policy impact. Raising health expenditure in many developing countries is constrained by fiscal constraints. While Dennis and Zuckerman (2008, p.296) generally observe that health expenditures are limited by the high level of debt servicing that poor countries are obliged to make, Rowden (2008) makes an explicit link between the levels of health expenditure and IMF-imposed expenditure targets. Rowden and Thapliyal (2007) present the findings of a quasi-independent evaluation of the IMF, which found that only US$3 in every US$10 in annual aid increases are spent, with the remainder being used to build up international reserves or draw down debt. Aside from global expenditure constraints, specific ceilings on the public sector wage bill have prevented the employment of additional health workers as well as wage increases to retain existing workers. Although the IMF issued a statement in 2007 that it would only operate wage ceilings where necessary, Rowden (2008, p.20) argues that the flexibility on ceilings has been 'the exception and not the rule'. Wage ceiling restrictions imposed by the IMF are particularly damaging, given that the public sector in many poor countries has been chronically underfunded for some time, with few donors paying recurrent salary costs (Rowden 2008, pp.20–1). Indeed, in their review of HIV/AIDS programmes, Dennis and Zuckerman (2008, pp.294–5) found that none of the four World Bank programmes they reviewed clearly supported recurrent health costs, focusing instead on expenditure on infrastructure, equipment, research and training. At the same time, the imposition of user fees and other cost-recovery mechanisms may reduce access to existing services. An obvious example is where user fees have led to the low take-up of anti-retroviral therapies (ARTs). Dennis and Zuckerman found that the Bank-funded Multisector HIV/AIDS Project in Ghana included cost recovery programmes, such as patient user fee co-payments for anti-retroviral drugs. They argue that these make the drugs unaffordable for the poor. The new World Bank Health Nutrition and Population strategy continues to promote user fees, despite Bank assurances that it does not support such fees for basic health care for the poorest (pp.296–7).

More generally, health services have undergone reform in many poor countries following advice from the World Bank. These reforms have revolved around privatised health systems, a new administrative rationality and fundamentally altered health financing (see also Chapters 5 and 11). In line with general neo-liberal principles, an underlying ideological belief prevails that private delivery is better than state delivery. A good example of the inadequacies of this approach, however, is provided by World Bank approaches to the HIV/AIDS programme itself. The World Bank Multi-Country AIDS Programme (MAP), which influenced the criteria for the much larger Global Fund (Putzel 2004, p.1132), requires that a country must have met certain requirements to be eligible for funds. These include: evidence of a strategic approach to HIV/AIDS; existence of a high-level HIV/AIDS coordinating body; an agreement by the government to channel funds directly to communities, civil society and the private sector; and an agreement by the government to use and fund multiple implementation agencies, especially community-based and non-governmental organisations (pp.1131–2). However, Putzel observes that, while some of the Bank's propositions were based on sound evidence, the proposals obscure the political reality of HIV/AIDS success stories. The Bank makes (p.1138):

> an implicit assessment of the inability of organizations *within* the state, or public authority, to implement HIV/AIDS programmes and an implicit, virtually ideological belief, that NGOs, religious organizations and private sector organizations will be able to do better. (original emphasis)

Instead, it is suggested that the success stories of Uganda and Senegal were driven by high-level government interest in a process fundamentally led by the Ministry of Health (pp.1134–5). The initiatives of the state and political organisations mobilised NGOs and civil society organisations, not vice versa. Thus, the Bank model overlooks the need for the centralised direction of health resources, led both by formal government and leading political organisations.

Another structural feature that is highlighted in the literature is the limited decision making power of women, given their relative economic and social disadvantage. A key policy conclusion is that HIV interventions need an explicit gender analysis and action plan to empower women with respect to sexual decision making, and this may also involve longer-term strategies to improve the economic and social status of women. However, World Bank HIV/AIDS interventions have not always encompassed these perspectives. Dennis and Zuckerman (2008, pp.294–5) sampled four World Bank projects to assess their gender focus. They found that only one was 'somewhat gender-sensitive' (p.294), but that its focus was exclusively on women, thereby overlooking gender relations. They argue that this fails to recognise men's influence on women's health, and men's own reproductive health needs.

Changes in trade and migration patterns may also affect HIV prevalence, but these have not been the focus of policy. As seen above, while border delays have been recognised as fuelling prostitution in some areas, policy responses have not sought to reduce delays, but rather to change the behaviour of individual truckers. Changes in trade and border policies and regulations, with the aim of reducing HIV risk, have not been proposed. In the same way, industrial and migration policies will clearly impact on the size of population movements, the stability of that movement, and its character. For example, the impact of migration on HIV prevalence is likely to be affected by the extent to which this migration is long term and whether migrants are able to move with their families. The character of sexual networks will be affected together with the corresponding HIV risk.

However, in proposing structural policies to reduce HIV prevalence, there can be no uniform menu, as evidenced by the false notion that greater educational access and attainment will be protective against HIV. Not only are there insufficient data to assess change over time, but, as we have seen, snapshot data also suggest that in some countries the more educated have higher HIV prevalence than the less educated. As a result, Gupta et al. (2008) correctly observe that no structural 'magic bullet' is likely to exist, and there is no single policy that would reduce HIV prevalence in all places among all social classes. Policies to reduce HIV prevalence need to be based on a clearer socio-economic profile of the pandemic for each country than is presently the case.

6.5 CONCLUSION

World Bank research on HIV prevalence has had a number of failings, and the policy recommendations drawn from it have been narrow and overly simplistic.[13] As a result, there are several reasons why the crisis-induced increase in health funding on the part of the Bank will not have a significant impact on HIV prevention. Such expenditure is likely to remain focused on education for individual behavioural change, failing to recognise the structural factors that drive HIV prevalence. Ministries of Health and the state, more generally, are unlikely to have a strong role in HIV/AIDS strategies and service delivery. Moreover, expenditure on HIV/AIDS in many poor countries is likely to be constrained by fiscal rules, with particularly negative implications for the recruitment of extra staff.

At the same time, the Bank itself is doing little to improve the evidence base for HIV/AIDS. Not only has it used data on HIV prevalence uncritically, it has also taken little action to improve the database used for formulating policy. While the Bank has sought to improve the availability of data for development policy in many areas, it has not done so for HIV/AIDS. It has, for example, sponsored a longitudinal household study in Kagera, Tanzania, to illustrate the impact of illness on households (see Ainsworth, Beegle and Koda 2005). However, this area does not have high HIV prevalence relative to other parts of Africa. Yet, without better data, either on the extent of HIV or the factors driving it, the policy debate is vulnerable to inappropriate or oversimplified conclusions. Indeed, Marks (2007) has argued that the debate on HIV and AIDS has been bedevilled with 'factoids – the intellectual viruses of quick and dirty synthetic studies' (p.861), where information is based on soft opinions and limited evidence.

This chapter also indicates that the conclusions of the Deaton evaluation report offered an unduly generous assessment of Bank research work on HIV/AIDS. Those involved may have been unaware of the concerns about HIV prevalence and self-reported sexual activity data in the reports that they praised. They may also have been unaware of the issues raised by those working in the disciplines of gender studies, social epidemiology and political economy. As such, they may not have recognised the narrow and simplistic focus of the Bank studies and their inability to describe the reality of HIV prevalence. In effect then, the architects of the Deaton evaluation made inappropriate choices about the composition of a team required to evaluate research in this area. It is both the complexity and the diversity of HIV prevalence and its contingent dependence upon wider social factors that may explain why the Deaton Report's economists should have viewed the Bank's research as satisfactory – to put it bluntly, through their own ignorance, not an individual but a systematic failure within economics.

Does this mean that economics has little to contribute to the analysis of HIV/AIDS? Mainstream approaches have struggled to address the key issues involved. However, this is to ignore the role that heterodox approaches could play in the HIV/AIDS policy debate. The evidence suggests powerful patterns of prevalence in terms of gender, geography, occupation and class, traditional concepts within political economy. Bujra (2006) has analysed these for Tanzania, and produced one of the earliest explanations for the pattern of high prevalence found there among the educated elite. However, the use of concepts such as class, social power and uneven economic development are absent from the World Bank dictionary, and this is likely to remain the greatest of obstacles to the Bank-sponsored work in credibly explaining HIV prevalence. In this respect, there is something more involved than long-running debates over the nature and causes of development and economic performance. In the case of HIV/AIDS, we are confronted with a new and devastating problem, for which imaginative research across methods and disciplines is essential, together with corresponding extension of the appropriately guided collection and use of evidence. The continuing poverty of World Bank (economic) research in this context, let alone that of effective policy response, whatever the appeal to economists, is cruelly exposed by the analytical issues involved.

NOTES

1. In earlier drafts, this chapter received helpful comments from a number of individuals, including Henry Bernstein, Chris Cramer, Kevin Deane, Justin Parkhurst and, of course, the editors of this book. As usual, I acknowledge any errors as my own.
2. The World Bank has a Global HIV/AIDS programme of action and five regional HIV and AIDS strategies. Dennis and Zuckerman (2008, pp.290–1) calculate that an average of 6 per cent of Bank expenditure went to HIV/AIDS programmes between 2003 to 2006, although the percentage decreased over time. At the same time, the World Bank plays only a small role in financing responses to the pandemic. In 2006, the Bank's main funding stream for HIV/AIDS, Multi-Country AIDS programme, accounted for only 7 per cent of all AIDS-related aid disbursements, Oomman, Bernstein and Rosenzweig (2007, p.3).
3. The main channel for World Bank funding, the Multi-Country AIDS Programme for Africa, MAP, is designed to deliver funds quickly to build a country's capacity to develop a national response to AIDS (Putzel 2004 and Oomman, Bernstein and Rosenzweig 2007). While it is difficult to determine the exact use of MAP funds, an estimated 74 per cent of funds over the period 2000–06 were spent on capacity development and prevention work (Oomman, Bernstein and Rosenzweig 2007, pp.48–50). Over that period, only 16 per cent of funds were spent on AIDS treatment and care.
4. These are yet another example of the kind of economics imperialism discussed by Fine (2002a) and Fine and Milonakis (2009).
5. The focus on choice has also been criticised by those writing more generally about the role that forced sexual activity has in HIV transmission (see Andersson 2006).
6. Nancy Birdsall (2006, p.3) rated the paper very highly and wanted the findings distributed widely within the Bank.

7. Shula Marks (2007, p.867) suggests that many young African women are 'choice-disabled', being dependent to a large extent on men for economic support and status, and thus engaging in risky sexual behaviour to secure their attentions and fatalistically accepting the concomitant risk of HIV and sexual violence as a necessary part of survival.

8. For example, local-level data have generated a debate about the extent to which risky sexual activity by women is the source of HIV infection among couples (see de Walque 2007). A parallel debate exists about the 'protective' role of marriage against HIV infection, with various competing interpretations of local-level studies (see Bongaarts 2007).

9. An analysis of HIV risk would assess current incidence rather than the 'stock' of HIV prevalence in a country.

10. Bennell (2004) has collected some examples of the divergence between prevalence estimates from UNAIDS and from population-based surveys: in Zambia the population-based estimate for 2001 was 15.6 per cent, compared to 21.5 for the clinic-based surveys; in South Africa, the gap was even bigger, with estimates of 16 per cent and 24 per cent, respectively; and in Burundi, the 2002 population-based survey suggested that the national prevalence rate was about 3 per cent, while the UNAIDS estimate for 2001 was 8.3 per cent.

11. Parkhurst (2010) has updated and extended this analysis of population-based surveys for Africa, finding a similarly complex relationship between wealth and prevalence.

12. Stillwaggon (2006) further suggests that broader structural change, such as the provision of clean water, reductions in border delays and more treatment for STIs, may be easier to accomplish than approaches that require individuals to change their sexual behaviour.

13. The discussion above points to the ideological and methodological reasons for this. Dennis and Zuckerman (2008, p.295) suggest that these explanations for the poor quality of Bank programmes might be supplemented by institutional arguments. In the health, nutrition and population (HNP) sector (which includes HIV and AIDS), the ranks of regular staff decreased by 40 per cent between 1999–2006, as permanent staff have been replaced by temporary or consultant staff. Dennis and Zuckerman (2008, p.295) argue that these new staff have lacked 'institutional memory and experience', and this is a major reason why an internal Bank review found that HNP was one of the poorest performing sectors of the Bank, with one-third of its projects rated 'unsatisfactory'.

7
Agriculture in the World Bank: Blighted Harvest Persists[1,2]

Carlos Oya

7.1 INTRODUCTION

The 2008 World Development Report (World Bank 2007a; hereafter WDR 2008), devoted to agriculture, opens with the bold statement that 'in the 21st century agriculture continues to be a fundamental instrument for sustainable development and poverty reduction' (p.1). The roles of agriculture and industry in development are amongst the oldest themes in development studies. Indeed, the two sectors lay at the heart of (the old or classic) development economics at its origins, and the economic and social history that preceded it. Both sectors, and particularly the relations between them, were perceived to be central to the economic and social transformations associated with development. For agriculture alone, the range and complexity of issues considered are significant. Explicitly, development was associated with transition to, or the failure of, capitalist agriculture, with the corresponding emergence of capitalist landlords and farmers, rural wage labour, and the socio-economic differentiation of a persistent peasantry by size of landholding, use of capital, forms of tenure, reliance upon wage labour, and so on. In other words, agrarian change is about the 'production' problematic of the classic agrarian question in political economy (Bernstein 2008). These issues were complemented by bigger ones such as the role of agriculture as a source of surplus for industrialisation in the provision of both resources and wage labour (the old 'accumulation' problematic), and by smaller ones concerning choice of technology and crop, access to markets and inputs, household survival and strategies, the impact of mechanisation, etc. Inevitably, whatever patterns of, or paths to, agricultural development could be identified from historical and continuing experience, these displayed considerable heterogeneity (the form of diverse paths of 'agrarian transition'; Byres 2003b), profound economic and social change, and drew attention to the exercise of power in the conflict between, and evolution of, classes attached to or detached from land.

Nevertheless, despite a seemingly renewed interest in agrarian issues reflected in the WDR 2008, the current state of mainstream development economics has itself undergone an extraordinary transformation, or transformations, by comparison with its precursors. First, agriculture no longer holds such a prominent position within the field. Second, to the extent that it continues to attract attention, it is as a sector both without deeper connection to the wider processes of development and subject to universally applied sets of principles derived from neoclassical economics, and particularly appealing for micro-econometric applications. Third, by the same token, attention to broader issues, 'agrarian questions' and other methods of analysis concerning the evolution of classes, the transition to capitalism, and the conflicts over these processes, has been more or less set aside. Fourth, in their place has been adopted a sequence of models concerned to apply theories of individual behaviour to agricultural performance and consequences, such as the emergence of agrarian 'institutions'. Fifth, for the latter, the focus has shifted towards the incidence of poverty and sustainability of rural livelihoods. Sixth, in line with the evolution of development economics more generally, the decline of agriculture as a central theme has been counterbalanced by the rise of the role of the state and of its policies as decisive (often negatively) in economic performance. While as a proportion of global production agriculture has declined significantly over the past 50 years, the weight of the world's population that remains dependent upon it has grown, and agriculture is decisive in the poorest countries.[3] Consequently, its decline and transformation within development economics resides uncomfortably beside the persistence of diversity, complexity and the economic, political and ideological salience of the agricultural sector in much of the developing world – not least as transnational agribusiness has come to dominate global food and agriculture markets.

These transformations have given the new development agricultural economics an idiosyncratic character. Whilst theory and methods have been rigid and narrow in drawing upon mainstream economics (as shown by the Bank's research outputs in the field, see Section 7.3), it has been impossible to set aside the concerns of the old development (structuralist) economics and classical political economy, given the specificities of agriculture – its attachment to land and landed property, its relationship with nature, its processes of class differentiation and exercise of power, its relationship to wage labour, migration and urbanisation, and the endemic intrusion of conflicts over how such issues are addressed politically (see Section 7.4 on how the new development economics has uncomfortably sought to reconcile itself to these issues).

In other words, neo-liberal and, to a lesser extent, post-Washington Consensus (PWC) perspectives have some but insufficient purchase even for their own purposes upon the issues raised by agriculture, even where it is marginalised as a topic. Taking the previously identified features together, the result has been for the literature to be marked by some general features drawn from mainstream economics, but for these to be complemented by an ad hoc mix of piecemeal analyses, focusing narrowly on specific issues, and drawing upon and making opportunistic allowance for ideological and political expediency in light of the potential threats of civil unrest arising out of the oppressive and conflictual natures of rural and agricultural lives, especially in the context of food crises (see Section 7.6). This is partly reflected in the World Bank's ready responsiveness to some NGO and neo-populist views on agriculture when they can be incorporated into its core analytical and methodological approach. Corresponding analyses and policy perspectives offer an amalgam of inconsistency and incoherence.

This chapter illustrates the propositions above through an overview assessment of the Bank's approach to, and experience with, agriculture, across three interrelated dimensions: research (scholarship), advocacy (rhetoric) and operational imperatives (policy). The following sections provide a mapping of the trends in the Bank's approach to (and research on) agriculture and rural development (ARD) since the 1960s. It highlights two main traditions that shaped current thinking and policy at the Bank, mainstream agricultural economics and neo-populism, and discusses the convenient but tense convergence between the two. While advocacy (rhetoric) currently contains several elements of NGO-like neo-populist dreams, research (scholarship) is led by very much narrower concerns and tools in the mainstream agricultural economics tradition in combination with insights from New Institutional (Development) Economics (NIE). The more recent period of the Bank's research on ARD, partly covered by the Deaton Report (1998–2005) and updated here (2006–09), is discussed in Section 7.3. This suggests that the Deaton Report offers limited critical commentary on Bank research by confining itself to the shared framework already revealed. In contrast, the final section points to alternatives, particularly in the wake of the crises of both food and finance – the one was quickly followed by the other at the end of the first decade of the new millennium (Section 7.6). The chapter also stresses the relative scarcity of output as well as the growing multiplication of agendas in World Bank research on ARD. This underlies the current Bank's tendency to provide incoherent messages, as manifested in the WDR 2008, 'Agriculture for Development', imbued by uneasy combinations of unwarranted pessimism and naive optimism (see Section 7.5). But amidst the apparent contradictions, tensions and multiplicity of agendas, there emerges a consistent pro-liberalisation message, articulated through research, operations and, especially, advocacy. It is remarkable how, after decades of neo-liberal experiments in developing countries, contradictory global tendencies and the latest global food crisis, the Bank remains strongly committed to market solutions and reluctant to promote a much bolder role for states in processes of agrarian transition. Thus the 'good governance' agenda is tactically incorporated into work on ARD to strengthen indirectly the case for 'market-friendly' approaches to agricultural development and the need for 'appropriate institutions' to make market liberalisation work.

Some of the arguments on advocacy, research and policy are illustrated with the example of the Bank's stance on the global food crisis of 2007–08 and its responses (see Section 7.6). The food crisis is significant insofar as, in its aftermath, the Bank is reclaiming prominence and space in agricultural policy debates in an attempt to improve its image and, more importantly, expand its portfolio of operations into an area that is likely to receive more donor support in the future. The scaling-up of funding to agriculture will reverse a trend initiated with the Washington Consensus, during which Bank resources towards ARD systematically declined to unprecedentedly low levels, showing that, at least until 2007, the Bank has been talking many talks but without really walking the walk (Section 7.5). Notably, the Bank's analysis of the food crisis denotes a selective preoccupation with the consequences and a selective treatment of the causes in line with the 'epistemic community' of mainstream economics.

7.2 MAPPING THE WORLD BANK'S APPROACH TO AGRICULTURE AND RURAL DEVELOPMENT

The Bank's approach to agriculture has evolved over time, particularly in terms of emphasis on specific themes and the nature of its operations in developing countries. However, a common denominator in this long and sometimes tortuous evolutionary path is the Bank's commitment to two permanent features: (a) the use of neoclassical economics for its theoretical and methodological choices in research, and (b) the entrenchment of a pro-market/neo-liberal ideology in its advocacy, though these have increasingly been masked by the rationalisation of 'progressive' and 'equity-sensitive' policies through the lens of neo-liberalism (Ferguson 2007).

Through different phases, the World Bank's core messages on agriculture have generally displayed, in different ways from the late 1970s, a committed belief in markets and the private sector as engines of growth and economic efficiency, and varying mistrust of state interventions, especially those that characterised agricultural policy in many developing countries before the onset of the Washington Consensus in the 1980s. During the Washington Consensus, when free-market messages were at their peak, the Bank moved from an initial phase (1981–89) centred on price incentives, deregulation and the ills of government failure (distortions, urban bias, rent-seeking, inefficiency, and so on) to one (1989–1990s) in which anti-state feelings were somewhat attenuated in favour of a state that should 'enable' markets and the private sector, with more focus on rural infrastructure and a role in research provision or facilitation. Interestingly, with the arrival of the more state-friendly PWC, the space for privatisation and deregulation has expanded, including the promotion of entry of the private sector (and NGOs) into the delivery of extension services and research, hitherto a realm of government's direct provision.[4] The operation of extension and other agricultural services, which have historically been provided by states in the vast majority of cases (Chang 2009), is now expected to follow a market-allocation logic, disguised by terms such as 'demand-led', in which agricultural producers are 'empowered' to decide rationally which services they need. In such a context, provision by the private sector is deemed preferable, following arguments that echo analogous support to private provision in health and education, for example.

On the operational side, from an initial, narrower, focus on physical investment and public goods for capital access, e.g. irrigation and agricultural modernisation, the Bank approach to agriculture has been to expand and diversify its portfolio of operations and messages towards a panoply of objectives and priorities that today are reflected in a variety of research, advocacy and operational documents produced over the past ten years: food production and agricultural credit (Woods phase); agriculture and basic needs with rural poverty as main focus; need for integrated non-sector focused programmes (McNamara phase); promotion of smallholder farming; smallholder productivity increase; elimination of price and macroeconomic distortions (structural adjustment); deregulation and privatisation of markets and ARD institutions and services (Washington Consensus phase); participation, ownership and community-driven rural development; rural governance and land administration; inequality and land markets; virtuous linkages between smallholders and transnational agribusiness; risk, uncertainty and insurance mechanisms. And the list could continue.[5]

The evolution sketched above has resulted in a dilution of agriculture and rural development into a myriad of micro-issues, well reflected in the way in which ARD is integrated into the Bank's current agenda, where research on agriculture and rural development falls under the umbrella of the broad research theme 'Sustainable Rural and Urban Development'. For the Bank, 'the research program on rural and urban development covers a *broad* set of topics including agriculture and rural development, environment and natural resource management, infrastructure, and urban development' (World Bank 2009b, p.23; emphasis added). Agriculture-related issues may also be addressed in other established themes such as 'Trade and Integration', or 'Poverty and Inequality'. The same report then recognises the wide range of issues covered: 'The agriculture and rural development research program focuses on a wide range of issues, including land policies, community driven development, irrigation water management, agricultural technology diffusion, rural finance, rural infrastructure, and trade policies.' This marks a move away from agriculture as a sectoral concern and towards a multiplicity of operational imperatives bearing on ARD since the 1990s, partly reflecting the growing popularity of the 'sustainable development' agenda.

This process denotes something that also emerges from the WDR 2008, which is a tendency towards shopping lists of issues that for one reason or another are included in the research and advocacy agendas without an explicit sense of what is central, what is tangential and the linkages between them. This tendency reflects growing incentives for 'talking many talks', as in adopting or co-opting other agendas, in order to reduce the scope for organised contestation, even if the price to pay is a proliferation of inconsistencies, vagueness and lack of focus. This is also in part an outcome of sequential overlapping agendas and priorities, led by institutional inertia and the need to respond to external pressures. This is manifested in the extent to which, for example, the Bank has moved on to new issues and priorities in the PWC era (institutional development, decentralisation, risk, producer organisations, poverty, vulnerability, environmental sustainability, etc.) while maintaining the core elements of the Washington Consensus.

A selective reading of both research outputs and advocacy messages over the past ten years or so, especially manifested in the flagship reports outlining the views and operational priorities of the Bank on ARD (for example 'Reaching the Rural Poor' in 2003, and 'Agricultural Growth for the Poor' in 2005) would *initially* suggest that a two-leg analytical approach has come to dominate current Bank thinking on ARD. This is essentially a neoclassical neo-populist (NCNP) approach that is in practice a marriage of convenience between two dominant tendencies in ARD studies, namely (1) a 'smallholder-first' or neo-populist approach and (2) an agricultural economics/new institutionalist economics framework grounded on neoclassical economics (Byres 2004, p.25).[6] We will consider these and their interaction in turn.

First, the 'smallholder-first' or neo-populist approach, also labelled by Bernstein (2009) as 'technicist' populism, in contrast to 'political' populism, emphasises the critical role of smallholder (family) farming in poverty reduction and development and advocates policies to support and privilege 'small farmers'[7] across the world.[8] The approach can be summarised in the belief that smallholder farming can deliver both *equity* and *efficiency* in a level playing field. This approach is also popular in OECD countries, where advocacy for smallholder 'sustainable' forms of production has gained ground over the past few decades (van der Ploeg 2008). An additional (and opportunistic) rationale is that small-scale (family-based) farming is seen as providing 'environmental services' and minimising the environmental footprint, a message that the Bank is willing to embrace actively, to square its environmental priorities with the promotion of smallholder farming (see World Bank 2007a and Woodhouse 2009).

Second, a mainstream agricultural economics field (partly linked to farm management studies), increasingly adopting insights and tools of the new institutionalist economics, is at the core of the analytical and empirical work of the Bank on ARD. This approach is essentially founded on neoclassical economics and draws on the notion of transaction costs and information asymmetries. The emergence of institutions and institutional change in response to market failures is analysed, and thus the hypothesis of perfect markets is rejected. The variants of this approach that pay more attention to institutional variations are superficially more amenable to the incorporation of history, in comparison with standard neoclassical economics applications.[9] Much of the Bank's *empirical* work, however, still remains framed in an old-style, conventionally neoclassical, agricultural economics tradition. This framework draws from the PWC and maintains the standard state–market dichotomy, but opens up more space for state intervention, especially for what is regarded as 'establishing the basics', in terms of macroeconomic stability, rural infrastructure, water access, education and health. Then, once 'basics' are in place, attention is given to market access and institutional innovations for input provision and risk management (see Dorward et al. 2004). In addition, from the 1990s, the World Bank enters a phase in which 'good governance' assumes a prominent role in the research–advocacy–policy triad, and is applied across the board, including in ARD, in what some authors have called an exercise of 'embedding neo-liberalism' (Harrison 2004).

A closer inspection of the most recent contributions of the Bank's work to ARD and, indeed, the substance of the WDR 2008 also suggest that the currently prevalent Bank view (and that of other important donors, such as the Department for International Development (DfID) and FAO/International Fund for Agricultural Development (IFAD), as reflected in their flagship reports on agriculture and rural poverty, DfID 2005 and IFAD 2001) is increasingly dominated by the second of the approaches above. This includes a bolder emphasis on 'good governance' (e.g. decentralisation, demand-driven services, and so on), sprinkled with some distilled elements of 'old' modernisation theory (notably when emphasis is put on agricultural productivity and irrigation projects) and ingredients of neo-populism, which are ever present in the rhetoric of their discourses and reports, particularly in flagship reports aimed for broad dissemination. For example, the advocacy for small farmers in the developing world recurs heavily in titles, initial statements and executive summaries (normally read by most people, especially development practitioners), while more substantive nuances are introduced in the main text or footnotes, often skipped by 'busy' readers. Indeed, critics of the WDR 2008, especially from NGOs, claim the Bank has failed smallholders, despite having 'paradoxically ... a long history of championing small farmers' (Havnevik et al. 2007, p.11).[10]

Similarly, a like-minded donor agency like DfID (2005, p.19) concedes that 'evidence shows that the optimal mix of farm size for growth varies according to a country's stage of development' and appears to suggest in other parts of the document that small farmers can *also* benefit from opportunities and growth, rather than being the main, let alone only, engines of agricultural growth. The World Bank, as shown in the WDR 2008, introduces several caveats on the prospects of small farming for survival in the context of globalisation and notes the challenges with more than usual emphasis, partly because it attempts to offer a longer-term perspective. Even Lipton (2006, p.66), the leading advocate of the small-farmer path, despite his continuous adherence to the ultimate superiority of small-scale farming in poverty reduction, now restricts this role to *initial* processes of mass poverty reduction and acknowledges that the empirical evidence to support some of the key assumptions underpinning the smallholder paradigm is scanty – insisting nevertheless that 'the small-farm logic' remains sound. In sum, while the classic neo-populist pro-smallholder stance remains alive in the Bank, this is increasingly being restricted to rhetorical statements.

7.3   ASSESSING WORLD BANK RESEARCH ON ARD: DEATON AND BEYOND

Chapter 2 has shown how the Bank, as a knowledge bank, strives to maintain a dominant position in development debates and in the production of knowledge and data on a wide range of issues. Its espousal of mainstream approaches not only serves as an instrument to validate operations, but also facilitates its emergence as an influential and 'authoritative' actor vis-à-vis mainstream academic communities in the field of development economics and related subjects. So what can we say about the quality and relevance of the Bank's research work on ARD? The answer to this question obviously depends on the perspective of the evaluator.

The Deaton Evaluation also assessed outputs and projects on ARD. However, these issues did not feature prominently in the main synthesis report, which devotes some of its most damaging criticisms to other areas, such as aid effectiveness and conflict (see Chapters 3 and 9). A reading of the individual evaluator reports for ARD outputs shows an overall mildly positive assessment, but with concerns over the unevenness in quality across projects and outputs (see Fafchamps 2006, Udry 2006 and Lin 2006). That ARD-related work seems to have been received with some indifference by the Deaton Evaluation (in terms of proportion of evaluated research projects and the tone of the individual evaluations) should be particularly worrying for a 'knowledge' institution aiming at setting norms and parameters across relevant debates. Moreover, a number of individual evaluator reports revealed substantive weaknesses from a technical point of view and a gap between evidence and policy messages, a tendency highlighted by the Deaton Report more generally (see also Chapter 2). Whilst papers/publications apparently reached 'sensible' conclusions, they were based on dubious methods (see Lin 2006). In other words, a group of very influential mainstream economists was not particularly impressed by the Bank research on ARD.[11] This is despite ideological congruence between the Deaton evaluators of agricultural research and the Bank advocacy.[12] For example, Justin Lin, now chief economist at the World Bank, revealed some of his own bias in asserting that '[the] Bank ought to be complimented for supporting greater openness in East Asia rather than protectionism in the wake of financial crisis' (Lin 2006, p.29). After having noted some important weaknesses in some of the Bank research, Lin ends by giving the 'knowledge bank' a pat on the back by noting that '[a]s the world is deluged with cheap capital, the greatest value of the Bank to developing countries will be its analytical capacity' (p.29). Congruence is also evident in the evaluation by Marcel Fafchamps, a frequent contributor to NIE analyses of agriculture who is especially interested in market failures and explicitly shares the Bank's basic preferences, in his praise of its work on land policies and its advocacy for market-led solutions to land inequalities and low productivity.

A tension arises between the focus of the Deaton Evaluation on outputs within a standard mainstream economics tradition and the fact that some of the work done by ARD research and operational units is bound to be inter-disciplinary and include non-economists, especially when operational imperatives to focus on 'community-driven development' matter. It is also noteworthy that some relevant material produced by the Bank in this field, and with significant outreach and implications, is either ignored or reviewed only superficially. This pertains to the operationally important work on 'distortions' and world agricultural trade liberalisation (see Anderson 2009 and Lloyd, Croser and Anderson 2009); the vast project on land policies and market-led land reform (Deininger 2003); and the work on the rural non-farm economy. All these projects substantially inform the content of strategy documents on ARD and, to a certain extent, the WDR 2008.

For promotional purposes Bank researchers look for 'resonance' with the main themes featured by the Bank (poverty reduction, trade, globalisation, integration, market-enabling environments, etc.) and aim to be as externally visible as possible, as in the case of employees of the Bank's research department (DEC): 'DEC professionals need to publish, ideally in both internal Bank publications and externally especially in academic journals' (Broad 2006, p.402).[13] Therefore, one way to assess whether the Bank's work on ARD issues has really had a substantial impact on mainstream debates, particularly within the agricultural economics field, is to look at how much and what has been published in well-known mainstream agricultural economics journals or in some of the most influential interdisciplinary development journals (such as *Development and Change* and *World Development*).

For this purpose, I looked at published articles in which at least one of the authors is associated with the Bank, or articles emerging from its research projects linked to the ARD unit, for the 2006–09 period. Table 7.1 summarises some of the main findings. It shows that in terms of the proportion of articles published in mainstream agricultural economics journals the performance is disappointing, given the otherwise substantial projection of the Bank's policy messages on agricultural matters in the development community. The expectation that the power of a leading institution like the Bank should be reflected in a significant presence in mainstream economics journals is not matched in the field of ARD. This might reflect a tendency of many of these journals to publish material that is not related to developing countries. However, the Bank's record in more development-oriented mainstream agricultural economics journals like *Food Policy* is not impressive either. It is also striking that published research fails overall to signal any clear focus on particular issues. The themes of the articles published vary substantially and cover issues that may or may not be central to current debates on ARD (see Table 7.1). There is clearly evidence of significant thematic dispersion, with a mixture of core advocacy concerns (agricultural liberalisation distortions), fashionable ideas (weather-indexed insurance mechanisms) and old questions (land reform and land administration). Moreover, a basic analysis of the core themes highlighted by the Bank's own website on ARD research also reveals a proliferation of themes, as 34 different ARD themes can be identified, dominated by work more directly linked

Table 7.1 World Bank-related articles published in selected journals (2006–09)

Journal	Hits/number of published papers with World Bank authorship	% all published papers with World Bank authorship	Main themes covered
Review of Agricultural Economics	4	2.1%	Integrated pest management; Doha and South-South trade; famine and overweight in China; world trade distortions – impact on agric. markets and farm income
Agricultural Economics	13	4.5%	Coping mechanisms in disasters; coffee liberalisation; market reform and prices; Doha agenda, food safety; global food crisis; off-farm labour and wages – rural non farm economy; sustainable agriculture
American Journal of Agricultural Economics	7	1.6%	Doha – impact on agriculture; price incentives; food prices; orphanhood; rainfall insurance; agro-processing wages prices unemployment
Journal of Agricultural Economics	2	1.5%	Crop variety demand of "semi-subsistence" households in Uganda; pesticide use in Bangladesh
Food Policy	6	3.3%	Food prices and marketing reforms; food aid
Journal of Agricultural and Resource Economics http://jareonline.org/	1	0.8%	Prices and price risk in cattle market
World Development (agriculture, rural development topics)	8	6.9%	Groundnut market liberalisation; conservation and resettlement; local governance; land certification and markets; rural income generation (non-farm income)
Development and Change (agriculture, rural development topics)	0	0.0%	Not applicable
European Review of Agricultural Economics	2	2.0%	Economic development in emerging Asian markets; impact of market and policy instability on price transmission
World Bank Research Observer	2	5.7%	Diarrhoeal diseases developing countries (referenced to rural areas); rural poverty
World Bank Economic Review	6	8.0%	2 articles on agriculture; 2 on land tenure; 1 on spatial poverty comparison; 1 on rainfall insurance

Source: Author's elaboration

to operations, such as irrigation and water management, as well as rural finance and land markets. The variety of themes identified in this website is also in tune with the variety of issues addressed by Policy Research Working Papers (PRWP), focused on ARD during the period 2006–09, where common property resource management, including land policies, and water management figure prominently.

The impact of the most significant advocacy tools on ARD, notably the WDR 2008, has not been impressive either. While the most common output for research on ARD is the PRWPs, it is interesting to note that the WDR 2008 makes relatively little use of them. In the voluminous list of references, only 28 entries are from the Bank's PRWP, which suggests that in-house production of 'knowledge' has not been influential.

A closer inspection of the contents reviewed for the period 2006–09, in conjunction with the results of the Deaton Report, broadly reveals the following features. First, there is not much in terms of quantity of research, despite the growing rhetoric about the huge importance of agriculture in the fight against poverty. In the Deaton Report, ARD occupied sixth place in a list of reviewed abstracts, accounting for only 9 per cent of the publications reviewed between 2001 and 2004. The research quantity deficit may well be a reflection of funding allocation patterns. As will be argued below, the Bank has until very recently not really put its money where its mouth is. Even though rural development and agriculture are frequently mentioned as central aspects of the poverty reduction agenda, relatively few resources have been devoted to this field. In the case of research budgets, data published by the World Bank show that on average only 6 per cent of the research budget (including research support to operations) was devoted to rural development (encompassing various themes apart from agriculture) during the period 2001–08, with funding increasing from 2005, partly as a result of the costs involved in preparating the WDR 2008 (World Bank 2009b).[14]

Significantly, though, despite the low percentages of *total* World Bank spending on research, an average annual budget of over US$2 million for rural development research is not negligible in *absolute* terms, compared to what academic institutions or think tanks may spend in a year. This spending has not resulted in an impressive output in terms of either peer-reviewed publications (both quantity and quality) or the quality of operations (see below). There is a curious consistency between the relatively meagre resources devoted to research on rural development (in proportional rather than absolute terms) and those dedicated to operations and projects in the same field.

Second, as indicated above, the relatively unimpressive resources devoted to research on ARD issues have been spread thinly. The research programme and outputs for the past ten years are heterogeneous in terms of themes and quality of output, with various unconnected streams of work leading to little impact in terms of academic outreach and operational links.

Third, much research on ARD is focused on micro-level specific issues, almost of a development-management or problem-solving kind (risk management arrangements, weather-indexed insurance, community-driven development, land certification, land market functioning, off-farm income generation by 'poor' households, rates of assistance/protection, etc.). Much less is spent on 'big' agrarian questions, such as the dynamic of agrarian change and linkages with industrialisation, which, according to one of the leading authors of the WDR 2008, have become 'obsolete' (de Janvry 2009).

Fourth, some (especially evaluative) research is directly linked to advocacy efforts to promote win–win scenarios, and less serious attention is paid to conflicts of interest and trade-offs. This is especially the case in research on linkages between private sector (agribusiness) and small farmers (contract farming, finance, insurance, extension, etc.) (World Bank 2007a, ch.6), which tend to focus on 'best practice' or 'success stories' of incorporation of smallholders into global value chains. These studies seldom make the point that, when linkages are established, they usually apply to small and shifting segments of the small-farming population, as independent research usually shows (see Dolan and Humphrey 2000, Amanor 2009 and Gibbon and Ponte 2005).

Fifth, the commitment to liberalisation and free markets is maintained through some high-profile research projects whose results have been widely disseminated. This is so in the case of the research project on 'distortions' to farm incentives (Anderson 2009), which attempts to take stock of the effect on agricultural producers of almost 50 years of changes in price policies and the gradual elimination of these distortions. The distortions are measured relative to allegedly 'more efficient' free markets, on the basis of limiting assumptions and analytical simplification.[15] This is a theme that has persisted with force since the early days of the Washington Consensus in the 1980s.

The new research agenda proposed by a recent flagship report (World Bank 2009a) describing the Bank's agriculture action plan for 2010–12 includes familiar topics such as productivity determinants, credit and insurance markets, international trade and agriculture, and returns on investments in rural infrastructure. These recurrent themes reflect the persistence of certain policy messages and operational imperatives (e.g. trying to maximise medium-term returns on infrastructure spending, whether irrigation or rural roads). In addition, a number of 'hot' topics are considered, such as the links between energy and food markets (sparked by the recent food crisis) and the consequences of climate change for farmers (p.66). This suggests that the Bank adds new themes as they become central in current debates on ARD, without dropping the core areas of work, in accordance with its drive to be a norm-setting knowledge institution.

Besides the specific nature and content of recent research, commented on above, the Bank's research on ARD is commonly influenced by the methodology and thematic emphasis of mainstream agricultural economics paired with NIE applied to agriculture in developing countries, as a basic element of the 'new development economics' (see Fine 2006 for a critique of the latter). From a political economy perspective, this analytical approach, according to Byres (2003a), applies a number of basic problematic beliefs: peasant rationality (understood in a broad rational-choice framework) and especially as reflected in responses to incentives; imperfect information underlying market failures and high transaction costs; opaque espousal of the efficient market hypothesis and the relevance of missing or failed markets; a positive view of agrarian institutions as functional, flexible (adaptable) and responsive to market failures; centrality of risk management in agrarian institutions; all implying that there is a role, albeit of a facilitating nature, for the state.

Mainstream NIE and World Bank approaches to agriculture and rural development have gradually transcended the most superficial assumptions about peasant homogeneity and do distinguish different groups of rural people, such as farmers, landless labourers, traders, moneylenders, etc. In Byres' (2003a) view, however, these groups do not amount to class divisions with class antagonisms, but merely to weakly defined occupational and/or income categories. This follows an implicit view of the peasantry and agricultural producers as still relatively homogeneous in the sense of facing similar constraints and welfare objectives. For example, for producers oriented to markets, we rarely see systematic and analytically driven distinctions between rich peasants, capitalist farmers and commercially oriented smallholders. They are most often all collapsed into the category of 'market-oriented farmers' as opposed to 'subsistence farmers' – a dichotomy that is very unhelpful, not least because the category of 'subsistence farmer' is empirically flawed.

Another problem is the consideration of social relations vertically along agricultural value chains and horizontally in rural areas simply in terms of (explicit or implicit) *contracts*. Power relations are then reduced to how people deal with information and how they use their relative endowments to bargain on contracts, as in the growing body of work on contract farming (see Little and Watts 1994). Empowerment is often addressed in vague terms of 'voice' and access to information, in a more or less technicist fashion. Social relations of production, and their appearance in 'contracts', follow the logic of 'mutual benefit', despite obvious evidence of rural inequalities. Production and exchange relations, therefore, are seldom seen in terms of relations of exploitation, where the exercise of power assumes a central role. In order to understand exploitation and conflict, a serious consideration of asymmetries of economic and political power (and not simply 'information') is central. In this context, the idea of 'bargaining' loses its analytical and empirical appeal, since disparities in power may be too great (Byres 2003a, p.247). Enforcement costs may also be exaggerated in situations of significant power disparity, where subordinate groups simply have little option vis-à-vis their patrons, employers, merchant capital, state officials, and so on.

From a political economy perspective, these are some of the most obvious problems in the dominant analytical frameworks underpinning World Bank research on ARD (see also below). Yet, despite these serious omissions and persistent neglect of an important critical (agrarian political economy) literature,[16] the Bank's prominent role in consolidating or advancing mainstream paradigms in ARD hinges on its reputation as a 'knowledge bank' (partly derived from a reputation of technical superiority), as well as on its financial muscle, which drags other donors towards 'shared' (research, advocacy and policy) agendas. In this way, Bank researchers may influence policy and operations both directly (through advice and feedback into operations/projects) and indirectly, via impact on the 'development community' (Deaton et al. 2006, p.14), while leaving substantive critics at the margin.[17]

7.4   THE EXPANDED AGENDA OF THE WDR 2008 AND ITS INCONSISTENCIES

This section explores the way in which the WDR 2008, as the latest instalment of the Bank's advocacy on agriculture, signals an expansion of the Bank's agenda on ARD issues, while at the same time providing continuity with core trends since the emergence of the PWC, resulting in some inconsistencies and tensions that further weaken the Bank's credibility in this field. The WDR 2008 presents the most up-to-date and detailed account of the Bank's approach to ARD, in a way that attempts to transcend the tendency of the Bank's previous rural development strategy reports towards dry shopping lists (World Bank 2003a and 2005a).[18]

There are two basic elements of continuity with the agenda set out during the Washington Consensus period and the subsequent rise of the PWC. First, as noted, there is the explicit liberalisation and anti-state stance that followed the crisis of the late 1970s and was reflected in the two reports that contained a substantial agricultural-related content, obsessively focused on state-created 'distortions' (see the 'Berg Report' (World Bank, 1981), World Bank 1982 and Anderson 2009). But the pro-liberalisation stance now co-exists with a less negative view of state interventions in agriculture and the gradual internalisation of neo-populist NGO-driven demands (e.g. smallholder farming promotion, land reform and community-driven development), as manifested in the WDR 2008 (World Bank 2007a, ch.11). Indeed, the two core strategic reports on ARD that preceded the WDR 2008 ('Reaching the Rural Poor', World Bank 2003a, and 'Agricultural Growth for Poverty Reduction', World Bank 2005a) celebrated the advances towards more liberal markets led by two decades of agricultural liberalisation and were very reluctant to acknowledge the various negative direct and indirect effects of structural adjustment in agriculture, despite a voluminous literature explaining the failures of adjustment in agriculture and the history of agricultural policies in successful capitalist transformations (Oya 2007 and Chang 2009).[19] The continuation of this imperative in the Bank's advocacy and research is manifest in the comprehensive study of the history of agricultural 'distortions' which has been recently published and has constituted one of the core research projects over the past few years (see World Bank 2009b and Anderson 2009).

The second element of continuity is the Bank's policy and operational commitment to the 'good governance' agenda incorporated into its ARD priorities (see Van Waeyenberge 2009 and Harrison 2004). 'Reaching the Rural Poor' and subsequent strategy documents have inserted 'good governance' elements by promoting decentralised and market-oriented land and natural resources management, the development of local land rental markets, and the formation of smallholder producer organisations, and by emphasising the usefulness of 'community driven development' approaches (and other ways to capture 'social capital'). 'Adequate' or 'good' governance is primarily advocated to ensure the sound implementation of agricultural policies – for which read the full implementation of the Washington Consensus agenda on agriculture, since one of the most frequent discourses articulated by the Bank on the impact of agricultural reforms in the 1980s and 1990s is that the reform agenda was only *partially* implemented (see World Bank 2007a, p.23, Kherallah et al. 2002 and Oya 2007). The WDR 2008, in contrast, broadly inherits this focus on 'good governance', without overly stressing the issue of 'partial implementation' of reforms.[20] The use of governance is coupled with recourse to notions of 'social capital' (see Chapter 5), particularly in the treatment of problems (for example, dealing with risk and increasing cohesion), which can have positive effects on agricultural performance.

On rural finance, perhaps one of the areas where the failures of structural adjustment were more evident (see Havnevik et al. 2007, Oya 2007 and Gibbon, Havnevik and Hermele 1993), the Bank responds with calls for financial innovations and demand-led approaches, consistent with a deepened liberalisation agenda and strong support for private financial institutions or private–public partnerships. The Bank is especially interested in being in the vanguard of new insurance mechanisms for commodity price risks, a particularly relevant aspect in the wake of the food crisis (see below). Though these are still experimental, the Bank shows almost blind faith in mechanisms such as 'innovative' and private sector-led weather-indexed or rainfall-based insurance services (see World Bank 2005a, pp.76–78, 2007a, p.149 and 2009a, p.26). Therefore, the Bank is adamant that old-style solutions such as 'supply-driven agricultural credit [have] proven unsustainable and unsuccessful and [are] no longer supported by the Bank' (World Bank 2003a, p.xix). Instead it opts to support 'financial instruments for income generation and reduction of financial risk [and] recognise the multiplicity of potential delivery mechanisms, suppliers, and users of rural financial services', i.e. microfinance and private sector- and demand-led insurance mechanisms – most of which are largely speculative and voluntaristic approaches lacking evidence to support them.[21]

Essentially, the WDR 2008 reproduces all the 'strategic elements' discussed above, but adds analytical substance, empirical detail, some nuances and a few more items for the shopping list – notably on more radical pathways out of poverty than own-account farming, such as non-farm rural employment and migration, a significant departure from typical neo-populist messages.[22] Significantly the WDR 2008 presents some 'findings' that had been partly ignored in previous advocacy reports: (a) the significance of agribusiness concentration in the international agro-food regime, both in output and input markets;[23] (b) the reality that not all smallholders are commercially viable (i.e. can successfully be integrated into ever demanding world markets for agricultural exports) and that a significant part of resource-poor smallholders are 'condemned' to migrate or to live off 'social safety nets' and targeted interventions to increase their food productivity (Havnevik et al. 2007). It follows from this, as various passages of the WDR 2008 confirm, that the state can have some role in kicking-off basics and correcting 'pervasive market failures', in line with some current mainstream economics thinking.

The WDR 2008 also attempts to make sense of the variety of possible rural development paths and interventions, through an analytical and empirical distinction between three groups of countries. It seeks, in a *static* classification, to capture patterns of agrarian change and economic transformation that are essentially *dynamic*.[24] Thus the Bank considers that three distinct groups of countries require relevant priorities, although an 'agriculture-first' and anti-urban bias advocacy permeates the core messages (see Kay 2009).[25] The distinction is thus made between

1. agriculture-based countries, largely coinciding with sub-Saharan Africa (SSA), where agricultural growth and food security are priority;
2. transforming countries, in transition and experiencing fast urbanisation with widening rural–urban gaps, many of which are found in Asia; and
3. urbanised countries, where the challenges are what to do with surviving smallholders and tackling rural poverty.

Unfortunately, this static typology, which is largely based on a crude selection of current structural data and questionable cut-off classificatory benchmarks, does not adequately reflect the dynamic of processes of agrarian change and socio-economic transformations in the twentieth and twenty-first centuries (Woodhouse 2009). Apart from the crude typology and the compression of history involved in this exercise (Austin 2008), the WDR 2008 is a good example of the sorts of tensions and inconsistencies arising from an advocacy approach that aims to expand the ARD agenda through selective internalisation of critics, but without renouncing the core tenets of the old pro-market liberal approach of the 1980s and 1990s. Here some examples are briefly presented.

First, the Bank faces the dilemma of how persisting in prioritising smallholder farming can be squared with the constraints and challenges of agrarian globalisation. Despite claims to the contrary by NGOs,[26] the Bank has not abandoned its advocacy to support smallholder farmers in developing countries. The logic is very simple, even superficial, and much related to the Bank's mandate of reducing poverty worldwide. The majority of the poor in the world are located in rural areas. Official statistics suggest they mostly depend on farming and most happen to be smallholders (very vaguely defined). If they mostly depend on their own farming then production and marketed surplus constitute their main means of survival. An increase in smallholder productivity is, therefore, logically imperative. However, the Bank concedes, the world of agricultural commodity markets and food provision is more complex than we think and, more 'strikingly', it is characterised by exceptional concentration of capital in a few transnational agro-food conglomerates (World Bank 2007a, p.135). From the point of view of the Bank, a keen advocate of a lightly regulated private sector (and implicitly of dynamic capitalism on a global scale), the question therefore is how smallholders in developing countries can interact with the global agro-food complex without questioning the logic of the global food regime and its market concentration. 'A dynamic private agribusiness sector linking farmers and consumers can be a major driver of growth in the agricultural and the rural nonfarm sectors. But growing agribusiness concentration may reduce its efficiency and poverty reduction impacts' (p.135).

The Bank unsurprisingly aims for win–win scenarios and solutions (contract farming, producer organisations, agribusiness-induced quality controls, innovative insurance to address transaction costs and risk, etc.) in a classic problem-solving fashion that is typical of the 'aid complex', in an attempt to reconcile a (pro-market) pro-capitalist stance with a pro-poor-small-farmer bias. But, despite imagination in the presentation of possible scenarios, it still has to acknowledge that not all smallholders can survive in the current context. This is when 'old development economics' stories of surplus labour, migration, agricultural surplus, and so on become handy, as the Bank timidly raises its head and reminds us that development is also about structural transformations that lead to the reduction in the number of agricultural producers and generally the gradual demise of the peasantry (p.27). Notwithstanding this apparent realisation, much of the Bank's advocacy and policy still operates as if the main issue at stake is supporting smallholders, implicitly assuming that they are here to stay and that they are likely to be a dynamic force in the development of capitalism. The main problem with the win–win scenarios of the Bank and WDR 2008 lies in the tendency, Oya (2009, p.598), to:

> neglect, silence or misrepresent power struggles, unequal and conflictual relations, which are pervasive among farmers, between farmers and their labourers, between farmers and traders and among so many participants in global value chains and clearly intrinsic to the structure of relations of production and extraction in contemporary capitalism, and which in some cases lead to violent outcomes.[27]

In general, the Bank's advocacy of smallholder farming is predicated upon the belief that increases in smallholder productivity can have massive impacts on rural poverty and quickly lead to significant poverty reduction. Much emphasis is placed on land productivity (see also below), with the Bank showing how the gap between farm trials and levels of productivity is large, suggesting that enormous potential exists. But is that potential to be fulfilled by smallholders? The evidence so far is not encouraging. Besides, the advocacy for smallholder productivity increases tends to be silent about labour productivity, which may be more important than land productivity in contexts of relative land abundance. As Woodhouse (2009, p.272) asserts: 'the question of labour productivity is of particular concern in many African contexts, where labour–land ratios have historically been low and control of labour in extended households has dominated the organization of production systems'. Moreover, one needs to reconcile the idea that small farmers are poor and in need of support with the Bank's advocacy for (market-oriented) demand-led agricultural services. Yet Woodhouse (2009, p.267) points out how the evidence counters World Bank dreams:

analysis of the implementation of this process ... suggests that it is less poor farmers who are most likely to benefit due to both their organisational capacity and political influence at local level, and central government officials' priority of raising aggregate production by supporting those farmers most capable of 'achieving results'.

A second, but related, inconsistency and tension is the advocacy for land reform. On land issues, the Bank unsurprisingly favours liberalisation of land rental markets as a solution to both equity and efficiency – again a market-induced win–win scenario in which trade-offs and conflict are missing (see Deininger 2003). At the same time, to match equity concerns, a timid support is given to redistributive land reform amongst small farmers. But the Bank is mostly concerned with a case for land reform on *efficiency* grounds, which takes it close to neo-populist positions. Thus contradictions emerge. The tension between advocacy for small farming and the empirical evidence used by the Bank itself is striking, particularly when the well-known 'inverse relationship' between farm size and (land) productivity is mentioned for the first time in the WDR 2008 (World Bank 2007a, pp.90–1).[28] In the first passage of that section some typical generalisations about the 'superiority' of smallholder farming are boldly presented. This is then astonishingly followed by two graphs that clearly show an increasingly *positive* relationship between farm size and productivity for staples (not even export crops) in Brazil and Chile, widely known as agricultural success stories. To square these two opposing views, the WDR 2008 suggests that the generally 'powerful' effect of lower labour supervision costs of family labour *may* be offset by large-scale advantages in accessing better technology, higher input applications, irrigation, and other yield-enhancing factors – all that as a result of 'market imperfections', the classic catch-all concept in the WDR 2008. Therefore, as the 'superiority' of small farming vanishes, the question of whether small farmers are becoming 'too small' arises (p.92; see Oya 2009). Moreover, the World Bank stance on land policies has other aspects of circle-squaring. First, it advocates land redistribution, assuming that land is the main constraint on survival and wealth creation,[29] based on a static interpretation of evidence on agrarian structures and productivity outcomes. Second, it believes that the market, which generally tends to display inegalitarian outcomes in land access and ownership, is the best way of redistributing land to the 'poor'. The consolidation and concentration mechanisms associated with market resource allocation (and clearly reflected in the recognised concentration of global agricultural-related markets) are therefore conveniently ignored (Borras 2007).

A third tension concerns the alternatives to smallholder farming in the context of an agriculture-for-development agenda. Thus, for the first time, the Bank stresses the importance of alternative paths of poverty reduction beyond smallholder farming, of which migration and rural labour markets stand out. This is a significant development that somewhat attenuates the hitherto substantial influence of neo-populist perspectives and NGO lobbies on World Bank advocacy.[30] However, the WDR 2008 mainly offers some descriptive evidence that illustrates the precarious working conditions of most agricultural wage workers in developing countries, going on to stress the importance of accessing global high-value markets to expand employment and to improve working conditions, while it makes no mention of how to empower workers through such labour market institutions as trade unions and minimum wages.[31] Indeed, the WDR 2008 solves the challenge with more wishful thinking and contradictions ('encourage formality while maintaining flexibility', World Bank 2007a, p.208) and retains its faith in corporate social responsibility to protect workers from the excesses of volatile capitalism (see Oya 2009 and Rizzo 2009 for critiques of this ambivalent and naive position).

To these broad advocacy targets contained in the WDR 2008, the Bank has recently added the need to improve food security through supply and demand actions as well as to pay more attention to the development of safety nets or 'coping mechanisms' for poorer vulnerable farmers in the face of spectacular volatility in global food markets and weather shocks associated with climate change (a point discussed in Section 7.6). These, again, add items to the expanding shopping list, and necessarily induce new trade-offs that, if ignored, further increase the set of tensions and contradictions discussed here. There are, however, some additional and substantive inconsistencies in the World Bank's relationship with agriculture. Indeed, the Bank has, until recently, responded with dwindling financial commitments to an increasingly active (internal) advocacy on ARD challenges, to which I now turn.

7.5   WORLD BANK ARD POLICY AND PRACTICE

This section aims to deal with the following question: is the World Bank as seriously committed to agriculture as its 'advocacy' (rhetoric), e.g. WDR 2008, press releases and other flagship reports, would suggest? The short answer, at least on the basis of the record until 2006, is 'no'. Generally OECD donor support to agriculture in developing countries has been declining steadily and rapidly since the early 1980s (see Figure 7.1). The trend in the percentage of aid that goes to agriculture has been consistent across bilateral and multilateral donors, and the Bank is no exception, with an increase until the early 1980s followed by a substantial decline until very recently, from 17 per cent in 1980–84 to only 6 per cent in 2000 (OECD 2001).[32] The Bank has clearly devoted dwindling financial resources to supporting agriculture, especially in African countries. Data show that from a peak of around 32 per cent of World Bank lending in 1976–78, the share of agriculture has consistently fallen below 10 per cent in the last 15 years or so, especially after the decline of sector adjustment loans (AGSECALs) (see Pincus 2001). More recently, from a 12 per cent average during the period 1990–2000 it has declined to only 6.5 per cent for the period 2000–05 – this is the third lowest sector share, behind industry and trade. This decline is in stark contrast with the substantial proportion of resources invested in 'good governance' programmes, the dominant operational imperative of the past 10–15 years (see Figure 7.2).

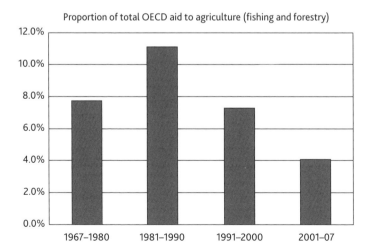

Figure 7.1 Overseas development assistance to agriculture, aggregate figures 1967–2007.

Source: Author's elaboration from OECD–DAC database.

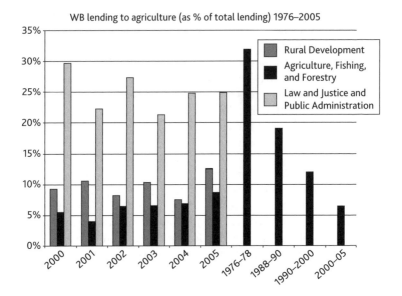

Figure 7.2   Bank lending priorities: governance versus agriculture.
Source: Author's elaboration from World Bank lending data.

Since 2003, however, allocations have somewhat increased. The 2003 ARD strategy, 'Reaching the Rural Poor' (World Bank 2003a), constituted a turning point, aiming to guide the World Bank's future rural lending operations, and ambitiously projecting 20 per cent annual increases. In reality, although the provisions for core components of agricultural lending have not met those targets since 2003, the Bank claims that if the contribution of 'other agriculture related investments' (which includes projects on land administration or market roads, for example) is taken into account, lending to agriculture is higher than is usually claimed (World Bank 2009a). The Bank now tries as far as possible to codify as ARD some of the operations from the expanding range of multi-sector projects, so that recently established targets are met.

Agriculture may not have been an operational priority for the Bank in the last 30 years, but the paradox is that the Bank remains a major single donor for agriculture in developing countries (typically representing between 18 and 25 per cent of total flows to agriculture), and the largest donor to agriculture in SSA (IEG 2007).[33] The Bank's financial muscle has directly and indirectly influenced agricultural policies in developing countries, particularly in Africa (Havnevik et al. 2007). Moreover, much of current aid to agriculture takes the form of policy advice (often counterproductive), technical assistance (not always effective or relevant), and the reinforcement of government structures dealing with rural development policies (more computers, cars and offices rather than manpower, due to public sector wage-bill ceilings) (see OECD 2001). It is striking that the WDR 2008 accuses developing-country 'governments' and 'donors' of failing agriculture in developing countries without a more explicit mea culpa. Apart from declining funding to ARD over the long period 1979–2003, two decades of macroeconomic and agricultural adjustment reforms resulted in, among other things, falling levels of public investment and agricultural research, which dropped in the list of priorities as a result of the Washington Consensus-induced fiscal squeeze.[34] This happened through the imperative of fiscal compression, with agricultural services as a necessary sacrifice, and through the weakening or dismantling of public agencies in charge of agricultural services, on the grounds of inefficiency and/or fiscal constraints.

The Bank's promises for 2010–12 are seemingly more radical and try to make amends: doubling or more of funding for the core agricultural programmes and additional increases in International Finance Corporation (IFC) funding for agribusiness, among other things. This implies, in the most optimistic scenario, that the World Bank would allocate up to US$8 billion annually in 2010–12 (including IFC funding) up from the estimated US$4.1 billion in 2006–08. This would make the World Bank, by a good margin, the largest single donor to agriculture and would thus enhance its clout on agricultural development priorities in developing countries. It is indeed a response to the call made after the global food crisis of 2007–08 (see below), and consistent with a desire to tap into a large part of the US$20 billion additional funding for agriculture in developing countries committed by the G20 in July 2009.[35]

Whilst a substantial increase in resources is of course highly necessary and welcome, some important questions remain. First, part of the problem, and perhaps a determinant of the Bank's declining interest in ARD, lies in the relatively low levels of satisfaction with, and low sustainability ratings of, its ARD projects, especially in SSA. A recent evaluation of the World Bank's work on agriculture in the region provides damaging evidence of the Bank's operational performance (IEG 2007). Moreover, the same report argues that background analytical work has been 'limited, scattered, of variable quality, and not easily available' (IEG 2007, p.xxv), despite the

Bank's usual operational and rhetorical emphasis on knowledge and technical advice.

Second, the Bank adds to the infamous volatility problem of aid flows. None of the top ten SSA borrowers of agricultural lending received consistent and simultaneous support across all critical sub-sectors. This meant that resources were often spread too thinly, thereby reducing potential long-term effectiveness, reproducing patterns observed with NGO projects. Moreover, the 'sprinkling' of lending across a diverse set of activities (research, extension, credit, seeds, policy reforms, etc.) was done with limited linkages between them and lacked any 'integrated' framework. In many of these areas, especially in one of the priority targets (access to credit and rural finance), the ineffectiveness of support is partly due to poor implementation of World Bank guidelines. On other forms of support, demand-led approaches to extension at the expense of public provision, the report points out that the sort of partnerships supported (PPP, demand-driven, NGOs) are neither cost-effective nor sustainable.

Third, little has been done to overcome one of the most significant constraints in African agriculture, the lack of irrigation. The Bank's evaluation report (IEG 2007, p.x) noted that the emphasis on irrigation (present in project documents and advocacy reports) has been accompanied by very little physical investment (see Figure 7.3). Instead, the Bank has focused on policy lending attached to structural reforms that, according to the evaluation report, 'fell short of producing the desired growth effects'. The report adds (p.xxvii):

Bank policy advice appears to have had far-reaching implications for the direction of agricultural development in African countries, in particular its policy advice associated with the adjustment agenda. However, results have fallen short of expectations because of weak political support and insufficient appreciation of reality on the ground, among other things.

More recently, lending has increasingly been directed to projects grounded in 'community-based approaches'. The latter have become a new article of faith, a convenient and politically correct method of delivery, despite there being little evidence that these approaches are able to respond to agro-ecological diversity (IEG 2007), let alone to socio-economic and political diversity (see also Bebbington et al. 2007).

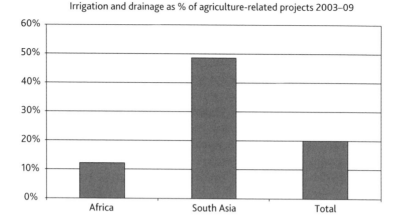

Figure 7.3   Uneven focus on irrigation investments: World Bank funding 2003–09.
Source: Author's elaboration from World Bank project database.

Overall, it is not clear then, from (a) current operational practices and imperatives, (b) management responses to critical evaluations[36] and (c) the record of shifting resource allocation, whether the Bank is seriously learning the lessons of past operations or simply following an operational inertia driven by an 'approval culture' (Wade 2006) coupled with ongoing policy imperatives. Over time the Bank has significantly shifted the pattern of resource allocation to agriculture, in response not so much to operational evaluations as to ideological and policy imperatives. For example, the proportion devoted to agricultural credit declined remarkably from 16 per cent in 1976–8 to 4.8 per cent in 1994–6 while the proportion allocated to agricultural sector loans (attached to programmes of market reforms in agriculture) increased from 0 per cent to almost 20 per cent over the same period (Pincus 2001). At the same time, agro-industry and crop support received marginal support in the 1990s, while irrigation/drainage has relatively resisted the vagaries of lending priorities in quantitative terms. However, in the case of irrigation, an examination of samples of relevant projects during the period 2003–09 reveals a move from large-scale physical investment towards 'soft' interventions, in the form of projects for 'community management' of water and irrigation infrastructure, and rehabilitation or forms of technical assistance for the management of access to irrigation (see also Inocencio et al. 2005). In other words, the creation of new physical irrigation infrastructure has been much less important compared to the alignment of irrigation projects within the overall good governance agenda and political correctness around community management and decentralisation. From the 1990s a focus on rural 'institutions' and the application of the good governance agenda to agricultural operations has been growing steadily. Thus, institutional innovations to support smallholder agriculture, community development initiatives, promotion of producer organisations and decentralisation of rural services have become central tenets of the PWC agricultural jargon in Bank operations, as most project documents tend to reflect.

World Bank operations in ARD are increasingly characterised by growing diversification of portfolio and a multiplication of themes, objectives and tools (Pincus 2001 and IEG 2007). This reflects two possible effects. First, the operational imperatives of portfolio expansion and 'approval culture', therefore loan disbursement, and the need to encroach on areas of work of other organisations (notably NGOs), partly in anticipation of declines in policy-related funding as the structural adjustment agenda is completed. Second, the 'Washington confusion' associated with the PWC, which results in the proliferation of shopping lists in the allocation of funding, particularly to low-income (African) countries. In order to test whether these and other features discussed above persist in current operational practice, a preliminary exploration of the project database for ARD in 2003–09 was carried out.[37] Some broad stylised facts emerge from this initial exploration.

First, a lack of focus and coherent operational line still stands out. The Bank disperses money over a wide range of sectors and themes, many of which are defined vaguely so that further proliferation of aims and methods is possible. Most projects included in the database are multi-sector and many include the usual themes common in the PWC agenda, namely public sector governance, decentralisation and administrative capacity building. Some phrases are often repeated in projects, including some of the largest items in the database, as revealed by the following selected excerpts, which are self-explanatory (emphasis added): 'priority *demand-driven community*-owned productive infrastructure investments of the public good type', 'support to empower ... *users* – farmers/pastoralists and other economic interest groups working within their organizations and through their local government councils – to purchase advisory services from both public and private sources', 'seed money to *empower* smallholder and poor farmers to acquire capital assets which they will use to undertake a wide range of small-scale income generating activities as well as improve farmers' access to markets and complementary support that add value to farm produce', and so on. As Bebbington et al. (2007) show, with reference to World Bank operations and 'organizational cultures', commitments to 'empowerment' enter the Bank's texts (dissemination reports and project documents) with relative ease; but their application is far more contingent, and their meanings diverse.[38]

Second, the proliferation of projects worth relatively small amounts by Bank standards (e.g. less than US$5 million per project) suggests that it is acting more like an NGO and less like a multinational development bank in projects that more or less relate to agriculture. For example, the average ARD project in the 2003–09 dataset amounts to US$19 million. (This is only US$14 million for the Africa region and has an overall median of US$5.5 million). Further, between 2003 and 2009, 64 per cent and 19 per cent of 733 projects with some ARD component did not allocate funds for ARD purposes in excess of US$10 million and US$1 million, respectively. The tendency towards a 'small is beautiful' approach, coupled with the proliferation of 'knowledge aid' or 'community grassroots' types of project, explains this pattern to some extent. This is in contrast with the Bank's comparative advantage as a centralised lender to the public sector; the Bank is unsuitable for successfully dealing with community-based programmes and not fit for purpose for 'participatory development', for reasons substantially explained by Pincus (2001).

Third, project proliferation can be consistent with skewness and concentration. A large proportion of the total funds committed to ARD (54 per cent) falls in the top bracket of more than US$100 million per project, which tend to go to general support projects, large multi-sector programmes including safety nets (many of them part of the Global Food Response Project; see below) and irrigation (though not to Africa) as significant categories.[39] These mega-projects are unevenly distributed and more common in transforming or urbanised countries, despite the enormous needs for scaled-up aid in agriculture-based countries (to use the WDR 2008 country typology). Thus African countries, where big-push interventions are clearly necessary and cannot be provided by NGOs, are even less favoured in this respect.[40] Out of the five largest-scale projects, each of which is worth more than US$500 million, only one went to Africa, namely to Ethiopia, and only 21 per cent of it was directed to ARD (the rest to all other priority sectors in the PRSP). Many of the large projects included in the database (16 out of 25) were classified under governance categories for the main sector, including themes like decentralisation, administrative reform, legal and environmental 'institutions', and so on. Regional disparities also emerge with respect to the nature of ARD support, with Africa receiving most projects focused on agriculture for general purposes, which in many cases include capacity-building institutional components that are also included in governance themes. In contrast, irrigation lending focuses on South Asia, which receives over 60 per cent of ARD projects that were related to irrigation and drainage in 2003–09, although many of these were about water community resource management with a lot of 'soft' elements (technical assistance). The neglect of Africa in irrigation funding is astonishing, considering that this is the region where the proportion of irrigated land is the lowest in the world (only 8 per cent of potentially irrigable land and 1.8 per cent of cultivated land, excluding the three largest irrigation countries, i.e. Sudan, Madagascar and South Africa) and where many of the current challenges on agricultural productivity could be partially addressed through substantial expansion of irrigated land (see IEG 2007 and World Bank 2007b). Only 12 per cent of relevant projects had some irrigation component in Africa between 2003 and 2009 (see also Figure 7.3).

Some of the above-mentioned mega-projects are associated with an apparent recent scaling up of resources for ARD, particularly between 2008 and 2009, and in line with some of the widely announced new commitments discussed before. Many of these large projects are part of the Bank's response to the global food crisis in 2007–08, an aspect of World Bank research, advocacy and policy to which the chapter now turns.

7.6   THE WORLD BANK AND THE GLOBAL FOOD CRISIS: SHORT-TERM EMERGENCY VERSUS SYSTEMIC FAILURE

At a time when the World Bank work on ARD was under pressure and subject to criticism (see IEG 2007 and Havnevik et al. 2007), the unravelling of the global food crisis[41] of 2007–08 provided the Bank with an opportunity to gain prominence in two main ways: first, by becoming a prime mover in the early debates on the causes, consequences and responses to the food crisis, together with FAO and IFPRI (International Food Policy Research Institute) (see Ivanic and Martin 2008, Mitchell 2008, von Braun 2008 and FAO 2008);[42] second, through the use of its well-established advocacy power within the donor community to lead the call for strengthened support to agriculture in developing countries, especially in low-income countries. It was a 'fortunate' coincidence that the food crisis exploded almost in tandem with the preparation of the WDR 2008 flagship report. This way its calls to increase aid to agriculture, especially in Africa, appeared bolder and timely. However, the Bank's response to the crisis is also a good reflection of the tensions discussed in previous sections of this chapter and of the complex interactions between research, advocacy and operational imperatives. This response also manifests some of the weaknesses and limitations of the Bank's approach to agricultural problems and the limitations of its support to 'win–win' scenarios in situations of acute crisis. It is remarkable how the focus has been much more on the consequences of the crisis than on its causes, especially its deep-rooted causes, as will be shown below.

Interestingly, much of the World Bank research work in this area (both published and unpublished) has mainly focused on *making a case* for the scaling up of aid to agriculture (in other words, fundraising), whereby global and country-level simulations aim to calculate the impact of food price increases on the number of people living below international and national poverty lines. In a way, it is the kind of work that NGOs or UN agencies would normally do to draw worldwide attention to a problem. The Bank has followed suit, and there is little controversy over the consequences, especially the likely increase in poverty incidence and the number of poor in the developing world – particularly in countries where food imports account for a significant proportion of domestic staple consumption (see Ivanic and Martin 2008).[43] Most agencies expected that a worsening of the nutritional status of poorer households, especially children, would be a lasting consequence of the world food crisis in several countries (Mitchell 2008 and IATP 2009).[44] This evidence was then used for calls to scale up agricultural funding, much of which is likely to be channelled through the World Bank. The call was successful, since subsequent commitments from large OECD donors, and indeed the recent October 2009 commitment to boost agricultural funding by the G20, will be implemented under the coordination of the World Bank.

It is not surprising that the World Bank has responded with a substantial promise of increased funds until 2012. A commitment is made to 'increase its agriculture support from US$4.1 billion annually in FY2006–08 to between US$6.2 and US$8.3 billion annually over the FY2010–2012 period – between 13 and 17 percent of total projected World Bank commitments'.[45] In particular, in response to the short-term effects of the food crisis, the World Bank, in May

2008, set up the Global Food Crisis Response Program (GFRP). This is expected to allocate up to US$2 billion for post-crisis recovery. The GFRP seeks to provide immediate relief to countries most affected by high food prices. It had already disbursed US$1164 million out of US$1190.4 million in 35 countries by October 2009, an amount that signals increasing commitment to agriculture in comparison with the previous 20 years. Most projects financed through the GFRP fall under the rubric of 'safety-net programmes', but they also include measures to promote the reduction of food taxes (further liberalisation), especially for imported food, supply-side interventions such as fertiliser and seed distribution (financing the costs associated with urgent procurement and distribution of fertilisers), and general budget support to ease fiscal constraints.

World Bank analyses of the food crisis mirror what has been published by other influential agencies and think tanks (especially FAO and IFPRI), but show greater focus on poverty implications. The methodology is generally one of simulations in a general equilibrium framework, the kind of analysis that is also fashionable in model simulations of the impact of the Doha agenda on developing countries (see Ivanic and Martin 2008 and World Bank 2008a). Bank researchers tend to see the crisis as a one-off episode underpinned by a combination of fairly recent developments: (a) the expansion of corn-based biofuel production, especially in the United States, at the expense of food production; (b) supply shocks in large producers/exporters (e.g. poor weather in Australia); (c) demand effects of diet shifts in large emerging countries like India and China; (d) energy price increases, at the expense of farming costs; and (e) export bans by grain exporter countries (Toye 2009, Mitchell 2008 and von Braun 2008). Mitchell (2008) and other Bank researchers estimate that 70 per cent of the large increase in biofuels production comes from grains and oilseeds in the United States and the European Union. Mitchell provides a significant twist in the explanation by noting that 'the large increases in biofuels production in the US and EU were supported by subsidies, mandates, and tariffs on imports'. In other words, 'distortions' to farm incentives are seen as a big part of the story, happily in line with World Bank's dominant pro-free-trade advocacy of the past 30 years.

This kind of assessment, based on simulations and attention to price 'distortions', contrasts with the type of analysis offered by alternative sources, such as the symposium on the world food crisis in the *Journal of Agrarian Change* 9(2), 2010. The contributions in this symposium tend to emphasise other more deeply rooted factors, namely the systemic features of capitalism, the role of financialisation, speculation, and the workings of global food chains. Taken together, these would suggest that the 2007–08 price crisis was only one extraordinary aspect of a slow, more latent, crisis in the global food regime (see Lang 2010, Van der Ploeg 2010 and Tickner 2008).

Apart from these broad features, these alternative accounts show that there are at least three aspects of the crisis that, by omission or commission, have not featured significantly or at all in World Bank assessments and responses. First, not much work has emerged on the *transmission mechanisms* of international price volatility and, for example, the extent to which there are asymmetries in price transmission – the 2008 drop was not reflected in similar proportional changes in local prices, which remained much higher than pre-crisis levels (Ghosh 2010). World Bank model simulations are based on simplifying assumptions about price transmission mechanisms that leave aside the importance of contingent power relations within global value chains and between importers, local traders and producers of different types in affected countries. The extent to which prices are transmitted or not, and who bears the burden of volatility, is an important political-economy aspect of the food crisis that remains seriously under-researched, despite the substantial resources put by the Bank into understanding the crisis and designing responses.

Second, on the issue of the causes, not enough linkages have been made between the event of sharp price movements and the structures, processes and relations induced by the global agribusiness revolution and the financialisation of the global economy before the onset of the crisis. The recent food crisis is not an unexpected episode to be treated simply as an 'emergency', but a consequence of the coupling of global agribusiness development/concentration and the uncontrolled financialisation of the global economy (UNCTAD 2009, IATP 2009, Ghosh 2010 and Fine 2010e). Supply factors may play a role, as some argue that food production in many poor countries has not been dynamic, and dependence on food imports may have increased to risky levels in some countries (Tickner 2008). Such problems can, however, be resolved through reliable sources of foreign exchange and price stabilisation mechanisms. However, despite frequent claims that increases in consumption (especially of meat) and changes in diet patterns in fast-growing economies such as India and China were important factors (von Braun 2008), the evidence contradicts the claims that the global food crisis is just a result of 'real' production and demand conditions (see Ghosh 2010 and IATP 2009 for a detailed account of world food balances in the crisis period). In particular, data on world production and trade of the commodities that have experienced the sharpest increases in prices (rice, maize, soybeans and wheat) do not show any significant imbalances between supply and demand. Even though for some of these commodities stocks declined more rapidly than usual in 2007/08, this hardly explains the sharp fluctuations in food prices in such a short time span. Ghosh (2010, p.77) puts it clearly: 'such wild swings in prices obviously cannot be explained by short-term supply and demand factors or any other "real economy" tendencies. Instead, these acute price movements are clearly the result of speculative activity in these markets'.

We are therefore left with two main plausible explanations, a combination of which brings us closer to an understanding of what happened. First, there is the supply-side story originating in the pressure that a rapid and heavily subsidised promotion of bio-fuels, as a result of energy security concerns in the USA and Europe, has exerted on the grain–livestock market by rapidly increasing demand for some grains (maize) or soybeans, which are therefore reallocated from food to energy destinations in processing (von Braun 2008 and Mitchell 2008). Second, and more important, is the role of financial speculation in driving price volatility in food markets. The novelty is that institutional investors (notably hedge funds, pension funds, etc.) and traders have rapidly moved into commodity markets once other sources of profit through speculation dried up, first after the dot-com bubble burst and afterwards with the toxic assets-led financial collapse of 2008. This was possibly due to the processes of financial deregulation that had accelerated after the Asian financial crisis in 1997. A key turning point was the Commodity Futures Modernization Act in 2000, which deregulated commodity trading in the United States and opened the door for all forms of financial engineering to be applied to commodity markets (Ghosh 2010). Futures markets, despite their supposed stabilising role in stifling speculation, have in reality fuelled it through the entry of institutional investors and traders with an eye on short-term gains. It is not surprising that volatility of commodity prices greatly increased during the past five years. This also explains why most commodity markets are strongly correlated today, regardless of their respective 'real trends', and the number one commodity for speculation, crude oil, leads the game, while others – and increasingly, as data show, food products – follow. The unprecedented price spikes experienced in 2007/08 for a wide range of commodities and the abrupt fall in the second half of 2008 are a signal that speculation and not supply–demand interactions accounts for the magnitude of such sudden changes. This thesis is unsurprisingly not supported by the Bank. Instead, Mitchell (2008) and other World Bank reports are more likely to emphasise the short-term role of export bans ('export bans and restrictions fuelled the price increases by restricting access to supplies', p.13) than the role of financial markets and investors.[46]

Moreover, there are other structural features of the global food system, not exposed by the 2007–08 crisis, but visible in the last two decades, which remain off the World Bank radar. These are the 'underlying tendencies within the food system leading not only to unaffordable food, and hence undernutrition, but also to the simultaneous production of malnutrition and obesity' (Johnston 2010, p.69, and Lang 2010). Though these are largely market outcomes, the World Bank is quick to put the blame on government distortions or reversible market imperfections.

On the operational side, the Bank has used its assessments of the global food crisis to enhance the marketing of what were some of its preferred products prior to the onset of the crisis. For example, renewed emphasis is put on 'innovative' private insurance mechanisms to deal with price and weather risks as well as on the promotion of rural financial markets to smooth risks faced by farmers (World Bank 2009a). Insurance remains therefore one of the favourite tools, in preference to older state-driven mechanisms such as stabilisation boards, which regulated producer prices in the 1960s and 1970s. In this sense, the World Bank demonstrates respect for its core deregulation agenda, while acknowledging the significance of market risk and volatility. It also reflects the commitment to products and innovations deriving from financial markets, manifesting embedded 'financialisation' in World Bank thinking. There are other mechanisms also supported by the Bank to address risks or transaction costs, as they also serve the purpose of linking smallholders with global value chains. One example is contract farming, which is effectively designed to replace old forms of government-led vertical integration (as in marketing boards) and induce incentives on both farmers and buyers to make output and input distribution more efficient.

The Bank's operations that are focused on smallholder productivity and the promotion of producer organisations to expand linkages with agribusiness also receive a boost as a consequence of the global food crisis, which has underscored the need for more solid ways of addressing food security in a context of massive global market volatility. The Bank states this boldly: [47] it is '[w]orking to help countries develop financial market insurance products and risk management strategies to ensure increased capacity to respond to future prices increases, such as weather derivatives and crop insurance'. In other words, palliative and market-friendly preventative measures to deal with risk and vulnerability are likely to assume more prominent roles in the Bank's and other donors' work as a result of the crisis.

7.7 CONCLUSIONS

The World Bank can be seen as adopting economic ideas and paradigms as instruments to validate its actions, while also being affected by 'real world' events, such as economic, financial and food crises, which may be absorbed and adapted to the core dominant paradigm (Sindzingre 2004, p.234). The recent evolution of Bank approaches to ARD and the even more recent incorporation of nuances and new messages from selected critics and inescapable events (like the 2007–08 global food crisis) confirm some of these tendencies.

It has been argued in this chapter that the proliferation and endless expansion of agendas gives rise to more tensions and contradictions, as well as shifting relations between research, advocacy and policy (operations). As noted in Chapter 2, these three elements 'are not necessarily mutually consistent with one another; but nor are they independent of one another; and they have a shifting relationship between one another over time and place and across issues'. Fine (2001a) and Chapter 2 argue that the apparent gaps or inconsistencies between advocacy and research may well be not only substantive (endemically so) but also functional (serving the purpose of paradigm maintenance), so that the World Bank can maintain its dominant position, and suppress criticism by ignoring, incorporating and managing it. This chapter addresses this issue by focusing on the latest report on agriculture, WDR 2008, and illustrating it through a brief exploration of the Bank's research and advocacy on ARD for the period 2003–09. However, despite the inconsistencies and tensions, an element of coherence is maintained throughout, and this is the commitment to a pro-free-market ideology that cuts across the research–advocacy–policy divide and is exemplified by the continuous work and emphasis on 'distortions' on farm incentives, usually caused by 'misguided' and 'costly' government interventions, past and present.

Remarkably, a recent paper by de Janvry (2009), one of the leading authors of the WDR 2008, exposes, possibly unwittingly, some of the main pitfalls of the Bank's approach to ARD. He recognises that knowledge on what works in ARD and what does not is limited and that methods and models used by the mainstream have so far not been good enough. He also considers policy and institutional 'fixes' to be problematic and open to test, while he emphasises the importance of trade-offs (win–win solutions are the exception rather than the rule!) and multiple development outcomes (context matters) in which heterogeneity and adaptation should be part of solutions. He considers the significance of the fact that pervasive market failures and the failures of two decades of reforms (1985–2005) have not really been acknowledged by the Bank. Finally he underscores the crucial need for long-term sustained and substantial additional finance for agriculture, beyond price and political (electoral) cycles (he forgets to mention the operational cycles of donors like the Bank itself). A serious consideration of some of these ideas would bring some radical changes in thinking and operations for ARD at the Bank. Thus, it appears that de Janvry's role as leading author of the WDR 2008 did not achieve much in this direction – not unlike the limited effect of Ravi Kanbur as lead author of the 2000/01 WDR, alluded to in Chapter 1.

A few years ago, consideration of the tensions between the Bank's operational imperatives and its ever growing and diversifying research and advocacy agenda led critics to see the Bank as thinking increasingly like an NGO, while continuing to act like a public sector bank (Pincus 2001, p.212). Thinking and acting like a large development bank devoted to funding economic transformations and agrarian change would require dealing with the agrarian questions that have long preoccupied agrarian political economists and which transcend the facile traps of neo-populism. This chapter started with an enumeration of some of these questions, especially what drives or hinders capitalist development in agriculture; how social transformations in rural areas are outcomes of historically contingent class struggles and state actions; the diverse role of agriculture in fuelling or hindering industrialisation; how agricultural development depends on the development and trans-formations of forces of production, notably technology, and how its diffusion is spurred or obstructed by social, economic and political factors. Addressing such questions requires a historically informed theory of uneven capitalist development, structural relations of inequality (such as class, gender, ethnicity, occupation, location, and other attributes), accumulation, inter-sector linkages and conflict, and thus a methodology to analyse systemic change. Indeed, these questions have been central to analyses rooted in historical materialist political economy and 'old development economics' approaches (see Fine 2006 and Jomo and Reinert 2005). However, these alternative approaches are either totally ignored by the Bank or simply dismissed for being superficially linked to the promotion of 'dirigiste development strategies'. The current World Bank's scholarship, advocacy and policy on agriculture and rural development issues at best scratch the surface of such longstanding problematics, as in the recent WDR 2008. At worst, they provide ahistorical guides and misleading win–win institutional and policy 'fixes' to the deep-rooted and long-term challenges facing developing countries today.

NOTES

1. I would like to acknowledge the excellent research assistance provided by Bernd Mueller and Helena Pérez-Niño.
2. This title is inspired by the similar title of an earlier critique of the Bank's impact on agricultural development in Africa (Gibbon, Havnevik and Hermele 1993).
3. The WDR 2008 states: 'three of every four poor people in developing countries live in rural areas ... and most depend on agriculture for their livelihoods' (World Bank 2007a, p.1).
4. In addition, the World Bank has expanded the pro-market liberalisation advocacy agenda (the 'unfinished liberalisation agenda'), partly by moving away from a focus on internal reforms in developing countries and towards multilateral trade talks on agriculture (the Doha agenda). In its more recent analyses of agricultural distortions, the Bank has directed its attention and concerns towards OECD countries that continue to introduce substantial distortions in their agricultural markets (see Anderson 2009, pt.2).
5. See Pincus (2001) for a detailed analysis of the evolution of the World Bank's approach to agriculture until 2000.
6. These are not the only current approaches to ARD. A relatively more holistic *livelihood framework*, partly embedded between neo-populism and neoclassical economics, has been and still is very influential in the development community, notably among NGOs and donors like DfID, but seems much less visible in World Bank intellectual production (on the evolution of this approach and the challenge it faces, see Scoones 2009). A Marxist-inspired *agrarian political economy* approach has strong following in some segments of the academic community, but is far from being known, understood or appreciated by the main 'actors' of the development aid business (see more below).
7. It is crucial to question the often vague use of the concept 'small farmer' or 'smallholder', though we do not have the space here to go into such a detailed discussion. See box 1 in Hazell et al. (2007, p.1) on various forms of defining scale in different contexts.

8. In academia, neo-populism is mostly exemplified by Michael Lipton's work (see Lipton 1977 and Byres' critique 1979; also Lipton 2006 for a more recent contribution).

9. For an earlier version in the neoclassical tradition of this kind of work applied to agrarian institutions, see Stiglitz (1974). For a critique of 'new' neoclassical development economics on agrarian issues, see Byres (2003a). See also Dorward, Kydd and Poulton (1998), Dorward et al. (2004) and Hazell et al. (2007) for this increasingly influential approach.

10. See also http://www.brettonwoodsproject.org/art-558763.

11. The evaluator Justin Lin later on became the Bank's chief economist. Reading between the 'polite' lines of his assessment for a number of projects reveals lack of enthusiasm about the relevance, rigour and integrity of the research undertaken. He also emphasises unevenness in quality and blames it on World Bank research being split between different units with different incentive systems and priorities. He notes: 'It seems that researchers in non-research departments are evaluated quite differently from those in the Research Department. The former have less incentive to conduct rigorous evidence-based analysis using micro data.'

12. See also Chapter 3, in the context of aid.

13. See also Chapter 1 of this volume.

14. The projects around the preparations of the WDR 2008 devoted to agriculture consumed a total of 52 per cent of the research funding for Rural Development in the 2006–08 period and 72 per cent in 2007 alone.

15. For a critique of mainstream studies of price distortions and agricultural incentives, totally ignored by the project, see Karshenas (2004).

16. See edited volume by Akram-Lodhi and Kay (2008) for a recent contribution to this literature.

17. This issue is covered in some detail in Chapters 1 and 2.

18. There is substantial critical literature on the WDR 2008. See the symposia papers in the *Journal of Agrarian Change* 9(2) (e.g. Amanor 2009) and in the *Journal of Peasant Studies* 36(3) (e.g. Oya 2009). See also Akram-Lodhi (2008) and NGO responses such as Patel (2008).

19. That ideology and advocacy depart from research in this regard is attested by how the Bank deals with the growing body of mainstream agricultural economics literature within the NIE tradition which has openly discussed the pitfalls of Washington Consensus agricultural reforms, especially in Africa, and emphasised the pervasiveness of market failures in Third World agriculture (see Dorward et al. 2004). While the Bank relies heavily on some of this literature for projects and research outputs, it also tends to neglect the most critical arguments.

20. Chapter 11 in the WDR 2008 is devoted to governance issues; the word 'governance' appears in over 150 instances throughout the document. For a critique of the incorporation of rural governance issues by the Bank, see Amanor (2009).

21. Remarkably, an article published in a World Bank feature issue on agriculture (Kloeppinger-Todd and Agwe 2008) acknowledges that rural credit has failed in the past three decades following the failure and closure of state-sponsored rural credit agencies in many developing countries. Although the blame is not directly attributed to structural adjustment reforms, it would be ironic to attribute it

to anything else, especially after the authors admit that 'private sector interest remained sporadic at best' after liberalisation (p.28).

22. This is an outcome of the diverse set of consultants and experts involved in the preparation of the WDR 2008 and, indeed, is also related to the intellectual history of the lead editors of the report, Derek Byerlee and Alain de Janvry (see Kay 2009).

23. The report provides evidence in this regard but does not venture into a deeper analysis of its drivers and consequences, which would amount to a much more heterodox understanding of global agriculture as the product of a global food regime dominated by TNC conglomerates (see Weis 2007).

24. In a recently published analytical piece that attempts to set out a new agenda for development, Lin (2010) has nothing much to say about agriculture and agriculture–industry linkages, despite his citing of classics like Hirschman (1958). See also Chapter 11.

25. See also Timmer (2009) for a similar but less static approach to structural transformation and the urban bias problematic.

26. See http://www.brettonwoodsproject.org/art-558763 and Patel (2008).

27. See also several chapters in Akram-Lodhi and Kay (2008).

28. See special issue of *Journal of Agrarian Change* (Byres 2004), and especially articles by Dyer (2004) and Sender and Johnston (2004) for detailed critiques of the 'inverse relationship' and the neoclassical neo-populist case for land reform. See also Collier and Dercon (2008) for another critical assessment of the evidence and a suggestion that the inverse relationship may only apply to comparisons within the smallholder range (i.e. a celebration of the 'small' among smallholders), excluding very large-scale farms.

29. Thereby ignoring the importance of labour productivity (see Woodhouse 2009 and above). See also Johnston (2005) and Sender and Johnston (2004) on the assumptions about poverty and the 'poor' that underpin this focus on assets and land.

30. For example, on the Bank's 2003 ARD strategy, 'Reaching the Rural Poor' (World Bank 2003a), the word 'wage' is only mentioned in three occasions in over 200 pages, and then only with reference to specific cases of processing activities.

31. It is also interesting how employment linkages between 'dynamic' smallholders and casual wage workers are not explored, and the discretion that different classes of farm employers use to impose exploitative working conditions on workers is not subject to analysis.

32. Updating these figures shows a further decline to 4.1 per cent for the most recent period 2001–07 (see Figure 7.2).

33. This paradox confirms how little agriculture has mattered for OECD donors.

34. This is even noted by de Janvry (2009), one of the leading authors of the WDR 2008 and closely associated with the Bank. He says that a greater focus on agriculture in the old industrialisation paradigm of the 1960s and 1970s was followed 'for 20 years (basically 1985 to 2005) by the neglect of agriculture ... This resulted in sharply declining public investment' (p.4). It is well known that this was the period of structural adjustment and World Bank-sponsored agricultural reforms in developing countries, especially in Africa.

35. The Bank was asked by the G20 to create a trust fund to increase agricultural investment in poor countries.

36. See, for example, the management response to the IEG Report (2007).

37. One challenge of such preliminary exploration is that there is a wide range of multi-sector projects with only one or two components related to ARD. For the purposes of this exercise any project with at least one of the cited sectors falling within the ARD group was included, resulting in around 750 projects for the 2003–09 period. The other challenge is to assign specific financing amounts to sub-sectors within each project. This was done on the basis of data on proportions by sector and theme.

38. Also, as Pincus (2001) argues, this is not really to the Bank's comparative advantage and results in organisational tensions.

39. For many of the largest projects there is a substantial degree of co-funding among various aid agencies of which the World Bank remains the leader. See, for example, the recent 'Ethiopia Protection of Basic Services Program Phase II Project' at http://web.worldbank.org/external/projects/main?pagePK=6431 2881&piPK=64302848&theSitePK=40941&Projectid=P103022.

40. South Asia is over-represented in the financially dominant US$100–500m category, which contains some of the few large-scale infrastructural projects present in the 2003–09 database.

41. The global food crisis of 2007–08 is usually defined 'in terms of a sharp increase in the international prices of most food products – with prices peaking in mid-2008 and then falling back significantly' (Johnston 2010).

42. For the first time, World Bank research was more prominently present in mainstream agricultural economics journals. A special issue was organised by the journal *Agricultural Economics* in 2008 to respond to the events. A record turnaround time of papers and reviews resulted in a selection of 14 papers that included 4 papers authored or co-authored by Bank-affiliated researchers.

43. Although producers could be beneficiaries of the large increases, most evidence suggests that the impact has been disproportionately borne by net food purchasers, according to available studies such as Ivanic and Martin (2008) and Tickner (2008). This is partly because some of the most affected commodities (rice, wheat) are not produced by smallholders in many low-income countries, especially in Africa, and partly because price transmission has been very uneven – rapid for imported food and much slower for domestically produced staples.

44. According to FAO data, an additional 24 million people suffered from malnutrition in 2007, which can to a great extent be attributed to the crisis.

45. See http://web.worldbank.org/WBSITE/EXTERNAL/NEWS/0,,contentMDK: 22359784~pagePK:64257043~piPK:437376~theSitePK:4607,00.html.

46. It is interesting that the research highlighted on the Bank's website on the food crisis (http://www.worldbank.org/foodcrisis/) stops in 2008 (i.e. no 2009 studies are featured). It would seem that the World Bank, driven by its need to build up advocacy in the face of rising prices, was no longer interested in the causes and consequences of the subsequent sharp drop in the second half of 2008 and early 2009. It is this massive swing that lends more credibility to the hypothesis that financial speculation plays an important role in the story.

47. See http://www.worldbank.org/foodcrisis/bankinitiatives.htm.

8
A Policy Wrapped in 'Analysis': The World Bank's Case for Foreign Banks

Paulo L. dos Santos

8.1 INTRODUCTION

> Cross-border banking supports the development of an efficient and stable financial system that offers a wide access to quality financial services at low cost.
>
> Claessens (2006a, p.1)
> World Bank Policy Research Working Paper, no.3854

> Foreign banks have also introduced improved risk management practices and 'imported' supervision from parent country regulators, thereby helped strengthen banking systems.
>
> Claessens and Lee (2003, p.1)

> Success demonstrated the viability of mortgage-backed securities as a funding alternative not only for BalAEF, but also for housing finance institutions throughout Central and Eastern Europe ... [T]he active role of the IFC, not only as an investor, but also as a structurer, helped BalAEF to create an issuance program which will enable the company to access cross-border investors.
>
> IFC summary report on support for BalAEF mortgage securitisation transaction in Latvia, December 2004.[1]

The financial and economic crises unfolding from the United States to the rest of the world since 2007 added considerable pertinence to critical assessments of the research and policy advocacy carried out by International Financial Institutions (IFIs). In a turn of supreme irony, the crises strengthened the position of IFIs, whose policies of international financial openness and liberalisation contributed directly to the economic and financial imbalances straining many developing and transition economies. In a setting of open capital accounts, loans by those institutions become vital for the maintenance of financial stability and the creation of even modest scope for monetary and fiscal responses to developing recessions. Irony turned to outright hypocrisy as the IFIs aggressively used the resulting policy leverage to promote orthodox fiscal, monetary and banking-sector policies, precisely while such measures were being abandoned by US and European governments seeking to minimise the economic and social costs of the crises.

The need for basic accountability and authoritative critiques of IFI work is particularly poignant in relation to the World Bank and its policy initiatives towards banking systems in developing and transition economies. By singularly leading the policy push in favour of the entry by leading private banks from developed economies (and the broader adoption of their lending and funding practices) in middle-income countries, the Bank contributed directly to the development of the financial vulnerabilities that have afflicted a number of developing and transition economies.[2] From the mid 1990s onwards, World Bank studies provided the core arguments in favour of foreign-bank entry into developing countries. As evidence mounted of the potential risks and imbalances arising from the lending and funding behaviour of foreign banks, the Bank again led the charge in downplaying or dismissing associated concerns.

Throughout these policy advocacy efforts, the World Bank put its research on the relationship between foreign banks and the performance of host economies at the heart of its interventions. This chapter offers a critical assessment of the content and process of this research. By so doing, it also affords a critical appreciation of the assessments of World Bank research on financial sector policy offered by the Deaton reports (see Chapter 2 of this volume for further discussion on the Deaton evaluation of World Bank research).

Some of the problems explored in the current chapter in this area of World Bank research parallel those identified by the Deaton reports. Specifically, influential empirical studies that shaped debates and policy on foreign-bank entry were founded on cross-country, panel data statistical estimations. Such methods were problematically used to infer the character of relationships between banking markets, bank behaviour, and aggregate economic activity that are in practice complex, changing, socially contingent and nationally specific. Results were pushed in support of policy, even though, as the Deaton reports noted, 'the policy takeaways of this research are often quite limited due to obvious interpretational issues' (Bertrand 2006, p.1).

But this chapter's examination of this area of Bank research identifies further and serious problems of content and conduct not discussed by the Deaton reports. First, empirical work on the impact of foreign-bank entry was grounded on an analytical framework – the structure–conduct hypothesis from industrial organisation – whose significant theoretical inadequacies for the study of banking industries had long been understood by mainstream economists, including Bank staff. Published World Bank research in this field simply omitted any discussion of the well-established limitations of the methods it used in making the case in favour of foreign-bank entry. Second, Bank research consistently ignored, dismissed or downplayed well-articulated concerns about the lending and funding behaviour of foreign banks. This included dismissing not just the concerns of academics and host-country policymakers, but also those expressed by staff at the IMF, the European Central Bank (ECB), the Federal Reserve and the Bank for International Settlements (BIS).

The readiness to ignore well-supported methodological and policy concerns, even when voiced by proponents of liberalisation, points to a compromised process of scientific research. Indeed, the discussion offered here strongly suggests that the Bank's optimism about foreign banks followed less from research outcomes than from a prior belief that the financial practices, regulators, ratings agencies and banks from the United States and Europe were not only superior to those of developing countries, but were somehow immune from speculative manias, bad lending and general malfeasance. On such bases, the World Bank promoted institutions such as Citigroup, HSBC, UBS, Raiffeisen, etc. as instrumental to financial-sector efficiency and stability in developing and transition economies. Along similar lines, the IFC financially and technically supported foreign-currency mortgage lending, securitisation and cross-border borrowing in Eastern Europe and Latin America, touting them as 'financial development'.[3]

Up to the time of writing, the Bank has failed to offer any reassessment of its policy prescriptions, or of the research output and methods that supported them. Instead, the central message from the World Bank concerning developing-country banking systems has been to oppose any moves in favour of an ongoing expansion of public ownership. Initial research papers, official documents and policy briefings[4] have argued that any state intervention into banking systems must be temporary, and that the principal lesson of the crisis is the need for better regulation that will ensure that banking 'markets work'. Even when confronted with a calamitous crisis created by the private banking markets, institutions and practices it supported, the Bank appears unwilling even to qualify its deep-seated policy bias in favour of 'free' banking markets and limited state intervention aimed at 'complementing' them with regulation. This unwillingness to think outside a well-defined ideological box taxes the scientific credibility of the Bank's 'research-based' policy agenda in this area of work.

The rest of this chapter proceeds as follows. Sections 8.2 and 8.3 document the role of the World Bank in the establishment of exclusively microeconomic metrics for the analysis of the impact of foreign-bank entry and discuss the widely known limitations and problems with the particular methodology adopted in such studies. Section 8.4 discusses the wide evidence of the reorientation of credit effected by foreign banks across middle-income economies, as well as the financial vulnerabilities developing from their funding and lending behaviour in Central and Eastern European (CEE) economies. Section 8.5 discusses the Bank's problematic reactions to this evidence, casting light on the Deaton reports' findings on the Bank's research on 'finance and private sector development'. Section 8.6 concludes with a discussion of the Bank's interventions on bank-sector policy since the international banking panic of late 2008. It suggests that the policy and theoretical biases evident in the Bank's foreign-entry work are ongoing and apparently unshakeable, underscoring the need for comprehensive, radical critiques of World Bank research, policy advocacy and operations.

8.2   ESTABLISHING A ONE-SIDED THEORETICAL FRAMEWORK

The liberalisation of foreign-bank entry into middle-income economies that started in the mid 1990s presented a historically novel situation. The level of financial integration represented by this process had not been seen since before the First World War and the collapse of the British-centred liberal financial and commercial order. Between 1920 and 1980, no country relaxed restrictions on the operations of foreign banks in its banking system, while a number of countries imposed or increased such restrictions.

Given the significant processes of indigenous industrialisation taking place in (and giving rise to) middle-income economies between 1914 and 1980, newly entering foreign banks would be developing unprecedented economic and social relations with existing indigenous industrial capital. In contrast, the operations of late-nineteenth- and early-twentieth-century financial capital in formal or informal colonies focused almost exclusively on credit to trading operations or to highly collateralised undertakings, usually involving home-country capitalists.[5]

The sheer novelty of this situation and the centrality of articulations between banks, state and industry to every successful case of belated capitalist development would suggest cautious and historically informed analytical approaches to the study of foreign-bank entry. The widely noted embeddedness of bank credit on broader social relations between lenders and borrowers would also suggest that this study be grounded on the specific national or even regional socio-economic realities shaping bank behaviour.[6] Both considerations motivated concerns about possible declines in relational lending to small, medium and growing firms central to economic development.

Yet the study of the impact of foreign-bank entry was approached with the brutal simplicity and comforting certainties of neoclassical analysis in its information-theoretic, market-complementing guises. If foreign banks helped improve the functioning of markets by making them more efficient and encouraging the development of institutions and government regulations targeting possible 'market imperfections', they were held ipso facto to contribute to the prospects of economic development. No further inquiry was necessary.

The World Bank played a central role in making this narrow case for foreign-bank entry. Its research became a central component of a broader push for foreign bank entry that started with the 1986 launch of the Uruguay Round, during which US negotiators started insisting on the liberalisation of financial services (Gelb and Sagari 1990). Around these discussions, papers arguing the potential benefits of foreign banks for developing countries started to appear in the policy literature of various multilateral agencies.[7]

This early literature made the case for foreign entry on traditional neoclassical grounds. Barriers to trade in banking services lead to inefficient allocations of productive resources, distorted consumption patterns and static and dynamic welfare losses. At the same time, papers rightly recognised potential macroeconomic risks and pitfalls arising from observed foreign-bank behaviour. Gelb and Sagari (1990) noted the observed bias of foreign banks towards servicing large clients, particularly subsidiaries of multinational corporations, and its possible contribution to the further segmentation of developing-country banking systems. They also discussed the possible role foreign banks might have in facilitating capital outflows in times of crisis, as well as how incumbent domestic banks might respond to competition from foreign entrants by charging higher prices to a shrinking customer base.

The World Bank joined early in the advocacy of foreign-bank entry, arguing in a 1988 assessment of the Philippine financial system that 'the strong domestic banks should not feel forever insulated from competition' (World Bank 1988, p.vi). By the mid 1990s the Bank was shaping the analytical and policy terms of an increasingly one-sided debate. This included providing the central theoretical arguments in favour of foreign-bank entry in the widely cited and influential study by then World Bank principal economist Ross Levine (1996). The Bank's intervention changed the analytical content and political tone of the debate, which no longer examined explicitly macro-level concerns such as those expressed by Gelb and Sagari (1990).

In this study, Levine offers an early illustration of post-Washington consensus thought and its problems. Explicitly rejecting macroeconomic metrics, including macro-level conceptualisations of bank output, the study established an exclusively microeconomic metric for assessing the impact of foreign-bank entry, while acknowledging the potential impact of market 'imperfections'. Those can be addressed through state regulation and institutions: 'As long as an adequate supervisory and regulatory system is in place to ensure the safety, soundness, and transparency of the financial system, most of the potential costs of foreign banks can be circumvented while still enjoying the benefits' (Levine 1996, p.226).

Levine advances an analytically disjointed, two-step approach to the assessment of the impact of foreign-bank entry. The first step is to examine whether financial development leads to higher rates of growth. This is established by relying on the cross-country panel estimations reported by King and Levine (1993), who claim that their regression results establish not only an association between financial development and higher rates of growth, but a causal relationship from the former to the latter. The second step is to examine whether foreign-bank entry leads to financial development. Once this is shown, a simple syllogism settles the question without the need for any attempt at a macro-level conceptualisation of the impact of the behaviour of foreign banks.

The paper argues that foreign banks promote financial development through a range of micro-level processes involving regulation, information and broader functioning of banking markets. Foreign banks 'may encourage the emergence of better rating agencies, accounting and auditing firms, and credit bureaus that acquire and process high-quality information on individuals, firms, and financial institutions' (Levine 1996, p.240). They may also 'intensify pressures on governments to enhance the legal, regulatory, and supervisory systems underlying financial activities' (p.225). Through such developments, foreign banks help create institutions and practices that ameliorate informational and other 'imperfections' in financial markets, paving the way for socially optimal allocations.

Levine also argues that foreign banks improve financial system functioning, as they (p.239):

[s]timulate improvements in transaction services by introducing credit cards or improving the payments system ... introduce, expand the availability of, and lower the cost of risk management mechanisms ... intensify credit assessment procedures and enhance information gathering techniques ... introduce improved mechanisms for monitoring firm and manager performance ... [and] intensify the competition for mobilizing domestic resources that would expand the mobilization of domestic saving and promote better resource allocation.

Levine readily dismisses macro-level concerns arising from the observed behaviour of foreign banks during crises. Their possible contribution to capital flight is shrugged off: 'foreign banks do not cause capital flight; the causes underlying capital flight are poor and inconsistent policies, political uncertainty, and high and variable taxes that make the domestic market an unattractive and risky place to invest' (p.245). More significantly, concerns that foreign banks only service particular market segments is dismissed, as 'evidence regarding foreign banks' picking market niches is more anecdotal and difficult to interpret' (p.246). In any event, '[b]usinesses attempt to find profitable markets, and this manifestation of market-based competition will promote improvements in the provision of financial services to domestic clients'. Levine also plays down concerns about foreign-bank entry, arguing that 'foreign banks are unlikely to play a dominant role in most countries because of cost advantages enjoyed by domestic banks in terms of acquiring information about firms, business conditions, and policy changes' (p.226).

Tellingly, neither Ross Levine nor other Bank researchers whose work explicitly relied on this paper have revisited or sought to correct the views it expresses. This is despite the widely acknowledged facts that, before the crisis, foreign banks came to play dominant roles in many countries, cherry-picked particular market niches, and, during the crisis, *caused* capital flight. This omission suggests that the principal concern of this research was to motivate policy, not accurately to describe the markets it sought to study.

8.3   RELYING ON QUESTIONABLE CONCEPTUAL AND EMPIRICAL TOOLS

This narrow microeconomic framework provided the foundation for a widely cited cluster of empirical studies, chiefly authored by World Bank economists, that has been used widely in World Bank and WTO policy advocacy of open banking systems.[8] At the centre of this literature stood the most widely cited and influential empirical and policy study on the effects of foreign-bank entry: 'How Does Foreign Entry Affect the Domestic Banking Markets?' by Claessens, Demirgüç-Kunt and Huizinga (2001).[9]

The broad thrust of this literature is that, so long as regulatory and supervisory functions are undertaken adequately, foreign banks 'can help countries build more robust and efficient financial systems by introducing international practices and standards; by improving the quality, efficiency, and breadth of financial services; and by allowing more stable sources of funds' (Claessens and Jansen 2000, pp.1–2). Explicit in this argument is the supposition that foreign banks, regulators and ratings agencies possess techniques and practices inherently superior to those available to host-country agents. As a 2003 World Bank study notes, '[f]oreign banks have also introduced improved risk management practices and "imported" supervision from parent country regulators, thereby helped [sic] strengthen banking systems' (Claessens and Lee 2003, p.1).

A number of these contributions make use of cross-country panel data statistical estimations and necessarily suffer from all the shortcomings associated with that method.[10] But this literature suffers from far deeper problems, even when statistical work is carried out on data from a single economy. These papers gave specific form to the general microeconomic metric offered in Levine (1996) by advancing bank operating ratios and price spreads as the central measures of banking sector performance. In doing this, they resuscitated the long-discredited structure, conduct and performance

(SCP) framework, whose problems and limitations had been widely documented in the 1970s and early 1980s. In fact, even from within the World Bank, research had emerged that was sharply critical of using cross-country bank operating ratios as a measure of sectoral performance (Vittas 1991; see below).

Uses of the SCP framework in the study of bank sector performance date back to a long strain of papers published in the late 1960s. Those papers sought to analyse the impact of deregulation of US banking markets on the basis of the structure–performance hypothesis: that the degree of market competition is shaped by the output concentration of the largest firms in the industry, as concentration is held to facilitate oligopolistic collusion. The hypothesis is tested by estimating the relationship between measures of market concentration and various negative measures of microeconomic efficiency, such as interest rate spreads and bank operating ratios, including bank profits and overhead costs normalised to bank assets. This is done with the use of linear regressions containing a range of ad hoc control variables.[11]

In seeking to make the case for foreign-bank entry, World Bank studies adapted the SCP framework to the measurement of the impact of foreign entry with little or no theoretical justification. In line with the framework, studies measured the microeconomic efficiency of banking sectors by interest rate spreads, profits and overhead costs normalised to some measure of bank assets. But the key market-structure measure used was not market concentration, but the degree of foreign-bank penetration, measured either as the asset share, branch share, or share of the total number of private banks accounted for by foreign banks. Linear regressions of the measures of market 'efficiency' on measures of market structure and on ad hoc vectors of control variables were estimated. Negative, statistically significant coefficients for measures of foreign presence were advanced as evidence of the positive impact of foreign banks.

The benchmark studies presented in Claessens, Demirgüç-Kunt and Huizinga (2001) derive coefficient estimates from a panel of firm-level data for banks in 80 developed and developing countries between 1988 and 1995. They establish that foreign presence is statistically associated with lower profitability, non-interest income and overhead costs for domestic banks. The interpretation provided of this finding is that foreign banks bring competitive pressure on domestic firms, forcing them to become more 'efficient', thus improving the performance of the banking system. On this basis the authors are favourable to the relaxation of restrictions on foreign entry.[12]

This study helped spawn dozens of similar papers based on the SCP methodology.[13] The resulting literature played an important role in World Bank policy advocacy. Early versions were central to arguments presented to a 1998 Bank of Korea conference promoting foreign-bank entry following the Asian crisis. Similarly in early 2001 the World Bank and the WTO launched the edited volume by Claessens and Jansen (2001), which was prominently billed as 'useful for policy makers considering further liberalizing their country's financial sector in the context of the new round of multilateral negotiations on services ... and for policy makers interested in strengthening financial systems around the world'.[14]

Yet for all its influence, this literature suffered from chronic analytical limitations, even when applied to a single economy. As with the earlier SCP bank studies, this literature did not offer any detailed discussion of the theoretical bases for the expected causal links between market-structure and micro-efficiency measures, or of the appropriateness of the particular empirical methods and measurements used to test such links. More broadly, it offered no theorisation of the nature of bank output, how it may be measured, and how it may be related to macroeconomic performance. The only theoretical arguments offered were those advanced by Levine (1996), discussed above.

The difficulties arising from this very simplistic outlook are manifold. A range of different processes and developments may account for different movements in the measures of microeconomic efficiency put forward by this literature. Different banking activities with different consequences for economic development may, for instance, inherently pose different overhead costs. Credit card lending on a sufficiently large scale typically exhibits very low costs per unit of money loaned, while soft-information relational lending between banks and small or medium enterprises is generally costly due to its irreducible labour intensity.[15] A shift in a banking system away from lending to small and medium enterprises (SMEs) in favour of mass credit-card lending would generally be associated with a fall in overhead costs (normalised by volume of business). But that cannot be taken, a priori or otherwise, as evidence of an improvement in banking and its contribution to economic development.

Similarly, as noted in Demsetz's (1973) early argument against SCP methods, lower profitability need not indicate higher efficiency. In fact, different levels of profitability across individual firms may point to differential firm efficiency, in which case higher profits accrue to more efficient firms. The view that high profitability is a symptom of inefficiency following from collusion is an extremely naive shibboleth of neoclassical 'perfect competition'.

At the broadest level, the relationships between the posited measures of microeconomic efficiency used in these studies and the various measures of market and economic structure are immensely complex. They are contingent on the type of banking activities undertaken by different individual banks. They probably vary over time. And they certainly vary from country to country. Consequently, it is very difficult to interpret estimated coefficients in cross-country SCP equations.[16] Even single-country SCP estimations are difficult to interpret without the support of corroborating evidence.

The broad problems with such approaches have been known for decades. Demsetz (1973) offered compelling arguments against the naive assumptions behind the structure–conduct hypothesis. Gilbert (1984) provided an extensive review and critique of the conceptual and empirical problems posed by SCP approaches to the study of banking, favouring the use of cost-function estimation methods instead.

Yet the most succinct and convincing exposition of the serious limitations of SCP methods, particularly when applied to cross-country bank studies, is provided in an earlier World Bank working paper by Dimitri Vittas (1991), titled 'Measuring Commercial Bank Efficiency: Use and Misuse of Bank Operating Ratios'. The paper's abstract reads:

> Measuring bank efficiency is difficult because there is no satisfactory definition of bank output. International comparisons based on operating costs and margins are fraught with problems. These stem from substantial differences in capital structure (leverage), business or product mix, range and quality of services, inflation rates, and accounting conventions (especially about the valuation of assets, the level of loan loss provisioning, and the use of hidden reserves). Facile and uncritical use of ratios cannot substitute for detailed knowledge and understanding of banking structure and practice.

Claessens, Demirgüç-Kunt and Huizinga (2001) effectively dismiss Vittas (1991), citing it in a perfunctory and distorting manner. The paper is not referred to in a discussion of the methodology adopted, but in a sub-section discussing the implications of different national accounting conventions for the quality of the data used in the statistical estimations. Readers are encouraged to 'see Vittas (1991) for an account of the pitfalls in interpreting international bank operating ratios' (Claessens, Demirgüç-Kunt and Huizinga 2001, p.6), and reassured that remaining national differences in accounting standards are dealt with through country dummy variables. No mention is made of Vittas's concern about different bank business mixes or product orientations, or of his warnings about the need for detailed knowledge of individual banking systems; both of which directly challenge the validity of the methodology adopted by the study.

Instead, Bank researchers made facile and uncritical use of bank operating ratios and of a methodology known by specialists to be highly problematic to motivate a very significant policy initiative across developing and transition economies. At no point did their papers offer any hint of the controversies or potential conceptual, theoretical and empirical problems posed by their studies, even when those had been highlighted by researchers inside the Bank itself. The analytical and policy debate, as shaped by the Bank, was highly problematic from the start.

8.4   THE IMPACT OF FOREIGN-BANK ENTRY

Despite its serious analytical pitfalls, this literature was successfully leveraged at times of financial crises to promote foreign-bank entry.[17] From South Korea to Mexico, the Bank and other IFIs strongly insisted that recapitalisation of distressed banking systems should be undertaken by private foreign banks, not through government intervention and control. As discussed below, the contrast between this advice and the policies implemented by US and European governments when their own banking sectors nearly imploded in 2008 as a result of bad lending and egregious risk management practices poses a considerable embarrassment for the Bank.

In the event, since the mid 1990s banks from the United States and Britain acquired significant market share across a range of countries, with Spanish and other continental institutions also establishing themselves in Latin American and CEE markets. Between 1995 and 2005 the market share of foreign banks rose from around 6 to 28.3 per cent in Brazil, and from about 10 to 15.7 per cent in the Philippines. By 2007, the foreign-bank market share had reached almost 40 per cent in Turkey (Ergüneş 2009). More significantly, by the middle of this decade foreign banks had come to control more than 70 per cent of the banking systems of Mexico and almost every single CEE economy.

A wide literature from many traditions in economic analysis has documented how the behaviour of foreign banks has changed banking credit across a range of middle-income economies. In line with theoretical expectations and policy concerns, foreign banks proved to lend less to small and medium enterprises than domestic banks.[18] At the same time they led the way in a boom of lending to households for consumption and mortgages in host economies. This was recognised by the IMF's (2006) Global Financial Stability Report, which noted that the recent rapid growth in credit to households in developing countries significantly followed from the 'increased presence of retail-lending-oriented foreign banks', which operate with 'well-developed consumer-lending strategies' (pp.46–8). A number of country-level studies support this assessment, pointing not only to foreign banks orienting credit towards individuals, but triggering a response by top domestic banks, which aggressively followed suit into these profitable markets.[19]

The resulting reorientation of credit is clearest in economies with the most substantial levels of foreign entry. In Estonia loans to individuals rose from 10.9 to 46.6 per cent of all lending between 1995 and February 2009. Between 2001 and 2008 such loans rose from 6.8 to almost 40 per cent of all loans by the top five banks in Bulgaria. In the Hungarian financial system, one third of all lending was allocated to households by early 2008, while such loans reached 49.8 per cent of all loans outstanding in Romania by January 2009. Poland saw loans to individuals rise from 15.5 per cent of all loans to non-financial agents in January 1997 to 54.1 per cent in January 2009. In Mexico mortgage and consumption lending rose in tandem with foreign-bank entry, from 15 to 45 per cent of all lending between 1999 and 2007.[20]

These reorientations of credit tend to have a detrimental overall impact on equity and economic development. Lapavitsas (2009) and dos Santos (2009) have emphasised how banks have profited considerably through such loans by appropriating growing portions of the income of households. In addition, a shift in credit allocation in favour of loans to households will tend to stimulate demand for goods, while possibly placing constraints on domestic productive capacities as credit is shifted away from productive investment. As a result it may be associated with current-account deteriorations as imports boom, rendering host economies increasingly dependent on capital inflows. This has been evident in many CEE economies (see

IMF 2006 and Duenwald, Gueorguiev and Schaechter 2005). Further, as even the World Bank recently noted, while credit to enterprises exhibits a positive association with per capita economic growth, credit to households does not.[21]

For the CEE economies, the reorientation of credit away from firms and towards households was exacerbated by a particular development: foreign banks increasingly relied on cross-border borrowing for funding their activities, introducing and promoting foreign-currency denominated loans, often extended to households. As Figure 8.1 shows, cross-border borrowing increased significantly across many countries in the region, particularly in the Baltics and Hungary, in the lead up to the current crisis.

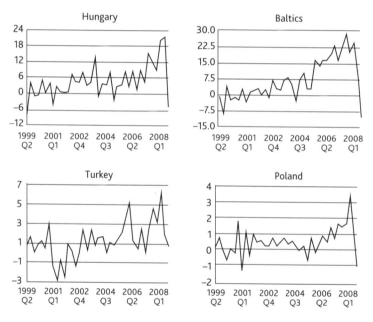

Figure 8.1 Quarterly change in cross-border loans from BIS banks (percentage of GDP). (Calculated from BIS, OECD and IMF data)

Figure 8.2 indicates how in Estonia and Poland much of this growth has been associated with a rise in loans to households denominated in foreign currencies.

Most other economies in the region witnessed similar increases in foreign-currency lending to households, which stood at very high levels in January 2009 (see Table 8.1).[22] A range of studies document the different factors contributing to this lending, including interest

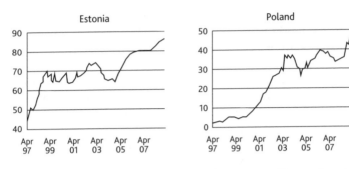

Figure 8.2   Foreign currency loans to households (percentage of all loans to households).
(Calculated from Eesti Pank and Narodowy Bank Polski data)

rate differentials, exchange-rate regimes and expectations of Euro entry.[23] At the same time, contributions from the IMF, BIS, and ECB have established links between foreign banks and the development of foreign currency lending.[24] As the IMF's (2006, pp.51–2) Global Financial Stability Report noted in relation to CEE economies: 'foreign banks have expanded their asset base faster than deposits, resulting in rising external and foreign currency debt, and an accumulation of currency risks by unhedged household borrowers'. More recently a detailed econometric study of lending behaviour in CEE economies published by the European Central Bank found that both foreign-bank presence and interest rate differentials are positively associated with foreign currency loans (Basso, Calvo-Gonzalez and Jurgilas 2007).

Table 8.1   Foreign currency loans to households, January 2009 (percentage of total)

Romania	Latvia	Hungary	Bulgaria
61	87.6	48.6	30

Calculated from national central bank data (figure for Bulgaria corresponds to the end of December 2008).

In addition to its contribution of financial vulnerabilities, this type of lending shared important predatory features with subprime mortgage lending in the United States.[25] Not only did it draw on abundant liquidity in international markets over the past few years, but it also placed households in risky financial positions, premised on speculation, in this case of eventual entry into the Euro. More significantly, it relied on the documented tendencies of borrowing households to focus almost exclusively on monthly repayments or higher loan volumes and not on the overall burden and risks posed by a loan.[26] These tendencies and the profitability of such lending ensured it continued growing, despite belated measures by Polish, Hungarian and Austrian authorities to curb it by forcing banks to inform borrowers of potential risks.[27]

In summary, quite apart from their impact on micro-level measures of efficiency, foreign banks and their lending behaviour created a number of economic problems and financial vulnerabilities in host economies across the world. This was highlighted by a wide literature, including studies by the IMF, the Federal Reserve, the ECB and the BIS. Yet none of this tempered the optimism of the World Bank. Having dismissed earlier concerns about the use of SCP methodologies for the study of banking-sector performance, Bank research contested, trivialised and dismissed this mounting evidence.

8.5   WHAT, ME WORRY?

The Bank's reaction to this evidence on the impact of foreign entry contained elements of denial, dogma and dubious empirical research. Bank papers argued that disappointing results followed from insufficient or ill-sequenced liberalisation,[28] or that the evidence presented was questionable on empirical or methodological grounds. It also offered a number of its own studies countering concerns about the potential problems created by the lending and funding behaviour of foreign banks on the basis of problematic cross-country studies with flimsy theoretical moorings, discussed below. More recently, World Bank research has argued, in a breathtaking act of self-exoneration, that levels of lending to households across countries have no relationship to policy initiatives, including foreign-bank entry (Beck et al. 2008). Throughout, the World Bank's scholarly response has suggested little capacity or willingness to engage meaningfully with evidence putting into question one of its important policy planks.

A series of World Bank studies suggested that the possible problems posed by foreign-bank entry follow from its incomplete character, noting that further liberalisation should address them. Flying in the face of country-level experience and evidence, Garcia-Herrero and Martinez Peria (2005) argued that cross-border borrowing was negatively related to the extent of foreign-bank presence and freedom of action in host economies. This result was established with the use of cross-country regressions estimating an empirical model of the share of total foreign claims on local economies held domestically by foreign banks across 100 host countries. As a result, according to the authors, host countries could reduce their exposure to cross-border claims by 'lowering regulatory barriers to bank activities and foreign-bank participation and by improving business opportunities in their market' (p.26). Similarly, Beck, Demirgüç-Kunt and Maksimovic (2004) attribute existing obstacles to the financing of enterprises, amongst other things, to the incomplete extent of liberalisation of foreign-bank entry. And Claessens (2006a) argues for the full inclusion of banking services into the WTO process as the best way to ensure foreign-bank entry delivers its full potential benefits.

A number of other papers took a different approach, arguing that foreign banks improve or maintain access to credit by small-scale enterprises (SMEs). Clarke et al. (2002, 2005) argued that once regressions control for an ad hoc list of 'factors that may affect lending' (Clarke et al. 2005 p.113),[29] many foreign banks in four Latin American countries are found to allocate no less credit to SMEs than comparable domestic banks. Large foreign banks in Colombia and Chile are found to lend proportionately more to SMEs than domestic banks once all factors are taken into account. The susceptibility of results in these papers to particular econometric specifications cast serious doubts on their findings, particularly in light of their weak theoretical foundations.[30]

Along similar lines Clarke, Cull, and Martinez Peria (2006) draw on a 1999 cross-country survey of perceptions of financing conditions by firm managers. The authors argue that in countries with significant foreign-bank presence, all enterprises report better access to and terms for banking credit, although the effect is stronger for larger enterprises.[31] Unfortunately, Clarke, Cull, and Martinez Peria do not discuss any country-level time series, investigating a single banking system's evolution as foreign banks gain market share. For instance, the Mexican monetary authorities have maintained a reliable and long-standing quarterly survey of credit market conditions facing firms in Mexico. The survey suggests a falling availability of bank credit following the full liberalisation of foreign-bank entry in 1998, hitting small and medium enterprises with particular force, as illustrated in Figure 8.3.[32]

A different approach was taken in relation to a 2006 theoretical and empirical study by IMF economists Enrica Detragiache, Thierry Tressel and academic Poonam Gupta. On the basis of an optimising model of foreign-bank behaviour,[33] the authors find support for their supposition that countries with more foreign-bank penetration have shallower banking sectors, and that foreign banks cherry-pick and service mainly large firms and have correspondingly less risky portfolios.

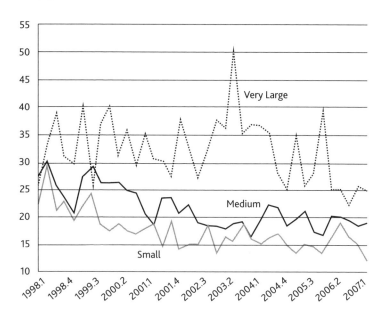

Figure 8.3   Surveyed Mexican firms with banks as main source of finance (per cent).

Source: Encuesta de Evaluación Coyuntural del Mercado Crediticio, Banco de México.

Claessens (2006b) offers comments on Detragiache, Gupta and Tressel (2006), focusing on possible omitted factors and considerations and possible data problems that may account for the findings. He argues that foreign-bank entry may run parallel with other developments, cherry-picking by foreign banks may be a positive development for financial stability, and that foreign entry may pose other trade-offs not captured in the study. Specifically in relation to policy, Claessens urges the authors to balance their findings with discussions of the 'overall value of foreign banks' to competition and stability.

He notes further that banking in general is moving away from soft-information lending across the developed world, and that there may not be any general alternatives to this development.[34] He concludes by finally considering the possibility that bank origin may affect lending behaviour, arguing in that case for a 'balanced entry strategy' by which some foreign banks focused on hard-information lending and some domestic banks focused on soft-information lending. Notably, this possible policy conclusion has never been further pursued in subsequent World Bank research on the issue.

From 2006 onwards Bank papers have deemed the evidence on foreign banks and access to credit by SMEs to be either 'inconclusive' or 'mixed'.[35] These formulations have been maintained even though, with one partial and problematic exception, all the cited papers claiming to find no unfavourable consequences of foreign-bank entry to SME lending have been produced by World Bank researchers.[36] This glaring skew in the evidence 'mix' is not noted in any of its research output on foreign banks.

A similar approach has been taken more recently in relation to lending to households. Beck et al. (2008) present evidence that while credit to enterprises has a statistical association with higher rates of per capita growth, credit to households has none. More significantly, the paper reports on regressions seeking to estimate the determinants of the share of credit to households in total lending on the basis of cross-country variations. The authors pursue an explicitly ad hoc approach to the specification of equations, noting that 'while the theoretical literature does not provide us with any direct guidance to which variables should explain best the composition of credit, we can use the basic intuition of models of endogenous financial intermediation' (p.12). This basic intuition leads the authors to a total of two dozen different variables that may explain the share of household credit.[37]

A number of regressions are carried out on subsets of explanatory variables, including simple cross-country estimations using average values for variables between 1994 and 2005 for each of 43 countries, and panel data estimates based on data from a subset of 23 countries. From these the authors conclude (p.19):

> These results suggest that the relative importance of bank lending to households and enterprises across countries is mostly driven by factors not immediately subject to policy decisions, but rather by differences in economic and financial structure. This also puts the previous finding of an insignificant impact of household lending on growth in a different light.

If these claims are to be taken at face value, it must be concluded that the dramatic growth of lending to households across Latin American and CEE economies in the last ten years followed not from foreign-bank entry, or any other policy, but from similarly explosive changes to domestic economic and financial structures.

The timing of these conclusions is notable. They are published as growing household debt across middle-income countries is proving to be a significant source of vulnerabilities. While a range of researchers have documented the role of foreign banks in the development of this debt, the institution most directly responsible for the policy of foreign-bank entry is declaring household debt to be independent of policy choice. The World Bank seems to be trying to say household debt is not a policy issue, not related to foreign banks, and most importantly, not its fault!

Some of the problems with the Bank studies reviewed above were identified and discussed in the Deaton reports, which documented many instances where Bank research was not only analytically problematic but also tailored to the needs of policy advocacy. While the Deaton reports on finance and private sector development did not directly address the various papers on foreign-bank entry included in the list under review, their criticisms were germane to this literature. As the more exhaustive of the two reports noted (Bertrand 2006, p.1):

> The cross-country approach that is adopted in much of the research I have reviewed suffers from serious limitations. While this research approach has established clear correlation patterns between many of the key variables of interest, the policy takeaways of this research are often quite limited due to obvious interpretational issues.

The report contrasts this reliance with the dearth of 'detailed case studies, where one can delve deeper into the specific experiences of a given country'. Such studies are desirable as appropriate research designs require 'a deep knowledge of a country's experience' (p.2).

Bertrand also levels strong criticisms at the recurring practice, in Bank research on the relationship between financial structure and economic development, of making policy recommendations based on the failure to establish statistical associations between measures of financial structure and economic development. As she points out, this betrays 'a strong tendency here to associate a lack of statistical evidence with a lack of economic evidence' (p.12). This criticism applies directly to the recent Bank claim that policy decisions have not influenced the share of credit that is allocated to households across different national economies.

Yet the discussion above points to an additional and in many ways more fundamental problem with World Bank research. The Bank's outright dismissal of the concerns voiced by Vittas (1991) on SCP methods, and of evidence provided by a range of researchers on some of the adverse impacts of foreign-bank entry, point to a research process impervious to serious internal and external criticism. It suggests that the policy bias castigated by the Deaton reports consciously informs not only the choice of research methodologies but also ex post assessments of policies promoted by the Bank. These findings raise serious questions about the analytical soundness of the Bank's research processes in this area, suggesting the need for stern scientific scepticism when engaging with its policy conclusions.

8.6   SACRED COWS AND DEAD HORSES

The Bank's policy interventions during the current international financial and economic crises appear to confirm this diagnosis. Faced with arguably the largest, most costly and clearest failure of private banking in the history of capitalism, the Bank's faith in private banking, and in the analytical tools and research that ostensibly supported its policy enthusiasm for them, remains unshaken.

The Bank has offered no attempt to examine critically the role and desirability of private banking institutions, and the possible usefulness of alternative institutional and governance mechanisms for developing (and developed) country financial systems. It has not tried to investigate the basis and character of the predatory practices by leading international banks that led to the subprime crisis in the United States and helped create the millstone of foreign-currency debt now tightly wrapped around the necks of many households in CEE and other economies. It has put forward no critical opinion of the destructive logic of financial competition, which impels private firms to occupy increasingly fragile financial positions, even while all know that such moves will end in disaster.[38] To the present date, the Bank has yet to take any responsibility for its role, through banking-sector research, policy and IFC programming, in contributing to financial vulnerabilities across a number of developing and transition economies.

Yet none of these failures has prevented the Bank from offering policy advice on banking systems to developing countries. In these interventions the Bank reveals a failure to question the analytical and policy orthodoxy that underpinned its own previous damaging interventions. The same poor methods are still being used to motivate the same damaging policies. Interventions have focused on arguments against public sector alternatives to private banks. Arguments have been founded on the simple assertion of an opposition between 'bad governments' and 'good markets', backed up by the usual litany of unenlightening cross-country statistical estimation exercises produced by the Bank itself.

In its 2008 Global Development Finance (GDF) report, the Bank implicitly concedes that the ability of foreign banks to borrow abroad contributed directly to externally fuelled credit booms, currency mismatches and a weakening of the ability of the authorities to control aggregate demand through monetary policy. But the admission of this patent fact is as close to a re-examination of previous research and policy outputs as the GDF report gets. The general policy recommendation it makes for developing countries is clear (World Bank 2008b, p.105):

> It is crucial that policy makers in emerging-market countries renew their commitment to the sound policies of the recent past and recognise the implications of changes in the financial climate. Sustaining and extending the structural changes and institution-building efforts that have made emerging markets' continued integration into global capital markets possible should command high priority, as should strengthening regulation and supervision aimed at limiting currency and maturity mismatches.

In other words, more of the same, except for *strengthened* financial regulation. Notably, the GDF report continues to draw on the problematic literature examined in section 8.5 above, to claim that foreign banks are beneficial to developing countries, since they 'helped ease credit constraints on firms' and 'improved the efficiency of domestic financial systems' (p.92).

The Bank's interventions have also sought to address the potential embarrassment posed by the extent of public intervention into banking systems in the US and Western European economies. Those interventions run directly counter to the policy maxim the IFIs have successfully imposed on developing countries facing banking crises over the past 20 years: that bank recapitalisation is not the business of governments and should be left to leading international private banks. During the current crisis, not only have states of the United States and Western Europe intervened directly into banking systems, but they have done so to rescue and prevent the failure of the very private institutions the IFIs had promoted as the cornerstone of sound and stable banking sectors in developing countries.

In response to this, the Bank and the IFC have intervened to underline the 'extraordinary' character of these interventions, lest the children pick up bad habits from the adults (Scott 2009, p.1):

> In most of the developed countries affected, governments initially improvised solutions that eventually led to substantial investments in systemically important banks. Not all their actions are worth emulating, especially those that undermine normal governance arrangements and the ability of all shareholders to hold the banks' board and management accountable.

Unfortunately, this admonition is not accompanied by any insights on the precise character of 'normal governance arrangements' of private banks, or on their role in the dissemination of the predatory and reckless lending and 'risk-management' practices that paved the way for the crisis.[39]

According to the Bank and the IFC, developing countries should be ready for the 'possibility of temporary ownership of financial institutions as a last resort', but must make it very clear that any such intervention is temporary (Scott 2009, p.6), and is necessary in order to 'avoid market distortions and reduce uncertainty'. Notably, the Bank offers no alternative to the same top international banks as the eventual private owners of banks following any such intervention.

The arguments against state ownership and in favour of policy orthodoxy have been put most clearly in the paper by Bank economists Asli Demirgüç-Kunt and Luis Servén (2009), 'Are all the Sacred Cows Dead?'. The paper's arguments offer no evidence of attempts to discuss in an open and critical manner the methodological premises and policy imperatives that made the Bank's intervention on banking systems so damaging to developing countries. In arguing in favour of private banking institutions, the authors rely on a series of past World Bank cross-country studies statistically establishing negative correlations between public bank ownership and various measures of 'financial development', including La Porta, Lopez-de-Silanes and Shleifer (2002), Barth, Caprio and Levine (2001) and Beck, Demirgüç-Kunt and Martinez Peria (2007, 2008). The authors also argue that public banks are corrupt, based on case studies that have established various degrees of political and managerial malfeasance in Pakistani and Indian banks.[40] No attempt is made to establish the basis for generalisation of those findings to all public banks in all developing countries. No discussion is offered on possible governance arrangements that may ensure public banks deliver on their stated social and developmental aims. And no comparison is pursued of the prevalence and costs of corruption and malfeasance in public banks with the costly, destructive and often corrupt practices of their private counterparts.

The authors' arguments are not made on deliberate consideration of the issue of public and private banks, but on very simplistic certainties about 'bad governments' and 'good private agents'. According to them, the problems of public banks are ultimately rooted in government officials that often 'lack the expertise to be effective managers' and face 'conflicts of interest' (Demirgüç-Kunt and Servén 2009, p 14). Indeed, ineffective government managers are to blame for the crisis (p.24):[41] 'The failure of private agents to exercise sufficient due diligence was rooted in the failure of government supervisors to challenge decisions made by private accountants and credit-rating organizations.' The analytical foundations of these arguments do not offer the bases to conduct rigorous inquiry into the relative merits of private and public governance mechanisms in banking and broader economic policy. The biases they reflect deprive not only the World Bank, but, most importantly, developing countries, of an honest debate, informed by the international crisis, on potential alternative frameworks for banking systems.

It is still too early definitively to characterise the Bank's post-crisis response in banking-sector research and policy. But these initial contributions strongly suggest these will continue to flog the same dead horses that underpinned its earlier work on the desirability and impact of foreign-bank entry. There is no evidence of Bank researchers questioning the analytical bases of their recent studies nor the policy positions they sustained, including in a June 2009 official assessment and directive document on its own research (World Bank 2009b). In light of the magnitude and significance of the current crisis, the Bank's hitherto lack of analytical curiosity, scepticism and imagination is not simply striking. It points to a scientific process compromised by prior policy aims. As this chapter has set out to argue, there are sound bases to treat the resulting 'research-based' prescriptions with the utmost scientific and policy scepticism.

NOTES

1. See http://www.ifc.org/ifcext/treasury.nsf/Content/Securitization. BalAEF is the Baltic American Enterprise Fund.
2. See dos Santos (2008) for an early exposition.

3. A typical example was the IFC's financial and technical support to the Baltic American Enterprise Fund (BalAEF). As described by the IFC's own documents celebrating support for BalAEF,

> Incorporating US-style mortgage lending practices, BalAEF has enjoyed strong growth and brought visibility to the housing markets while strengthening the prospects for securitization in the international markets. The mortgage loans are provided in Euros, US dollars, and local currency for terms up to 20 years.

   See http://www.ifc.org/ifcext/treasury.nsf/Content/Securitization.
4. See Demirgüç-Kunt and Servén (2009), World Bank (2008b) and Scott (2009), respectively.
5. See Bairoch and Kozul-Wright (1996), Gelb and Sagari (1990) and Bordo, Eichengreen and Kim (1998).
6. The importance of such factors has been widely noted, in sociology by Uzzi (1999), in Marxist political economy by Lapavitsas (2003), and by mainstream economists in Faini, Galli and Gianni (1993), Cuadrado, de la Dehesa and Precedo (1993) and Berger and Udell (2002).
7. Terrel (1986), Blejer and Sagari (1987) and Gelb and Sagari (1990) are the salient early examples.
8. See the contributions in Bank of Korea (1998), Claessens and Jansen (2000) and Litan, Masson and Pomerleano (2001), for instance.
9. The series of working papers published by the Bank since 1998 that culminated in the 2001 version published in the *Journal of Banking and Finance* had registered 671 citations in other published papers according to Google Scholar, as of 27 March 2009.
10. Centrally, the supposition that the complex and nationally specific relationships being estimated are homogeneous not only across time, but also across countries. See Arestis and Demetriades (1997), for instance.
11. For reviews of early applications of the SCP framework to the banking industry, see Guttentag and Herman (1967), Greenbaum (1967) and Heggestad (1977).
12. That the study's findings include the observation that foreign banks draw higher profits than domestic banks in developing countries does not temper the authors' support for foreign banks on the grounds of microeconomic efficiency.
13. See, for instance, Denizer (2000) for Turkey, Barajas, Steiner and Salazar (2000) for Colombia, Clarke et al. (2000) for Argentina, Lee (2002) for MENA economies, Unite and Sullivan (2003) for the Philippines, and Naarborg and Lensink (2008) for CEE and Central Asian economies. See also Levine (2003) and Lensink and Hermes (2004) for additional multi-country panel data exercises, and the individual contributions to the collections offered by Claessens and Jansen (2000).
14. WTO Press Release 208, 19 February 2001.
15. See Mester (1997), Uzzi (1999) or Lapavitsas and dos Santos (2008).
16. The attendant difficulties are illustrated by Lensink and Hermes (2004), who argue in favour of the benefits of foreign-bank entry on the basis of an established positive association between measures of foreign entry and domestic bank overhead costs. The association is held to point to investments in new technologies and systems by domestic banks in response to foreign competition.
17. Mathieson and Roldós (2001) estimate that on average, between 1991 and 1999 banking crises were followed by increases in foreign-bank market share of about 10 per cent.

18. See, for instance, Gormley (2007) for evidence from India, Bleger and Rozenwurcel (2000) and Berger, Klapper and Udell (2001) for Argentina, Mian (2006) for Pakistan, dos Santos (2007) for the Philippines, and Detragiache, Gupta and Tressel (2006) for a large sample of poor economies; see also BIS (2005).

19. Including Haber and Musacchio (2005) for Mexico, Mohanty, Schnabel and Garcia-Luna (2004) and Lapavitsas and dos Santos (2008) for a range of developing countries, Hapitan (2001) for the Philippines, and Ergüneş (2009) for Turkey.

20. Calculated from central banks' data, except for Mexico, where data from the Comisón Nacional Bancaria y de Valores are used.

21. Beck et al. (2008). See below for a discussion of the problematic interpretation of these results by the study's authors.

22. The three regional exceptions are the Czech Republic and Slovakia, where foreign currency lending has remained low, and Croatia, where it has remained confined to enterprises.

23. See Jeanne (2003) and Rosenberg and Tirpak (2008).

24. See Moreno and Villar (2005), IMF (2006) and Basso, Calvo-Gonzalez and Jurgilas (2007).

25. See Blackburn (2008), Dymski (2009) and Lapavitsas (2009) for rich descriptions of this lending.

26. See Miles (2004) and Campbell and Cocco (2003).

27. See the study by UNECE economists Palacin and Shelburne (2005).

28. See Bayraktar and Wang (2004), Čihák and Podpiera (2005), Claessens and Lee (2003 Beck, Demirgüç-Kunt and Maksimovic (2004) and Garcia-Herrero and Martinez Peria (2005).

29. The factors include, among others, the bank's size, a vector of variables measuring returns on assets, overhead costs to total assets, level of capitalisation, share of non-performing loans, and a series of dummy variables for foreign ownership and form of entry (de novo, merger, or outright purchase). No robust theorisation is advanced to justify this collection of variables other than indications of evidence that they affect bank behaviour.

30. Clarke et al. (2002) find that foreign banks allocate a lower share of their loans to small and medium enterprises in all countries, but this difference is most pronounced with small foreign banks. With slight changes to the econometric specification, Clarke et al. (2005) find that the earlier result only holds for Chile and Peru, while in Colombia and Argentina foreign banks tend to allocate similar proportions of their loan portfolios to SMEs.

31. This is on the basis of estimated probit models of responses on the availability and price of credit as functions of a range of more than 20 variables, including indices for a country's 'electoral competitiveness', 'rule of law', and a dummy variable indicating a British legal origin, motivated without reference to any theory.

32. See Encuesta de Evaluación Coyuntural del Mercado Crediticio, published by Banco de México.

33. The theoretical justification for such a model is drawn from Allen Berger et al. (2005).

34. See Lapavitsas and dos Santos (2008) for a discussion of this shift in bank behaviour and its relationship to foreign-bank entry.

35. See Clarke, Cull, and Martinez Peria (2006), Claessens (2006b) and Beck and Martinez Peria (2008), for instance. Other papers studying the financing of SMEs have opted for simply not investigating or mentioning the possible role of foreign banks in that process. See Beck, Demirgüç-Kunt and Martinez Peria (2008) on this account.

36. The only partial exception to this result is the study by Giannetti and Ongena (2005), published by the ECB. The study concludes that in CEE economies (p.33):

> foreign lending stimulates growth in firm sales, assets, and leverage, but that the effect is dampened for small firms. Even though foreign banks favour entry, lack of local knowledge remains a handicap. Indeed we find that small firms have a lower market share and a lower proportion of total assets in countries with stronger foreign bank presence.

A number of World Bank studies have misrepresented these findings, including the official Global Development Finance Report of 2008 (World Bank 2008b). The GDF suggests that Giannetti and Ongena (2005) conclude that 'the presence of foreign banks *increases* access to credit' (p.94; my emphasis). As with other Bank studies citing Giannetti and Ongena (2005), the GDF also omits any mention of the second finding, concerning the lower market share and asset proportion of small firms, which is reported in the paper's abstract.

37. These include share of urban population, size of informal sector, share of manufacturing output, volume of capital-market transactions relative to size of banking sector, a range of variables describing various aspects of the 'legal environment', a composite measure of 'institutional development' put forward by Kaufman, Kraay and Mastruzzi (2004), size of the banking sector, proportion of government banks, concentration of the banking industry, market share of foreign banks, measures of restrictions on bank activities, the deductibility of mortgage interest payments, and dummy variables for the origin of the country's legal system and for its majority religion.

38. Captured in the unselfconscious July 2007 remarks by then Citigroup CEO, Chuck Prince, on the leveraged buyout boom: 'When the music stops, in terms of liquidity, things will be complicated. But as long as the music is playing, you've got to get up and dance'. See also, of course, Minsky (1992).

39. On this, Alan Greenspan offered far greater candour during his 23 October 2008 remarks to the US House Committee of Government Oversight and Reform, in which he admitted that 'those of us who have looked to the self-interest of lending institutions to protect shareholder's equity (myself especially) are in a state of shocked disbelief'. World Bank output is yet to offer a similarly candid assessment of the 'normal governance arrangements' of private banks.

40. Cole (2004), Dinc (2005) and Khwaja and Mian (2005).

41. Demirgüç-Kunt and Servén (2009, p.24). The bases on which inexperienced and ineffective state managers should have been able to challenge decisions made by (presumably experienced and effective) private accountants and ratings agencies are unfortunately not discussed by the authors.

9
Hard Science or Waffly Crap? Evidence-Based Policy versus Policy-Based Evidence in the Field of Violent Conflict

Christopher Cramer and Jonathan Goodhand

9.1   INTRODUCTION

The cliché has it that truth is the first casualty of war; rather, truth, or reliable evidence at any rate, is one of the principal battlefields of war. And the site of conflict spreads from localised claims and counter-claims to competing interests, claims to scientific rigour, and explanations internationally.

We hope to highlight some features of the various relationships between policy and research or evidence and to discuss some of the factors that affect these relationships. The relationship is often seen as strained. As Andy Mack put it (2002, p.515):

> the academic conflict research community has far less impact on the policy community than the importance of its work deserves. This is so for a number of reasons. First, the scholarly and policy communities communicate badly – the former rarely seeking to make their work more accessible to the latter. This is particularly true of the work of the econometricians, which few in the policy community understand.

He listed other reasons, including the claim that since policymakers do not understand econometrics, if someone criticises the work of an econometrician they might reject it for the wrong reasons; the argument that policymakers are confused by multiple and conflicting conflict datasets (as well they might be);[1] the claim that policymakers do not have the time to select between competing explanations of the causes of conflict; and the argument that there is no genuine interdisciplinarity or communication across government departments. Our discussion tallies in some ways with Mack's, but also departs from it: in arguing that there can be a close relationship between academics, indeed even econometricians, and policymakers; and in putting greater emphasis on the role of interests, be they individual, institutional or political, in shaping policy and filtering, shaping, encouraging, and drawing upon or excluding research.

The study of violent conflict is not unique in these respects and often in its substance and in its methods provides heightened examples of trends, and deficiencies, common in other fields. It offers a particularly good example of the proliferation of what Barnett and Prins (2005, p.7) dub factoids, 'the intellectual viruses of quick and dirty synthetic studies' that produce information based on soft opinion and a very narrow evidential base and that get transformed into fact through constant citation (see also Chapter 6). They were writing about the social science literature on HIV/AIDS, but the process is central to recent debates on violent conflict in developing countries too. In addition, soft opinion and a narrow evidence base can be translated into apparent fact by constant repetition, but also by the mechanism of laying claim to 'hard science'. For example, as Suhrke and Samset pointed out about the world of peace building, where pressure for standardisation of policy measures has been building and there are bureaucratic pressures on policymakers to ask for formulaic solutions (2007, p.199): 'Conclusions based on sophisticated statistical methods convey certainty and factual "truth" even though this may be false security'.

Arguably, this desire for security and control is accentuated in environments affected by violent conflict, in which policymakers (and others) cling to 'hard facts' while they are buffeted by events, heightened risk and uncertainty, and interruption or damage to normal information production. Meanwhile, there is an increased risk that they will be detached from reality as they retreat into secure compounds and gated communities because of safety concerns, and their world contracts to that small universe of technocrats conversant in the language of good governance, good policy, and so on. There may be a form of intellectual gated compound in which aid officials and policymakers take refuge behind the security barrier of the assumption that they are doing good. Several writers have looked at the various forms of denial deployed by aid workers in order to deal with cognitive dissonance (Walkup 1997, Marriage 2006, Goodhand 2006 and Caddell and Yanacopulos 2006). Forms of distancing, reality distortion and the creation of false illusions may be understood as important ways of coping with high levels of stress, uncertainty and the pressure to intervene in the face of the irresolvable.[2]

The chapter begins in Section 9.2 by introducing the work of the World Bank on violent conflict or civil war in developing countries and discusses the way Deaton et al. (2006) assessed this work. Section 9.3 branches out to discuss the international intervention in Afghanistan from 2001 onwards, and Section 9.4 addresses the particular issue of opium. Finally, the chapter highlights some general issues that arise from the preceding discussion.

9.2   THE DEATON REPORT AND WORLD BANK RESEARCH ON CIVIL WARS

The World Bank's 2003 report 'Breaking the Conflict Trap' (World Bank 2003d) was submitted to the evaluation panel for Deaton et al. (2006) as one of the Policy Research Reports it was to assess, along with other work, such as the two volumes of *Understanding Civil War* (Collier and Sambanis 2005). The evaluator assigned to this work also looked at papers that formed a cornerstone of the Bank's work, written by the report's lead author, Paul Collier. This work has been influential, intellectually and in policy circles, though it is difficult to assess the nature and degree of influence involved. First, his work has had a powerful effect in shaping debates across at least some disciplines on the causes and characteristics of violent conflicts in developing countries – a field that has expanded rapidly since the end of the Cold War; and, second, he has had the ear of a number of international development agencies, including DfID, the World Bank, and NORAD, the Norwegian aid agency. A Norwegian official, for example, once told one of the authors of this chapter that Collier had been 'beatified' by the development minister there. Yet there is equally widespread scepticism about the veracity of Collier's claims and the rigour of his methods as well as the degree of influence exerted in official agencies.

Before looking at how Deaton et al. assessed the Bank's work on civil war, we highlight two particular areas of work and claims made by Collier, of special interest to the uninitiated. The first is more widely known and is the argument about greed versus grievance in causing civil wars. The second is the claim that countries emerging from recent civil wars have a 50 per cent chance of returning to war within the first few years of the end of a war.

A great deal has been written about the greed versus grievance debate. This is not the place to rehash the substance of the debate, so we simply highlight some of the issues and the history of the debate. Collier, with Anke Hoeffler, wrote a number of papers reporting variations on a model that purported to test whether civil wars were caused by 'greed' or 'grievance', using regression analysis. This involved forging a sharp distinction between these two categories of motivation, finding quantifiable proxy variables for each, and then assessing the correlation between observations for these variables and observations from a dataset on civil wars, taken from the Correlates of War project. Lo and behold, the surprising finding for these intrepid social scientists was that the greed proxies were more likely than grievance to explain (in probabilistic terms) the onset of civil war. To this the authors added an explanation, derived from the tenets of methodological individualism, inspired theoretically by the neoclassical economist Jack Hirshleifer and by Mancur Olson's propositions about collective action. To summarise the core idea: there are grievances or grounds for violent complaint aplenty, but they do not produce sufficient conflict to clear the market. The market, as it were, would be cleared at an equilibrium level of conflict where excess pressure of grievances (demand for change) had been soaked up by supply of change. This is because equality, rights, freedom from injustice, etc., are all public goods and therefore undersupplied in an unregulated world because of free-rider problems, time-consistency complications and credibility gaps among suppliers. Access to direct material rewards to individuals – loot – overcomes the collective-action problem and clears the market.

In the best traditions of social science, this appealed to many people because it was controversial and apparently surprising. Conventional wisdom may tell us that grievances cause wars; but statistics reveal the opposite. Thus, it was not just the finding itself that accounted for the renown of the work, but its claims to objectivity. 'Every time a civil war breaks out, some historian traces its origin to the 14th century and some anthropologist expounds on its ethnic roots', Collier argued (2003, p.40). Suggesting that motivations are clouded by a self-serving 'narrative of grievance', Collier disavowed anthropological or other field-related methods and took what he pointed out was the conventional approach in social science, i.e. 'to infer motivation from patterns of observed behaviour' (Collier 2000b, p.92).

An apparently surprising finding, revealed by objective social science methods, was combined with excellent branding and a clear storyline – greed causes civil wars in developing countries. This combination helped propel the work to the forefront of a growing social science interest in developing-country violent conflicts. It also provoked a series of critiques. Although none of these critiques was ever openly acknowledged by Collier and his associates, at one level they appear to have had some effect. At the very least the tone of the argument shifted and Collier began to argue that it was not greed so much as opportunity that caused civil wars, though the underlying model and rationale remained much the same. That there was a debate, and considerable criticism, was implied in a contradiction within the World Bank report, 'Breaking the Conflict Trap' – one that the evaluators of Deaton et al. (2006) did not pick up on. For, on the one hand, there is an intriguing sentence in the report that reads: 'While the prevalence of natural resource secessions suggests that greed cannot be entirely discounted, it does not appear to be the powerful force behind rebellion that economic theorists have assumed' (p.64).[3] On the other hand, the book is built on precisely the econometric model that propounded the greed thesis so clearly in the first place.

The second example concerns civil war recurrence. Here we briefly summarise Suhrke and Samset's article (2007, p.195) on the way that academic findings can be 'converted into conventional wisdom and effectively inserted into the policy debate, even though the findings themselves are unstable'. Collier and Hoeffler (2002, p.17) found that 'shortly after a conflict, on average, countries face a 50 percent risk of renewed conflict during the next five years'. In World Bank (2003d, p.83) this idea reappeared as: 'The typical country reaching the end of a civil war faces around a 44 percent risk of returning to conflict within five years'. Groups within the UN that wanted a stronger commitment to peace building and then to the setting up of the UN Peacebuilding Commission seized on this claim and repeatedly stated that half or nearly half of countries emerging from civil war returned to war within the first five years of peacetime. The claim was equally useful to other interests favouring a surge in post-conflict aid, often supported by packages of far-reaching post-conflict economic reforms. The Commission for Africa (2005), chaired by Tony Blair, was among others that repeated the phrase and, as the claim became conventional wisdom, it lost any awkward caveats of probability and appeared as factual certainty. Many academics also recycled the claim in one form or another.

Suhrke and Samset show how the very meaning of the phrase is unclear and might be interpreted in different ways. They also show how, accepting the most obvious interpretation (that the claim refers to the risk that a country that has had a war has another civil war within five years after the end of the first one), the data in fact show a much lower statistical risk, i.e. something like 26 per cent rather than 44 or 50 per cent. In more recent work, Collier and Hoeffler in one paper find a 20–23 per cent risk of recidivism among post-civil war countries in the first four years; but then stretching the period to ten years they find, in another, a roughly 34 per cent risk and in another paper a roughly 40 per cent risk. More importantly, there is never any careful discussion of methodology or changes in datasets used or methods applied. As Surhke and Samset conclude (2007, p.200):

if three out of four post-civil war countries are likely to remain peaceful during the first five years, and nearly two out of three during the first decade, it would seem to warrant less intrusive and more targeted – although still distinctive – international engagement.

As a small aside, a source in the World Bank told one of the authors of this chapter recently, when asked about Deaton et al. (2006), 'yeah, this is interesting but we just don't have time to read or think about things like that'. The same source, a well-trained economist, repeated the 50 per cent civil war recidivism claim as unquestioned.

Again, the particular success in converting research findings into conventional wisdom in the policy and even academic world owes a great deal to the *appearance* of rigorous social science objectivity when this produces easily digestible findings or storylines and when these are convenient for those interests driving particular reforms or resource-allocation agendas (see also Chapter 3). This claim to science is important. The sharpest statement, in this context, came in a keynote speech that Collier (2006) gave to a conference on the role of the private sector in post-conflict reconstruction in Berlin. He began:

The post-conflict field is relatively new and as a consequence it is full of crap. Science is only just catching up and policy makers have meanwhile persuaded themselves that what they want to believe is true.

So there is a lot of nice sounding waffly crap, which in other fields of policy has been driven out by hard science, but is still saturating this topic. And this topic is bloody important. So we have got to drive all the crap out. And that will be painful. You have to unlearn a lot of what you think you know.

There is much truth here, but it should apply equally to self-proclamations of scientific rigour.

What did Deaton et al. (2006) have to say about the Bank's work in this field? First, at a general level, the final report argues that Bank researchers 'have taken the lead in working on topics, such as civil wars, aid effectiveness, doctor and teacher absenteeism, or pollution in developing countries that other researchers have unduly neglected' (p.37). The report, drawing on the background paper by Daron Acemoglu, suggests that work on the causes and consequences of civil war 'may be the most important question for development in sub-Saharan Africa, and perhaps in other parts of the world' (p.64). Second, however, the final report notes that Acemoglu also criticised the work for its lack of an appropriate conceptual and empirical framework. As a result, the regression results cannot be used to support the conclusions they ostensibly reach. Thus, as the final report sums it up, 'an important and promising topic was marred by poor execution' (p.64).

Acemoglu's (2006) background report looks at the underlying work by Collier that set up the larger book projects (*Understanding Civil Wars*, vols 1 and 2 and *Breaking the Conflict Trap*) and, in particular, at the well-known greed and grievance paper. Acemoglu observes that this paper draws on the crime and punishment literature to divide potential factors into grievance and opportunity factors. Answering the questions: Was the methodology appropriate and well executed? Was it innovative? Acemoglu answers (p.9):

No. The theoretical framework is rather simple and does not build on anything that has been done in the past 20–25 years. The econometric framework is very deficient. It has a number of serious conceptual and methodological problems. First of all, at the end the regression is one of endogenous variables on endogenous variables. But all of the results are interpreted as causal effects. The main regression models pool data across different periods, but run simple OLS regressions without including time dummies, country dummies or adjusting the standard errors for the fact that there are multiple observations from the same country without any type of fixed or random country effects.

Asked if the Bank's work in this field reflects awareness of existing knowledge from other research and whether it reflects good understanding of the countries in question, Acemoglu ignores the question about country understanding and interprets the other bit of the question in terms of econometric techniques. Thus, he argues that Collier's work is not at the frontier of econometrics or applied research; in particular, it does not draw on the work of econometricians on endogeneity problems (reciprocal influence between variables).

Asked if the data are reliable Acemoglu says he thinks the dataset on civil wars is reliable and very useful. This is rather cavalier, especially given the misgivings of one of the contributors to Bank research, Sambanis, about the sensitivity of civil war datasets to minor changes in coding rules, not to mention the arguments made by some that there are serious deficiencies, when trying to understand global conflict trends, in relying exclusively on datasets on civil wars.[4] Acemoglu argues that the regressions do not test any well-specified hypothesis and the correlations that are interpreted as causal effects are nothing more than correlations. Indeed, twisting the knife a little more, he argues that Collier's papers might be published in an international relations journal, but would not be published in any second- or third-tier economics journal. So the *Understanding Civil War* books would have worked better if they had not used this econometric model.

So much for hard science. But it is one thing for an economist to be hoist on the petard of his own discipline and arguments about economic methodology. It is another altogether to develop a richer critique or a more useful way of responding to the critiques. It is highly unlikely that Acemoglu's criticisms will have any effect. And it is disappointing that his evaluation was so extraordinarily restricted in scope. It was narrowly econometric in its interest, failed to interrogate even the reliability of the data in the models, and showed no interest whatsoever in the possibility that understanding civil wars, if that is what they are, in developing countries might warrant research methods that at the very least combine econometrics and economic theory with other insights and methods. Therefore, this evaluation itself managed to miss a great deal of work that has been done in recent years, showing itself unable properly to address questions about whether the Bank's work reflected, let alone advanced upon, existing knowledge.[5] The evaluation merely reflects back the narcissistic gaze of Bank research in this field during the period under review in Deaton et al. (2006).

And so much for the Deaton et al. evaluation. Research (and policy thinking and operational decisions) within the World Bank on issues linked to violent conflict is far more complex than is captured by the terrain covered in the evaluation. That there are those in the Bank who take an interest in recent research from different disciplinary perspectives is clear from the ongoing work of the team producing the Bank's 'World Development Report 2011' (going to print as this chapter is written), on conflict, security and development. That there is often a more complex interplay of interests, ideas and evidence is also true from a closer look at the case of Afghanistan, to which the chapter now turns.

9.3   AFGHANISTAN

The United States alone is spending over 800 million dollars a year on counter-narcotics. We have gotten nothing out of it, nothing … It is the most wasteful and ineffective programme I have seen in 40 years in and out of the government.

Ambassador Richard Holbrooke
Brussels Forum conference, March 2009

If there was ever a case in which external intervention – drawing on grandiose ideas of creating, in poor and war-affected countries, societies resembling fantasy images of Western market democracies, through military intervention, democracy promotion and state-building efforts (Cramer 2006 and Stewart 2009) – might have been one of the causal factors in conflict recidivism, it would be Afghanistan. This section focuses on policy narratives there and on interventions related to the opium economy. We discuss how the policy processes of international agencies have engaged with, shaped and selectively used research, to justify particular 'state building' and counter-narcotics interventions. This section identifies a tendency among some actors to neglect sophisticated, empirical research that does not support institutional and political interests. Indeed, this has also afflicted detailed and innovative World Bank research, which has often been used selectively or ignored by other actors when its findings had inconvenient implications for them. As with the more global claims discussed in Section 9.1, interventions in Afghanistan have often been accompanied by smothering reality in factoids and misleading clichés – for example about greedy rebels. The discussion of Afghanistan highlights the tendency for policy-based evidence to trump evidence-based policy. This discussion also shows how sweeping claims apparently based on scientific method can mesh with both institutional imperatives and specific interests when applied to particular policy contexts, such as the Taliban and narcotics in Afghanistan.

To understand better the policy discourse–research nexus around poppy, it is first necessary to identify some of the wider political and institutional influences on knowledge creation and use in Afghanistan. Reliable, national-level data have always been scarce there. The pre-war Afghan state was centralised but weak, and its influence in the countryside often extended little beyond the government compound. Its limited outreach meant that rural society was never made legible through cadastral surveys, census making and so forth. To a large extent, the rural economy remained statistically unknown.[6] This was compounded by the war-induced crisis of the state, followed by its collapse in the 1990s and the flight of the Afghan intelligentsia to the west or to neighbouring countries. Furthermore, over the last 30 years, Afghanistan virtually fell off the research map; the corpus of research on the country, up until 2002, was extremely limited, even when compared to other environments affected by, or emerging from, conflict. Apart from problems of security, access and the lack of hard data, researchers grappled with the analytical challenge of researching the highly informalised and often invisible processes and institutions that evolved during wartime. To evade the enumerators and to remain outside the record books and archives has been an age-old strategy of Afghan peasants and local elites. Furthermore, there were no large multilateral or bilateral development donors operational in Afghanistan during the war years, with the World Bank, for instance, keeping a watching brief from neighbouring Pakistan. So, following the Bonn agreement of December 2001, when government officials and aid bureaucrats established their line ministries and new offices in Kabul, they had very little hard data or research to go on. A joint UN–World Bank needs assessment in 2002 was conducted largely by foreign consultants based in Islamabad and, to a great extent, new policies and programmes for the country were developed in an informational vacuum.

The situation improved steadily after 2002, reflecting investments in building up the institutions and capacities of the Afghan state, and the demands of aid agencies, the military and diplomats for more accurate, detailed and timely data about the country and its people. Afghan technocrats, such as Ashraf Ghani, an ex-World Bank official and the minister of finance between 2002 and 2004, were instrumental in leading efforts to centralise and strengthen state functions, including improved data collection and analysis. A series of government planning documents and needs assessments was developed, including the National Development Framework in 2002, 'Securing Afghanistan's Future' in 2004, the Interim Afghanistan National Development Strategy (I-ANDS) in 2006 and the Afghanistan National Development Strategy (ANDS) in 2008, which the government also used as its Poverty Reduction Strategy Paper (PRSP). International agencies also made a significant investment in surveys,[7] data collection and policy-relevant research. UNDP produced two Afghan Human Development Reports, in 2004 and 2008, the World Bank and the IMF wrote a series of overview and thematic studies and individual NGOs like CARE International invested heavily in research and advocacy, as did NGO coordination bodies such as the Agency Coordination Body for Afghan Relief (ACBAR) and NGO alliances such as the Afghan Civil Society Forum (ACSF). Within this increasingly crowded field there are also specialist research bodies, the most significant being the Afghan Research and Evaluation Unit (AREU), as well as international and Afghan consultancy firms, including Cooperation for Peace and Unity (CPAU) and the Afghan Analysts Network. As noted by Suhrke et al. (2008, p.7), a market has emerged for research, monitoring and evaluation. Beyond the development industry, there are a plethora of other bodies and institutions from the military and diplomatic communities, who conduct their own analyses and research (openly or covertly) to guide their interventions and programmes. For example, the US military from 2007 started employing anthropologists – the so-called human terrain teams – to ensure that their forces were more sensitive to, and better able to engage with, local culture and politics. Finally, in contrast to its orphaned status during the war years, Afghanistan became a favoured site for international researchers, leading to a rash of research projects and publications on subjects to do with post-conflict peace building, state building, reconstruction, security sector reform, aid programming, etc.

Consequently, a typical Kabul-based aid official can today draw upon a wealth of published and grey information and data when compared, for example, to an NGO worker living there in the 1990s. But to what extent are the data and analysis accurate, representative and reliable? Do they meet the criteria of 'hard science'? Or are they mostly 'waffly crap'? To what extent, drawing upon Alex de Waal's (1997) critique of humanitarianism, is there a kind of Gresham's Law operating in the field of research and analysis, whereby the 'debased' research is disseminated and recycled and undermines the credibility of 'authentic' research? Whilst these questions deserve a more thorough treatment than can be offered here, a number of points are highlighted.

First, data collection and analysis are for the most part funded by donors and, consequently, shaped by their (often short-term) interests and policy agendas, as explored further in the next section. For example, public opinion polls on a range of issues, from the popularity of the government to Afghan attitudes towards the United States, are often of very dubious credibility. Second, the data, if not actually collected by expatriates, are usually analysed and written up by them, mostly in English. In the development sector, research and analysis are dominated by expatriates or English-speaking émigré Afghans. Most of the key policy documents, including 'Securing Afghanistan's Future', I-ANDS and ANDS, were produced by foreign consultants.[8]

A foreign-funded, expatriate-dominated research community reinforces the wider problem of a dual public sector, in which talent and capacities – including academics at Kabul University and statisticians in government departments – are actively sucked out of the state sector into better-paying positions with think tanks, consultancy firms, NGOs and donor agencies. As Suhrke et al. note (2008, p.1), there has been limited investment in building Afghan capacities for independent research, and a 'demand for immediate policy-relevant knowledge to serve reconstruction and statebuilding initially led to much short-term importation of skills'. The study continues, the 'general impression is of a set of highly unequal (some would say colonial) relationships that inhibit the growth of an independent Afghan research community'. In the long term this hinders institutional learning and the building up of deep knowledge, particularly given the short contracts and rapid turnover of many expatriates. This problem is accentuated by the fragmented, competitive nature of the international effort in Afghanistan, leading to information hoarding and poor communication. Finally, dependence on expatriates has accentuated the restrictions that growing insecurity have placed on serious fieldwork. Expatriates have increasingly retreated into their compounds, and DfID personnel, for instance, must travel with close protection teams in Kabul and, in the south, cannot venture beyond their militarised bases and compounds.

Therefore, a low starting base, domestic capacity deficits and an unruly foreign-dominated institutional environment have all contributed to the uneven quality of research and analysis in Afghanistan. But technical and institutional weaknesses only tell part of the story. To understand how and why data are generated, analysed and used to reinforce particular policy discourses and interventions, attention must turn to an analysis of the political economy of war and intervention in Afghanistan.

International geopolitical, particularly US, interests, have shaped the intervention environment and in turn influence the kind of research that is encouraged, listened to and used to reinforce and legitimise particular policy narratives. State building is occurring in the context of an ongoing war, with foreign troops involved in active combat operations. Western domestic politics constantly intrudes upon (and frequently trumps) intervention strategies supposedly based on Afghan priorities and concerns. The need to sell a success story back home may influence which research is funded and how seriously its findings are taken. Research and policy advice that tells a story of complexity, that generates findings that are difficult to operationalise, and that identifies less than optimal choices will be quietly left to one side. Whilst it is always the case that high politics impinges upon the positions and choices of aid organisations and the funding environment for research, it is clear that room for manoeuvre in such intensified political engagements is more limited and the struggles for legitimacy more intense. In the case of the UK government, the Cabinet Office (along with the Foreign and Commonwealth Office and the Ministry of Defence) takes a far more active interest in the work of DfID than would be the case for other less strategic countries. Some interpret this positively, as being part of a necessary thrust towards 'joined-up' policy, complemented by 'joined-up' thinking; but conversely there may be strong overt or covert pressures for research to be 'integrated' or made 'coherent' with a particular government position or set of priorities. It is not coincidental that much recent research funding has been channelled towards topics related to counter-insurgency, Islamic radicalisation and the role of development in winning hearts and minds. This is not to argue that there is one hegemonic discourse or that development agencies and researchers are simply the handmaidens of govern-mentality – there are clearly major differences within and between western countries involved in Afghanistan, and these divisions are becoming more apparent, particularly as the death toll of foreign troops and Afghan civilians has mounted. And debates within troop-providing countries, such as Canada, the Netherlands, Germany and the United Kingdom, have become more heated about the purposes and costs of intervention.

Besides these geopolitical interests, the research–policy nexus is also influenced by the funding environment and the nature of aid markets. Aid flows to Afghanistan amount to more than half of GDP. The funding environment is extremely complex, involving multiple donors and delivery mechanisms. Roughly two-thirds of aid money is delivered off-budget, circumventing the Afghan state, and involves complex subcontracting arrangements linking public, commercial and not-for-profit actors. For instance, USAID funding for school reconstruction can involve up to eight layers of contractors, including for-profit organisations such as Creative Associates or DAI, private security companies like Dyncorp, as well as several international and Afghan NGOs. As in Iraq, there has been a massive (and poorly regulated) transfer of funds from the public to the private sector. So, Afghanistan is characterised by an extremely unregulated and unruly aid market. As Cooley and Ron have noted elsewhere (2002), given the way aid markets are structured, rent-seeking, information-hoarding and lack of coordination are rationally induced forms of behaviour for aid organisations. Institutional interests, notably competition for profile and market share, are significant factors in influencing how data are used and interpreted.

9.4 THE OPIUM INDUSTRY

The opium industry is a highly politicised and contested arena generating particular research and policy debates and, unsurprisingly, characterised by a high 'factoid quotient'. Focus here is on three interrelated policy narratives: first, that opium is driving the neo-Taliban insurgency; second, that opium cultivation is no longer connected to the problem of rural poverty; third, that reductions in opium cultivation are linked to successful counter-narcotics measures. These narratives are underpinned by problematic assumptions and assertions, which are bolstered through the selective deployment of research findings to legitimise particular interventions. In spite of high-quality research in Afghanistan that counters such assertions,[9] these policy narratives have remained surprisingly resilient, constituting a good example of the foregrounding of policy-based evidence. After providing some background on the drugs industry in Afghanistan, we analyse the policy debates and ask what factors explain the emergence and persistence of these narratives.

The evolution of the drug economy during the war years has been dealt with elsewhere (Rubin 2000, Goodhand 2004 and 2005 and McDonald 2007). Afghanistan's emergence as the global leader in opium production was based upon a triple comparative advantage of favourable physical, political and economic conditions: a cultivation environment that produces opium poppies with a high morphine content; chronic insecurity and institutional weakness, which have meant inadequate or non-existent forms of regulation; and poor infrastructure and rural poverty that constrain the development of alternative licit livelihoods. Over the years, as Goodhand shows (2008), Afghans have developed the know-how, expertise and market connections to build upon these comparative advantages to survive, accumulate and wage war.

For a brief period, Afghanistan lost its position as the primary producer of opium, after the Taliban ban for the growing season of 2000/01. However, following US-led military intervention in October 2001 and the apparent collapse of the Taliban, there was a massive increase in the volume and geographic spread of poppy cultivation in Afghanistan.[10] By 2005 poppy cultivation had spread to all 34 provinces, including regions with no previous tradition or expertise in poppy cultivation. However, from 2006, cultivation has become more concentrated in the traditional poppy-growing (and insurgency-affected) areas of the south, as the number of 'poppy-free' provinces in the north and centre grew. Total production and hectarage also began to show a slight decline from 2007/08, with the 2009 UNODC report suggesting a 22 per cent decrease in cultivation and a 10 per cent decrease in production.

The vast bulk of value added in the drug industry is generated outside Afghanistan, as Byrd and Jonglez show (2006, p.130). In 2005/06 the total export value of opiates produced in Afghanistan equalled about 38 per cent of non-drug GDP, down from 47 per cent of the previous year due to growth of the non-drug economy. Byrd and Jonglez report growing market integration, with Helmand and Kandahar becoming centres of gravity that influence prices in other markets. As Giustozzi argues (2007a, p.79), for political entrepreneurs, the drug economy is a vehicle for accumulating power. Shaw (2006) charts the emergence of a complex system of patronage, which provides state protection to criminal trafficking.[11]

In October 2002, the Afghan Government established the Counter Narcotics Directorate (CND), which reported to the National

Security Council. CND was responsible for counter-narcotics (CN) strategy development and coordination. It was supported by the UK government, the lead nation for counter-narcotics, one of five pillars in the Security Sector Reform (SSR) strategy.[12] Over time there has been a broadening of the CN agenda, with a greater focus on institution building and 'mainstreaming' CN so that all areas of intervention are drug sensitive. Also US involvement in CN policies as a funder and instigator has increased, with an overall thrust to push for a more coercive and eradication-led strategy.

Therefore, the opium economy has moved from the periphery to the centre of policy debates on state building, counter-insurgency and stabilisation. Three interconnected policy narratives are symptomatic of this shift. First, opium revenues provide the tax base for the insurgency; there appears to be a growing geographical correlation between the intensity of poppy cultivation and the intensity of insurgency. According to UNODC, about 98 per cent of Afghanistan's 7,700 tonne opium yield in 2008 came from regions affected by Taliban insurgency. Poppy cultivation, it seems, has become an index of insecurity. Just as the Taliban taxed the opium trade in the 1990s, insurgent groups are reportedly imposing transit and protection fees in the range of 15 to 18 per cent on both drugs and precursor chemicals (Jalali, Oakley and Hunter 2006, p.2). There has reportedly been a shift from opportunistic taxation towards a growing nexus in the south between the insurgency and the drugs trade. The study by Gretchen Peters (2009) promotes such a policy narrative, arguing that insurgents act more like mafiosi than mujahideen and are motivated more by profit than religion or ideology (pp.5–6). UNODC (2008) estimated that the Taliban derived US$400 million annually from taxation of the drug economy. The neo-Taliban is characterised by some commentators as a 'narco-insurgency', and coercive eradication is justified, because removing poppy will undermine the insurgency. This reflects a broader intellectual climate, as well as serving particular functions within Afghanistan. It resonates with rebel-centric understandings of civil wars and a focus on 'lootable resources' in isolation from broader political and social contexts. The Taliban according to this narrative mobilise around an anti-government Islamist discourse to mask their underlying 'greedy' motivations.

A second policy narrative is the assertion that there is no causal linkage between poverty and poppy cultivation. Antonio de Costa, head of UNODC, has made this point repeatedly, arguing that there is no linkage between where poppy is grown and the highest levels of poverty. The central highlands and parts of the north for example, though historically regions with high levels of chronic poverty, are currently either poppy-free or have achieved low levels of cultivation. This can be contrasted with the primary poppy-producing areas of the south, where there is more irrigated land, and larger land holdings – a picture reinforced by UN poverty assessments, which tend to show lower levels of poverty in these areas compared to many of the poppy-free provinces. Again, this policy narrative justifies eradication-led interventions, and is based on a similar model of utility-maximising peasants, driven by the unassailable profitability of poppy compared to other crops.

Third, as more provinces in the north and centre became poppy-free, it has been increasingly asserted that *successful CN efforts have led to widespread reductions in poppy cultivation.* The sticks and carrots of CN policies have raised the risks and costs of poppy cultivation, whilst increasing the incentives to grow alternative licit crops. A range of instruments, including eradication, interdiction, provision of alternative livelihoods, good-performance initiatives, the removal of uncooperative provincial governors, and so forth, have changed the costs and benefits of poppy production and trafficking. This policy narrative suggests that where the full gamut of CN policies have been implemented, they have achieved their goals, justifying a policy of pressing ahead with 'more of the same'.

Yet there is a growing body of high-quality research on the opium industry in Afghanistan which does not support, and largely contradicts, these three policy narratives. First, the evidence base on the drugs–insurgency linkage is extremely thin and circumstantial. Big claims are based on evidence that is far from robust. The same anecdotes and so-called intelligence are frequently cited and recycled until they become part of received wisdom (these are the micro-level, country-specific analogues of the 50 per cent civil war recidivism claim discussed above). Historically, we know that drugs were never a significant part of the Taliban's war chest and, whilst not denying that today's taxation of the drugs economy is an important source of funding, this is not the same as arguing that drugs are driving the insurgency – this is to confuse correlation with causality. A recent US Senate Committee Report, based on evidence provided by the CIA and DIA (Defense Intelligence Agency), calculated that the amount of drug money flowing to the Taliban was some US$70 million, much less than previously estimated. Furthermore, there was no evidence of a significant amount going to Al Qaeda. Giustozzi

(2007b) similarly argues that the importance of drugs money to the Taliban has been overstated; far more important has been external funding from state and non-state actors in Pakistan and the Gulf states. The evidence suggests that governmental actors are far more important players in the drugs economy than the Taliban (Shaw 2006). Furthermore, the most direct connection between drugs and conflict is the destabilising impact of wrong-headed government eradication policies. The selective and transparently corrupt implementation of these policies has undermined the legitimacy of the state and, in turn, provided the Taliban with the opportunity to stand as the protectors of the peasantry. Therefore, the Taliban–drugs connection is primarily a story of *politics* rather than *economics*. This rebel-centric focus on drugs and the Taliban serves a number of functions – not least in shifting the focus away from links between actors within the Afghan state and the drugs industry.

Second, the denial of a poverty–poppy cultivation linkage is equally problematic. It draws on a narrowly economic model of Afghan poppy cultivators; essentially the calculation about whether to grow or not boils down to one of profitability – poppies are grown because the profit margins are so great in comparison to licit crops. This ignores research that shows the complex multifunctional role that poppy plays in the livelihood strategies of Afghan farmers – the decision to grow, how much, which varieties and when are influenced by a range of variables, including access to land, water, labour and credit, prices of other crops, the transport and marketing infrastructure, and so on. Most importantly, the decision to grow or not is never made on a purely economic cost–benefit analysis. It is based upon complex *political* negotiations involving state and non-state actors, influenced by the wider power relations and the security environment, whose shifting determinants, content and meanings are not reducible to, nor to be taken as exogenous constraints on, optimising farmers. Far from being largely about profit, the most important factor is the need to spread risk (economic and political), with poppy being essentially a low-risk crop in a high-risk environment. A simplistic model of profit-maximising farmers legitimises an eradication-led strategy, but it is certainly not a case of evidence-based policy. Such sweeping generalisations about the poppy–poverty linkage are often based on aggregate figures of questionable reliability. They ignore the extreme variability of conditions between and within districts in Afghanistan. As Mansfield argues (2006), there is a need for more disaggregated analysis. Household surveys show that there are pockets of extreme poverty in Helmand just as there are in Hazarjat. Also, whilst it is true that landownership patterns are different in the south and there are more large landowners in Helmand, sharecroppers and landless labourers depend on the poppy harvest. At the farm-gate level at least, it is nonsense to argue that 'greed' is driving the opium economy. Furthermore, longitudinal analysis in Nangahar suggests that poppy eradication efforts perversely consolidate the link between poppy and poverty by pushing people further into debt, due to the loss of labour days, the selling of assets and subsequent migration to Pakistan. In 2004/05, this led to a rebound effect the next season. And it has played a role in pushing the peasantry closer to the Taliban, by increasing their grievances against government.

Third, the policy narrative that reduction in poppy cultivation in large swathes of the country is related to effective CN measures has been questioned, most convincingly in an AREU paper by Mansfield and Pain (2008) entitled the 'Failure of Success'. They argue that shifts in cultivation patterns have less to do with the (dis)incentives created by CN policies than changes in terms of trade, the security environment and local governance. For instance Mansfield (2007), comparing Baharak and Jurm districts in Badakshan, shows that in 2007 changed livestock and wheat prices, combined with higher labour rates and improved security and governance in Baharak, account for the decline in cultivation there when compared to Jurm. Mansfield and Pain question the sustainability of the decline in poppy cultivation, which has been primarily due to increased wheat prices, combined with a decline in farm-gate poppy prices. For the first time in decades, in certain parts of the country it is more profitable to cultivate wheat. However, shifts in terms of trade are only part of the story; farmers continued to grow poppy in insurgency-affected areas even though other crops appeared to be more profitable. They did so because the risks associated with getting licit crops to market were too high, due to growing insecurity and proliferating road blocks. Since opium was purchased by traders at the farm gate, poppy farmers were not exposed to such risks. Finally, it seems unlikely that the current favourable terms of trade for wheat will continue and more likely that opium prices will recover. CN policies in themselves do not address the underlying factors related to market conditions, governance and security. Significant declines in poppy cultivation, rather than being a once-and-for-all measure, must be understood as being a part of the bargaining between the central state and peripheral elites. In Nangarhar and Balkh, for instance, provincial governors have cleverly exploited their success in poppy elimination or reduction to extract resources and buy greater political autonomy from the centre. They, in turn, have negotiated with, bought off or coerced district-level elites to enforce opium bans. It is also important to note that some of the so-called 'opium-free provinces' remain important transit routes for opiates, with provincial leaders benefiting from the revenues this creates.

Given that there is a large body of research questioning these policy myths, why have they proved so resilient? One answer may be the failure of researchers to communicate findings to policymakers in a convincing way – the research may be better at showing the complexities and nuances of the drugs industry than at providing compelling alternative policy narratives. However, policymakers are dismissive and deliberately neglectful of this body of research and its implications for action, ignoring research that diverges from their world view and creates dissonance. That there is no magic bullet – decreasing Afghanistan's reliance on poppy will take decades and involves complex dilemmas and a mixture of context-specific interventions – is not a prescription that most policymakers want to hear, cf. Paris and Sisk (2008). The data and research are melded to meet the needs of the end user – a case of policy-based evidence, in which there are strong political and institutional pressures to implement policies that have little to do with the realities in Afghanistan. Interestingly, the Senlis Council, which has persistently advocated a policy of legalisation, draws upon the same evidence to argue for a very different story. Both analyses – from those arguing for prohibition and those who advocate legalisation – are based on a policy agenda that largely treats Afghanistan as a blank slate. Both offer magic-bullet solutions and create an evidence base to back up their prescriptions. The Bush administration's push for aerial eradication and the Senlis Council's advocacy for legalisation neatly mirror one another, even though they are situated at opposite extremes of the policy spectrum.[13]

Mainstream policy narratives on drugs perform a range of functions for a diverse set of actors. We have identified some of these interests, including geo-political agendas relating to security and the war on terror, and institutional/economic interests with individuals and organisations generating rents around the war on drugs. Dyncorp, for example, earned over US$1 billion in poppy eradication contracts (Nathan 2010). Afghan politicians talk up the dangers of a 'narco-state' to ensure continued western funding, whilst local strongmen deploy drugs-eradication policies to take out competitors in the drugs industry. Like the drugs industry itself, the CN industry involves complex assemblages of actors and networks with differing sets of interests and agendas. Making policy in practice involves processes of negotiation, bargaining, brokerage and 'translation' – it frequently looks very different when it 'hits the ground'. Explanations for certain policy outcomes have less to do with 'high politics' than with prosaic questions related to competition for budgets and individual power battles. Also, for individual policymakers, operating in a context of complexity and unpredictability, clear policy narratives provide a reassuring sense of security.

In the field of development, identifying a problem is intimately linked, as Mosse argues (2005), to distilling a solution. Experts are trained to frame problems in technical terms and, for drugs specialists working in UNODC or the British Embassy, the process of making policy involves defining problems and rendering them technical. This necessarily requires simplification, making the problem visible, defining boundaries and screening out discordant information. Li (2008) shows how problems rendered technical are simultaneously rendered apparently non-political. To some extent, screening out the political in a highly politicised context is a necessary strategy in order to maintain a neutral space for research. Significantly, the World Bank has been extremely good at doing this and producing or funding some of the best technical research on the drugs economy (Buddenberg and Byrd 2006 and Byrd 2008, for example). And this was due in no small part to the individuals involved, who had deep knowledge of the context and were committed to high quality research and evidence-based policy.[14]

9.5   CONCLUSIONS

This chapter began by drawing attention to World Bank research and to Deaton et al. (2006). World Bank research also featured in our discussion of research, policy, and advocacy in Afghanistan, though the chapter has had a wider scope than just the Bank. Overall, in our examples, we have argued that there is a tension between evidence-based policy and policy-based evidence, that is, the privileging of certain empirical claims (and methods) at the expense of other research, driven by institutional dynamics, policy preferences, political interests and ideologies. One thing that emerges is that the World Bank is far from being the cartoon villain of the piece. Flagship World Bank research on conflict has in some respects led the way and encouraged broader debate; the research covered by Deaton et al. (2006) showed evidence of internal debates, which is itself healthy; and, since that research, the Bank's interests in and approach to conflict-affected countries has moved on. Further, in the particular case of Afghanistan and the opium economy, the Bank has produced some of the very best research that exists. Even though this has not necessarily translated neatly into policy reforms, the Bank's research did shape policy debates on drugs, and most importantly helped to shift the emphasis away from eradication-led strategies. Nonetheless, this chapter has made clear that the Bank – at the general level of research on violent conflict within the period under review in Deaton et al. (2006) – has fallen a long way short of reasonable expectations of what a 'knowledge bank' might be.

The relationship between the research community and donor agencies and policymakers (not to mention NGOs and others) is a complex one. We argue that it cannot be reduced either to the inabilities of researchers effectively to communicate their findings or to the constraints on the ability of policymakers to understand econometrics or weigh up competing explanations.[15] These may well often be relevant factors. There are other factors at play. These include the institutional pressures on policymakers,[16] a persuasive (at least until recently) discourse privileging economics, and in particular econometrics, as the exclusive source of rigorous and objective social science,[17] and coalitions of political (and material) interest and broad ideology.[18] They also include highly specific issues such as the role, for good or ill, of particular individuals and relationships. Together these factors often lead to policy-based evidence trumping efforts to build a foundation for policymaking from credible evidence. The weaknesses and gaps in evidence in conflict contexts undermine the scope for effective policymaking. But the problem, we have argued, goes beyond lack of evidence to the sorting, packaging and selling of evidence.

NOTES

1. To give two examples: first, Sambanis (2004) explores neatly the variations in different versions of a single database (the Correlates of War Project) over time and the way that these variations have substantive effects on the degree of significance and sign of correlation between the incidence of 'civil war' and each of a number of common independent variables such as democracy or level of GDP; second, Restrepo, Spagat and Vargas (2004) explain how trends and levels of conflict-related violence in Colombia vary between commonly used international datasets, such as the Uppsala Conflict Data Project and a

Colombia-specific dataset that trawled Spanish language sources as well as English language reporting.

2. There may also be strong inclinations – in high pressure conditions of uncertainty – to apply variants of the 'anchoring', availability, and stereotyping biases identified in the influential work of Tversky and Kahneman (1974).

3. This in a subsection of the report on whether or not greed is the key causal factor in civil wars, which makes no mention at all of Collier's contribution to the argument that it might be.

4. See Cramer (2006) and Østerud (2008) for example.

5. Among the many contributions to empirical and analytical understanding of the political economy of violent conflict in recent years are Gutiérrez Sanín (2003), Keen (2005), Heimer (1979), Richards (2004), Wood (2003), Besteman (1996), Weinstein (2006), Korf (2005), some of the contributions of the Crisis States Research Centre (www.crisistates.com) and Stewart (2008).

6. Notwithstanding the important study by Fry (1974) of the pre-war Afghan economy.

7. The most important of these surveys has been the Afghanistan national household survey (NRVA), which has allowed standard poverty analysis to be conducted.

8. Though it is important to note that where there was effective supervision by the Afghan leadership – as in the case of 'Securing Afghanistan's Future' – this was reflected in more grounded and higher-quality documentation.

9. See for example Byrd and Buddenberg (2006), Mansfield (2006) and Mansfield and Pain (2008).

10. The reasons behind this increase include: the Taliban prohibition which led to a tenfold increase in prices, whilst pushing the poor rural householder further into indebtedness; the initial laissez-faire approach of international forces towards the opium industry, because of the prioritisation of the war on terror; and policy interventions such as a poppy buy-out scheme, which compensated farmers who grew poppy, thereby encouraging them to do so.

11. For example, one former mujahideen commander, Din Muhammed Jurat, became a general in the Ministry of the Interior and is widely believed to be a major figure in organised crime (Rubin 2007).

12. A recent UK government Foreign Affairs Select Committee report argued that the United Kingdom had effectively been handed a 'poisoned chalice' as the lead nation for CN in 2001.

13. The absence of magic-bullet solutions and the need to avoid eradication-led strategies has been stressed in several World Bank publications, including Byrd and Ward (2004), Byrd (2008) and Ward et al. (2008).

14. It is perhaps not coincidental that World Bank staff have tended to stay longer in post than for most other agencies. The average time of senior Bank staff working in Afghanistan has been well over four years.

15. It is still frequently claimed that academics have problems in communicating their findings. While this is obviously often true, it ignores the possibility that their findings may be well communicated but simply irreducible to the neat sound bites and one-liners that officials think they need (e.g. to 'persuade their minister').

16. And also capacity constraints. The UK National Audit Office (2008, p.14) argues that capacity 'to use large amounts of development aid effectively may be limited in insecure environments'.

17. Lack of dialogue within the social sciences is another problem. A conference call on the methodological and ethical challenges of conducting research on violence in sub-Saharan Africa drew a substantial response from anthropologists and some others, but none at all from economists working on conflict/violence (see Cramer, Hammond and Pottier, forthcoming).

18. Stewart (2009, p.3) argues neatly that projecting a dystopian vision of Afghanistan, for example, is combined functionally with 'implausibly optimistic' responses – citing Gordon Brown's statement that in July 2009 '(t)here can only be one winner: democracy and a strong Afghan state' – and that the ideology of liberal peace building and state building is

> broad enough to include Scandinavian humanitarians and American special forces; general enough to be applied to Botswana as easily as to Afghanistan; sinuous and sophisticated enough to draw in policy makers; suggestive enough of crude moral imperatives to attract the *Daily Mail*; and almost too abstract to be defined or refuted.

10
The Washington Consensus and the China Anomaly

Dic Lo

10.1 CHINA AND WORLD BANK RESEARCH

World Bank research on China has been something like the Cheshire Cat from Alice in Wonderland.[1] From time to time, its head alone appears and grins benevolently upon the policy framework to be adopted. But there is little sign of a substantial body of analysis of any depth and, at other times, neither cat nor grin is to be seen at all.

This is unfortunate, not least as the position of China in the world economy and in economic analysis has become increasingly prominent, rapidly so in the wake of the global crisis. A coherent research approach would incorporate three important issues. First is to identify the sources and, equally, the nature of China's success. Second is to shed light on the causes and course of the current crisis and China's role within it. Third, across each of these issues, is to learn lessons for other developing countries from China's experience, both to respond to the crisis in the short term and to promote development in the longer term.

In view of the significance of these issues, it is regrettable, if unsurprising, that China comes and goes in Bank's research in line with the institution's advocacy needs. For China is troublesome for the Bank: as a case study, its record of success can only be fitted into the Bank's prognostications through distortion and oversight that stretch credibility beyond breaking point. Indeed China has attracted a huge research effort on the part of the mainstream policy establishments of the world, including the IMF and the Bank. But, as far as 'advocacy' is concerned, the heyday of highlighting the Chinese experience has long gone. This is especially notable in the so-called 'economics of transition', as promoted by the International Financial Institutions. China traditionally figured prominently in work on this emanating from the World Bank and the IMF. Since the late 1990s, however, China has become a nonentity in these institutions' systematic accounts of transition. This reflects a fundamental shift in the treatment of China in advocacy. For the approach adopted before the shift is one of selective interpretation of the Chinese experience to fit it into policy doctrines for transition – what might be termed the 'selection' approach. The approach after the shift, in contrast, is characterised by excluding China altogether when the institutions attempt to defend their (traditional) policy doctrines in the face of the awkwardness posed by the Chinese experience of transition. It is as if China no longer exists as a transition economy. This oversight might be dubbed the 'exclusion' approach.

What are the (advocacy) arguments into which China must fit or from which it must be excluded? The Washington institutions' policy doctrines with regard to systemic transition have been a manifestation of the broader canon for development known as the Washington Consensus – hence Stiglitz's reference (1999b) to the 'Washington Consensus doctrines of transition'.[2] Yet, policies in practice have been more complex. They have not always strictly adhered to the Washington Consensus, especially when Stiglitz himself sought to influence World Bank ideas by injecting notions of pervasive market failures (around the post-Washington Consensus). Nevertheless, as far as the treatment of China is concerned, the exclusion approach has prevailed over the last decade. Since the late 1990s, the enormous amount of research on China conducted by the Washington institutions is almost entirely composed of piecemeal analyses on specific issues, with little reference to its overall experience of economic transition.

This is also characteristic to some degree of the way in which China features in the Deaton evaluation process (see Section 2.3 for more details on the Deaton Report). There is little sense in the report of the striking significance of China as a model of development and transition nor of its impending significance for (understanding) the world economy. Nonetheless, despite overall support for World Bank research, considerable criticism is directed towards the way in which the Chinese experience has been treated. For example, Acemoglu (2006), in his evaluation of the World Bank report on privatisation in China, while sharing its exclusively microeconomics-based, one-sided affirmation of privatisation, still remarks: 'Again, there is too much of a tendency to jump to policy conclusions' (p.4). Lin (2006), in his evaluation of a range of World Bank research outputs on China's rural–agricultural reforms, was understandably dissatisfied with the piecemeal analyses, and concludes: 'I suggest that the World Bank have a more thorough evaluation of the social impacts of land allocations in China' (p.13). In his overview of the Deaton Report, Stiglitz highlights that it is undesirable, indeed unacceptable, that the World Bank has excluded China from its research on transition – but he adds little himself about the more general importance of the Chinese experience.[3]

This chapter is divided into five sections. The following section begins by showing that China's experience of transition does not conform to the policy doctrines of the World Bank, which are themselves questionable. The Bank misunderstands transition in general and, further, misapplies its misunderstanding to China itself. This account is then reinforced in Section 10.3 by demonstrating how well China has performed in relation to other transition and developing countries (where World Bank policies have prevailed over at least two lost decades for development). In addition, the context for China's success is highlighted in terms of the challenges posed by global developments around trade and finance over the last 30 years. Attention is focused on the special relationship, or 'symbiosis', between China and the United States, related to their trade and capital account imbalances. Section 10.4 demonstrates how far China departs from World Bank policies in practice and how inappropriate is the Bank's frame of analysis. This is done on the basis of a closer look at forms of enterprise ownership and control, recent developments in labour markets, and a brief but rapidly abandoned experiment in neo-liberal policies. The section illustrates how neither the paradigm of 'leave as much as possible to the market' nor that of 'rely on piecemeal correction of market and institutional imperfections' is able to capture the systemic functioning and requirements of Chinese development and policymaking. The concluding remarks tease out broader lessons that can be drawn from the Chinese experience (as opposed to using – or distorting – the Chinese experience to confirm lessons already predetermined).

10.2   THE TRANSITION ORTHODOXY IN FACE OF THE CHINESE PUZZLE

To what extent is the Chinese experience of economic transformation a conundrum for the mainstream doctrines of economic development and systemic change? The orthodoxy tends to emphasise market forces, while the Chinese economy has been characterised by the continuing presence of non-market influences. Indeed, do such doctrines have any purchase upon transformation or transition as systemic change, given the superficial dogma of relying upon the market as both means and goal of economic development?[4]

Attempts to interpret China in a way that is consistent with the so-called transition orthodoxy – i.e. the 'Washington Consensus doctrines of transition' – have coalesced around the following two propositions. The first proposition (Proposition 1) concerns *institutions*: China's reformed economic institutions have been a mix of market-conforming and market-supplanting elements; its developmental achievements have been ascribable to the conforming elements while the accumulated problems have been ascribable to the supplanting elements; and the problems have tended to outweigh the achievements as Chinese economic transformation proceeds from the allegedly easy and earlier pre-industrial phase to the difficult later post-industrial phase. The second proposition (Proposition 2) concerns *development*: different countries have entered transition at different levels of development and this largely explains the contrast between China's sustained rapid growth in its industrialising phase as opposed to the depression in countries of the former Soviet bloc in their post-industrial phase. So contrasting comparative performances are deemed to be largely unrelated to differences in strategies of systemic transformation.[5]

The main thrust of Proposition 1 is adherence to the principles of individualistic property rights. The so-called 'market-supplanting elements' refer to institutional arrangements that violate these principles: discrete government intervention in economic affairs (the state–business relationship), soft budget constraints (the finance–industry relationship) and rigid employment and compensation systems (the worker–enterprise relationship). The negation of these arrangements is necessary for justifying the orthodox policy prescriptions of mass privatisation and of subjecting ownership to market trading via liberalisation of domestic and international finance. It is asserted time and again that, should the market-supplanting elements continue, the future prospects for the Chinese economy are at best uncertain, but more likely to be crisis-prone. The only way to avoid this looming crisis is to 'complete the transition to the market', as speedily as possible.[6]

Proposition 1 does not fare well against the evidence. Early on, Martin Weitzman (1993, p.549) observed:

According to almost any version of standard mainstream property rights theory, what has been described as the 'East

European model' basically represents the correct approach to transformation, while what we are calling the 'Chinese model' should represent a far-out recipe for economic disaster … The central paradox is the enormous success of the Chinese model in practice, contrasted with the spluttering, tentative, comparatively unsuccessful experience with the East European model.

Almost ten years later, in reviewing the persistent contrast between 'East Asian transition economies' (China and Vietnam) and transition economies in Europe and the Commonwealth of Independent States (countries of the former Soviet bloc), Stanley Fischer (2001) makes a similar comment: 'Most indicators suggest that progress of structural reform in East Asia has been relatively modest, yet output performance has been far superior to even the best reformers in Europe and the CIS' (p.5). The Chinese experience indicates that the principles of individualistic property rights are neither necessary nor sufficient for generating sustained rapid economic growth or, indeed, for avoiding economic disaster.

Proposition 2 is thus needed for the transition orthodoxy. In its first systematic report on the economics of transition, the World Bank (1996, p.5) pondered:

Do differences in transition policies and outcomes reflect different reform strategies, or do they reflect primarily country-specific factors such as history, the level of development, or, just as important, the impact of political changes taking place at the same time?

Proposition 2 provides the answer. Its implied message is that the transformation experiences of China and countries of the former Soviet bloc are not essentially comparable and, insofar as there is a limited scope of comparability, this supports rather than undermines the transition orthodoxy. Moreover, once committed to the argument of incomparability, the World Bank (2002b) could exclude China in its second systematic report on the economics of transition. The IMF (2000) and the OECD (2005), meanwhile, explicitly charted the implications of the limited scope of comparability. This was done following Sachs and Woo (1994), who had argued early on that, unlike countries of the former Soviet bloc, China was just fortunate to be at a low level of industrialisation at the beginning of its reforms. It had been able to generate economic growth via labour transfer from the rural–agricultural sector to industry, whilst postponing the needed, unavoidably painful reforms.

What underpins each of the orthodox propositions is the belief that economic development is dictated by the principles and workings of the market and that performance naturally ebbs and flows with levels of development. But Stiglitz (1999b), during his brief stint as chief economist at the World Bank, sought to direct the mainstream away from these presuppositions. Regarding the economics of transition, he argued that China faced a task of economic transformation far *more* demanding than that faced by countries of the former Soviet bloc. This is because China's task encompassed both systemic reform and economic development, rather than systemic reform alone. In other words, for Stiglitz, China had performed extremely well despite, not because of, its lower level of development.

His judgement fares far better than the transition orthodoxy when set in the context of broader comparisons. For China's growth performance stands in sharp contrast, not only with countries of the former Soviet bloc, but also with most parts of the developing world. And the record of world development in the three decades since the late 1970s, i.e. during the era of neo-liberal globalisation, has been dismal. In any case, the initial conditions of China's economic transformation is not one of under-industrialisation. In 1980, industrial value-added accounted for an astonishingly high proportion of China's GDP, 44 per cent. This is lower than the Soviet Union in the same year (54 per cent), on a par with Brazil (44 per cent), but higher than South Korea (40 per cent) and India (24 per cent) (data from the World Bank's World Development Indicators database). Thus, despite starting with one of the highest industry-to-GDP ratios in the world, China has exceptionally been able both to sustain very rapid industrial growth throughout the reform era and to absorb labour transferred from the rural–agricultural sectors.

10.3 THE ASIA–EUROPE DIVIDE IN TRANSITION AND LATE DEVELOPMENT

Interestingly, in early 2001, a working paper emerged from the Bank's research department with the provocative title: 'The Lost Decades: Developing Countries' Stagnation in Spite of Policy Reform 1980–1998' (Easterly 2001b). The 'lost decades' refers to the era of globalisation and the Washington Consensus. Associating 'lost decades' with market reform was truly unprecedented in World Bank research (but Easterly was about to lose his job; see Chapter 1). Far more standard has been neglect of the uncomfortable conclusions that follow from the economic trends in the developing world over those decades, and the implicit questions these raise.

The data in Table 10.1 show a disappointing picture of economic stagnation in the developing world over the 1980s and 1990s. The average annual real growth rate of per capita income for all low- and middle-income economies put together is 1.3 per cent in the 1980s and 1.8 per cent in the 1990s. This pace of growth is at best sluggish, and it is also substantially slower than that of high-income economies. The promise of globalisation, that the working of the world market would promote the convergence of the income levels of developing countries towards the levels of advanced countries, did not materialise. It is therefore no exaggeration when the 1980s and 1990s are called the 'lost decades of development', especially when excluding China and, to a lesser extent, India.

Table 10.1   Average annual real growth rate of per capita GDP (per cent)

	1980–90	1990–2000	2000–07
China	8.8	9.3	9.0
India	3.6	4.2	6.0
USSR/Russia	1.3	−4.7	7.0
Low-income economies	2.2	1.2	3.9
Middle-income economies	1.2	2.2	4.8
Low- and middle-income economies	1.3	1.8	4.5
Countries of former Soviet bloc	1.2	−1.7	5.8
High-income economies	2.7	2.2	1.7

Source: World Bank, World Development Indicators database.

Note: Countries of former Soviet bloc = 'Low- and middle-income economies in Europe and Central Asia' in World Bank statistical classification.

The Asia–Europe divide in transition, i.e. the contrast between the transition experience of China and that of countries of the former Soviet bloc, is, further, indicative of development lost under globalisation. First, the divide represents the extremes of unevenness in late development worldwide. The growth performance of countries of the former Soviet bloc was especially catastrophic in the 1990s. Table 10.1 indicates how the average annual real growth rate of per capita income is −1.7 per cent for the bloc as a whole, and −4.7 per cent for Russia alone. This miserable performance was also associated with a serious negative impact on social development. Table 10.2 gives the relevant data of life expectancy at birth, a most important indicator of social development capturing the impact of nutrition, health care and work. Between 1990 and 2000, life expectancy in China increased by three years, while that in all low-income and middle-income economies increased by two years. In contrast, during this period, life expectancy in countries of the former Soviet bloc decreased by one year, while that in Russia alone decreased by four years.[7]

Table 10.2 Life expectancy at birth (years)

	1980	1990	2000	2007
China	66	68	71	73
India	56	60	62	65
USSR/Russia	67	69	65	68
Low-income economies	51	54	56	57
Middle-income economies	62	65	68	70
Low- and middle-income economies	60	63	65	67
Countries of former Soviet bloc	67	69	68	70
High-income economies	73	76	78	79

Source: World Bank, World Development Indicators database.

Note: Countries of former Soviet bloc = 'Low- and middle-income economies in Europe and Central Asia' in World Bank statistical classification.

Second, as can be seen from Table 10.3, the Asia–Europe divide in transition reflects the huge gap between the market-fundamentalist approach to systemic transformation and the realities of transition and development in practice. On the one hand, with their rapid 'structural reforms', the institutions of most East and Central European transition economies had by the late 1990s become indistinguishable, at least formally, from those of advanced capitalist economies. This contrasts with China, assigned a low indicator as 'reformers'. On the other hand, in 1999, after a decade of transition, the vast majority of countries of the former Soviet bloc had not recovered output to their initial levels. For Russia, output in 1999 was only 0.55 of its 1989 level, while China's was 2.52 times higher. In a sense, China had outperformed Russia almost five times over (a ratio of 2.52 to 0.55)!

Third, what of the post-2000 rebound in economic growth and social development across major regions of the developing world, including countries of the former Soviet bloc? For the years 2000–07, the average annual real growth rate of per capita income for all low- and middle-income economies reached 4.5 per cent. This was more than double that for high-income economies. For countries of the former Soviet bloc the rate increased to 5.8 per cent. Life expectancy in these countries increased by two years, on a par with all low- and middle-income economies. In Russia, it increased by three years. Are these indications that, finally, the promise of globalisation is being realised? Or, do these trends reflect no more than a recovery from the lost decades? It is too early to form a firm judgement on these questions. But the current recession, which has emanated from the advanced capitalist countries and engulfed the world economy as a whole since 2008, gives cause for pessimism.

Table 10.3   Transition and output change

	Real output ratio, 1999/1989	EBRD aggregate transition indicator, 1999
EU accession countries	0.95	3.3
Baltic countries	0.68	3.2
Other southeast Europe countries	0.77	2.5
CIS	0.53	2.3
Russia	0.55	2.5
China	2.52	2.1

Source: International Monetary Fund, World Economic Outlook, October 2000, ch.3.

Note: The European Bank for Reconstruction and Development (EBRD) transition indicators 'range from 1 to 4+, where 4+ indicates that the country's structural characteristics are comparable to those prevailing on average in the advanced economies, and 1 represents conditions before reform in a centrally planned economy with dominant state ownership of means of production ... the transition indicators are linearized by assigning a value of +0.3 to a "+" sign and a value of –0.3 to a "–" sign.' (IMF 2000, p.179)

Whatever the nature and profundity of the post-2000 rebound, and of the ongoing world recession, there is the singular importance of China. The relations between China and the United States loom large, and more so since the crisis struck and the recession bit. Indeed, what I call the 'China–USA economic symbiosis' has often been raised as an important driving force behind the post-2000 economic rebound as well as the subsequent recession. China has been seen successively as the driver of the world (and US) economy, as its weak point, and now as its potential saviour, with the position shifting to suit circumstances and political, economic and policy interests.

The 'China–USA symbiosis' takes the form of China exporting cheap manufactures to the United States, in exchange for the latter's government debt. This has allowed for demand for industrial inputs from the broader East Asian region and for commodities from the rest of the world. With fast productivity growth in Chinese industry, the symbiosis also lowers the cost of production for the world economy as a whole. All these have helped to underpin the post-2000 rebound. Yet, this symbiosis also has its intrinsic contradiction in the form of the so-called 'global imbalances' – the ballooning current-account surplus of China (together with Germany and Japan) and the corresponding deficits of the United States. The inability of the United States to raise its productive capacity to match its appetite for consumption forms the major factor in the financial crisis and the ensuing world recession.

This 'China–USA economic symbiosis' is not necessarily desirable for Chinese or world development, and its breakdown could pave the way for the formation of an alternative, more desirable world economic order. Further, the symbiosis and the 2000–07 rebound should be evaluated alongside two other concurrent world economic trends: the accumulation of foreign exchange reserves on an unprecedented scale in developing countries, and the serious deterioration of the terms of trade against manufacturing-oriented developing countries. China has borne the brunt of both of these trends.

The accumulation of official reserves is a response to the vulnerability to capital flight in the world economy, an insurance policy against the lessons learnt by developing countries from the 1997–98 East Asian financial crisis (and a consequence of enforced liberalisation of capital controls under Washington Consensus policies). As shown in Figure 10.1, the official holding of foreign exchange reserves by developing countries, expressed as a ratio to the monthly average of import values, has far exceeded that of developed countries. Further, the gap between the two country groups has widened substantially in recent years. Between 2000 and 2007, the average ratio of reserves to imports for all developing countries increased from 9.5 months to 14.8 months, whereas that for all developed countries basically stayed at the level of two months. For China, it increased from 8.8 months to 18.9 months. Given the very low interest yield on official reserves, their accumulation implies a massive transfer of seigniorage from the developing world to the advanced countries that issue reserve currencies, primarily the United States.[8]

The trend of deteriorating terms of trade against manufacturing-oriented developing countries is indicated in Figure 10.2. Between 1998 and 2007, the measure for China fell by almost 30 per cent, while that for the East Asian newly industrialising economies (Hong

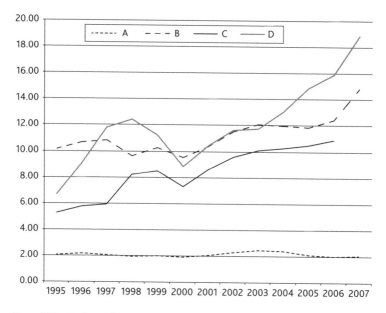

Figure 10.1   Foreign exchange reserves as ratios of average values of monthly imports.

Sources: International Monetary Fund, COFER 2007, and World Economic Outlook, April 2007; Asian Development Bank databank.

Notes: Data are end-of-year foreign exchange reserves of central bank divided by the monthly average import value of the past 12 months. A = developed countries ('industrial countries' for foreign exchange holding and 'advanced countries' for imports in the IMF categorization); B = developing countries; C = East Asian economies (Mainland China, Hong Kong, Taiwan, South Korea, Singapore, Malaysia, Thailand, Indonesia and the Philippines); D = China (Mainland China, not including Hong Kong, Macau and Taiwan).

Kong, Singapore, South Korea and Taiwan) fell by almost 20 per cent. These figures stand in contrast to the almost unchanged and persistently favourable position of advanced countries, and the almost 30 per cent gain of all developing countries combined. Within the literature, there is a prominent argument that the deterioration of the terms of trade against developing countries reflects a situation of systemic demand deficiency in the world economy.[9] This suggests a current worldwide excess supply of manufactures. Thus, whilst the evolution of the terms of trade in the world market after the late 1990s has benefited a handful of commodity-exporting developing countries, it has been unfavourable for late industrialisation on a world scale.

From the perspective of Chinese economic development, these two trends in the world economy – differential impact of shifting terms of trade against manufacturing and the high costs of reserves

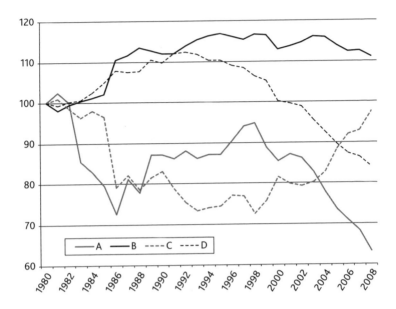

Figure 10.2   Net barter terms of international trade in goods (1980 = 100).

Sources: Chinese data from World Bank, World Development Indicators database; others from International Monetary Fund, World Economic Outlook database.

Notes: A = China; B = developed countries ('industrial countries' in the IMF categorisation); C = developing countries; D = East Asian newly industrialising economies (i.e. Hong Kong, Taiwan, South Korea and Singapore).

– have imposed a heavy cost. But they need to be balanced against how benefits have accrued to China from its increasing integration into the world market. China has achieved remarkable productivity growth over recent years: its average annual growth rate of per worker real GDP in 2000–07 is a hefty 9.3 per cent. Elsewhere, Lo (2007) and Lo and Zhang (2009) have argued that this success has been mainly based on China's *internal* dynamics, through a rapid process of capital deepening and industrial upgrading. Insofar as external conditions have contributed, these took the form of technology import, and were not primarily due to the symbiosis in the form of export demand on which most emphasis has been placed. Nevertheless, the symbiosis contributes to the acknowledged expansion of China's export-oriented, labour-intensive industries which, albeit with slow productivity growth, create jobs and ease the problem of unemployment.

Whatever the nature and contribution of the symbiosis in the past, it cannot continue into the future in the wake of the global crisis.

What alternative paths are open? At the domestic level, the main ingredients of a new path could include a continuation of the process of capital deepening and industrial upgrading, with the transfer of surplus from productivity gains being used to promote the development of the 'services' sectors, creating more jobs, and a more skilled and productive workforce. From the perspective of world development, the contribution of a new Chinese *external* dynamics could take at least two forms. First, if released from the China–USA symbiosis, China's high level of foreign exchange reserves (almost two trillion dollars by the end of 2008) could provide a valuable source of finance for the rest of the developing world, not only for natural resource extraction but, more importantly, for industrial development. Second, upgrading of the labour-intensive part of Chinese industry could release space for other developing countries to embark on a path of industrialisation. Significantly, measures corresponding to these prospects have already been incorporated into Chinese policies since 2008, particularly through the renowned 4 trillion yuan fiscal package, which addresses long-term development more than short-term demand stimulation. Whether this will be sustained and succeed remains to be seen.

10.4   GRADUAL MARKETISATION, NEO-LIBERALISATION AND THE QUEST FOR ALTERNATIVES

Outcomes, however, will depend upon continuing extensive state intervention. This exposes the deep divide between the postures of the Washington Consensus and Chinese realities, for both the past and the future. What mainstream development economics considers as market-supplanting elements of the Chinese economy ultimately concerns the nature and role of the public sector. For it is widely agreed that the operation of Chinese state-owned enterprises (SOEs) has significantly deviated from the principles of the market economy, particularly with regard to individualistic property rights. In the orthodox literature, China's enterprise reform has generally been portrayed as a process of the state attempting to induce entrepreneurial activities by management. But this process has occurred in a broader context in which various stakeholders of enterprises – local governments, workers, local communities, the banks and other business partners – have been involved, to form a web of checks and balances governing the operation and development of enterprises. This systemic feature is visible not only in SOEs (Lo 1999) but also in enterprises of other types of public ownership, including the renowned collectively owned township and village enterprises (or TVEs) (Smyth 1998).

Enterprises of such a 'dubious' nature have dominated the Chinese economy, at least for a major part of the reform era. In 1992, for instance, SOEs and collectively owned enterprises combined to account for 86 per cent of the output of Chinese industry as a whole. By the turn of the century, the share still remained at 64 per cent, with the rest being accounted for by the catch-all category of enterprises of 'other ownership types', which include private firms and various types of joint-ownership firms. Even for shareholding firms that are not formally state-controlled, a significant proportion (mainly those listed in the stock market) is governed by agents of the state as the ultimate owner–controller.

Yet, ownership aspects aside, China did shift towards embracing Washington Consensus doctrines for at least a short period during the reform era. In the mid 1990s, there was a high tide of neo-liberalism in China. This mainly took the form of the 1993–95 financial liberalisation and the 1995–97 enterprise downsizing drive. There were also policies adopted during these years of working towards liberalising external finance and balancing the state budget by the turn of the century (see Lo 2007).

The 1995–97 downsizing of state-owned enterprises had especially far-reaching implications. Initiated by the state leadership with an objective of transforming large and medium enterprises into modern corporations and small-scale enterprises into shareholding cooperatives, the drive was seized upon by local authorities of different levels simply to sell off state assets while unilaterally defecting on the state's obligation for job security of workers (and passing the liabilities of the sold enterprises on to state banks and, ultimately, to the central government). Consequently, unemployment surged, consumption expansion slowed and investment growth stagnated. Together with the worsening external environment caused by the 1997–98 East Asian financial crisis, China was plunged into deflation at the macro level, and worsening financial performance of enterprises and banks at the micro level.

The response was a fundamental policy reversal in 1998. The leadership adopted four major categories of anti-crisis policies between 1998 and 2002. First, it launched several Keynesian-type fiscal packages for expanding investment demand, which were financed by issuing of debt on an unprecedented scale. Second, it implemented a range of welfare-state policies aimed at reversing the trend of stagnant consumption expansion. Third, it adopted policy measures to revitalise the state sector, with the objective of improving the financial conditions of state-owned enterprises and the balance sheets of state banks. Fourth, it adopted a cautious approach to reforming the regime of external transactions – in particular, the target of liberalising the capital account was in effect shelved. As an anti-crisis strategy, these policies embodied the idea of helping enterprises as well as the government itself to 'grow out of indebtedness'. The robust growth of the economy in the crisis-prone years of 1998–2002, as well as the substantial decrease in the indebtedness (as ratios of GDP) of state finance, state banks, and state-owned enterprises, indicate that the adoption of these market-supplanting policies was both justified and successful.

Further, while only intended as short-term, anti-crisis measures, these policies turned out to be consistent with the long-term social and economic development strategy for the new century. This strategy, known as 'constructing a harmonious society', emphasises the need to reverse the trend of increasing social polarisation under market reforms, especially the secular trend of decline of labour compensation as a share of national output. Although the growth process had not been based mainly on cheap labour, popular opinion to the contrary, labour compensation has experienced sluggish growth over most of the reform era. As can be seen from Figure 10.3, until the turn of the century, the growth of the real urban wage rate (the formal sector of the Chinese economy) had lagged far behind that of per capita real GDP. This has, however, been reversed over the past decade through deliberate state efforts to improve labour compensation. These include enhancing labour rights protection, working towards the target of establishing collective bargaining in all enterprises, enforcing the establishment of unions in all enterprises, and enforcing a new employment contract law – all breaking with the previous laissez-faire approach towards employment.

These labour-enhancing policies have solid underpinnings because they are consistent with the prevailing economic growth path attached to capital deepening. The same applies to the broader policies for income redistribution and social welfare provision, and attempts to reconstruct a government-funded health-care system for society as a whole, including the rural population. These measures have become major elements in the state's policy package announced in late 2008 – both for promoting long-term social and economic development, and for coping with the prevailing financial crisis and looming recession in the world economy.

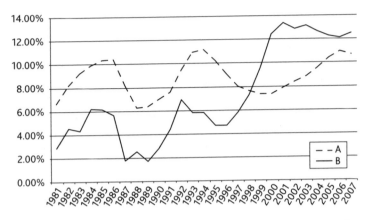

Figure 10.3   Annual growth rate of per capita real GDP and real urban wage rate (5-year moving average, per cent).

Sources: National Bureau of Statistics, China Statistical Yearbook, various years.

Notes: A = per capita real GDP; B = urban real wage rate.

The nature of the country's foray into Washington Consensus policies, and its subsequent retreat, highlight the fundamental difference in the way in which the state engages in economic affairs in China as compared with the measures promoted by the International Financial Institutions (IFIs). Putting it unduly crudely, the neo-liberal turn in China was a policy *choice* and not the extensive subordination of the economy to the systemic global tendencies associated with the neo-liberal era. This is brought out clearly by the relationship between China and the leading index of neo-liberalism, not least as dramatically revealed by its current crisis, namely financialisation (see introduction and conclusion to this volume). For neo-liberal globalisation has been marked by the extraordinary expansion of financial markets *and* their extension into ever more areas of economic and social life, in dysfunctional ways in which the imperatives of accumulation of fictitious capital, stakeholder value, and so on, have been at the expense of real accumulation and, through each and every aspect of policy and provision, the economic and social conditions underpinning economic performance.

At one level, China seems to have shared, even to have been at the forefront of the process of financialisation. For the extent to which its economic activities are mediated by banking is astonishing, with corporate dependence on banking for finance for example standing at 95 per cent in the mid 2000s (Carney 2009, p.91). Banks control the economy – or do they? But this is to conflate finance with financialisation. For the Chinese financial system has not so much been regulated (or not) as controlled and dictated to by the state's policy goals – one of the most open violations of the Washington Consensus' proscription on directed finance.

10.5   CONCLUDING REMARKS

In many respects, understanding China's economic success is not rocket science once one is freed from analytical and empirical prejudices. For China has gone through a classic process of (latecomer) industrialisation and development even if, as always, with peculiar features of its own. The country has had high rates of savings, the formation of an urban and industrial workforce out of rural and agricultural origins, the expansion of both domestic and export markets, the upgrading of technology, not least through international cooperation, and so on. The issue then is to get right not so much the first step of what China did, but the second step of how it did it. The 'grin and bear it' stance of the Washington Consensus – if it is not hurting, it is not working – is as vacuous in both of these respects as the Cheshire Cat's body. First and foremost, the Chinese state has been instrumental in undertaking non-market-conforming interventions in bringing about China's transition; and the same is so of corporate governance, where China has been and remains peculiar and peculiarly successful, and on a grand scale. This is a lesson which could and should have already been realised from the experience of East Asian industrialisation (and the lost decades as negative mirror image).

Second, then, China explicitly experimented with and rejected neo-liberal policies. At most, in their favour, it might be argued that such policies offered an opportunity to shake up the economy and propel it forward once they were abandoned. But such shock therapy, as it is more popularly known, can hardly prevail other than dysfunctionally over two or more decades without these being lost to development, as evidenced by the comparative experience of transition between east and west.

What is much more significant of the neo-liberal experiment in China is precisely that this is what it was, reflecting the extent to which the state retained control over the economy whilst embracing, however temporarily, orthodox policies. Similarly, the financial system is managed to support economic policy rather than the other way round. This is not to suggest that China has been immune from the consequences of neo-liberalism on a global scale, as has been indicated by reference to the preferred notion of symbiosis. The imbalances that this has involved are now well recognised and have been variously blamed or praised for sustaining global accumulation and underpinning its crisis, alongside the presumed role of cheap labour and goods as either supporting or undermining economies elsewhere.

In these respects, China has three lessons to offer. The first is how adjustment to changed global circumstances at a national level inevitably involves state intervention to facilitate and promote economic activity both across and within the divides between internal and external markets (and in supporting social provision through domestic mobilisation of resources). The second is to point to the need to wrest control from finance so that it should serve the economy rather than vice versa. And the third is to acknowledge the need for total reform of the world financial and trading systems in which the two pillars of the US dollar (and capital account deficit) as reserve currency and the US trade deficit as a major element of global demand are fundamentally transformed, if not abolished.

For the latter, there is every reason to believe that China can, and will, play a major role, not least because of its position as US creditor in trade and finance. Its corresponding symbiosis with the US, though, leaves it in an ambiguous position in terms of its own interests and strategy, since any devaluation of the US dollar lessens the value of China's reserves and the demand for its exports. But there are also two unambiguous prospects which bear upon the role to be played by China. One is that the systemic transformation of the roles of the US dollar, the US economy and financialisation more generally is an essential factor in the prospects of developing countries that do not have the political or the economic conditions to allow for the sort of strategy that appears to be open to China. The other is that World Bank research, by virtue both of its past record and its continuing direction in the wake of the crisis, and despite the enhancement, as a knee-jerk response to the crisis and recession, of its and the IMF's role, is set to contribute nothing to the processes of reform at the global and national levels. Indeed, its stances into the future, as in the past, will prove an obstacle both in and of themselves, as well as in obfuscating and disorganising the potential for alternatives that will inevitably emerge from more progressive quarters.

NOTES

1. 'The Cheshire Cat's grin is reminiscent of the vagaries of human character or of a trickster', http://en.wikipedia.org/wiki/Cheshire_Cat#cite_note-1.
2. The IMF (2000) itself refers to 'market fundamentalism in transition'.
3. Joseph Stiglitz: http://siteresources.worldbank.org/DEC/Resources/84797-1109362238001/726454-1164121166494/JES-bankResearchReviewanjesfin.pdf
4. This section draws on Lo and Zhang (2009).
5. See IMF (2000), OECD (2005) and World Bank (2002b), all containing main elements of these two propositions. For Proposition 1, see also Lardy (1998) and Steinfeld (2000). For Proposition 2, the pioneering work is Sachs and Woo (1994).
6. Examples of such claims abound, for example *The Economist* 24–30 October 1998, pp.15–16 and pp.23–28, together with the citations listed in the previous endnote.
7. Stuckler, King and McKee (2009), for example, suggest that the mass privatisation programmes in Eastern Europe increased the short-term adult male mortality rate by a staggering 12.8 percent.
8. See Rodrik (2006) for an account of the costs to developing countries of holding foreign exchange reserves.
9. Singh (1992). See also Ram (2004) for a review of the more recent literature.

Part III
Continuity or Change?

Whilst the Deaton Report was the initial prompt to the alternative evaluations that have given rise to this book, its presence has increasingly faded into the background (though it has by no means vanished altogether) as each individual chapter has evolved. Bear in mind that whilst our response to the report was more or less immediate, the published results of our endeavours have only materialised some five years after the Deaton Report itself. In part, the role of Deaton as subsequent point of departure is a response to events, not least the need to take account of the crisis and its aftermath in material terms and in assessing research itself. In part, it was a consequence of the imperative of taking a broader approach than the Deaton evaluations themselves, narrowly confined as these were in (inter)disciplinary reach and contextual location of World Bank research, in its mutual influence upon scholarship, rhetoric and policy in practice – if inconsistently and, on occasion, incoherently so. But, first and foremost, the reason why, to some extent both to our surprise and to our disappointment, we should have back-burnered the Deaton Report, as it were, is because it has had such a limited impact throughout the development community. Everyone concerned with development should know of its results and, thereby, hold to a sceptical attitude on all past and future World Bank research. Yet, despite offering, on its own terms, swingeing criticism from established figures of World Bank research, both in its substance and in its role in advocacy, the Deaton Report has more or less vanished without trace. Indeed, most practitioners have not even heard of it. As such, to take Deaton as a starting point for a more wide-ranging and penetrating critique of the World Bank is intellectually compelling but strategically self-defeating.

And, of course, this state of affairs is not new, as the World Bank has long enjoyed an incredibly powerful immunity from criticism, even from within. This is not to say that its research and postures do not evolve; far from it. But it does serve notice that the role of criticism is limited, especially in the absence of other pressures for change. And, as witnessed by the aftermath of the shift from the Washington to the post-Washington Consensus, the response to such external pressures, whether of progressive movements or of evidence of sheer failed developmental initiatives (most marked in light of the global crisis), is both uncertain, diverse and limited, but rarely transparent. For this reason, continuing critical regard of World Bank research, and the development of alternatives, remains crucial, not least because those engaging with the Bank need to be forewarned and forearmed. Their ideas and alternatives must derive from somewhere, and the sources for alternatives have been seriously depleted by the increasing breadth and depth of the World Bank's reach across all aspects of development, not least as its policy, research and advocacy portfolios have grown prodigiously – the last two especially in its role as knowledge bank, thereby dictating agendas and incorporating scholars, activists, NGOs and other aid agencies engaged in the business of development.

This is the context in which the single chapter of this final part assesses the future prospects for World Bank research. We observe the Bank's continuing failure to take account of alternatives, to offer serious reassessment of its own role or of the nature of development in light of the global crisis, and to depart from the reductionist methods of mainstream neoclassical economics (other than to allow for token and opportunistic incorporation of the non-economic). Indeed, the crisis might be seen to have strengthened the Bank's role in scholarship, advocacy and policy, as well as available funding, through the simple expedient of engaging in minimal mea culpa.

Such is certainly the more immediately apparent response deriving from the Bank's partner in consensus, the IMF. Whilst it continues to impose draconian measures on adjusting countries in the wake of the crisis, not least in Greece and eastern Europe, it proceeds to confess it was mistaken over the verities of past policy to which it stuck so dogmatically (in scholarship and advocacy, if not, it should be emphasised, in policy in practice). For Blanchard, Dell'Ariccia and Mauro (2010, p.3) confess that 'we thought of monetary policy as having one target, inflation, and one instrument, the [interest] policy rate'; and they admit that financial deregulation may have had unanticipated macroeconomic effects – indeed, global crisis and recession. What is striking here is how limited is the span of self-criticism, both in intellectual substance and in breadth and depth of account of policy interventions and their impact. And, of course, the mea culpa certainly does not run so far as self-examination, to enquire how they could have done and thought what they did – without which it is not clear why they should be trusted to continue to hold the reins of finance; nor, by the same token, why the World Bank should continue to hold the reins of development knowledge.

11
Whither World Bank Research?

Ben Fine, Elisa Van Waeyenberge and Kate Bayliss

11.1   INTRODUCTION

The chapters in this volume offer a detailed and far-reaching critique of World Bank research. Each bases its assessment on a body of literature in a particular area, shining light on broader policy issues. This chapter seeks to draw these together and to consider the ramifications for the Bank's role as a 'knowledge bank'.

Throughout this volume, four themes have been prominent. One is that the World Bank's research is part and parcel of a broader, shifting but often inconsistent amalgam of ideology (rhetoric or advocacy), scholarship and policy. Second is that the shifts involved have been loosely attached to the putative displacement of the Washington Consensus by the post-Washington Consensus (PWC). Third, however critical it was, the Deaton Report offers only a narrow prism through which to view Bank research. And, fourth, the current crisis offers the opportunity for a reassessment of World Bank research in the past and in prospect. In this closing chapter, we seek to push these themes further and also pose alternatives to World Bank research and researching.

We begin by observing that, as a knowledge bank, the Bank has been less than scholarly in interpreting its assets (although much more careful in preserving and accumulating them under its contested attempts at exclusive ownership), rarely moving beyond the notion of knowledge as a public good, with, at most, occasional and token deference to indigenous, and hence contextual, sources and meanings of knowledge. This lack of both introspection and extrospection is compounded by the substantive content of its approach. For World Bank research is deeply grounded in mainstream economics, which is inadequate both as a theory of the capitalist economy and as a frame for understanding development (or lack of it), across both its economic and social dimensions and the inevitable intersections between the two. Consequently, the social (both as the non-economic and the non-individual) tends to be reduced to the economic (market imperfections or their consequences), and the economic subsequently or simultaneously to be reduced to the individual. In some respects, this indicates a striking weakness of mainstream economics – an implicit confession that it is incapable of addressing the economy on its own terms, but needs to gather concepts and factors that have traditionally been located within the domains of other social sciences. But this weakness and fragility have, remarkably, been transformed into an extraordinary triumph in which the core principles of economics, sorely inadequate though they are for understanding the economy alone, have been projected in application across the social sciences as a whole. More generally, this process has been dubbed economics imperialism (Fine and Milonakis 2009). But it takes the form of the new development economics, whose evolution and presence have been heavily and increasingly influenced by the Bank, not least as its original application with the Washington Consensus gave way to the more refined and palatable post-Washington Consensus (Fine 2002d and 2010b).

Bank research has overseen the displacement of the old development economics by the new, the shift from critically exploring and explaining development to advocacy and policy projection (and corresponding attachment to the donor community), and the increasing, if far from absolute, subordination of development studies to development economics on these terms of engagement (Fine 2009c). These shifts are indicative more of the knowledge bank's closure to alternative ideas and approaches than of its openness to new ideas, not least with regard to continuities from the past as inherited from the Washington Consensus. This persists with the latest attempt by the Bank's chief economist to redefine its development paradigm (Lin 2010; see below).

Further, these fundamental shortcomings have a set of concrete implications regarding the way the Bank exercises its knowledge role. These have been highlighted in various contributions to this book and are further explored in this chapter by way of conclusion. First, certain approaches crucial to the study of development have been excluded from Bank analysis or, when they are incorporated, this is done in an opportunistic and/or token fashion. Second, Bank research tends to be characterised by lack of context or of attention to specificities. This allows unchanging policy imperatives to be attached continuously to changing analytical stances, with the promotion of private sector interests persistently dominating Bank policy. Third, Bank scholarship is characterised by the lack of an understanding of the systemic, and this allows the Bank to chart a role for itself in areas where it has itself contributed to (and often perpetuates) the underlying problem it is allegedly seeking to address. We explore this with particular reference to more recent Bank interventions, both in scholarship and advocacy, on the subjects of the financial crisis and climate change. Finally, we consider the Bank's new strategic research direction in light of our preceding analysis.

11.2 FRAMEWORK SELECTION BIAS

Regarding the absence of crucial approaches and, correspondingly, topics from Bank research or discourse, consider the 'developmental state paradigm' (DSP). This was a prominent and effective factor in criticising the Washington Consensus by pointing incontrovertibly to the empirical evidence of the East Asian Newly Industrialised Countries (NICs) as having been heavily dependent for their success upon state intervention, especially through industrial policy. Whatever the merits of the DSP on its own terms,[1] its *exclusion* from World Bank discourse is most significant. At most, it has been denuded and incorporated as an aspect of correction of market and institutional imperfections in a way that precludes systemic consideration of the role of the state.

Much the same is true of industrial policy (Fine 2010c). With the Washington Consensus, industrial policy was defined negatively in terms of leaving everything as far as possible to the free market, especially through trade liberalisation to promote competition and privatisation. At most, though, the PWC, especially within the Bank, has taken such postures as point of departure, suggesting there can be a role for the state in promoting the market (see Pack and Saggi 2006). This is, though, to take an extraordinarily narrow view of industrial policy. What is notably absent is any reference to industrial policy as a systemic contributing factor to development as industrialisation, with attention to the corresponding formation and exercise of class interests. This paves the way for the state to support piecemeal interventions, but the analytical and policy weaknesses remain. Industrial policy is primarily seen in terms of the state providing an enabling environment for entrepreneurs to exploit their position to engage in self-discovery of their best opportunities.[2] The analysis remains based on the optimising behaviour of individuals at the expense and implicit rejection of any other method and, thereby, leaves aside major issues of power, class, conflict and economic and social transformation, other than through some accidental outcome of 'aggregation of purposeful behaviour by individuals' (Rodrik 2007, p.3).

The preceding chapters demonstrate the extension of individualism beyond the limits of credibility. For example, the World Bank analysis of war and violence assumes rational individualism whereby grievances are topped up by a level of individual greed to achieve an equilibrium level of conflict. Anthropological and historical inputs are set aside. Similarly, in the Bank's analysis of HIV/AIDS, individuals are assumed to optimise their level of exposure to the virus, suggesting that sexual interactions are the result of freely informed decisions and ignoring, for example, gender-based norms that pressure women to engage in risky activities. Equally narrow is the Bank's preoccupation with economists to the neglect of other expertise. Johnston, for example, shows how analysis of HIV/AIDS needs to consider the work of epidemiologists, gender specialists and political economists so that the target to reduce prevalence would be based on class-based social norms and sexual networking patterns, geographic mobility and access to health care rather than just on individual behaviour and general development.

In agriculture, the analytical framework is based on an assumption of peasant rationality as reflected in responses to incentives, imperfect information, underlying market failures and high transaction costs. While at least the most superficial assumption of peasant homogeneity has been eroded, the distinctions between different commercial farm activities is based entirely on occupational and income status, so individual constraints and welfare objectives are still considered to be more or less homogeneous. There is an absence of distinction between rich peasants, capitalist farmers and commercially-oriented smallholders. These are typically collapsed into the category of market-oriented farmer in opposition to poor 'subsistence farmer'. In reality, unequal conflictual relations are pervasive among farmers and traders and participants in global value chains and are intrinsic to the structure of relations of production and extraction in global capitalism. An approach based on structural parameters such as class and power relations would have greater relevance.

11.3 FROM GENERAL TO SPECIFIC: OR VICE VERSA?

While the World Bank has in general become increasingly sensitive to the issue of *context*, it has done so in part as a response to the criticism that one (neo-liberal) model fits all and in part as a way of introducing the effect of institutions and market imperfections. As discussed above, a heavy dose of economic rationality linked to incentives is involved.

The Bank, nevertheless, prides itself on the strong empirical content of its research, with the latter, in the Bank's own words, preoccupied with 'results on the ground' (World Bank 2009b, p.16). Its engagement with empirical realities remains characterised, however, by a predilection for quantitative econometric analysis, often prone to poor technique, poor data and weak underlying analytical frameworks. The chapters in this volume have highlighted that the widespread use in World Bank research of large-scale econometric studies and sophisticated statistical methods gives the illusion of science and certainty, when in reality the underlying data and theory are often weak. Typically findings are quantified to appear as factual truths. The preceding chapters cite a number of such studies, in which questionable data and methods are processed through econometric manipulation to reach an apparently precise association which is presented as having universal application. For example, shortly after civil war the typical country faces a 44 per cent risk that it will return to conflict within five years; a $2,000 increase in per capita income is associated with a reduction of about 4 per cent in the HIV prevalence; and water privatisation is associated with a 54 per cent increase in residential connections per worker. All of these assertions are made without reference to the specifics of the context in which they are situated.

The lack of specificity or context to the Bank's analysis, nevertheless, serves to support continuing policy imperatives that can easily be attached to shifting analytical stances. Let us return to health, to explore this issue a little further (see also Chapters 5 and 6). Significantly, for a World Bank study, Das and Hammer (2005, p.1) begin with a vignette which concludes with a doctor's explanation of treatment known to be inappropriate:[3]

> But if I tell the mother that she should go home and only give the child water with salt and sugar, she will never come back to me; she will only go to the next doctor who will give her all the medicines and then she will think that he is better than me.

This is to enter the world of health beliefs on which there is no commentary as opposed to shifting the incentives of those offering treatment. It is hardly remedied by offering 'Six sizes fit all' as a model for health and nutrition services (World Bank 2004c, p.155). This is not, however, to prioritise health beliefs over material factors, but to see them both as attached to a health *system*.[4] As argued elsewhere, especially Bayliss and Fine (2008), health and other public services are subject to systemic provision and need to be addressed analytically and through policy as such. Yet, in practice, ranging over health and social security, Iriart, Merhy and Waitzkin (2001, p.1250) point to a new ideological 'common sense' that is being used to reconstruct 'fundamentals' from which to 'rethink the system'. This comprises the following elements:

- the crisis in health stems from financial causes;
- management introduces a new and indispensable administrative rationality to resolve the crisis;
- it is indispensable to subordinate clinical decisions to this new rationality if cost reduction is desired;
- efficiency increases if financing is separated from service delivery, and if competition is generalised among all subsectors (state, social security, and private);
- the market in health should be developed, because it is the best regulator of quality and costs;
- demand rather than supply should be subsidised;
- making labour relationships flexible is the best mechanism to achieve efficiency, productivity and quality;
- private administration is more efficient and less corrupt than public administration;
- payments for social security are each worker's property;
- deregulation of social security allows the user freedom of choice, to be able to opt for the best administrator of his or her funds;
- the passage of the user/patient/beneficiary to client/consumer assures that rights are respected;
- quality is assured by guaranteeing the client's satisfaction.

This ideology is being pushed, especially in the context of critical economic performance, the conditionalities imposed by international agencies, and the privatisation of health-care provision, smoothing the entry of multinational corporations into health and social security provision.

Thus, instead of the PWC and now post-crisis posture – that everything depends upon everything else and aspects of policy can be picked up on ad hoc and piecemeal basis to rationalise the use of the state to promote private capital in the process of provision – health as social policy more generally needs to be attached to contextual specificities and, most promisingly, within a broader framework of developmental state welfarism (for which, see Fine 2009a, d and f and work from UNRISD referenced there).[5] Whilst the notion of the developmental welfare state remains ambiguous, it does provide an alternative overarching ethos and framework within which to push for more progressive and effective policies than those currently being pursued and promoted by the Bank.

For, as is readily apparent, this new 'common sense' in health policy has no purchase whatsoever either on the *specificity* of health itself or on the particular problems faced by the poorest economies. Such considerations have been 'taken out' and have been replaced by a 'black box' of neo-liberal perspectives. By contrast, an alternative perspective based around the 'public sector system of provision approach' would take the view that health care needs to incorporate the following insights, and more:[6]

- Health is highly dependent on socio-economic and sociocultural determinants and is not just a consequence of the direct provision of health services.
- A distinction must be drawn between preventative, primary and curative services, recognising and addressing systemic tendencies for curative services to be promoted at the expense of the others, especially where commercial imperatives arise.
- Provision of health care itself ranges over diverse activities, from supply of buildings to training (and retention) of staff, and supply of drugs and equipment.
- Different conditions arise and require response in different ways according to both medical and social circumstances. The 'externalities' across health itself, and with other conditions affecting welfare, are widespread, with considerable economies of scale and scope that need to be identified and accommodated in practice.
- The practices, ethos or culture surrounding health are complex, both for citizens and for health staff.

Thus, in the context of social policy (and development) more generally, the shift from Washington Consensus to PWC across ideology, scholarship and policy in practice requires careful untangling and undoing. The uncompromising push for commercialisation and user charges associated with the Washington

Consensus has been beaten back, although it might be thought to have achieved its purpose of smoothing the way for what can be presented as a less extreme, more reasonable, nuanced and balanced approach to the roles of public and private sectors in provision, based on promoting the private sector under the guise of state intervention to correct market imperfections and enhance efficiency. An astonishing example and rationale is provided by the provision of an elite hospital in Afghanistan. Whilst it is accepted that '[t]he government's new health initiatives have been focused on primary care, particularly in rural areas', the IFC is investing US$4.5 million in a complementary investment to provide just 36 beds, alongside training of medical staff, etc.; the rationale is to 'benefit people who usually go abroad for treatment, helping stem the outflow of foreign exchange and reduce travel costs for patients and their families' (IFC 2009a). Not, to put it mildly, your typical rural peasant in need of primary and preventative services.

Further, in the wake of the crisis, whilst both the World Bank and the IMF have emphasised the necessity of providing safety nets to the vulnerable and of preserving economic and social infrastructure, the suspicion must be that this is designed to rationalise state support to private provision. Either the private sector is already in the bag as far as privatisation is concerned, or it is not a source of profit following the crisis, so the best bet is to make money out of social security and economic and social infrastructure. The presence and significance of such strategy is revealed with stunning clarity by the post-crisis report on health provision in Africa (IFC 2009b) (p.15):[7]

This report estimates that private sector entities have the potential to deliver between 45 and 70 percent of the needed increase in capacity ... For health care companies looking for markets in which to expand, and for investors looking to invest in health care businesses, this $11–$20 billion in private health care expansion represents a significant opportunity ... governments needing the support of the private sector to fund the expected growth in health care demand must create an environment supportive of significant private sector investment ... Health policy makers will have to recognize the reality that private sector entities have a significant role to play in health care. Many have concerns about private sector involvement in this field, and governments and policy makers must ensure that the sector is properly regulated to achieve high-quality health outcomes. Similarly, governments needing the support of the private sector to fund the expected growth in health care demand must create an environment supportive of significant private sector investment.

Not surprisingly, then, the five priorities of the IFC when it comes to health services in Africa are (p.17):[8]

1. Developing mechanisms for creating and enforcing quality standards for health services and medical product manufacturing and distribution;
2. Including as many of the population as possible in risk-pooling programs;
3. Channeling a portion of public and donor funds through the private health sector;
4. Enacting local regulations that are more encouraging of a private health care sector; and
5. Improving access to capital, including by increasing the ability of local financial institutions to support private health care enterprises.

Of these, the first is innocuous enough, the last three reinforcing the role to be played by the private sector. As for the second, we could not agree more; for the welfare state, not the private sector, has traditionally been seen as the mode of risk pooling par excellence, as against the private sector serving as the source of the risk to be pooled, not least as forcibly brought home by financial instability and its consequences. But, of course, the World Bank has other ideas: it wants the state to support collectives of citizens in pooling their resources to promote private and privatised provision.

11.4   NEW FRONTIERS: OLD PARADIGMS

Bank research has been characterised by a dramatic lack of systemic understanding of the fundamental issues pertaining to the current challenges that face developing countries. This is obvious in the context of new developments in financialisation and climate change. The new and heterodox concept of 'financialisation' has sought to explain in systemic fashion why the last 30 years have been marked by sluggish growth (and corresponding lost decades of development) and have ultimately given way to the current crisis; yet this remains absent from Bank research and discourse.

Financialisation has been variously defined and understood as: the phenomenal expansion of financial assets relative to real activity; the proliferation of different types of assets; the absolute and relative expansion of speculative as opposed to real investment; a shift in the balance of productive to financial imperatives within the private sector, whether financial or not; increasing inequality in income, arising out of the weight of financial rewards; consumer-led booms based on credit; the penetration of finance into ever more areas of economic and social life, such as pensions, education, health, and provision of economic and social infrastructure; the emergence of a neo-liberal culture of reliance upon markets and private capital, and corresponding anti-statism. Financialisation is also associated with the continued role of the US dollar as world money despite, at least in the current crisis, its deficits in trade, capital account, the fiscus, and consumer spending, and minimal rates of interest (Fine 2010d and 2011).

The consequences of financialisation have also been hypothesised in terms of: reductions in overall levels and efficacy of real investment as financial instruments and activities expand at its expense, even if excessive investment does take place in particular sectors at particular times (as with the dot-com bubble of a decade ago); prioritising shareholder value, or financial worth, over other economic and social values; pushing of policies towards conservatism and commercialisation as far as possible; extending influence of finance more broadly, both directly and indirectly, over economic *and* social policy; placing more aspects of economic and social life at the risk of volatility from financial instability and, conversely, placing the economy and social life at risk of crisis from triggers within particular markets (as with the food and energy crises that immediately preceded the financial crisis, but were overshadowed by it).Whilst, then, financialisation is a single word, it is attached to a wide variety of different forms and effects of finance, with the United States and Britain to the fore.

Accordingly, different countries have experienced financialisation differently, and this is especially true of the developing world. It has, for example, been much less affected by international transmission mechanisms associated with toxic financial assets than through the slowdown in growth, corresponding export demand, and capital flows from direct foreign investment, aid and migrant remittances. Nonetheless, financialisation has been important in the developing world, with corresponding diversity of impacts on the way in which and the extent to which financial interests have been formed and have influenced policy. This has rendered responses to the crisis, as with the United States and Britain, highly attuned to the interests of finance, with business as usual in many respects in terms of conditionalities imposed by the IFIs in its crisis packages.[9] What financialisation points to is the systemic and global dysfunction of finance, and the need to insulate developmental goals from its determining influence, as has been demonstrated in the case of China (Chapter 10). In contrast, the World Bank's approach remains deeply embedded in the notion that crises are temporary malfunctions that require austerity plus safety nets (the latter at most in principle) in the short run and better policy (financial regulation) in the longer term.

Such short-termism within the Bank, and with those with whom it interacts, leads various chapters in this volume to illustrate how recent crises in food and finance have given greater legitimacy to the World Bank and its pro-market approach, with a strong role for the IFC in the crisis response. This is despite the reality that the policies of international financial openness and liberalisation promoted by the IFIs contributed directly to the economic and financial imbalances straining many developing and transition economies. In agriculture, the food crisis has led to scaling up of Bank activities and further marketing of its products, such as 'innovative' private insurance mechanisms. A similar commitment to products and services derived from financialisation is evident in infrastructure policy, in which a large component of the Bank's response is to support the private sector's infrastructure investments, and the Bank's array of financial products and insurances are offered to mitigate private sector risk.

The failure to appreciate or tease out systemic issues also transpires sharply in the Bank's analytical, rhetorical and policy role pertaining to the environment. Indeed, the issue of climate change, although not dealt with separately within this volume, exposes probably more than any other the extraordinary weaknesses and inconsistencies in the Bank's positions within and across its ideology, scholarship and policy in practice. In this respect, it is worth quoting initially from the Deaton Report on the issue, not least in its passing commentary that '[c]urrently, there is very little frontline academic work being done by economists in such important areas as urban economics, transportation, climate change, and infrastructure' (Deaton et al. 2006, p.15).[10]

This neatly reveals the way in which work by non-economists does not count for the report (for climate and beyond), and an astonishing failure to broach both the work of non-economists and the relationship between the World Bank's research and its policy, which, both directly and indirectly, has made a major impact on the environment. The Bank has itself, for example, been a major source of finance for those industries most implicated in causing climate change, even continuing in this role as supporter of fossil fuel projects despite the research and recommendations of its own Extractive Industries Review of 2004, and failing to meet its own social and environmental safeguard policies, which are deemed to be compulsory.[11] It has also served as a major player in carbon markets, gaining commission of over 10 per cent through its dealings. And it has taken a leading role in the Clean Development Mechanism which defines which new projects count as satisfying a clean bill of health as far as the environment is concerned.[12]

These observations need to be put into a broader perspective. On carbon trading, for example, the World Development Report for 2010 (World Bank 2009f, hereafter WDR 2010), 'Development and Climate Change', as cited in Baudienville (2009, p.1), estimates that

> [m]itigation in developing countries could cost between $140 to $175 billion per year over the next 20 years, with adaptation investments rising to an average of $30 to $100 billion a year between 2010 and 2050. Yet efforts to raise funding for mitigation and adaptation have been inadequate, and, to date, amount to less than 5% of projected needs.

Indeed, there is the prospect that carbon trading will become the single largest financial market, dealing in trillions of dollars in the right to pollute.[13] And, in terms of investments, the ambiguous role of the Bank has been highlighted by the continuing controversy over its proposed support for (dirty) coal-fired electricity power stations in South Africa. As much as $5 billion has been committed, the largest ever loan on the African continent. As reported in the foreword to Hallowes (2009, p.3):[14]

> While some news reports suggest that the loan is needed to ensure universal access to electricity in South Africa, the shocking record of World Bank oil loans to Africa tells another story. 80% of projects that the World Bank invested in between 1992 and 2003 were designed to export oil to Western Europe, Canada, the U.S., Australia, New Zealand and Japan. Couple this with South Africa's export led economy and one has to ask whether the loan is really going to be used for ensuring that all people in South Africa will have access to affordable energy, or is it going

to be used to protect South Africa's export led, energy and carbon intensive development considering that around 80% of our energy is used by industry and commerce.

As indicated, then, business as usual for the Bank as far as the environment is concerned, with an inclination to overlook its own contributions to pollution with one hand whilst busily alleviating it, or making money out of doing so, with the other.

This is more of a blind eye than a blind spot or apocalypse now. In its World Development Report for 2009, 'Reshaping Economic Geography', reference to the need for a more favourable *business* climate attracts many more references than the *climate* itself which is notable for its more or less total absence (Fine 2010b). Inevitably the gathering myopia and inconsistencies could no longer be entirely avoided in WDR 2010, given its chosen subject matter. But what could be avoided was any systemic analysis of the sources of environmental degradation in capitalist development and of its reliance upon a fossil fuel economy over hundreds of years. Heavy reliance is not surprisingly placed upon 'cap and trade' and offset mechanisms, the idea that, at least in principle, pollution can be contained by trading a fixed quantum in financial markets, supplemented by higher quotas in case of support for use of less polluting technologies elsewhere (usually in the developing world). This has, however, all been heavily criticised, not least in practice, for allocating property rights in permission to continue to pollute to the polluters of the past and present, the lack of binding constraints within the quotas set, and in promoting the growing stock of pollutants through offset mechanisms based on business as usual, as long as matched by (poorly overseen and corrupt) support for projects nominally polluting proportionately less severely than otherwise (see Lohman and Sexton 2010 for a brief account).

Such mechanisms lie at the heart of the Bank's postures. As the WDR 2010 puts it (p.320), '[m]any policies to address adaptation and mitigation are already known. Secure property rights, energy-efficient technologies, market-based eco-taxes and tradable permits – all have been piloted and studied over decades'. It does, however, acknowledge their limited impact both in the past and prospectively, for

implementing them still proves difficult. Their success relies not just on new finance and new technology but also on complex and context-specific social, economic, and political factors normally called institutions – the formal and informal rules affecting policy design, implementation, and outcomes.

More specifically, the Bank is worried about 'institutional inertia', if not its own. Its approach is not, however, to derive institutional imperatives, or lack of them, from the demands of business and the systemic drive for profit. Instead, it draws implicitly upon the new institutional economics and its wide-ranging application to development, rooted in the behaviour of individuals. For, '[f]irst, myriad private acts of consumption are at the root of climate change. As consumers, individuals hold a reservoir of mitigation capacity' (p.321). This is followed by an account of the psychological and other factors that prevent individuals from pursuing more satisfactory behaviour and policies towards the environment. There is simply no recognition that the consumers' and the citizens' huge reservoir of mitigation capacity might simply be appropriated by business for more of the same.

Nonetheless, the WDR does, at least by its own standards, admit of the need for apocalyptic change, not least under a heading, 'Bringing the state back in'. It argues, with no sense of irony for its own culpability that (p.30)

[o]ver the past 30 years the role of the state has been cut back in various domains key to addressing the climate challenge, such as energy research. The retreat from direct intervention occurred with a switch from 'government' to 'governance' and an emphasis on the state's role in steering and enabling the private sector.

And, again with no sense of rewriting its own past stances on the issue of the developmental state, it accepts that:

This general trend hides a complex picture. Twentieth-century Europe saw various forms and degrees of state capitalism. The rise of East Asian economies, including China's, demonstrated the pre-eminence of the state in 'governing the market' to deliver the most successful example of accelerated development.

And, in order to drive home the point of a renewed role for the state, it observes that '[m]ost recently, the 2008 financial crisis showed the pitfalls of deregulation and unrestrained markets – and triggered renewed emphasis on bringing back the state'.

So, in order to ensure action on climate change, a greater role is projected for the state, and even rationalised on the basis both of its success for East Asian NICs and the failings of the global financial system. But, as is immediately made apparent, this is not to be a democratic state with freedom of manoeuvre. Rather, the state is merely to be the instrument of what is to be determined by the 'arrangements' of others: 'Political and institutional arrangements can help avoid shifting action on climate change from the living to the unborn by making it difficult to reverse climate policy. Such arrangements could include constitutional amendments and climate-change laws' (p.341). And, as if the troubles with the financial system had already been forgotten, the text immediately continues by effectively suggesting arrangements through an independent climate tribunal, along the lines of the independent central banks that have overseen the spectacular rise and crisis of financialisation: 'But they can also involve the establishment of independent institutions that take a longer-term view, in the same way that monetary institutions control inflation'.

In this light, it is hardly surprising that the Bank's bid to take the lead in climate change finance for development should be viewed with dismay by developing countries and activists alike, especially in the wake of the (failed) Copenhagen conference. It is a recipe for continuing largesse towards the developed world's polluting and the thick end of a wedge already in place in applying conditionalities to World Bank finance more generally. By the same token, the implications for research are transparent, with similar tensions as are derived for agriculture (Oya, Chapter 7). Scholarship, ideology and policy in practice are stretched to breaking point and only mutually accommodated by a degree of incoherence and populism that is scarcely sustainable.

11.5   THE FUTURE FOR DEVELOPMENT RESEARCH?

The onset of the recent crises in agriculture and finance provides a good opportunity for a reassessment of both policy and research. This is a view expressed by the World Bank (2009b) in its plans for future research and by the Bank's current chief economist, Justin Lin (2010), and one with which the authors of this volume concur. However, careful reading of the Bank's position indicates that the underlying failings discussed in the preceding chapters will continue to be unaddressed.

The Bank's prospective research programme aims to clarify what appropriate development priorities, policies and structures are for countries at different stages of development (World Bank 2009b). The research programme is inspired by the work of Lin, who has proposed a 'new structural economics'.[15] In this conceptual framework, the starting point of the analysis is an economy's endowments (of capital, labour and natural resources), which are assumed to be given at any specific point in, but changeable over, time (Lin 2010, p.12). In almost tautological fashion, it is asserted how

> [c]ountries at different stages of development tend to have different economic structures due to their differences in their endowments. Factor endowments for countries at the early stages of development are typically characterised by a relative scarcity in capital and relative abundance in labour or resources. (p.13)

Crucially, the 'new' framework considers these structural differences between developed and developing countries 'to be in large part endogenous to their endowment structures and determined by market forces, rather than resulting from the distribution of power or other exogenously determined rigidities as assumed by the old structural approach' (p.3).

So, endowments are given rather than the result of particular historical trajectories, and structural differences between countries derive from the former rather than from the fact that they need to be situated in the broader context of the international and domestic political, economic, financial and commercial realities within which economic outcomes, progressive or otherwise, take form. From this starting point of given and differential endowments between rich and poor countries, the argument continues that these endowment differentials imply comparative advantages in different types of industries and production activities. Hence, '[g]iven the endogeneity of industrial structure at each stage of development, the targets of industrial upgrading and infrastructure improvement in a developing country should not necessarily refer to the industries and infra-structure that are in place in high-income countries' (p.3). Further, 'economic development as the dynamic process of moving from one stage to the next requires industrial diversification, upgrading and corresponding improvements in hard and soft infrastructure'.

Drawing on propositions from new growth theory regarding innovation generating public knowledge, and combining this with the more traditional public-good arguments around infrastructure-yielding externalities, Lin suggests that 'in addition to an effective market mechanism, the government should play an active, facilitating role in the industrial diversification and upgrading process and in the improvement of infrastructure' (p.3). More specifically, according to the new structural economics, the role of the state in industrial upgrading (p.21):

> should be limited to the provision of information about the new industries, the coordination of related investments across different firms in the same industries, the compensation of information externalities for the pioneer firms, and the nurturing of new industries through incubation and encouragement of foreign direct investment.

Yet, at each stage of development a competitive market should remain the economy's fundamental mechanism to allocate resources (p.16). And, while the state needs to play a 'facilitating role' in industrial upgrading, it also has to focus on how to exit from the distortions it creates to the market mechanism (p.17). As such, Lin offers an extremely weak and narrow frame for addressing development, with an exclusive reliance on neoclassical economics and contingent market-supporting policies and institutions to assist in structural transformation that itself remains poorly understood.

Lin further derives a few preliminary policy insights. Regarding fiscal policy, the new structural economics supports counter-cyclical policy, to be put in the service of infrastructure upgrading (p.22). Revenues from commodities in resource-rich countries should be used to invest in human, infrastructural and social capital to facilitate the diversification and upgrading of industry, rather than being solely channelled into foreign reserve accumulation (p.23). In monetary policy, low interest rates could encourage investments in infrastructure, rather than interest rates being set solely with the purpose of price stability (p.25). Emphasis is put on appropriate sequencing in the liberalisation of domestic finance and foreign trade. It is further argued that the optimal financial structure of a country varies with its stage of development. For poorer countries, local banks should be the backbone of their financial system. With industrial upgrading the financial structure changes and large banks and sophisticated equity markets gain in prominence (p.26). A differential policy environment is prescribed to regulate foreign direct investment compared to portfolio investment. This would favour the former and not the latter; but capital controls remain absent from the narrative (p.27). Finally, the new structural economics highlights the importance of well-designed policy on 'human capital' development. This goes beyond the traditional (neoclassical) emphasis on education, to include measures that foster skills to facilitate the upgrading of industries (p.28).

The policy recommendations offer slightly more progressive stances than the conceptual framework. Yet, four features are striking. First, there is no reference to the PWC in the entire document. This is remarkable given that the PWC was posited by one of Lin's predecessors as chief economist at the Bank, with the PWC itself being committed to a matrix of policies incorporating an overlapping content across its various elements (see Stiglitz 1998a). Second, Lin's summary of policies will not necessarily translate into any corresponding alteration of the Bank's overarching policy matrix, with the divergence between Bank scholarship and practice as highlighted across the chapters in this book likely to persist, if unevenly. This is most apparent in the continuing commitment of Bank management to the CPIA (Country Policy and Institutional Assessment), which sets the policy framework within which the Bank engages with its low-income clients and remains committed to core neo-liberal policies (see Chapter 3). Third, leaving aside a passing reference to finance, this new framework is constructed as if the financial crisis at the end of the noughties had never happened, let alone had any role to play in revealing the nature of (the prospects for) development. And, fourth, in particular on this latter score, this is studiously a *national* framework in which all can become developed if only they adopt appropriate policies (a mix of the market and a facilitating, if weak, state – public ownership does not figure at all). In a sense, globalisation and internationally systemic factors are wished away, other than as constraints and opportunities.

In terms of the Bank's future research programme, three strategic directions emerge from Lin's propositions (World Bank 2009b, pp.52–4). The first is to elaborate the analytical framework described above, with its emphasis on stages of development and corresponding industrial structure. Second, the role of the state at each stage of the development process will be investigated along the lines of whether the state and market mix should be different in developing as compared to developed countries; whether government should play a more proactive role towards institutional change in developing countries; and whether and how the government's role changes as development proceeds (p.53). Finally, a major preoccupation of

Bank research will be to assess economic distortions and identify clear exit strategies for governments. For the priority remains 'to create space for private sector dynamism, [and hence] to study exit strategies for governments in various sectors. Governments can take a lead role in defining the exit strategy and, thereby, providing space for market adjustments' (p.54).

While both Lin (2010) and the World Bank (2009b) recognise the need for a rethink in the light of the crisis, the Bank reveals no capacity for such an endeavour. Its strategic directions for research indicate no radical change, while the opportunity provided by the dramatic circumstance of the global crisis lies fallow and the Bank persists in favouring more of the same.

11.6 CONCLUDING REMARKS

The chapters in this book bring out underlying elements in the approach of the World Bank to research, which apply across a range of topics. In essence the authors take issue with the neo-liberal framework and systematically demonstrate its failings across a set of areas. The chapters illustrate that the policy context and agendas, both overt and implicit, of those undertaking research are important determinants of findings. Yet, the Bank itself is apparently unaware of the contexts and power relationships within which its policies and research are undertaken, instead assuming impartial neutrality. Even lending is often governed by an agenda in which disbursement takes priority over ex post evaluation, with little appreciation of the conflict of interest between the roles of lender and analyst. Much of this is ignored in Bank research which (implicitly) assumes no agendas, history, power or politics, and where decisions are understood to be based on rationality, cool unbiased calculation and honourable motivation.

From the point of view of future research, then, the lessons from this volume are simple. First, the nature and role of research (at the Bank but also more widely) should not be assessed in isolation from its rhetorical and policy context. Second, the Bank's own research has had the effect of precluding more radical approaches from consideration, especially those underpinned by political economy, incorporating corresponding interdisciplinarity (as opposed to mainstream economics) and systemic understandings of development. Third, the growing momentum behind state support for private sector provision in practice has tended to be disguised behind a rhetoric and scholarship of being pro-poor and even-handed when it comes to the role of the state. Fourth, certainly for the foreseeable future, whether within or without the Bank, scholarly integrity in engaging with its research is preferable to the delusion that intellectual and broader reform can be won through a subtle pandering to the Bank's economists. And, fifth, the veracity (and vanity) of the scholar is as nothing compared to the weight of progressive movement and organisation in underpinning material, ideological and intellectual change.

NOTES

1. See Fine, Saraswati and Tavasci (2011) on problems pertaining to the DSP.
2. These arguments have been strongly articulated by Dani Rodrik, who has been in the forefront of the charge against the industrial policy of the Washington Consensus, with 'self-discovery' promoting entrepreneurship as the weapon of choice (see Hausman and Rodrik 2003).
3. This, as do other micro-level studies of health, attracts considerable praise from the Deaton process.
4. As a Deaton Report assessor, Birdsall's (2006, p.5) conclusion is intriguing:

    Of all the potential research that could be done with health, I would put the highest priority for Bank research ... on health *systems*. The Bank is probably better placed, because of its depth in economics, than other institutions to address health financing, organization and other system issues. And it is probably better placed than most economists in academe because its operations by their nature tend to provide support to and through the health systems of member countries. Good research on health systems has as much or more chance to lead to policy changes in the way systems are organized and financed as other kinds of health research, even on inequalities. Research on health systems can be useful for program design within the constraints of health systems but less useful on the non-marginal issues that health system problems pose.

    Note that '(health) system' appears eight times in this paragraph! The meaning of the last clause is unclear, but may point to the need to examine the interaction of health systems with economic and social reproduction more generally. (For an account of the treatment of health within the Deaton Report, not fully incorporated into this volume, see Fine 2008a.)

5. As Fine (2009d) observes, the World Bank has a major influence over social policy at the cost of $1 per *year* per person, compared for example with needed health care costs of $12, with much of its budget supporting its own consultants.
6. For this approach in general, see Fine (2002c and 2009d and e), Bayliss and Fine (2008) and Fine and Hall (2011), and for differences in health systems in the context of globalisation, see Labonté and Schrecker (2007a–c). For the contrasting fortunes of the Colombian and Cuban health systems in the era of neo-liberalism, see de Groote et al. (2005) and Vos (2005), respectively.
7. For a similar push for private provision within education, see World Bank (2009d) and Patrinos, Barrera-Osorio and Guáqueta (2009); these studies allow for discretion – and so for private participation – in the practice of education. See also special issue of *Compare*, vol.39, no.2, 2009.

8. We do not address the role of private donor agencies in health, with the Gates Foundation to the fore, which provide levels of funding that are now dominating official aid quantitatively and, to some extent, qualitatively. Irrespective of their own stances towards private versus public provision in principle, their impact, given current conditions, is in practice more attuned towards private and clinically driven provision. As McCoy et al. (2009, p.1651) comment on Gates' funding of the World Bank:

> More controversial is the award of two grants to the International Finance Corporation, whose mandate is to support private sector development. The reasons why the International Finance Corporation needs philanthropic funding are not clear, but this donation suggests that the Gates Foundation is keen to promote the growth of private health-care providers in low-income and middle-income countries, and is consistent with views that have been expressed by the foundation and the observation that private foundations generally view the public sector with scepticism and disinterest.

Note also how the World Bank's interventions into health have been at the expense of the World Health Organisation, with 'more than 80 per cent of WHO's funding ... dependent on voluntary or so called extra budgetary resources' (Koivusalo 2009, p.289). See also Baum (2008, pp.461–2): 'Since the publication of the World Bank's Investing in health report (World Bank 1993), WHO has no longer enjoyed the automatic position as the leading global voice on public health.'

9. See Van Waeyenberge, Bargawi and McKinley (2010) for an assessment of the IMF's crisis response in low-income countries.

10. Note that the assessor for the evaluation, Heal (2006), is extremely positive (at least over the less than four pages submitted). Heal mainly focuses on impact studies, not the causes of climate change, excuses promotional material (for clean development mechanisms) and highlights the Bank's role in promoting carbon markets (see below).

11. See Redman (2008) for a critique, and visit http://web.worldbank.org/WBSITE/EXTERNAL/TOPICS/EXTOGMC/0,,contentMDK:20605112~menuPK:3369 36~pagePK:148956~piPK:216618~theSitePK:336930,00.html

12. Note that the multiplicity of competing roles within the Bank is characteristic of the collective handling of the environment across other institutions; see Newell, Jenner and Baker (2009) on how these roles are uncoordinated, incoherent, uneven, subject to blind spots (or should that be eyes?) and weak on process. See also Brooks, Grist and Brown (2009, pp.752–3), who observe that '[n]ot only do existing development models fail to address long-term climatic and environmental variability and change, but they also frame current approaches to adaptation ... A new approach to development, and a new vision of adaptation, are urgently needed.'

13. For a simple account, see Lohman and Sexton (2010).

14. On the issue of meeting energy poverty, note that, as reported by Radford (2009), '[o]f the approximate $7.5 billion allocated for the World Bank's energy portfolio in fiscal year 2008, only $1.4 billion was spent on the neediest countries'.

15. See also Monga (2009) for a putative post-macroeconomics which is little more than a mish-mash of old orthodoxies, distinguished at most by minimal departure from neo-liberal postures.

References

Acemoglu, D. (2006) 'Evaluation of World Bank Research', background report for the Deaton evaluation, http://siteresources.worldbank.org/DEC/Resources/84797-1109362238001/726454-1164121166494/3182920-1164133928090/Daron-Acemoglu.pdf.

Adam, A.-H. and K. Bayliss (2011) 'Where Have all the Alternatives Gone? The Shrinking of African Water Policy Options', in McDonald and Ruiters (2011).

Addison, T. and F. Tarp (2009) 'The Triple Crisis and the Global Aid Architecture', UNU-WIDER, mimeo.

Ainsworth, M., K. Beegle and G. Koda (2005) 'The Impact of Adult Mortality and Parental Deaths on Primary Schooling in North-Western Tanzania', *Journal of Development Studies*, vol.41, no.3, pp.412–39.

Akram-Lodhi, H. (2008) '(Re)Imagining Agrarian Relations? The *World Development Report 2008: Agriculture for Development*', *Development and Change*, vol.39, no.6, pp.1145–161.

—— and C. Kay (eds) (2008) *Peasants and Globalization: Political Economy, Rural Transformation and the Agrarian Question*, London: Routledge.

Alatas, V., L. Pritchett and A. Wetterberg (2002) 'Voice Lessons: Local Government Organizations, Social Organizations, and the Quality of Local Governance', World Bank Policy Research Working Paper no.2981.

Almedom, A. (2005) 'Social Capital and Mental Health: An Interdisciplinary Review of Primary Evidence', *Social Science and Medicine*, vol.61, no.5, pp.943–64.

Amanor, K. (2009) 'Global Food Chains, African Smallholders and World Bank Governance', *Journal of Agrarian Change*, vol.9, no.2, pp.247–62.

Anderson, K. (ed.) (2009) *Distortions to Agricultural Incentives: A Global Perspective 1955–2007*, New York: Palgrave Macmillan for the World Bank.

Andersson, N. (2006) 'Prevention for Those Who Have Freedom of Choice – Or Among the Choice-Disabled: Confronting Equity in the AIDS Epidemic', *AIDS Research and Therapy*, vol.3, no.23, pp.1–3, http://www.ncbi.nlm.nih.gov/pmc/articles/PMC1592104/pdf/1742-6405-3-23.pdf.

Arestis, P. and P. Demetriades (1997) 'Financial Development and Economic Growth: Assessing the Evidence', *Economic Journal*, vol.107, no.442, pp.783–99.

Ashman, S., B. Fine and S. Newman (2010) 'The Crisis in South Africa: Neoliberalism, Financialisation and Uneven and Combined Development', *Socialist Register*, 2011, in Panitch, Albo and Chibber (2010).

Austin, G. (2008) 'The "Reversal of Fortune" Thesis and the Compression of History: Perspectives from African and Comparative Economic History', *Journal of International Development*, vol.20, no.8, pp.996–1027.

Bairoch, P. and R. Kozul-Wright (1996) 'Global Myths: Some Historical Reflections on Integration, Industrialization, and Growth in the World Economy', UNCTAD Discussion Paper no.113.

Bangura, Y. (2000) 'Public Sector Restructuring: The Institutional and Social Effects of Fiscal, Managerial and Capacity-Building Reforms', UNRISD Occasional Paper 3, Geneva.

Bank of Korea (1998) *The Implications of Globalization of World Financial Markets*, Seoul: Bank of Korea.

Barajas, A., R. Steiner and N. Salazar (2000) 'Foreign Investment in Colombia's Financial Sector', in Claessens and Jansen (2000).

Barfield, C. (ed.) (1996) *International Financial Markets: Harmonization versus Competition*, Washington, DC, AEI Press.

Barnett, T. and G. Prins (2005) *HIV/AIDS and Security: Fact, Fiction and Evidence – A Report to UNAIDS*, London: LSEAIDS.

Barth, J., G. Caprio and R. Levine (2001) 'Banking Systems around the Globe: Do Regulations and Ownership Affect Performance and Stability?', in Mishkin (2001).

Basso, H., O. Calvo-Gonzalez and M. Jurgilas (2007) 'Financial Dollarization, the Role of Banks and Interest Rates', European Central Bank Working Paper no.748.

Baudienville, G. (2009) 'Beyond Grants: Climate Finance in Developing Countries', ODI Opinion no.141, December, http://www.odi.org.uk/resources/download/4538.pdf.

Baum, F. (2008) 'The Commission on the Social Determinants of Health: Reinventing Health Promotion for the Twenty-First Century?', *Critical Public Health*, vol.18, no.4, pp.457–66.

Bayliss, K. (2003) 'Utility Privatisation in Sub-Saharan Africa: A Case Study of Water', *Journal of Modern African Studies*, vol.41, no.4, pp.507–31.

—— (2006) 'Privatisation Theory and Practice: A Critical Analysis of Policy Evolution in the Development Context', in Jomo and Fine (2006).

—— (2008) 'Water and Electricity in Sub-Saharan Africa', in Bayliss and Fine (2008).

—— (2009) 'Private Sector Participation in African Infrastructure: Is It Worth the Risk?' International Policy Center for Inclusive Growth Working Paper no.55, UNDP, Brasilia.

—— and B. Fine (eds) (2008) *Whither the Privatisation Experiment? Electricity and Water Sector Reform in Sub-Saharan Africa*, Basingstoke: Palgrave MacMillan.

—— and D. Hall (2001) 'A PSIRU Response to the World Bank's "Private Sector Development Strategy: Issues and Options"', Public Services International Research Unit, School of Computing and Mathematical Sciences, University of Greenwich, www.psiru.org/reports/2001-10-U-wb-psd.doc.

Bayraktar, N. and Y. Wang (2004) 'Foreign Bank Entry, Performance of Domestic Banks and Sequence of Financial Liberalization', World Bank Policy Research Working Paper no.3416.

Bebbington, A. (2004) 'Social Capital and Development Studies I: Critique, Debate, Progress?', *Progress in Development Studies*, vol.4, no.4, pp.343–49.

—— (2007) 'Social Capital and Development Studies II: Can Bourdieu Travel to Policy?', *Progress in Development Studies*, vol.7, no.2, pp.155–62.

—— (2008) 'Social Capital and Development Studies III: Social Capital and the State (Seen from Peru)', *Progress in Development Studies*, vol.8, no.3, pp.271–80.

—— S. Guggenheim, E. Olson and M. Woolcock (2004) 'Grounding Discourse in Practice: Exploring Social Capital Debates at the World Bank', *Journal of Development Studies*, vol.40, no.5, pp.33–64.

—— Woolcock, M., Guggenheim, S., and E. Olson (eds) (2006) *The Search for Empowerment: Social Capital as Idea and Practice at the World Bank*, Bloomfield: Kumarian Press.

—— D. Lewis, S. Batterbury, E. Olson, and M.S. Siddiqi (2007) 'Of Texts and Practices: Empowerment and Organisational Cultures in World Bank-Funded

Rural Development Programmes', *Journal of Development Studies*, vol.43, no.4, pp.597–621.

Beck, T. and M. Martinez Peria (2008) 'Foreign Bank Acquisitions and Outreach: Evidence from Mexico', World Bank Policy Research Working Paper no.4467.

—— A. Demirgüç-Kunt and V. Maksimovic (2004) 'Bank Competition and Access to Finance: International Evidence', *Journal of Money, Credit and Banking*, vol.36, no.3, pp.627–48.

—— A. Demirgüç-Kunt and M. Martinez Peria (2007) 'Reaching Out: Access to and Use of Banking Services across Countries', *Journal of Financial Economics*, vol.85, no.2, pp.234–66.

—— —— —— (2008) 'Banking Services for Everyone? Barriers to Bank Access and Use around the World', *World Bank Economic Review*, vol.22, no.3, pp.383–96.

—— B. Büyükkarabacak, F. Rioja and N. Valev (2008) 'Who Gets the Credit? and Does it Matter? Household vs. Firm Lending across Countries', World Bank Policy Research Working Paper no.4661.

Benjamin, B. (2007) *Invested Interests: Capital, Culture and the World Bank*, Minneapolis: University of Minnesota Press.

Bennell, P. (2004) 'Is UNAIDS Right? Levels and Trends in HIV Prevalence in Sub-Saharan Africa', ELDIS Discussion Paper, http://www.eldis.org/fulltext/unaids_bennell.pdf.

—— and T. Pearce (1998) 'The Internationalisation of Higher Education: Exporting Education to Developing and Transitional Economies', IDS Working Paper no.74, University of Sussex, Brighton.

Berdal, M. and D. Malone (eds) (2000) *Greed and Grievance: Economic Agendas in Civil Wars*, Boulder and London: IDRC/Lynne Rienner.

Berger, A. and G. Udell (2002) 'Small Business Credit Availability and Relationship Lending: The Importance of Bank Organisational Structure', *Economic Journal*, vol.112, no.477, pp.F32-F53.

—— L. Klapper and G. Udell (2001), 'The Ability of Banks to Lend to Informationally Opaque Small Businesses', *Journal of Banking and Finance*, vol.25, no.12, pp.2127–67.

—— N. Miller, M. Petersen, R. Rajan and J. Stein (2005) 'Does Function Follow Organizational Form? Evidence from the Lending Practices of Large and Small Banks', *Journal of Financial Economics*, vol.76, no.2, pp.237–69.

Bergesen, H.O. (1999) *Dinosaurs or Dynamos? The UN and the WB at the Turn of the Century*, London: Earthscan.

Bernstein, H. (2008) 'Agrarian Questions from Transition to Globalization', in Akram-Lodhi and Kay (2008).

—— (2009) 'V.I. Lenin and A.V. Chayanov: Looking Back, Looking Forward', *Journal of Peasant Studies*, vol.36, no.1, pp.55–81.

Bertrand, M. (2006) 'Evaluation of World Bank Projects', background report for the Deaton evaluation, http://siteresources.worldbank.org/DEC/Resources/84797-1109362238001/726454-1164121166494/3182920-1164133928090/Marianne-Bertrand.pdf.

Besteman, C. (1996) 'Local Land Use Strategies and Outsider Politics: Title Registration in the Middle Jubba Valley', in Besteman and Cassanelli (1996).

—— and L. Cassanelli (eds) (1996) *The Struggle for Land in Southern Somalia: The War Behind the War*, Boulder: Westview.

Beynon, J. (2001) 'Policy Implications for Aid Allocations of Recent Research on Aid Effectiveness and Selectivity', paper presented at the Joint Development Centre/

DAC Experts Seminar on Aid Effectiveness, Selectivity and Poor Performers, OECD, Paris, 17 January 2001, www.oecd.org/dataoecd/15/62/2664833.pdf.

Birdsall, N. (2006) 'Evaluation of World Bank Research Projects: Perspectives on AIDS', background report for Deaton evaluation, http://siteresources.worldbank. org/DEC/Resources/84797-1109362238001/726454-1164121166494/3182920-1164133928090/Nancy-Birdsall.pdf.

—— (ed.) (2006) *Rescuing the Bank*, Washington, DC: Center for Global Development.

BIS (2005) 'Foreign Direct Investment in the Financial Sector: Experiences in Asia, Central and Eastern Europe and Latin America', Committee on the Global Financial System Publications no.25, Bank for International Settlements.

Bischof, G., H. Rumpf, U. Hapke, C. Meyer and U. John (2003) 'Types of Natural Recovery from Alcohol Dependence: A Cluster Analytic Approach', *Addiction*, vol.98, no.12, pp.1737–46.

Blackburn, R. (2008) 'The Subprime Crisis', *New Left Review*, no.50: 63–106.

Blakely, T., J. Atkinson, V. Ivory, J. Wilton and P. Howden-Chapman (2006) 'No Association of Neighbourhood Volunteerism with Mortality in New Zealand: A National Multilevel Cohort Study', *International Journal of Epidemiology*, vol.35, no.4, pp.981–89.

Blanchard, O., G. Dell'Ariccia and P. Mauro (2010) 'Rethinking Macroeconomic Policy', IMF Staff Position Note SPN/10/03, 12 February, http://www.imf.org/external/pubs/ft/spn/2010/spn1003.pdf.

Bleger, L. and G. Rozenwurcel (2000) 'Financiamiento a las Pymes y Cambio Estructural en la Argentina: Un Estudio de Caso Sobre Fallas de Mercado y Problemas de Información', *Desarrollo Economico*, vol.40, no.157, pp.45–71.

Blejer, M. and S. Sagari (1987) 'The Structure of the Banking Sector and the Sequence of Financial Liberalization', in Connolly and Gonzalez-Vega (1987).

Boelens R. (2009) 'The Politics of Disciplining Water Rights', *Development and Change*, vol.40, no.2, pp.307–31.

Bongaarts J. (2007) 'Late Marriage and the HIV Epidemic in Sub-Saharan Africa', *Population Studies*, vol.61, no.1, pp.73–83.

Bordo, M., B. Eichengreen and J. Kim (1998) 'Was There Really an Earlier Period of International Financial Integration Comparable to Today?', in Bank of Korea (1998).

Borras, S.J. (2007) *Pro-Poor Land Reform: A Critique*, Ottawa: University of Ottawa Press.

Bourguignon, F. (2006) 'Chief Economist's Response: An Evaluation of World Bank Research, 1998–2005', World Bank, http://siteresources.worldbank.org/DEC/Resources/84797-1109362238001/726454-1164121166494/Research-Evaluation-2006-Chief-Economist-Response-11-27-06-FINAL.pdf.

Brahmbhatt, M., E. Ley, P. Paci, N. Sinha, V. Suri, M. Verhoeven and N.R. Zagha (2008) 'Weathering the Storm: Economic Policy Responses to the Financial Crisis', http://siteresources.worldbank.org/NEWS/Resources/weatheringstorm.pdf.

Braun, J. von (2008) 'Food and Financial Crises: Implications for Agriculture and the Poor', Washington, DC: IFPRI.

Bridgen, P. (2006) 'Social Capital, Community Empowerment and Public Health: Policy Developments in the UK since 1997', *Policy and Politics*, vol.34, no.1, pp.27–50.

Broad, R. (2006) 'Research, Knowledge, and the Art of "Paradigm Maintenance": the World Bank's Development Economics Vice-Presidency (DEC)', *Review of International Political Economy*, vol.13, no.3, pp.387–419.

—— and J. Cavanagh (2009) *Development Redefined: How the Market Met Its Match*, Boulder: Paradigm Publishers.

Brooks, N., N. Grist and K. Brown (2009) 'Development Futures in the Context of Climate Change: Challenging the Present and Learning from the Past', *Development Policy Review*, vol.27, no.6, pp.741–65.

Bujra, J. (2006) 'Class Relations: AIDS & Socioeconomic Privilege in Africa', *Review of African Political Economy*, vol.33, no.107, pp.113–29.

Buddenberg, D. and W. Byrd (eds) (2006) *Afghanistan's Drug Industry. Structure, Functioning, Dynamics and Implications for Counter-Narcotics Policy*, UNODC and the World Bank.

Burnside, C. and D. Dollar (1997) 'Aid, Policies and Growth', World Bank Policy Research Working Paper no.1777.

—— —— (2000) 'Aid, Policies and Growth', *American Economic Review*, vol.90, no.4, pp.847–68.

Byrd, W (2008) 'Responding to Afghanistan's Opium Economy Challenge: Lessons and Policy Implications from a Development Perspective', World Bank Policy Research Working Paper no.4545.

Byrd, W. and D. Buddenberg (2006) 'Introduction and Overview' in Buddenberg and Byrd (2006).

—— and O. Jonglez (2006) 'Prices and Market Interactions in the Opium Economy', in Buddenberg and Byrd (2006).

—— and C. Ward (2004) 'Drugs and Development in Afghanistan', Social Development Papers, Conflict Prevention and Reconstruction Unit, paper no.18, World Bank.

Byres, T. (1979) 'Of Neo-Populist Pipe Dreams: Daedalus in the Third World and the Myth of Urban Bias', *Journal of Peasant Studies*, vol.6, no.2, pp.210–40.

—— (2003a) 'Agriculture and Development: the Dominant Orthodoxy and an Alternative View', in Chang (2003).

—— (2003b) 'Paths of Capitalist Agrarian Transition in the Past and in the Contemporary World', in Ramachandran and Swaminathan (2003).

—— (ed.) (2004) 'Redistributive Land Reform Today', special issue of *Journal of Agrarian Change*, vol.4, nos 1–2.

Caddell, M. (1999) 'What Knowledge for Development? Some Thoughts on the *1998–1999 World Development Report, Knowledge for Development*', *Norrag News*, no.24, pp.13–16.

—— and H. Yanacopulos (2006) 'Knowing but Not Knowing: Conflict, Development and Denial', *Conflict, Security, Development*, vol.6, no.4, pp.557–79.

Campbell, C. and C. McLean (2002) 'Ethnic Identities, Social Capital and Health Inequalities: Factors Shaping African–Caribbean Participation in Local Community Networks in the UK', *Social Science and Medicine*, vol.55, no.4, pp.643–57.

Campbell, J. and J. Cocco (2003) 'Household Risk Management and Optimal Mortgage Choice', *Quarterly Journal of Economics*, vol.118, no.4, pp.1449–94.

Carlsson, J. and L. Wohlgemut (eds) (2000) *Learning in Development Co-operation*, Stockholm: Expert Group on Development Issues.

Carney, R. (2009) 'Chinese Capitalism in the OECD Mirror', *New Political Economy*, vol.14, no.1, pp.71–99.

Carpiano, R. (2006) 'Towards a Neighborhood Resource-Based Theory of Social Capital for Health: Can Bourdieu and Sociology Help?', *Social Science and Medicine*, vol.62, no.1, pp.165–75.

—— (2007) 'Neighborhood Social Capital and Adult Health: An Empirical Test of a Bourdieu-Based Model', *Health and Place*, vol.13, no.3, pp.639–55.

Chang, H.-J. (ed.) (2001) *Joseph Stiglitz and the World Bank: The Rebel Within*, London: Anthem Press.

—— (ed.) (2003) *Rethinking Development Economics*, London: Anthem Press.

—— (2009) 'Rethinking Public Policy in Agriculture: Lessons from History, Distant and Recent', *Journal of Peasant Studies*, vol.36, no.3, pp.477–515.

Cheng, H.-S. (ed.) (1986) *Financial Policy and Reform in Pacific Basin Countries*, Lexington: Lexington Books.

Cheung, Y. and N. Cheung (2003) 'Social Capital and Risk Level of Post-Treatment Drug Use: Implications for Harm Reduction among Male Treated Addicts in Hong Kong', *Addiction Research and Theory*, vol.11, no.3, pp.145–62.

Čihák, M. and R. Podpiera (2005) 'Bank Behavior in Developing Countries: Evidence from East Africa', IMF Working Paper no.05/129.

Claessens, S. (2006a) 'Competitive Implications of Cross-Border Banking', World Bank Policy Research Working Paper no.3854.

—— (2006b) 'Comments on "Foreign Banks in Poor Countries: Theory and Evidence"', International Monetary Fund, http://www.imf.org/external/np/res/seminars/2006/arc/pdf/claess.pdf.

—— and M. Jansen (eds) (2000) *The Internationalisation of Financial Services*, London: Kluwer Law International.

—— and J. Lee (2003) 'Foreign Banks in Low-Income Countries: Recent Developments and Impacts', in Hanson, Majnoni and Honohan (2003).

—— A. Demirgüç-Kunt and H. Huizinga (2001) 'How Does Foreign Entry Affect Domestic Banking Markets?', *Journal of Banking and Finance*, vol.25, no.5, pp.891–911.

Clarke, G., R. Cull, and M. Martinez Peria (2006) 'Foreign Bank Participation and Access to Credit Across Firms in Developing Countries', *Journal of Comparative Economics*, vol.34, no.4: pp.774–95.

Clarke, G., K. Kosec and S. Wallsten (2009) 'Has Private Participation in Water and Sewerage Improved Coverage? Empirical Evidence from Latin America', *Journal of International Development*, vol.21, no.3, pp.327–61.

—— —— L. D'Amato and A. Moliniari (2000) 'On the Kindness of Strangers? The Impact of Foreign Entry on Domestic Banks in Argentina', in Claessens and Jansen (2000).

—— —— M. Martinez Peria, and S. Sanchez (2002) 'Bank Lending to Small Businesses in Latin America: Does Bank Origin Matter?', World Bank Policy Research Working Paper no.2760.

—— —— —— —— (2005) 'Bank Lending to Small Businesses in Latin America: Does Bank Origin Matter?', *Journal of Money, Credit, and Banking*, vol.37, no.1, pp.83–118.

Cole, S. (2004) 'Fixing Market Failures or Fixing Elections? Elections, Banks, and Agricultural Credit in India', Harvard Business School, Cambridge, MA, http://www.hbs.edu/research/pdf/09-001.pdf.

Collier, P. (1997a) 'The Failure of Conditionality', in Gwin and Nelson (eds) (1997).

—— (1997b) 'Aid and Economic Development in Africa', Centre for the Study of African Economies, Department of Economics, University of Oxford.

—— (2000a) 'Conditionality, Dependence and Coordination: Three Current Debates in Aid Policy', in Gilbert and Vines (2000).

—— (2000b) 'Doing Well Out of War: An Economic Perspective', in Berdal and Malone (2000).

—— (2003) 'The Market for Civil War', *Foreign Policy*, 136: pp.38–45.

—— (2006) Keynote Address to conference on 'Private Sector Development and Peacebuilding: Exploring Local and International Perspectives', Berlin, September, www.businessenvironment.org/dyn/be/besearch.details?p_phase_id=108&p_lang=n&p_phase_type_id=6.

—— (2007) *The Bottom Billion: Why the Poorest Countries Are Failing and What Can Be Done About It*, Oxford: Oxford University Press.

—— and S. Dercon (2008) 'African Agriculture in 50 Years: Smallholders in a Rapidly Changing World', FAO Expert Meeting on How to Feed the World in 2050, 24–26 June 2009.

—— and D. Dollar (1999) 'Aid Allocation and Poverty Reduction', World Bank Policy Research Working Paper no.2041.

—— —— (2001) 'Can the World Cut Poverty in Half. How Policy Reform and Effective Aid can Meet IDGs', *World Development*, vol.29, no.11, pp.1787–802.

—— —— (2002) 'Aid Allocation and Poverty Reduction', *European Economic Review*, vol.46, no.8, pp.1475–1500.

—— —— (2004) 'Development Effectiveness: What Have We Learnt?', *Economic Journal*, vol.114, no.496, pp.244–71.

—— and J. Gunning (1999) 'Explaining African Economic Performance', *Journal of Economic Literature*, vol.37, no.1, pp.64–111.

—— and A. Hoeffler (2002) 'On the Incidence of Civil Wars in Africa', *Journal of Conflict Resolution*, vol.46, no.1, pp.13–28.

—— and N. Sambanis (eds) (2005) *Understanding Civil War: Evidence and Analysis* (2 vols), Washington, DC: World Bank.

—— P. Guillaumont, S. Guillaumont and J. Gunning (1997) 'Redesigning Conditionality', *World Development*, vol.25, no.9, pp.1399–1407.

Commission for Africa (2005) *Our Common Interest - Report of the Commission for Africa*, http://allafrica.com/sustainable/resources/view/00010595.pdf.

Connolly, P and C. Gonzalez-Vega (eds) *Economic Reform and Stabilization in Latin America*, London: Greenwood Press.

Cooley, A. and J. Ron (2002) 'The NGO Scramble: Organisational Insecurity and the Political Economy of Transnational Action', *International Security*, vol.27, no.1, pp.5–39.

Coraggio, J.-L. (2001) 'Universities and National Knowledge-Based Development: An Alternative to a Global Knowledge Bank', in Gmelin, King and McGrath (2001).

Cramer, C. (2006) *Civil War Is Not a Stupid Thing: Accounting for Violence in Developing Countries*, London: Hurst.

—— L. Hammond and J. Pottier (eds) (forthcoming) *Ethical and Methodological Challenges of Researching Violence in Africa*, Leiden: AEGIS/Brill.

Crosby, R. and D. Holtgrave (2006) 'The Protective Value of Social Capital against Teen Pregnancy: A State-Level Analysis', *Journal of Adolescent Health*, vol.38, no.5, pp.556–59.

—— —— R. DiClemente, G. Wingood and J. Gayle (2003) 'Social Capital as a Predictor of Adolescents' Sexual Risk Behavior: A State-Level Exploratory Study', *AIDS and Behavior*, vol.7, no.3, pp.245–52.

Cuadrado, J., G. de la Dehesa and A. Precedo (1993) 'Regional Imbalances and Government Compensatory Financial Flows: The Case of Spain', in Giovannini (1993).

Das, J. and J. Hammer (2005) 'Money for Nothing: The Dire Straits of Medical Practice in Delhi, India', World Bank Policy Research Working Paper no.3669.

de Groote, T. et al. (2005) 'Colombia: In Vivo Test of Health Sector Privatization in the Developing World', *International Journal of Health Services*, vol.35, no.1, pp.125–41.

De Silva, M.S. Huttly, T. Harpham and M. Kenward (2007) 'Social Capital and Mental Health: A Comparative Analysis of Four Low Income Countries', *Social Science and Medicine*, vol.64, no.1, pp.5–20.

—— T. Harpham, T. Tuan, R. Bartolini, M. Penny and S. Huttly (2006) 'Psychometric and Cognitive Validation of a Social Capital Measurement Tool in Peru and Vietnam', *Social Science and Medicine*, vol.62, no.4, pp.941–53.

de Waal, A. (1997) *Famine Crimes: Politics and the Disaster Relief Industry in Africa*, London: James Currey /African Rights.

Deaton, A. (2003) 'Health, Inequality, and Economic Development', *Journal of Economic Literature*, vol.41, no.1, pp.113–58.

—— (2009a) 'The World Development Report at Thirty: A Birthday Tribute or a Funeral Elegy', in Yusuf (2009).

—— (2009b) 'Instruments of Development: Randomization in the Tropics, and the Search for the Elusive Keys to Economic Development', the Keynes Lecture, British Academy, October 9th, 2008, http://www.princeton.edu/~deaton/downloads/Instruments_of_Development.pdf.

—— A. Banerjee, N. Lustig and K. Rogoff (2006) 'An Evaluation of World Bank Research, 1998–2005', http://siteresources.worldbank.org/DEC/Resources/84797-1109362238001/726454-1164121166494/RESEARCH-EVALUATION-2006-Main-Report.pdf.

Debt Relief International (2002) 'Implementing HIPC II', Declaration of the 6th HIPC Ministerial Meeting, London, March, http://www.development-finance.org.

Deininger, K. (2003) *Land Policies for Growth and Poverty Reduction*, Oxford and New York: World Bank and Oxford University Press.

Demirgüç-Kunt, A. and L. Servén (2009) 'Are All the Sacred Cows Dead? Implications of the Financial Crisis for Macro and Financial Policies', World Bank Policy Research Working Paper no.4807.

Demsetz, H. (1973) 'Industry Structure, Market Rivalry, and Public Policy Source', *Journal of Law and Economics*, vol.16, no.1, pp.1–9.

Denizer, D. (2000) 'Foreign Entry in Turkey's Banking Sector, 1980–1997', in Claessens and Jansen (2000).

Denning, S. (2000) 'What is Knowledge Management?', http://www.stevedenning.com/what_is_knowledge_management.html.

—— (2001) 'Knowledge Sharing in the North and South', in Gmelin, King and McGrath (2001).

Dennis, S. and E. Zuckerman (2008) 'Mapping Multilateral Development Banks' Reproductive Health and HIV/AIDS Spending', *Gender & Development*, vol.16, no.2, pp.287–300.

Dethier, J. (2007) 'Producing Knowledge for Development: Research at the World Bank', *Global Governance*, vol.13, pp.469–78.

Detragiache, E., P. Gupta and T. Tressel (2006) 'Foreign Banks in Poor Countries: Theory and Evidence', paper presented at the 7th Jacques Polak Annual Research

Conference, International Monetary Fund, http://www.imf.org/external/np/res/seminars/2006/arc/pdf/tressel.pdf.

DfID (2005) *Growth and Poverty Reduction: The Role of Agriculture*, London: Department for International Development.

DHS (2005) 'Tanzania: AIS, 2003–04', HIV Fact Sheets no.HF10. Calverton, MD: Measure DHS, ICF Macro, http://www.measuredhs.com/pubs/pdf/HF10/Tanzania_HIV_factsheet.pdf.

DiClemente, R., R. Crosby and M. Kegler (eds) (2002) *Emerging Theories in Health Promotion Practice and Research*, San Francisco: Jossey-Bass/Pfeiffer.

Dinc, S. (2005) 'Politicians and Banks: Political Influences on Government-Owned Banks in Emerging Countries', *Journal of Financial Economics*, vol.77, no.2, pp.453–79.

Djamba, Y. (2003) 'Social Capital and Premarital Sexual Activity in Africa: The Case of Kinshasa, Democratic Republic of Congo', *Archives of Sexual Behavior*, vol.32, no.4, pp.327–37.

Dolan, C. and Humphrey, J. (2000) 'Governance and Trade in Fresh Vegetables: The Impact of UK Supermarkets on the African Horticulture Industry', *Journal of Development Studies*, vol.37, no.2, pp.147–76.

Dollar, D. (2001) 'Some Thoughts on the Effectiveness of Aid, Non-Aid Development Finance and Technical Assistance', *Journal of International Development*, vol.13, no.7, pp.1039–55.

—— and W. Easterly (1999) 'The Search for the Key: Aid, Investment and Policies in Africa', *Journal of African Economies*, vol.8, no.4, pp.546–77.

—— and A. Kraay (2002) 'Growth is Good for the Poor', *Journal of Economic Growth*, vol.7, no.3, pp.195–225.

—— S. Devarajan and T. Holmgren (2001) 'Overview', in World Bank (2001b).

Doornbos, M. (2000) '"Good Governance": The Rise and Decline of a Policy Metaphor?', *Journal of Development Studies*, vol.37, no.6, pp.93–108.

Dorward, A., J. Kydd and C. Poulton (1998) *Smallholder Cash Crop Production under Market Liberalisation: A New Institutional Economics Perspective*, Wallingford: CAB International.

—— —— J. Morrison and I. Urey (2004) 'A Policy Agenda for Pro-Poor Agricultural Growth', *World Development*, vol.32, no.1, pp.73–89.

Douglas, J., S. Earle and S. Handsley (eds) (2007) *A Reader in Promoting Public Health*, London: Sage.

Drukker M., C. Kaplan, F. Feron and J. van Os (2003) 'Children's Health-Related Quality of Life, Neighbourhood Socio-Economic Deprivation and Social Capital: A Contextual Analysis', *Social Science and Medicine*, vol.57, no.5, pp.825–41.

Duenwald, C., N. Gueorguiev and A. Schaechter (2005) 'Too Much of a Good Thing? Credit Booms in Transition Economies: The Cases of Bulgaria, Romania, and Ukraine', IMF Working Paper no.05/128.

Duflo, E. (2006) 'Evaluation of World Bank Research', background report for the Deaton evaluation, http://siteresources.worldbank.org/DEC/Resources/84797-1109362238001/726454-1164121166494/3182920-1164133928090/Esther-Duflo.pdf.

Dutt, A. and K. Jameson (eds) (1992) *New Directions in Development Economics*, Aldershot: Edward Elgar.

Dyer, G. (2004) 'Redistributive Land Reform: No April Rose. The Poverty of Berry and Cline and GKI on the Inverse Relationship', *Journal of Agrarian Change*, vol.4, nos 1–2, pp.45–72.

Dymski, G. (2009), 'Racial Exclusion and the Political Economy of the Subprime Crisis', *Historical Materialism*, vol.17, no.2, pp.149–79.

Easterly, W. (2001a) *The Elusive Quest for Growth: Economists' Adventures and Misadventures in the Tropics*, Cambridge: MIT Press.

Easterly, W. (2001b) 'The Lost Decades: Developing Countries' Stagnation in Spite of Policy Reform 1980–1998', World Bank Policy Research Working Paper no.2272.

—— (2002) 'How Did Heavily Indebted Poor Countries Become Heavily Indebted? Reviewing Two Decades of Debt Relief', *World Development*, vol.30, no.10, pp.1677–96.

—— (2003) 'Can Foreign Aid Buy Growth?', *Journal of Economic Perspectives*, vol.17, no.3, pp.23–48.

—— R. Levine and D. Roodman (2003) 'New Data, New Doubts: A Comment on Burnside and Dollar's "Aid, Policies and Growth"', *American Economic Review*, vol.92, no.4, pp.1126–37.

Ebrahim, S. (2004) 'Social Capital: Everything or Nothing?', *International Journal of Epidemiology*, vol.33, no.4, p.627.

Ellaway, A. (2004) 'Commentary: Can Subtle Refinements of Popular Concepts Be Put into Practice?', *International Journal of Epidemiology*, vol.33, no.4, pp.681–2.

Ellerman, D. (2001) 'From Sowing to Reaping: Improving the Investment Climate(s)', http://www.ellerman.org/Davids-Stuff/Memos/SOW&REAP.PDF.

Ergüneş, N. (2009) 'Global Integration of the Turkish Economy in the Era of Financialisation', Research on Money and Finance Working Paper no.8.

Estache, A. and E. Kouassi (2002) 'Sector Organization, Governance, and the Inefficiency of African Water Utilities', World Bank Policy Research Working Paper no.2890.

—— and M. Rossi (2002) 'How Different is the Efficiency of Public and Private Water Companies in Asia?' *World Bank Economic Review*, vol.16, no.1, pp.139–48.

Fafchamps, M. (2006) 'Evaluation of World Bank Research', background report for the Deaton evaluation, http://siteresources.worldbank.org/DEC/Resources/84797-1109362238001/726454-1164121166494/3182920-1164133928090/Marcel-Fafchamps.pdf.

Faini, R., G. Galli and C. Gianni (1993) 'Finance and Development: The Case of Southern Italy', in Giovannini (1993).

Fall, M., P. Marin, A. Locussol and R. Verspyck (2009) 'Reforming Urban Water Utilities in Western and Central Africa: Experiences with Public Private Partnerships', Report no.48730, Vol. 1 Water Sector Board Discussion Paper Series 13, World Bank, Washington, DC.

FAO (2008) *The State of Food Insecurity in the World 2008*, Rome: FAO.

Farr, J. (2004) 'Social Capital: A Conceptual History', *Political Theory*, vol.32, no.1, pp.6–33.

—— (2007) 'In Search of Social Capital', *Political Theory*, vol.35, no.1, pp.54–61.

Ferguson, J. (2007) 'Formalities of Poverty: Thinking about Social Assistance in Neoliberal South Africa', *African Studies Review*, vol.50, no.2, pp.71–86.

Ferguson, K. (2006) 'Social Capital and Children's Well-Being: A Critical Synthesis of the International Social Capital Literature', *International Journal of Social Welfare*, vol.15, no.1, pp.2–18.

Fine, B. (1999) 'The Developmental State is Dead: Long Live Social Capital?', *Development and Change*, vol.30, no.1, pp.1–19.

—— (2001a) *Social Capital versus Social Theory: Political Economy and Social Science at the Turn of the Millennium*, London: Routledge.

—— (2001b) 'Neither the Washington nor the Post-Washington Consensus: An Introduction', in Fine, Lapavitsas and Pincus (2001).

—— (2002a) 'Economic Imperialism: A View from the Periphery', *Review of Radical Political Economics*, vol.34, no.2, pp.187–201.

—— (2002b) 'Review of C. Gilbert and D. Vines, *The World Bank: Structure and Policies*', *Journal of Agrarian Change*, vol.2, no.1, pp.130–2.

—— (2002c) *The World of Consumption: The Material and Cultural Revisited*, London: Routledge.

—— (2002d) 'Economics Imperialism and the New Development Economics as Kuhnian Paradigm Shift', *World Development*, vol.30, no.12, pp.2057–70.

—— (2003) 'Social Capital: The World Bank's Fungible Friend', *Journal of Agrarian Change*, vol.3, no.4, pp.586–603.

—— (2006) 'The New Development Economics', in Jomo and Fine (2006).

—— (2007a) 'Social Capital Goes to McDonald's', plenary address, Critical Management Studies Conference, University of Manchester, July 2007, http://www.mbs.ac.uk/research/organisationstudies/cms5/documents/benfine.pdf.

—— (2007b) 'Social Capital', *Development in Practice*, http://www.informaworld.com/smpp/title~content=t713412875~db=all~tab=issueslist~branches=17-v1717(4 & 5), pp.566–74.

—— (2007c) 'Eleven Hypotheses on the Conceptual History of Social Capital', *Political Theory*, vol.35, no.1, pp.47–53.

—— (2007d) 'Financialisation, Poverty, and Marxist Political Economy', Poverty and Capital Conference, 2–4 July 2007, University of Manchester, https://eprints.soas.ac.uk/5685/1/brooks.pdf.

—— (2008a) 'Social Capital and Health: The World Bank through the Looking Glass after Deaton', paper for presentation on 12 March 2008 at seminar for School of Oriental and African Studies/London International Development Centre, eprints.soas.ac.uk/5623/.

—— (2008b) 'Social Capital in Wonderland: The World Bank behind the Looking Glass', *Progress in Development Studies*, vol.8, no.3, pp.261–9.

—— (2009a) 'Financialisation and Social Policy', prepared for conference on 'Social and Political Dimensions of the Global Crisis: Implications for Developing Countries', 12–13 November 2009, UNRISD, Geneva, https://eprints.soas.ac.uk/7984, shortened and revised version in Utting, Razavi and Buchholz (2011).

—— (2009b) 'Social Capital versus Social History', *Social History*, vol.33, no.4, pp.442–67.

—— (2009c) 'Development as Zombieconomics in the Age of Neo-Liberalism', *Third World Quarterly*, vol.30, no.5, pp.885–904.

—— (2009d) 'Social Policy and the Crisis of Neo-Liberalism', prepared for conference on 'The Crisis of Neo-Liberalism in India: Challenges and Alternatives', Tata Institute of Social Sciences (TISS) Mumbai and International Development Economics Associates (IDEAs), 13–15 March 2009, networkideas.org/ideasact/jan09/ia27_International_Conference.htm.

—— (2009e) 'Neo-Liberalism in Retrospect? It's Financialisation, Stupid', conference on 'Developmental Politics in the Neo-Liberal Era and Beyond', 22–24 October 2009, Center for Social Sciences, Seoul National University, https://eprints.soas.ac.uk/7993/.

—— (2009f) 'Political Economy for the Rainbow Nation: Dividing the Spectrum?', prepared for 'Making Sense of Borders: Identity, Citizenship and Power in South

Africa', annual conference of the South African Sociological Association, June/ July, Johannesburg, https://eprints.soas.ac.uk/7972/.

—— (2010a) *Theories of Social Capital: Researchers Behaving Badly*, London: Pluto Press.

—— (2010b) 'Flattening Economic Geography: Locating the World Development Report for 2009', *Journal of Economic Analysis*, vol.1, no.1, pp.15–33.

—— (2010c) 'Industrial Policy', mimeo, available upon request from author.

—— (2010d) 'Neo-Liberalism as Financialisation', in Saad-Filho and Yalman (2010).

—— (2010e) 'Looking at the Crisis through Marx: Or Is It the Other Way about?', in Kates (2010).

—— (2011) 'Neo-Liberalism in Retrospect? It's Financialisation, Stupid', in Fine, Chang and Weiss (2011).

—— and D. Hall (2011) 'Terrains of Neoliberalism: Constraints and Opportunities for Alternative Models of Service Delivery', in McDonald and Ruiters (2011).

—— and D. Milonakis (2009) *From Economics Imperialism to Freakonomics: The Shifting Boundaries Between Economics and Other Social Sciences*, London: Routledge.

—— K.-S. Chang and L. Weiss (eds) (2011) *Developmental Politics in Transition: The Neoliberal Era and Beyond*, in preparation.

—— C. Lapavitsas and J. Pincus (eds) (2001) *Development Policy in the Twenty-First Century. Beyond the Post-Washington Consensus*, London: Routledge.

—— Saraswati, J. and D. Tavasci (eds) (2011), *Beyond the Developmental State*, London: Pluto Press, forthcoming.

Fischer, S. (2001) 'Ten Years of Transition: Looking Back and Looking Forward', *IMF Staff Papers*, vol.48 (special issue), pp.1–8.

Folland, S. (2007) 'Does "Community Social Capital" Contribute to Population Health?', *Social Science and Medicine*, vol.64, no.11, pp.2342–54.

Forbes, A. and S. Wainwright (2001) 'On the Methodological, Theoretical and Philosophical Context of Health Inequalities Research: A Critique', *Social Science and Medicine*, vol.53, no.6, pp.801–16.

Foster, V. and C. Briceño-Garmendia (2010) *Africa's Infrastructure: A Time for Transformation*, Washington, DC: World Bank.

Fraser, A. (2005) 'Poverty Reduction Strategy Papers: Now Who Calls the Shots?', *Review of African Political Economy*, vol.104, no.5, pp.317–40.

Fry, M. (1974) *The Afghan Economy: Money, Finance and Critical Constraints to Development*, Leiden: Brill.

Fulkerson, G. and G. Thompson (2008) 'The Evolution of a Contested Concept: A Meta-Analysis of Social Capital Definitions and Trends (1988–2006)', *Sociological Inquiry*, vol.78, no.4, pp.536–57.

Galal, A., L. Jones, P. Tandon and O. Vogelsang (1994) *Welfare Consequences of Selling Public Enterprises: An Empirical Analysis*, World Bank and Oxford University Press: Oxford.

Galea, S., A. Karpati and B. Kennedy (2002) 'Social Capital and Violence in the United States, 1974–1993', *Social Science and Medicine*, vol.55, no.8, pp.1373–83.

Galiani, S. (2006) 'World Bank Evaluation Report', background report for Deaton evaluation, http://siteresources.worldbank.org/DEC/Resources/ 84797-1109362238001/726454-1164121166494/3182920-1164133928090/ Sebastian-Galiani.pdf.

—— P. Gertler and E. Schargrodsky (2005) 'Water for Life: The Impact of the Privatisation of Water Services on Child Mortality', *Journal of Political Economy*, vol.113, no.1, pp.83–120.

Gallagher, K. (2009), 'The Economic Crisis and the Developing World: What Next? Interview with Robert Wade and José Antonio Ocampo', *Challenge*, vol.52, no.1, pp.27–39.

Garcia-Herrero, A. and M. Martinez Peria (2005) 'The Mix of International Banks' Foreign Claims: Determinants and Implications', World Bank Policy Research Working Paper no.3755.

Gassner, K., A. Popov and N. Pushak (2008) 'Does the Private Sector Deliver on Its Promises? Evidence from a Global Study in Water and Electricity', Gridlines, World Bank PPIAF note no. 36.

—— —— —— (2009) 'Does Private Sector Participation Improve Performance in Electricity and Water Distribution?', Trends and Policy Options no.6, World Bank and PPIAF, IBRD, Washington, DC.

Gavin, M. and D. Rodrik (1995) 'The World Bank in Historical Perspective', *American Economic Review*, vol.85, no.2, pp.329–34.

Gelb, A. and S. Sagari (1990) 'Banking', in Messerlin and Sanvant (1990).

—— B. Ngo and X. Ye (2004) 'Implementing Performance-Based Aid in Africa: The Country Policy and Institutional Assessment', World Bank Africa Region Working Paper no.77, Washington, DC.

Ghosh, J. (2010) 'The Unnatural Coupling: Food and Global Finance', *Journal of Agrarian Change*, vol.10, no.1, pp.72–86.

Giannetti, M. and S. Ongena (2005) 'Financial Integration and Entrepreneurial Activity: Evidence from Foreign Bank Entry in Emerging Markets', European Central Bank Working Paper no.498.

Gibbon, P., and S. Ponte (2005) *Trading Down: Africa, Value Chains, and the Global Economy*, Philadelphia: Temple University Press.

—— K. Havnevik and K. Hermele (1993) *A Blighted Harvest: The World Bank and African Agriculture in the Eighties*, London: James Currey.

Gilbert, C. and D. Vines (eds) (2000) *The World Bank: Structure and Policies*, Cambridge: Cambridge University Press.

—— A. Powell and D. Vines (1999) 'Positioning the World Bank', *Economic Journal*, vol.109, no.459, pp.598–633.

Gilbert, R. (1984) 'Bank Market Structure and Competition: A Survey', *Journal of Money, Credit and Banking*, vol.16, no.4, pp.617–45.

Giovannini, A. (ed.) (1993) *Finance and Development: Issues and Experience*, Cambridge: Cambridge University.

Giustozzi, A. (2007a) 'War and Peace Economies of Afghanistan's Strongmen', *International Peacekeeping*, vol.14, no.1, pp.75–89.

—— (2007b) *Koran, Kalashnikov and Laptop: The Neo-Taliban Insurgency in Afghanistan*, London: Hurst.

Gmelin, W., K. King and S. McGrath (eds) (2001) *Development Knowledge, National Research and International Cooperation*, Edinburgh: CAS.

Gold, R., B. Kennedy, F. Connell and I. Kawachi (2002) 'Teen Births, Income Inequality, and Social Capital: Developing an Understanding of the Causal Pathway', *Health and Place*, vol.8, no.2, pp.77–83.

Goodhand, J. (2004) 'Afghanistan in Central Asia', in Pugh, Cooper and Goodhand (2004).

—— (2005) 'Frontiers and Wars: The Opium Economy in Afghanistan', *Journal of Agrarian Change*, vol.5, no.2, pp.191–216.

—— (2006) *Aiding Peace: The Role of NGOs in Armed Conflict*, Boulder: Lyne Reinner.

—— (2008) 'Corrupting or Consolidating the Peace? The Drugs Economy and Post Conflict Peacebuilding in Afghanistan', *International Peacekeeping*, vol.15, no.3, pp.405–23.

Gormley, T. (2007) 'Banking Competition in Developing Countries: Does Foreign Bank Entry Improve Credit Access?', Washington University, St Louis, John M. Olin School of Business, mimeo.

Greenbaum, S. (1967) 'Competition and Efficiency in the Banking System: Empirical Research and Policy Implications', *Journal of Political Economy*, vol.75, pp.461–79.

Grootaert, C. (1997) 'Social Capital: The Missing Link?', in World Bank (1997c), reproduced as World Bank, Social Capital Initiative, Working Paper no.3.

Gupta, G., J. Parkhurst, J. Ogden, P. Aggleton and A. Mahal (2008) 'Structural Approaches to HIV Prevention', *The Lancet*, vol.372, no.9640, pp.52–63.

Gutiérrez Sanín, F. (2003) 'Criminal Rebels? A Discussion of War and Criminality from the Colombian Experience', Crisis States Programme Working Paper no.27, DESTIN.

Guttentag, J. and E. Herman (1967) 'Banking Structure and Performance', New York University Bulletin nos 41–3, New York: New York University.

Gwin, C. (1994) 'US Relations with the WB 1945–1992', Brookings Occasional Paper, Brookings Institution, Washington, DC.

—— and J. Nelson (eds) (1997) *Perspectives on Aid and Development*, Washington, DC: Overseas Development Council.

Haber, S. and A. Musacchio (2005) 'Foreign Banks and the Mexican Economy, 1997–2004', Stanford Center for International Development Working Paper no.267.

Hall, D. (2008) 'Economic Crisis and Public Services', Public Services International Research Unit, note 1, December, http://www.psiru.org/reports/2008-12-crisis-1.doc.

—— and E. Lobina (2006) *Pipe Dreams: The Failure of the Private Sector to Invest in Water Services in Developing Countries*, Public Services International Research Unit Report, University of Greenwich.

Hallowes, D. (2009) 'The World Bank and Eskom: Banking on Climate Destruction', Pietermaritzburg: groundWork, http://www.bicusa.org/en/Issue.Resources.48.aspx.

Halpern, D. (2005) *Social Capital*, London: Polity.

Hanson, J., G. Majnoni and P. Honohan (eds) (2003) *Globalization and National Financial Systems*, Washington, DC: World Bank.

Hapitan, R. (2001) 'Reactions to the Entry of Foreign Banks in the Philippines', APEC Study Center Network Discussion Paper no.2001-09.

Harrison, G. (2004) *The World Bank and Africa*, London: Routledge.

Hausman, R. and D. Rodrik (2003) 'Economic Development as Self-Discovery', *Journal of Development Economics*, vol.72, no.2, pp.603–33.

Havnevik, K., D. Bryceson, L. Birgegard, P. Matondi and A. Beyene (2007) 'African Agriculture and the World Bank: Development or Impoverishment?' Policy Dialogue no.1, Nordic Africa Institute, Uppsala.

Hawe, P. and A. Shiell (2000) 'Social Capital and Health Promotion: A Review', *Social Science and Medicine*, vol.51, no.6, pp.871–85.

Haynie, D., S. South and S. Bose (2006) 'Residential Mobility and Attempted Suicide among Adolescents: An Individual-Level Analysis', *Sociological Quarterly*, vol.47, no.4, pp.693–721.

Hazell, P., C. Poulton, S. Wiggins and A. Dorward (2007) 'The Future of Small Farms for Poverty Reduction and Growth', IFPRI 2020 Discussion Paper no.42, Washington, DC.

Heal, G. (2006) 'World Bank Research Evaluation: Environmental Research', background report for Deaton evaluation, http://siteresources.worldbank.org/DEC/Resources/84797-1109362238001/726454-1164121166494/3182920-1164133928090/Geoffrey-Heal.pdf.

Heggestad, A. (1977) 'Market Structure, Risk and Profitability in Commercial Banking', *Journal of Finance*, vol.32, no.4, pp.1207–16.

Heimer, F. (1979) *The Decolonization Conflict in Angola, 1974–76: An Essay in Political Sociology*, Geneva: Institut Universitaire des Haute Études Internationales.

Hemenway, D., B. Kennedy, I. Kawachi and R. Putnam (2001) 'Firearm Prevalence and Social Capital', *Annals of Epidemiology*, vol.11, no.7, pp.484–90.

Hirschman, A.O. (1958) *The Strategy of Economic Development*, New Haven, CT: Yale University Press.

Hyyppä, M. and J. Mäki (2003) 'Social Participation and Health in a Community Rich in Stock of Social Capital', *Health and Education Research*, vol.18, no.6, pp.770–9.

IATP (2009) *Betting Against Food Security: Futures Market Speculation*, Trade and Governance Programme Paper, Minneapolis, MN: Institute for Agriculture and Trade Policy.

IDA (2003) 'Progress on Economic and Sector Work in IDA Countries', October, http://siteresources.worldbank.org/IDA/Resources/MTRESW.pdf.

—— (2004) 'Working Together at the Country Level: The Role of IDA', September, http://siteresources.worldbank.org/IDA/Resources/WorkingTogether.pdf.

—— (2006) 'Economic and Sector Work Progress Report', Operations Policy and Country Services, October, http://siteresources.worldbank.org/IDA/Resources/Seminar%20PDFs/73449-1164920192653/ESW.pdf.

—— (2007) 'Aid Architecture: An Overview of the Main Trends in Official Development Assistance Flows', Resource Mobilization, February, http://siteresources.worldbank.org/IDA/Resources/Seminar%20PDFs/73449-1172525976405/3492866-1172527584498/Aidarchitecture.pdf.

—— (2009) 'Proposal for a Pilot IDA Crisis Response Window', IDA Resource Mobilisation Department, November, Washington, DC :World Bank.

IEG (2007) *World Bank Assistance to Agriculture in Sub-Saharan Africa: An IEG Review*, Washington, DC: World Bank.

—— (2009) 'The World Bank's Country Policy and Institutional Assessment: An Evaluation', June, Washington, DC: World Bank.

IFAD (2001) *Rural Poverty Report 2001: The Challenge of Ending Rural Poverty*, Rome: FAO/IFAD.

IFC (2001) 'Investing in Private Education: IFC's Strategic Directions', Health and Education Group, Washington, DC.

—— (2007) 'Strategic Directions FY08–10: Creating Opportunity', http://www.ifc.org/ifcext/mena.nsf/AttachmentsByTitle/IFC_SDP_full/$FILE/IFC_SDP_full.pdf.

—— (2009a) 'IFC Helps Expand Health Care in Afghanistan', http://www.ifc.org/ifcext/media.nsf/Content/Afghanistan_HealthCare_Feb09.

—— (2009b) 'The Business of Health in Africa', http://www.ifc.org/ifcext/healthinafrica.nsf/Content/FullReport.

ILO (2010) 'Global Employment Trends: January 2010', Geneva: ILO.

IMF (2000) *World Economic Outlook: October 2000*, Washington, DC: International Monetary Fund.

—— (2006) *Global Stability Report 2006*, Washington, DC: International Monetary Fund.

IMF/World Bank (2004) 'Strengthening the Foundations for Growth and Private Sector Development: Investment Climate and Infrastructure Development', background paper for the Development Committee Meeting, September, Washington, DC.

—— (2010) 'Global Monitoring Report 2010: The MDGs after the Crisis', background report for the Development Committee Meeting, April, Washington, DC: IBRD/World Bank.

INFRA (2009) 'Impact of Global Crisis on Infrastructure PPP Projects: What Are the Issues at Stake and What Can the World Bank Group Do to Help?', INFRA Guidance Note, May 2009, Washington, DC: World Bank.

—— (2010a) 'Infrastructure Recovery and Assets (INFRA) Platform: A Response to Support Infrastructure during the Crisis', http://siteresources.worldbank.org/INTSDNET/Resources/5944695-1247775731647/InfrastructureRecoveryandAssets_overview_01.12.2010.pdf.

—— (2010b) 'Incorporating Social Dimensions in the Infrastructure Recovery and Assets (INFRA) Platform', January 2010, Washington, DC: World Bank.

Inocencio, A., M. Kikuchi, D. Merrey, M. Tonosaki, A. Maruyama, I. de Jong, H. Sally and F. Pennig de Vries (2005) 'Lessons from Irrigation Investment Experiences: Cost-Reducing and Performance-Enhancing Options for Sub-Saharan Africa', report submitted by the International Water Management Institute for implementation of the Collaborative Program on 'Investments in Agricultural Water Management in Sub Saharan Africa: Diagnosis of Trends and Opportunities', http://siteresources.worldbank.org/RPDLPROGRAM/Resources/459596-1170984095733/IWMICostsIrrigationProjects.pdf.

Iriart, C. , E. Merhy and H. Waitzkin (2001) 'Managed Care in Latin America: The New Common Sense in Health Policy Reform', *Social Science and Medicine*, vol.52, no.8, pp.1243–53.

Islam, M., U. Gerdtham, B. Gullberg, M. Lindström and J. Merlo (2008) 'Social Capital Externalities and Mortality in Sweden', *Economics and Human Biology*, vol.6, no.1, pp.19–42.

Ivanic, M. and W. Martin (2008) 'Implications of Higher Global Food Prices for Poverty in Low-Income Countries', World Bank Policy Research Working Paper no.4594.

Jalali, A., R. Oakley and Z. Hunter (2006) 'Combating Opium in Afghanistan', Strategic Forum no.224, Institution for National Strategic Studies, National Defence University, November.

Janvry, A. de (2009) 'Agriculture for Development: New Paradigm and Options for Success', Elmhirst Lecture, IAAE Conference, Beijing, 16–22 August, http://ageconsearch.umn.edu/bitstream/53202/2/Elmhirst%20IAAE%20Beijing%20de%20Janvry2.pdf.

Jeanne, O. (2003) 'Why Do Emerging Economies Borrow in Foreign Currency?', International Monetary Fund Working Paper no.03/177.

JMP (2008) 'Joint Monitoring Programme Progress Report on Drinking Water and Sanitation', UNICEF, WHO.

Johnston D. (2005) 'Poverty and Distribution: Back on the Neoliberal Agenda', in Saad-Filho and Johnston (2005).

—— (2010) 'Introduction to a Symposium on the 2007–8 World Food Crisis', *Journal of Agrarian Change*, vol.10, no.1, pp.69–71.

Jomo, K. and B. Fine (eds) (2006) *The New Development Economics: After the Washington Consensus*, Delhi: Tulika and London: Zed Press.

—— and E. Reinert (2005) *The Origins of Development Economics: How Schools of Economic Thought Have Addressed Development*, Delhi: Tulika and London: Zed Press.

Jones, P. (2004) 'When "Development" Devastates: Donor Discourses, Access to HIV/AIDS Treatment in Africa and Rethinking the Landscape of Development', *Third World Quarterly*, vol.25, no.2, pp.385–404.

Kanbur, R. (2001a) 'Economic Policy, Distribution and Poverty: The Nature of Disagreements', Department of Economics, Cornell University, http://www.ifad.org/poverty/lecture.pdf.

—— (2001b) 'Cross-Border Externalities, International Public Goods and Their Implications for Aid Agencies', Department of Economics, Cornell University, http://people.cornell.edu/pages/sk145/papers/IPGWB.pdf.

—— (2002) 'IFIs and IPGs: Operational Implications for the World Bank', Department of Economics, Cornell University, www.arts.cornell.edu/poverty/kanbur/IFI-IPG.pdf.

Kapur, D. (2002) 'The Changing Anatomy of Governance of the World Bank', in Pincus and Winters (2002).

—— (2003) 'Do as I Say Not as I Do: A Critique of G-7 Proposals on Reforming the Multilateral Development Banks', G-24 Discussion Paper no.20, UNCTAD, Geneva.

—— (2006) 'The 'Knowledge' Bank', in Birdsall (2006).

—— J. Lewis and R. Webb (1997) *The World Bank: Its First Half Century. Vol.1: History*, Washington, DC: Brookings Institution Press.

—— —— —— (eds) (1997) *The World Bank: Its First Half Century. Volume II: Perspectives*, Washington, DC: Brookings Institution Press.

Kariuki, M. and J. Schwartz (2005) 'Small-Scale Private Service Providers of Water Supply and Electricity: A Review of Incidence, Structure, Pricing and Operating Characteristics', World Bank Policy Research Working Paper no.3727.

Karshenas M. (2004) '"Urban Bias", Intersectoral Resource Flows and the Macroeconomic Implications of Agrarian Relations: The Historical Experience of Japan and Taiwan', *Journal of Agrarian Change*, vol.4, nos 1–2, pp.170–89.

Kates, S. (ed.) (2010) *The Meltdown of the World Economy: Alternative Perspectives on the Global Financial Crisis*, Edward Elgar: Cheltenham.

Katz, A. (2009) 'Time to Get beyond the Sex Act: Reflections on Three Decades of AIDS Reductionism', *Social Medicine*, vol.4, no.1, pp.1–7.

Kaufman, D., A. Kraay and M. Mastruzzi (2004) 'Governance Matters III: Governance Indicators for 1996–2002', *World Bank Economic Review*, vol.18, no.2, pp.253–87.

Kaul, I., I. Grunberg and M. Stern (eds) (1999) *Global Public Goods: International Cooperation in the 21st Century*, New York: Oxford University Press for UNDP.

Kavanagh, A., G. Turrell and S. Subramanian (2006) 'Does Area-Based Social Capital Matter for the Health of Australians? A Multilevel Analysis of Self-Rated Health in Tasmania', *International Journal of Epidemiology*, vol.35, no.3, pp.607–13.

Kawachi, I. (2001) 'Social Capital for Health and Human Development', *Development*, vol.44, no.1, pp.31–5.

—— and S. Wamala (eds) (2007) *Globalization and Health*, Oxford: Oxford University Press.

—— B. Kennedy, K. Lochner and D. Prothrow-Stith (1997) 'Social Capital, Income Inequality, and Mortality', *American Journal of Public Health*, vol.87, no.9, pp.1491–8.

—— D. Kim, A. Coutts and S. Subramanian (2004) 'Commentary: Reconciling the Three Accounts of Social Capital', *International Journal of Epidemiology*, vol.33, no.4, pp.682–90.

Kay, C. (2009) 'Development Strategies and Rural Development: Exploring Synergies, Eradicating Poverty', *Journal of Peasant Studies*, vol.36, no.1, pp.103–37.

Keen, D. (2005) *Conflict and Collusion in Sierra Leone*, Oxford: James Currey.

Kessides, I. (2004) *Reforming Infrastructure: Privatization, Regulation and Competition*, World Bank Policy Research Report, co-publication of the World Bank and Oxford University Press, Washington, DC: IBRD/World Bank.

Kherallah, M., C. Delgado, E. Gabre-Madhin, N. Minot and M. Johnson (2002) *Reforming Agricultural Markets in Africa*, London: Johns Hopkins University Press.

Khwaja, A. and A. Mian (2005) 'Do Lenders Favor Politically Connected Firms? Rent Provision in an Emerging Financial Market', *Quarterly Journal of Economics*, vol.120, no.4, pp.1371–411.

King, K. (2001a) '"Knowledge Agencies": Making the Globalisation of Development Knowledge Work for the North and the South?', in Gmelin, King and McGrath (2001).

—— (2001b) '"Knowledge Agencies": Making the Globalisation of Development Knowledge Work for the North and the South?', *Norrag News*, no.28, pp.17–18.

—— and S. McGrath (2004) *Knowledge for Development: Comparing British, Japanese, Swedish and World Bank Aid*, Zed Books: London.

King, R. and R. Levine (1993) 'Finance and Growth: Schumpeter Might be Right', *Quarterly Journal of Economics*, vol.108, no.3, pp.717–37.

Kirkpatrick, C., D. Parker and Y.-F. Zhang (2004) 'State Versus Private Sector Provision of Water Services in Africa: A Statistical, DEA and Stochastic Cost Frontier Analysis', Centre on Regulation and Competition Working Paper no.70, University of Manchester.

Kjellen, M. (2006) 'From Public Pipes to Private Hands: Water Access and Distribution in Dar es Salaam, Tanzania', Department of Human Geography, Stockholm University.

Kloeppinger-Todd, R. and J. Agwe (2008) 'Pilot Innovations Could Reignite Anemic Rural Finance', *Development Outreach*, vol.10, no.3, pp.27–30.

Koivusalo, M. (2009) 'The Shaping of Global Health Policy', in Panitch and Leys (2009).

Korf, B. (2005) 'Rethinking the Greed–Grievance Nexus: Property Rights and the Political Economy of War in Sri Lanka', *Journal of Peace Research*, vol.142, no.2, pp.201–17.

Kremer, M. (2006) 'Evaluation of World Bank Research Projects: Infrastructure', background report for Deaton evaluation, http://siteresources.worldbank.org/

DEC/Resources/84797-1109362238001/726454-1164121166494/3182920-1164133928090/Michael-Kremer.pdf.

Kreuter, M. and N. Lezin (2002) 'Social Capital Theory: Implications for Community-Based Health Promotion', in DiClemente, Crosby and Kegler (2002).

Krueger, A. (1998), 'Whither the World Bank and the IMF?', *Journal of Economic Literature*, vol.36, no.4, pp.1983–2020.

Kunitz, S. (2004) 'Social Capital and Health', *British Medical Bulletin*, vol.69, no.1, pp.1–13.

La Porta, R., F. Lopez-de-Silanes and A. Shleifer (2002) 'Government Ownership of Commercial Banks', *Journal of Finance*, vol.57, no.1, pp.265–301.

Labonté, R. and T. Schrecker (2007a) 'Globalization and Social Determinants of Health: Introduction and Methodological Background', *Globalization and Health*, vol.3, no.1, http://www.globalizationandhealth.com/content/3/1/.

—— —— (2007b) 'Globalization and Social Determinants of Health: The Role of the Global Marketplace', *Globalization and Health*, vol.3, no.1, http://www.globalizationandhealth.com/content/3/1/6.

—— —— (2007c) 'Globalization and Social Determinants of Health: Promoting Health Equity in Global Governance', *Globalization and Health*, vol.3, no.1, http://www.globalizationandhealth.com/content/3/1/7.

Lagarde, E., B. Auvert, M. Caraël, M. Laourou, B. Ferry, E. Akam, T. Sukwa, L. Morison, B. Maury, J. Chege, I. N'Doye, A. Buvé, and the Study Group on Heterogeneity of HIV Epidemics in African Cities (2001) 'Concurrent Sexual Partnerships and HIV Prevalence in Five Urban Communities of Sub-Saharan Africa', *AIDS*, vol.15, no.7, pp.877–84.

Lang, T. (2010) 'Crisis? What Crisis? The Normality of the Current Food Crisis', *Journal of Agrarian Change*, vol.10, no.1, pp.87–97.

Lapavitsas, C. (2003) *Social Foundations of Markets, Money and Credit*, London: Routledge.

—— (2009), 'Financialised Capitalism: Crises and Financial Expropriation', *Historical Materialism*, vol.18, no.2, pp.114–48.

—— and P. dos Santos (2008), 'Globalization and Contemporary Banking: On the Impact of New Technology', *Contributions to Political Economy*, vol.27, no.1, pp.31–56.

Lardy, N. (1998) *China's Unfinished Economic Revolution*, Washington, DC: Brookings Institution Press.

Lee, J. (2002) 'Financial Liberalization and Foreign Bank Entry in MENA', World Bank, http://siteresources.worldbank.org/INTMNAREGTOPTRADE/Resources/MENA-Financial-Sector-R3.pdf.

Leeder, S. (1998) 'Social Capital and Its Relevance to Health and Family Policy', www.pha.org.au/social.htm.

Leiteritz, R. and C. Weaver (2005) '"Our Poverty is a World Full of Dreams": Reforming the World Bank', *Global Governance*, vol.11, no.3, pp.369–88.

Lensink, R. and N. Hermes (2004) 'The Short-Term Effects of Foreign Bank Entry on Domestic Bank Behaviour: Does Economic Development Matter?' *Journal of Banking and Finance*, vol.28, no.3, pp.553–68.

Levine, R. (1996) 'Foreign Banks, Financial Development and Growth', in Barfield (1996).

—— (2003) 'Denying Foreign Bank Entry: Implications for Bank Interest Margins', Banco Central de Chile Documentos de Trabajo no.222.

Li, T. (2008) *The Will to Improve: Governmentality, Development and the Practice of Politics*, Durham, NC: Duke University Press.

Lin, J. (2006) 'Evaluation of World Bank Research Projects: Finance and Private Sector Development', background report for Deaton evaluation, http://siteresources.worldbank.org/DEC/Resources/84797-1109362238001/726454-1164121166494/3182920-1164133928090/Yi-Fu-Lin.pdf.

—— (2010) 'New Structural Economics: A Framework for Rethinking Development', World Bank Policy Research Working Paper no.5197.

—— and H.-J. Chang (2009) 'Should Industrial Policy in Developing Countries Conform to Comparative Advantage or Defy It? A Debate between Justin Lin and Ha-Joon Chang', *Development Policy Review*, vol.27, no.5, pp.483–502.

Lindström, M. (2004) 'Social Capital, the Miniaturization of Community and Cannabis Smoking among Young Adults', *European Journal of Public Health*, vol.14, no.2, pp.204–8.

—— (2005) 'Social Capital, the Miniaturization of Community and High Alcohol Consumption: A Population-Based Study', *Alcohol and Alcoholism*, vol.40, no.6, pp.556–62.

—— (2006) 'Social Capital and Lack of Belief in the Possibility to Influence One's Own Health: A Population-Based Study', *Scandinavian Journal of Public Health*, vol.34, no.1, pp.69–75.

—— (2008) 'Social Capital, Anticipated Ethnic Discrimination and Self-Reported Psychological Health: A Population-Based Study', *Social Science and Medicine*, vol.66, no.1, pp.1–13.

Lipton, M. (1977) *Why Poor People Stay Poor. A Study of Urban Bias in World Development*, London: Temple Smith.

—— (2006) 'Can Small Farmers Survive, Prosper, or Be the Key Channel to Cut Mass Poverty?' *Electronic Journal of Agricultural and Development Economics*, vol.3, no.1, pp.58–85.

Litan, R., P. Masson and M. Pomerleano (2001) *Open Doors: Foreign Participation on Financial Systems in Developing Countries*, Washington, DC: Brookings Institution Press.

Little P. and M. Watts (eds) (1994) *Living Under Contract: Contract Farming and Agrarian Transformation in Sub-Saharan Africa*, Madison: University of Wisconsin Press.

Lloyd, P., J. Croser and K. Anderson (2009) 'Global Distortions to Agricultural Markets: New Indicators of Trade and Welfare Impacts', Policy Research Working Paper no.4865, Washington, DC: World Bank.

Lo, D. (1999) 'Reappraising the Performance of China's State-Owned Industrial Enterprises, 1980–96', *Cambridge Journal of Economics*, vol.23, no.6, pp.693–718.

—— (2007) 'China's Quest for Alternatives to Neo-Liberalism: Market Reform, Economic Growth, and Labor', *Kyoto Economic Review*, vol.76, no.2, pp.193–210.

—— and Y. Zhang (2009) 'Making Sense of China's Economic Transformation', *Review of Radical Political Economics*, forthcoming.

Lofors, J. and K. Sundquist (2007) 'Low-Linking Social Capital as a Predictor of Mental Disorders: A Cohort Study of 4.5 Million Swedes', *Social Science and Medicine*, vol.64, no.1, pp.21–34.

Lohman, L. and S. Sexton (2010) 'Carbon Markets: The Policy Reality', *Global Social Policy*, vol.10, no.1, pp.3–6.

Lubker, M., G. Smith and J. Weeks (2002) 'Growth and the Poor: A Comment on Dollar and Kraay', *Journal of International Development*, vol.14, no.5, pp.555–71.

Luke, N. (2006) 'Exchange and Condom Use in Informal Sexual Relationships in Urban Kenya', *Economic Development and Cultural Change*, vol.54, no.2, pp.319–48.

MacFarlan, M. and S. Sgherri (2001) 'The Macroeconomic Impact of HIV/AIDS in Botswana', IMF Working Paper no.01/80.

Macinko, J. and B. Starfield (2001) 'The Utility of Social Capital in Studies on Health Determinants', *Milbank Quarterly*, vol.79, no.3, pp.387–428.

Mack, A. (2002) 'Civil War: Academic Research and the Policy Community', *Journal of Peace Research*, vol.39, no.5, pp.515–25.

Mansfield, D. (2006) 'Responding to the Diversity in Opium Poppy Cultivation', in Buddenberg and Byrd (2006).

—— (2007) 'Governance, Security and Economic Growth: The Determinants of Opium Poppy Cultivation in the Districts of Jurm and Baharak, Badakshan', report for GTZ/AKDN.

—— and A. Pain (2008) 'Counter-Narcotics in Afghanistan: The Failure of Success?', Afghanistan Research and Evaluation Unit (AREU), Kabul.

Mansyur, C., B. Amick, R. Harrist and L. Franzini (2008) 'Social Capital, Income Inequality, and Self-Rated Health in 45 Countries', *Social Science and Medicine*, vol.66, no.1, pp.43–56.

Marin, P. (2009) *Public–Private Partnerships for Urban Water Utilities: A Review of Experiences in Developing Countries*, PPIAF/World Bank, Trends and Policy Options No. 8.

—— and A.-K. Izaguirre (2006) 'Private Participation in Water: Toward a New Generation of Projects?', Gridlines, World Bank PPIAF note no.14.

Marks, S. (2007) 'Science, Social Science and Pseudo-Science in the HIV/AIDS Debate in Southern Africa', *Journal of Southern African Studies*, vol.33, no.4, pp.861–74.

Marmot, M. and R. Wilkinson (eds) (1999) *Social Determinants of Health*, Oxford: Oxford University Press.

Marriage, Z. (2006) *Not Breaking the Rules, Not Playing the Game: International Assistance to Countries at War*, London: Hurst.

Mathieson, D. and J. Roldós (2001) 'Foreign Banks in Emerging Markets', in Litan, Masson and Pomerleano (2001).

McCoy, D., G. Kembhavi, J. Patel and A. Luintel (2009) 'The Bill and Melinda Gates Foundation's Grant-Making Programme for Global Health', *The Lancet*, vol.373, no.9675, pp.1645–53.

McDonald, D. (2007) *Drugs in Afghanistan: Opium, Outlaws and Scorpion Tales*, London: Pluto Press.

—— and G. Ruiters (eds) (2011) *Alternatives to Privatization: Exploring Non-Commercial Service Delivery Options in the Global South*, forthcoming, papers from Muncipal Services Project, http://www.municipalservicesproject.org/.

McDonald, S. and J. Roberts (2006) 'AIDS and Economic Growth: A Human Capital Approach', *Journal of Development Economics*, vol.80, no.1, pp.228–50.

McGillivray, M., S. Feeny, N. Hermes and R. Lensink (2006) 'Controversies over the Impact of Development Aid: It Works; It Doesn't; It Can, but That Depends …', *Journal of International Development*, vol.18, no.7, pp.1031–50.

McLean, S., D. Schultz and M. Steger (eds) (2002) *Social Capital: Critical Perspectives on Community and 'Bowling Alone'*, New York: New York University Press.

Meadowcroft, J. and M. Pennington (2007) *Rescuing Social Capital from Social Democracy*, London: Institute of Economic Affairs.

Mehta, L. (1999) 'From Darkness to Light? Critical Reflections on the World Development Report 1998/99', *Journal of Development Studies*, vol.36, no.1, pp.151–61.

—— (2001) 'The World Bank and its Emerging Knowledge Empire', *Human Organisation*, vol.60, no.2, pp.189–95.

—— (2006) 'Reinventing Development Research', IDS 40th Anniversary Conference Report, IDS, University of Sussex, Brighton, www.ids.ac.uk.

Menard, C. and G. Clarke (2002) 'A Transitory Regime: Water Supply in Conakry, Guinea' in Shirley (2002).

Messerlin, P. and K. Sanvant (eds) (1990) *The Uruguay Round: Services in the World Economy*, Washington, DC: World Bank.

Mester, L. (1997) 'What is the Point of Credit Scoring?', *Federal Reserve Bank of Philadelphia Business Review*, September–October, pp.3–16.

Mian, A. (2006) 'Distance Constraints: The Limits of Foreign Lending in Poor Economies', *Journal of Finance*, vol.61, no.3, pp.1465–505.

Miles, D. (2004) *The UK Mortgage Market: Taking a Long-Term View*, London: HM Treasury.

Miller, D., R. Scheffler, S. Lam, R. Rosemberg and A. Rhupp (2006) 'Social Capital and Health in Indonesia', *World Development*, vol.34, no.6, pp.1084–98.

Milyo, J. and J. Mellor (2003) 'On the Importance of Age-Adjustment Methods in Ecological Studies of Social Determinants of Mortality', *Health Services Research*, vol.38, no.6, pt.2, pp.1781–90.

Minsky, H. (1992) 'The Financial Instability Hypothesis', Levy Institute Working Paper no.74.

Mishkin, F. (ed.) (2001) *Prudential Supervision: What Works and What Doesn't*, Chicago: University of Chicago Press.

Mishra, V., S. Bignami, R. Greener, M. Vaessen, R. Hong, P. Ghys, T. Boerma, A. Van Assche, S. Khan and S. Rutstein (2007) 'A Study of the Association of HIV Infection with Wealth in Sub-Saharan Africa', DHS Working Paper no.31, USAID/Measure, Calverton, MD.

Mitchell (2008) 'A Note on Rising Food Prices', World Bank Policy Research Working Paper no.4682.

Mkandawire, T. (1997) 'The Social Sciences in Africa: Breaking Local Barriers and Negotiating International Presence', the Bashorun M.K.O. Abiola Distinguished Lecture, presented to the 1996 African Studies Association Annual Meeting, *African Studies Review*, vol.40, no.2, pp.15–36.

—— (2000) 'Non-Organic Intellectuals and "Learning" in Policy-Making Africa', in Carlsson and Wohlgemut (2000).

—— (2002) 'Incentives, Governance and Capacity Development in Africa', in UNDP (2002).

Mohanty, S., G. Schnabel and P. Garcia-Luna (2004) 'Banks and Aggregate Credit: What Is New?', BIS Papers, vol.28, no.2, pp.11–39.

Monga, C. (2009) 'Post-Macroeconomics: Reflections on the Crisis and Strategic Directions Ahead', World Bank Policy Research Working Paper no.4986.

Mooney, G. (2005) 'Addictions and Social Compassion', *Drug and Alcohol Review*, vol.24, no.2, pp.137–41.

Morduch, J. (2006) 'Evaluation of World Bank Research Projects: Financial Sector and Development', background report for Deaton evaluation, http://siteresources.worldbank.org/DEC/Resources/84797-1109362238001/726454-1164121166494/3182920-1164133928090/Jonathan-Morduch.pdf.

Moreno, R. and A. Villar (2005) 'The Increased Role of Foreign Bank Entry in Emerging Markets', BIS Papers, vol.23, no.1, pp.9–16.

Morgan, M., R. Hooper, M. Mayblin and R. Jones (2006) 'Attitudes to Kidney Donation and Registering as a Donor among Ethnic Groups in the UK', *Journal of Public Health*, vol.28, no.3, pp.226–34.

Morrissey, M. (2006) 'Community, Social Capital and Indigenous Health in the Northern Territory', *Ethnicity and Health*, vol.11, no.3, pp.229–46.

Morrissey, O. (2000) 'Introduction: Assessments of *Assessing Aid*', *Journal of International Development*, vol.12, no.3, pp.371–3.

Mosse, D. (2005) *The Aid Effect: Giving and Governing in International Development*, London: Pluto Press.

—— (2006) 'Anti-Social Anthropology? Objectivity, Objection, and the Ethnography of Public Policy and Professional Communities', *Journal of the Royal Anthropological Institute*, vol.12, no.4, pp.935–56.

—— (2008) 'Epilogue: The Cultural Politics of Water – A Comparative Perspective', *Journal of Southern African Studies*, vol.34, no.4, pp.937–46.

Mozumder, P. and A. Marathe (2007) 'Role of Information and Communication Networks in Malaria Survival', *Malaria Journal*, vol.6, no.1, http://www.malariajournal.com/content/pdf/1475-2875-6-136.pdf.

Mulvaney, C. and D. Kendrick (2005) 'Depressive Symptoms in Mothers of Pre-School Children: Effects of Deprivation, Social Support, Stress and Neighbourhood Social Capital', *Child: Care, Health and Development*, vol.31, no.4, p.489.

Mundy, K. (2002) 'Retrospect and Prospect: Education in a Reforming Bank', *International Journal of Educational Development*, vol.22, no.5, pp.483–508.

Muntaner, C. (2004) 'Commentary: Social Capital, Social Class, and the Slow Progress of Psychosocial Epidemiology', *International Journal of Epidemiology*, vol.33, no.4, pp.674–80.

—— and J. Lynch (2002) 'Social Capital, Class Gender and Race Conflict, and Population: An Essay Review of *Bowling Alone*'s Implications for Social Epidemiology', *International Journal of Epidemiology*, vol.31, no.1, pp.261–7.

—— —— and G. Davey Smith (2001) 'Social Capital, Disorganised Communities, and the Third Way: Understanding the Retreat from Structural Inequalities in Epidemiology and Public Health', *International Journal of Health Services*, vol.31, no.2, pp.213–37.

Naarborg, I. and R. Lensink (2008) 'Banking in Transition Economies: Does Foreign Ownership Enhance Profitability?', *European Journal of Finance*, vol.14, no.7, pp.545–62.

Narayan, D. and L. Pritchett (1997) 'Cents and Sociability: Household Income and Social Capital in Rural Tanzania', World Bank Policy Research Working Paper no.1796.

Nathan, J. (2010) 'Poppy Blues: The Collapse of Poppy Eradication and the Road Ahead', *Defence and Security Analysis*, vol.24, no.4, pp.331–53.

National Audit Office (2008) *Department for International Development: Operating in Insecure Environments*, London: The Stationery Office.

Nattrass, N. (2009) 'Poverty, Sex and HIV', *AIDS and Behavior*, vol.3, no.5, pp.833–40.

Navarro, V. (2004) 'Commentary: Is *Capital* the Solution or the Problem?', *International Journal of Epidemiology*, vol.33, no.4, pp.672–4.

—— (2005) 'Social Capital: Response', *International Journal of Epidemiology*, vol.34, no.2, pp.480–1.

—— (ed.) (2007) *Neoliberalism, Globalization, and Inequalities: Consequences for Health and Quality of Life*, Amityville, NY: Baywood.

Newell, P., N. Jenner and L. Baker (2009) 'Governing Clean Development: A Framework for Analysis', *Development Policy Review*, vol.27, no.6, pp.717–39.

Norrag News (1998) 'Knowledge Generation in Higher Education: New Challenges for North–South International Cooperation', *Norrag News*, no.23.

—— (2000) 'Knowledge, Research and International Co-operation', *Norrag News*, no.27.

Nustad, K. and O. Sending (2000) 'The Instrumentalisation of Development Knowledge', in Stone (2000).

Nyqvist, F., F. Finnäs, G. Jakobsson and S. Koskinen (2008) 'The Effect of Social Capital on Health: The Case of Two Language Groups in Finland', *Health and Place*, vol.14, no.2, pp.347–60.

OECD (2001) *Aid to Agriculture*, http://www.oecd.org/dataoecd/40/43/2094403. pdf.

—— (2005) *Economic Survey of China 2005*, Organisation for Economic Co-operation and Development, Paris, September, http://www.oecd.org/docume nt/21/0,2340,en_2649_201185_35331797_1_1_1_1,00.html.

—— (2006) 'Keeping Water Safe to Drink', Policy Brief, March 2006.

Oirere, S. (2009) 'Kenya's Water Sector Reforms under Threat', *Water Utility Management International*, vol.4, no.1, p.5.

Oksanen, T., A. Kouvonen, M. Kivimäk, J. Pentti, M. Virtanen, A. Linna and J. Vahtera (2008) 'Social Capital at Work as a Predictor of Employee Health: Multilevel Evidence from Work Units in Finland', *Social Science and Medicine*, vol.66, no.3, pp.637–49.

Oomman, N., M. Bernstein and S. Rosenzweig (2007) 'Following the Funding for HIV/AIDS: A Comparative Analysis of the Funding Practices of PEPFAR, the Global Fund and World Bank MAP in Mozambique, Uganda and Zambia', report for HIV/AIDS Monitor and Centre for Global Development.

Østerud, Ø. (2008) 'Towards a More Peaceful World? A Critical View', *Conflict, Security and Development*, vol.8, no.2, pp.223–40.

Oya, C. (2007) 'Agricultural Maladjustment in Africa: What Have We Learned After Two Decades of Liberalisation?', *Journal of Contemporary African Studies*, vol.25, no.2, pp.275–97.

—— (2009) 'The World Development Report 2008: Inconsistencies, Silences, and the Myth of "Win–Win" Scenarios', *Journal of Peasant Studies*, vol.36, no.3, pp.593–601.

Pack, H. and K. Saggi (2006) 'Is There a Case for Industrial Policy? A Critical Survey', *World Bank Research Observer*, vol.21, no.2, pp.267–97.

Palacin, J. and R. Shelburne (2005) 'The Private Housing Market in Eastern Europe and the CIS', UNECE Discussion Paper no.2005-5.

Palitza, K. (2009) 'Global Financial Crisis Leads to HIV Budget Cuts', 18 May, Inter Press Service News Agency, http://ipsnews.net/news.asp?idnews=46882.

Panitch, L. and C. Leys (eds) (2009) *Morbid Symptoms: Health under Capitalism*, *Socialist Register 2010*, London: Merlin Press.

—— G. Albo and V. Chibber (eds) (2010) *Socialist Register 2011*, London: Merlin Press.

Paris, R. and T. Sisk (2008) *The Dilemmas of Statebuilding*, London and New York: Routledge.

Parkhurst, J. (2010) 'Understanding the Correlations between Wealth, Poverty and Human Immunodeficiency Virus Infection in African Countries', *Bulletin of the World Health Organization*, vol.88, no.7, pp.519–26.

Patel, R. (2008) 'The World Bank and Agriculture: A Critical Review of the World Bank's WDR 2008', Action Aid discussion paper, October.

Patrinos, H., F. Barrera-Osorio and J. Guáqueta (2009) *The Role and Impact of Public–Private Partnerships in Education*, Washington, DC: World Bank.

Pattussi, M., R. Hardy and A. Sheiham (2006) 'The Potential Impact of Neighborhood Empowerment on Dental Caries among Adolescents', *Community Dentistry and Oral Epidemiology*, vol.34, no.5, pp.344–50.

Peet, R. (2003) *Unholy Trinity: The IMF, the World Bank and the WTO*, London: Zed Books.

Peters, G. (2009) *How Opium Profits the Taliban*, Washington, DC: United States Institute of Peace.

Philipson, T. and R. Posner (1995) 'The Microeconomics of the Aids Epidemic in Africa', Population and Development Review, vol.21, no.4, pp.835–48.

Picciotto, R. (2002) 'Development Cooperation and Performance Evaluation: The Monterrey Challenge', Washington, DC: World Bank.

Pincus, J., (2001) 'The Post-Washington Consensus and Lending Operations in Agriculture: New Rhetoric and Old Operational Realities', in Fine, Lapavitsas and Pincus (2001).

—— and J. Winters (eds) (2002) *Reinventing the World Bank*, London: Cornell University Press.

Ploeg, J. van der (2008) *The New Peasantries: Struggles for Autonomy and Sustainability in an Era of Empire and Globalization*, London: Earthscan.

Prasad, N. (2007) 'Social Policies and Water Sector Reform', Markets, Business and Regulation Programme Paper no.3, United Nations Research Institute for Social Development.

Pugh, M. and N. Cooper, with J. Goodhand (eds) (2004) *War Economies in a Regional Context: Challenges for Transformation*, London: International Peace Academy/Lynne Rienner.

Putnam, R. (1993) *Making Democracy Work: Civic Traditions in Modern Italy*, Princeton: Princeton University Press.

—— (2004) 'Commentary: "Health by Association": Some Comments', *International Journal of Epidemiology*, vol.33, no.4, pp.667–71.

—— (2007) '*E Pluribus Unum*: Diversity and Community in the Twenty-First Century', the 2006 Johan Skytte Prize Lecture', *Scandinavian Political Studies*, vol.30, no.2, pp.137–74.

Putzel, J. (2004) 'The Global Fight Against Aids: How Adequate Are The National Commissions?', *Journal of International Development*, vol.16, no.8, pp.1129–140.

Radford, P. (2009) 'Foreign Policy: Coal for Christmas – The World Bank Is Still Subsidizing One of the World's Dirtiest Fuels', Bank Information Center, http://www.bicusa.org/en/Article.11699.aspx.

Ram, R. (2004) 'Trends in Developing Countries' Commodity Terms-of-Trade since 1970', *Review of Radical Political Economics*, vol.36, no.2, pp.241–53.

Ramachandran, V.K. and M. Swaminathan (eds) (2003) *Agrarian Studies: Essays on Agrarian Relations in Less Developed Countries*, New Delhi: Tulika Books.

Ranis, G. (2003) 'The MDBs and the Nation State', Carnegie Conference Papers, http://www.yale.edu/macmillan/globalization/ranis.pdf.

Rao, V. and M. Woolcock (2007a) 'Disciplinary Monopolies in Development Research: A Response to the Research Evaluation Process', http://siteresources.worldbank.org/INTPOVRES/Resources/DisciplinaryMonopoly.pdf?resourceurl name=DisciplinaryMonopoly.pdf.

—— —— (2007b) 'Disciplinary Monopolies in Development Research', *Global Governance*, vol.13, no.4, pp.479–84.

Rasheed, S. (1994) 'Social Sciences and Policy Making in Africa: A Critical Review', *Africa Development*, vol.19, no.1, pp.91–118.

Razzell, P. and C. Spence (2005) 'Social Capital and the History of Mortality in Britain', *International Journal of Epidemiology*, vol.34, no.2, pp.477–8.

Redman, J. (2008) 'Dirty Is the New Clean: A Critique of the World Bank's Strategic Framework for Development and Climate Change', Institute for Policy Studies, http://www.ips-dc.org/reports/.

Restrepo, J., M. Spagat and J. Vargas (2004) 'The Severity of the Colombian Conflict: Cross-Country Datasets versus New Micro Data', Working Paper Conflict Analysis Resource Centre (CERAC), http://personal.rhul.ac.uk/pkte/126/Documents/Docs/Severity%20of%20Col%20Conflict.pdf.

Richards, P. (ed.) (2004) *No Peace, No War: An Anthropology of Contemporary Armed Conflicts*, Oxford: James Currey.

Rigg, J., A. Bebbington, K. Gough, D. Bryceson, J. Agergaard, N. Fold and C. Tacoli (2009) 'The World Development Report 2009 Reshapes Economic Geography: Geographical Reflections', *Transactions of the Institute of British Geographers*, vol.34, no.2, pp.128–36.

Rizzo, M. (2009) 'The Struggle for Alternatives: NGOs' Responses to the *World Development Report 2008*', *Journal of Agrarian Change*, vol.9, no.2, pp.277–90.

Robinson, W. (2010) 'Global Capitalism Theory and the Emergence of Transnational Elites', WIDER-UNU Working Paper no.2010/02, http://www.wider.unu.edu/publications/working-papers/2010/en_GB/wp2010-02/.

Rodriguez, F. and D. Rodrik (2000) 'Trade Policy and Economic Growth: A Skeptic's Guide to the Cross-National Literature', revised May 2000, Department of Economics, University of Maryland, https://www.hec.unil.ch/docs/files/40/285/trade_policy_and_economic_growth.pdf.

Rodrik, D. (2006) 'The Social Cost of Foreign Exchange Reserves', *International Economic Journal*, vol.20, no.3, pp.253–66.

—— (2007) *One Economics, Many Recipes*, Princeton: Princeton University Press.

Rosenberg, C. and M. Tirpak (2008) 'Determinants of Foreign Currency Borrowing in the New Member States of the EU', IMF Working Paper no.08/173.

Rowden, R. (2008) 'Blocking Progress: The IMF and HIV/AIDS', *Global Social Policy*, vol.8, no.1, pp.19–24.

—— and N. Thapliyal (2007) 'IMF Still Blocking Progress on HIV/AIDS, Health and Education: New Report Outrages Aid Advocates', *Policies and Priorities*, vol.2, no.1, http://www.ifiwatchnet.org/?q=en/node/2731.

Rubin, B. (2000) 'The Political Economy of War and Peace in Afghanistan', *World Development*, vol.28, no.2, pp.1789–803.

—— (2007) 'Saving Afghanistan', *Foreign Affairs*, vol.86, no.1, pp.57–78.

Ryrie, W. (1995) *First World, Third World*, New York: St. Martin's Press.

Saad-Filho, A. and D. Johnston (eds) (2005) *Neoliberalism: A Critical Reader*, London: Pluto Press.

—— and G. Yalman (eds) (2010) *Transitions to Neoliberalism in Middle-Income Countries: Policy Dilemmas, Economic Crises, Mass Resistance*, London: Routledge.

Sachs, J. (2001) *Macroeconomics and Health: Investing in Health for Economic Development*, Geneva: WHO.

—— and W. Woo (1994) 'Structural Factors in the Economic Reforms of China, Eastern Europe, and the former Soviet Union', *Economic Policy*, vol.9, no.18, pp.101–45.

Saghir, J. (2009) 'Water for Development: Tackling Global Water Challenges', presentation at World Bank Water Week 2009, http://info.worldbank.org/etools/BSPAN/PresentationView.asp?PID=2384&EID=1075.

Salmi, J. (2002) *Constructing Knowledge Societies: New Challenges for Tertiary Education*, Washington, DC: World Bank.

Sambanis, N. (2004) 'What Is Civil War? Conceptual and Empirical Complexities of an Operational Definition', *Journal of Conflict Resolution*, vol.48, no.6, pp.814–58.

Samoff, J. (1992) 'The Intellectual/Financial Complex of Foreign Aid', *Review of African Political Economy*, vol.19, no.53, pp.60–87.

—— and C. Bidemi (2003) 'From Manpower Planning to the Knowledge Era: World Bank Policies on Higher Education in Africa', paper prepared for the UNESCO Forum on Higher Education, Research and Knowledge, 15 July, http://aafaq.kfupm.edu.sa/features/Carrol.pdf.

—— and N. Stromquist (2001) 'Managing Knowledge and Storing Wisdom? New Forms of Foreign Aid?', *Development and Change*, vol.32, no.4, pp.631–56.

Santos, P. dos (2008), 'The World Bank, the IFC and the Antecedents of the Financial Crisis', Bretton Woods Update no. 63.

—— (2009), 'On the Content of Banking in Contemporary Capitalism', *Historical Materialism*, vol.17, no.2, pp.180–213.

Scherrer, C. (2005) 'GATS: Long-Term Strategy for the Commodification of Education', *Review of International Political Economy*, vol.12, no.3, pp.484–510.

Scoones, I. (2009) 'Livelihoods Perspectives and Rural Development', *Journal of Peasant Studies*, vol.36, no.1, pp.171–96.

Scott, D. (2009) 'Banks in Crisis: When Governments Take Temporary Ownership', Crisis Response, Public Policy for the Private Sector, Note no.9, World Bank and IFC.

Sender, J. and D. Johnston (2004) 'Searching for a Weapon of Mass Production in Rural Africa: Unconvincing Arguments for Land Reform', *Journal of Agrarian Change*, vol.4, nos 1–2, pp.142–64.

Shaw, M. (2006) 'Drug Trafficking and the Development of Organized Crime in Post-Taliban Afghanistan', in Buddenberg and Byrd (2006).

Shirley, M. (ed.) (2002) *Thirsting for Efficiency: The Economics and Politics of Urban Water System Reform*, London: Elsevier Publications.

Sierra, K. (2009) 'The Economic Crisis and the Water Sector: Rising to the Challenge', Keynote Address, 5th World Water Forum, Istanbul, 2009, http://siteresources.worldbank.org/INTWAT/Resources/03132009-RM-Fifth_World_Water_Forum-KS-TPs.pdf.

Sindzingre, A. (2004) '"Truth", "Efficiency" and Multilateral Institutions: A Political Economy of Development Economics', *New Political Economy*, vol.9, no.2, pp.233–49.

Singh, A. (1992) 'The Actual Crisis of Economic Development in the 1980s: An Alternative Policy Perspective for the Future', in Dutt and Jameson (1992).

Smith, G. and J. Lynch (2004) 'Commentary: Social Capital, Social Epidemiology and Disease Aetiology', *International Journal of Epidemiology*, vol.33, no.4, pp.691–700.

Smyth, R. (1998) 'Township and Village Enterprises in China: Growth Mechanism and Future Prospects', *Journal of International Economic Studies*, no.12, pp.101–17.

Squire, L. (2000) 'Why the World Bank Should Be Involved in Development Research', in Gilbert and Vines (2000).

Standing, G. (2000) 'Brave New Words? A Critique of Stiglitz's World Bank Rethink', *Development and Change*, vol.31, no.4, pp.737–63.

Steinfeld, E.S. (2000) *Forging Reform in China: The Fate of State-Owned Industry*, Cambridge: Cambridge University Press.

Stephens, C. (2008) 'Social Capital in Its Place: Using Social Theory to Understand Social Capital and Inequalities in Health', *Social Science and Medicine*, vol.66, no.5, pp.1174–84.

Stern, N. and F. Ferreira (1997) 'The World Bank as "Intellectual Actor"', in Kapur, Lewis and Webb (eds) (1997).

Stewart, F. (ed.) (2008) *Horizontal Inequalities and Conflict: Understanding Group Violence in Multiethnic Societies*, London: Palgrave Macmillan.

Stewart, R. (2009) 'The Irresistible Illusion', *London Review of Books*, 9 July, http://www.lrb.co.uk/v31/n13/stew01_.html.

Stiglitz, J. (1974) 'Incentives and Risk Sharing in Sharecropping', *Review of Economic Studies*, vol.41, no.2, pp.219–55.

—— (1998a) 'More Instruments and Broader Goals: Moving toward the Post-Washington Consensus', WIDER Annual Lecture, Helsinki, 7 January, reprinted in Chang (2001).

—— (1998b) 'Towards a New Paradigm for Development Strategies, Policies and Process', 1998 Prebish Lecture at UNCTAD, Geneva, 19 October, reprinted in Chang (2001).

—— (1999a) 'Knowledge as a Global Public Good', in Kaul, Grunberg and Stern (1999).

—— (1999b) 'Whither Reform? Ten Years of the Transition', paper presented at the Annual Bank Conference on Development Economics, Washington, DC: World Bank.

—— (1999c) 'The World Bank at the Millennium', *Economic Journal*, vol.109, no.459, pp.577–97.

—— (2008) 'Turn Left for Sustainable Growth', *Economists' Voice*, September, pp.1–3.

Stillwaggon, E. (2006) 'Reducing Environmental Risk to Prevent HIV Transmission in Sub-Saharan Africa', *Africa Policy Journal*, vol.1, pp.1–21, http://www.hksafricapolicyjournal.com/sites/default/files/Stillwaggon.pdf.

Stone, D. (ed.) (2000) *Banking on Knowledge: The Genesis of the Global Development Network*, London: Routledge.

—— (2003) 'The "Knowledge Bank" and the Global Development Network', *Global Governance*, vol.9, no.1, pp.43–61.

—— (2007) '"Going Over to the Dark Side?": Responsible Scholarship, Intellectual Capture and the World Bank', University of Warwick, mimeo.

—— and C. Wright (eds) (2007) *The World Bank and Governance: A Decade of Reform and Reaction*, London: Routledge.

Stuckler, D., L. King and M. McKee (2009) 'Mass Privatisation and the Post-Communist Mortality Crisis: A Cross-National Analysis', *The Lancet*, vol.373, no.9661, pp.399–407.

Subasat, T. (2003) 'Does the Dollar Index Really Measure Outward Orientation?', *International Review of Applied Economics*, vol.17, no.3, pp.309–26.

Suhrke, A. and I. Samset (2007) 'What's in a Figure? Estimating Recurrence of Civil War', *International Peacekeeping*, vol.14, no.2, pp.195–203.

—— T. Chaudary, K. Harpikven, A. Sarwari and A. Strand (2008) 'Applied Social Science Research in Afghanistan: An Overview of the Institutional Landscape', Bergen: Christian Michelson Institute.

Sundquist, J., S. Johansson and M. Yang (2006) 'Low Linking Social Capital as a Predictor of Coronary Heart Disease in Sweden: A Cohort Study of 2.8 Million People', *Social Science and Medicine*, vol.62, no.4, pp.954–63.

Sundquist, K. (2004) 'Social Participation and Coronary Heart Disease: A Follow-up Study of 6900 Women and Men in Sweden', *Social Science and Medicine*, vol.58, no.3, pp.615–22.

—— and M. Yang (2007) 'Linking Social Capital and Self-Rated Health: A Multilevel Analysis of 11,175 Men and Women in Sweden', *Health and Place*, vol.13, no.2, pp.324–34.

Szreter, S. (1997) 'Economic Growth, Disruption, Deprivation, Diseases and Death: On the Importance of the Politics of Public Health for Development', *Population and Development Review*, vol.23, no.4, pp.693–728.

—— (2002a) 'Health, Class, Place and Politics: Social Capital and Collective Provision in Britain', *Contemporary British History*, vol.16, no.3, pp.27–57.

—— (2002b) 'The State of Social Capital: Bringing Back in Power, Politics and History', *Theory and Society*, vol.31, no.5, pp.573–621.

—— (2004) 'Author's Response: Debating Mortality Trends in 19th Century Britain', *International Journal of Epidemiology*, vol.33, no.4, pp.707–8.

—— (2005) 'Response', *International Journal of Epidemiology*, vol.34, no.2, pp.479–80.

—— and G. Mooney (1998) 'Urbanization, Mortality, and the Standard of Living Debate: New Estimates of the Expectation of Life at Birth in Nineteenth-Century British Cities', *Economic History Review*, vol.51, no.1, pp.84–112.

—— and M. Woolcock (2004a) 'Health by Association? Social Capital, Social Theory, and the Political Economy of Public Health', *International Journal of Epidemiology*, vol.33, no.4, pp.650–67.

—— —— (2004b) 'Rejoinder: Crafting Rigorous and Relevant Social Theory for Public Health Policy', *International Journal of Epidemiology*, vol.33, no.4, pp.700–4.

Tan, C. (2007) 'The Poverty of Amnesia: PRSPs in the Legacy of Structural Adjustment', in Stone and Wright (2007).

Tarp, F. (2001) 'Aid and Reform in Africa' (review of World Bank volume by S. Devarajan, D.R. Dollar and T. Holmgren), *Journal of African Economies*, vol.10, no.3, pp.341–53.

Taylor, A., C. Williams, E. Dal Grande and M. Herriot (2006) 'Measuring Social Capital in a Known Disadvantaged Urban Community: Health Policy

Implications', *Australia and New Zealand Health Policy*, BioMedCentral, http://www.anzhealthpolicy.com/content/pdf/1743-8462-3-2.pdf.

Terrel, H. (1986) 'The Role of Foreign Banks in Domestic Banking Markets', in Cheng (1986).

Tickner, V. (2008) 'Africa: International Food Price Rises and Volatility', *Review of African Political Economy*, vol.35, no.117, pp.508–14.

Timmer, P. (2009) *A World without Agriculture: The Structural Transformation in Historical Perspective*, Washington, DC: AEI Press.

Torres, R.-M. (2001) '"Knowledge-Based International Aid": Do We Want It, Do We Need It?', in Gmelin, King and McGrath (2001).

Toye, John, (2009) 'Development with Dearer Food: Can the Invisible Hand Guide Us?', *Journal of International Development*, vol.21, no.6, pp.757–64.

Tversky, A. and D. Kahneman (1974) 'Judgement under Uncertainty: Heuristics and Biases', *Science*, vol.185, no.4157, pp.1124–31.

Udry, C. (2006)) 'Evaluation of World Bank Research Projects: Agriculture and Rural Development', background report for Deaton evaluation, http://siteresources.worldbank.org/DEC/Resources/84797-1109362238001/726454-1164121166494/3182920-1164133928090/Christopher-Udry.pdf.

UNAIDS (1999) 'Factsheet on Differences in HIV Spread in African Cities', UNAIDS, http://data.unaids.org/Publications/IRC-pub03/lusaka99_en.html.

—— UNFPA and UNIFEM (2004) *Women and HIV/AIDS: Confronting the Crisis*, Geneva and New York: UNAIDS, UNIFEM, UNFPA.

UNCTAD (2009) *The Global Economic Crisis: Systemic Failures and Multilateral Remedies*, Geneva: UNCTAD.

UNDP (2002) *Capacity for Development: New Solutions for Old Problems*, New York: UNDP.

Unite, A. and M. Sullivan (2003) 'The Effect of Foreign Entry and Ownership Structure on the Philippine Domestic Banking Market', *Journal of Banking and Finance*, vol.27, no.12, pp.2323–45.

Utting, P., S. Razavi and R. Buchholz (eds) (2011) *Global Crisis and Transformative Social Change*, London: Routledge, in press.

UN (2003) 'The Impact of AIDS', working paper no. ESA/P/WP.185, Department for Economic and Social Affairs, Population Division, United Nations, New York.

—— (2009a) 'Report of the Commission of Experts of the President of the United Nations General Assembly on Reforms of the International Monetary and Financial System', 21 September, New York.

—— (2009b) 'The Millennium Development Goals Report 2009', New York: United Nations.

UNODC (2008) 'Afghanistan Opium Survey 2008', New York: United Nations Office on Drugs and Crime.

Uzzi, B. (1999) 'Embeddedness in the Making of Financial Capital: How Social Relations and Networks Benefit Firms Seeking Financing', *American Sociological Review*, vol.64, no.4, pp.481–505.

Vaa, M. (2003) 'Urban Research Agendas, Modes of Financing Research and Considerations of Quality', *Forum of Development Studies*, vol.30, no.1, pp.108–19.

—— (2010) 'The Food Crisis, Industrialized Farming and the Imperial Regime', *Journal of Agrarian Change*, vol.10, no.1, pp.98–106.

Van Waeyenberge, E. (2007) *Exploring the Emergence of a New Aid Regime: Selectivity, Knowledge and the World Bank*, Ph.D. thesis, University of London.

—— (2009) 'Selectivity at Work: Country Policy and Institutional Assessments at the World Bank', *European Journal of Development Research*, vol.21, no.5, pp.792–810.

—— H. Bargawi and T. McKinley (2010) 'Standing in the Way of Development: A Critical Survey of the IMF's Crisis Response in Low Income Countries', a Eurodad and Third World Network Report, April.

Veenstra, G., I. Luginaah, S. Wakefield, S. Birch, J. Eyles and S. Elliott (2005) 'Who You Know, Where You Live: Social Capital, Neighbourhood and Health', *Social Science and Medicine*, vol.60, no.12, pp.2799–818.

Vittas, D. (1991) 'Measuring Commercial Bank Efficiency, Use and Misuse of Bank Operating Ratios', World Bank Policy Research Working Paper no.806.

Vos, P. (2005) '"No One Left Abandoned": Cuba's National Health System since the 1959 Revolution', *International Journal of Health Services*, vol.35, no.1, pp.189–207.

Wade, R. (1996) 'Japan, the World Bank, and the Art of Paradigm Maintenance: The East Asian Miracle in Political Perspective', *New Left Review I*, no.217, pp.3–37.

—— (2002) 'US Hegemony and the World Bank: The Fight over People and Ideas', *Review of International Political Economy*, vol.9, no.2, pp.215–43.

—— (2006) 'The IMF and the World Bank under Stress: Renewal or Swansong?', *Review of International Organizations*, vol.1, no.4, pp.397–400.

Wakefield, S. and B. Poland (2005) 'Family, Friend or Foe? Critical Reflections on the Relevance and Role of Social Capital in Health Promotion and Community Development', *Social Science and Medicine*, vol.60, no.12, pp.2819–32.

Walkup, M. (1997) 'Policy Dysfunction in Humanitarian Organizations: The Role of Coping Strategies, Institutions and Organizational Culture', *Journal of Refugee Sudies*, vol.10, no.1, pp.37–60.

Walque, D. de (2007) 'Sero-Discordant Couples in Five African Countries: Implications for Prevention Strategies', *Population and Development Review*, vol.33, no.3, pp.501–23.

Walters, W. (2002) 'Social Capital and Political Sociology: Re-imagining Politics?', *Sociology*, vol.36, no.2, pp.377–97.

Ward, C., D. Mansfield, P. Oldham and W. Byrd (2008) 'Afghanistan Incentives and Development Initiatives to Reduce Opium Production', World Bank/DfID.

Weinstein, J. (2006) *Inside Rebellion: The Politics of Insurgent Violence*, Cambridge: Cambridge University Press.

Weis, T. (2007) *The Global Food Economy: The Battle for the Future of Farming*, London: Zed Books.

Weisbrot, M., D. Baker, R. Naiman and G. Neta (2000) 'Growth May Be Good for the Poor: But Are IMF and World Bank Policies Good for Growth?', Centre for Economic and Policy Research, briefing paper draft, Washington, DC.

Weitzman, M. (1993) 'Economic Transition: Can Theory Help?', *European Economic Review*, vol.37. nos 2–3, pp.549–55.

Wellings, K., M. Collumbien, E. Slaymaker, S. Singh, Z. Hodges, D. Patel and N. Bajos (2006) 'Sexual Behaviour in Context: A Global Perspective', *The Lancet*, vol.268, no.9558, pp.1706–28.

Williamson, J. (1990) 'What Washington Means by Policy Reform', in Williamson (1990).

—— (ed.) (1990) *Latin American Adjustment: How Much Has Happened?* Washington, DC: Institute for International Economics.

Wojcicki, J. (2005) 'Socioeconomic Status as a Risk Factor for HIV Infection in Women in East, Central and Southern Africa: A Systematic Review', *Journal of Biosocial Science*, vol.37, no.1, pp.1–36.

Wolfensohn, J. (1996a) 'People and Development', address to the Board of Governors at the Annual Meetings of the World Bank and the IMF, October, Washington, DC.

—— (1996b) 'The World Bank as a Global Information Clearinghouse', Annual World Bank Conference on Development Economics, Washington, DC: World Bank.

—— (1999) 'A Proposal for a Comprehensive Development Framework', discussion draft, Washington, DC: World Bank.

Wood, E. (2003) *Insurgent Collective Action and Civil War in El Salvador*, Cambridge: Cambridge University Press.

Wood, L., B. Giles-Corti and M. Bulsara (2005) 'The Pet Connection: Pets as a Conduit for Social Capital', *Social Science and Medicine*, vol.61, no.6, pp.1159–73.

—— —— —— and D. Bosch (2007) 'More than a Furry Companion: The Ripple Effect of Companion Animals on Neighborhood Interactions and Sense of Community', *Society and Animals*, vol.15, no.1, pp.43–56.

Woodhouse, P. (2009) 'Technology, Environment and the Productivity Problem in African Agriculture: Comment on the World Development Report 2008', *Journal of Agrarian Change*, vol.9, no.2, pp.263–76.

Woolcock, M. (1998) 'Social Capital and Economic Development: Toward a Theoretical Synthesis and Policy Framework', *Theory and Society*, vol.27, no.2, pp.151–208.

—— S. Szreter and V. Rao (2009) 'How and Why Does History Matter for Development Policy?', Brooks World Poverty Institute at the University of Manchester, BWPI Working Paper no.68.

World Bank (1981) 'Accelerated Development in Africa: An Agenda for Action', Washington, DC: World Bank.

—— (1982) 'World Development Report 1982: International Development Trends, Agriculture and Economic Development', Washington, DC: World Bank.

—— (1988) 'Philippines: Financial Sector Study', report no.7177-PH, Washington, DC: World Bank.

—— (1994) 'Adjustment in Africa: Reforms, Results and the Road Ahead', Washington, DC: World Bank.

—— (1996) 'World Development Report 1996: From Plan to Market', Oxford University Press, New York.

—— (1997a) 'Adjustment Lending in Sub-Saharan Africa', Operations Evaluation Department Update Report 16594, Washington, DC.

—— (1997b) 'Confronting AIDS: Public Priorities in a Global Epidemic', Washington, DC: World Bank.

—— (1997c) 'Annual Report 1997', Washington, DC: World Bank.

—— (1998a) 'Assessing Aid: What Works, What Doesn't and Why', New York: Oxford University Press for the World Bank.

—— (1998b) 'World Development Report 1998/9: Knowledge for Development', Oxford University Press for the World Bank, New York.

—— (2001a) 'World Development Report 2000/1: Attacking Poverty', Oxford University Press for the World Bank, New York.

—— (2001b) 'Aid and Reform in Africa', Washington, DC: World Bank.

—— (2002a) 'A Case for Aid: Building a Consensus for Development Assistance', Washington, DC: World Bank.

—— (2002b) 'Transition – The First Ten Years: Analysis and Lessons for Eastern Europe and the Former Soviet Union', Washington, DC: World Bank.

—— (2002c) 'Private Sector Development Strategy: Directions for the World Bank Group', April 9, Washington, DC: World Bank.

—— (2003a) 'Reaching the Rural Poor: A Renewed Strategy for Rural Development', Washington, DC: World Bank.

—— (2003b) 'Sharing Knowledge: Innovations and Remaining Challenges', Operations Evaluation Department, October 8, Washington, DC.

—— (2003c) 'Strategy Update Paper for FY04–06: Implementing the World Bank's Strategic Framework', 7 March, Washington, DC.

—— (2003d) 'Breaking the Conflict Trap', Washington, DC: World Bank.

—— (2004a) '2003 Annual Review of Development Effectiveness: The Effectiveness of Bank Support for Policy Reform', Washington, DC: World Bank.

—— (2004b) 'Annual Report on Portfolio Performance: Fiscal Year 2003', Quality Assurance Group, Washington, DC.

—— (2004c) 'World Development Report 2004: Making Services Work for Poor People', Oxford University Press, Oxford.

—— (2005a) 'Agricultural Growth for the Poor: An Agenda for Development', Washington, DC: World Bank.

—— (2005b) '2004 Annual Review of Development Effectiveness: The Bank's Contributions to Poverty Reduction', Washington, DC: World Bank.

—— (2006) 'Implementation Completion Report (IF-N0170 PPFI-Q0170 IDA-35660) on an Interim Fund Credit Report No: 36083-GUIz', http://www-wds.worldbank.org/external/default/WDSContentServer/WDSP/IB/2006/07/26/000090341_20060726092636/Rendered/INDEX/36083.txt.

—— (2007a) 'World Development Report 2008: Agriculture for Development', Washington, DC: World Bank.

—— (2007b) 'Investment in Agricultural Water for Poverty Reduction and Economic Growth in Sub-Saharan Africa: A Synthesis Report', Washington, DC: World Bank.

—— (2007c) 'Meeting the Challenges of Global Development: A Long Term Strategic Exercise for the World Bank Group', Washington, DC: World Bank.

—— (2008a) 'Food Price Crisis in Africa', *World Bank Research Digest*, vol.3, no.1, pp.1, 8.

—— (2008b) 'Global Development Finance: The Role of International Banking', Washington, DC: World Bank.

—— (2008c) 'Implementation Completion and Results Report (IDA-34760 IDA-3476A) on a Credit in the Amount of SDR 55 Million to Burkina Faso for the Ouagadougou Water Supply Project Report No: ICR0000705', http://www-wds.worldbank.org/external/default/WDSContentServer/WDSP/IB/2008/11/11/000333037_20081111224358/Rendered/PDF/ICR7050ICR0P0003060Box334091B01PUBLIC1.pdf.

—— (2008d) 'Lessons from World Bank Research on Financial Crises', World Bank Policy Research Working Paper no.4779.

—— (2009a) 'Implementing Agriculture for Development: World Bank Group Agriculture Action Plan, FY2010–2012', http://siteresources.worldbank.org/INTARD/Resources/Agriculture_Action_Plan_web.pdf.

—— (2009b) 'Report on the World Bank Research Program for Fiscal Years 2006, 2007 and 2008 and Future Directions', Washington, DC: World Bank.

—— (2009c) '2009 Annual Report', Washington, DC: World Bank.

—— (2009d) 'Abolishing School Fees in Africa: Lessons from Ethiopia, Ghana, Kenya, Malawi, and Mozambique', with UNICEF, Washington, DC: World Bank.

—— (2009e) 'Averting a Human Crisis During the Global Downturn: Policy Options from the World Bank's Human Development Network', Washington, DC: World Bank.

—— (2009f) 'World Development Report 2010: Development and Climate Change', Oxford University Press, Oxford.

—— (2009g) 'Global Development Finance: Charting a Global Recovery', IBRD, Washington, DC.

—— (2010a) 'New World, New World Bank Group: (I) Post-Crisis Directions', February, http://siteresources.worldbank.org/DEVCOMMINT/ Documentation/22553954/DC2010-0003(E)PostCrisis.pdf.

—— (2010b) 'Global Economic Prospects: Crisis, Finance and Growth', IBRD, Washington, DC.

—— (2010c) 'Transforming the Bank's Knowledge Agenda: A Framework for Action', Knowledge Strategy Group, Washington, DC.

—— (2010d) 'New World, New World Bank Group: (II) Internal Reform Agenda', February, http://siteresources.worldbank.org/DEVCOMMINT/Documentation/ 22553917/DC2010-0004(4)InternalReform.pdf.

World Bank Institute (2009) 'Annual Review 2008: Learning for Development', http://siteresources.worldbank.org/WBI/Resources/WBIAR08-fullsmallersize.pdf.

WSP (2006) 'Getting Africa on Track to Meet the MDGs on Water and Sanitation: A Status Overview of Sixteen African Countries', report prepared by Water and Sanitation Programme, Nairobi.

Yamaoka, K. (2008) 'Social Capital and Health and Well-Being in East Asia: A Population-Based Study', *Social Science and Medicine*, vol.66, no.4, pp.885–99.

Yusuf, S. (ed.) (2009) *Development Economics through the Decades: A Critical Look at 30 Years of the World Development Report*, Washington, DC: World Bank.

Zoellick, R. (2008) 'Modernizing Multilateralism and Markets', 6 October, Washington, DC, http://web.worldbank.org/WBSITE/EXTERNAL/NEWS/0,,c ontentMDK:21927552~pagePK:34370~piPK:42770~theSitePK:4607,00.html.

—— (2009) 'The World Bank Group Beyond the Crisis', 6 October, Istanbul, Turkey, http://web.worldbank.org/WBSITE/EXTERNAL/NEWS/0,,contentMDK:22340 541~pagePK:34370~piPK:34424~theSitePK:4607,00.html.

Index

Compiled by Sue Carlton

Mehta, L. 31–2
Menard, C. 76
Merhy, E. 268
Mexico, and foreign banks 200, 204
Millennium Development Goals
(MDGs) 12, 43, 91, 92, 101, 136,
139
Miller, D. 114–15
Mishra, V. 137–8
Mitchell, D. 178, 181
Mkandawire, T. 66
Morduch, J. 76
Mosse, D. 88–9, 235
Multi-Country AIDS Programme
(MAP) 141
Multilateral Investment Guarantee
Agency (MIGA) 10
Multisector HIV/AIDS Project (Ghana)
140
Muntaner, C. 113

National Riflemen's Association 111
Nattrass, N. 134, 137
neo-liberalism 1, 6, 7–9, 32, 267, 269,
272, 280, 281
and agriculture 20, 148, 149, 150,
153
and aid allocation 52, 60, 62, 70
and China 241, 244, 252, 254,
255–6
and health sector 140–1
and social capital 18, 119
and water sector 18, 83, 89, 91, 94,
97
new development economics 1, 3,
147–8, 160, 264
New Institutional (Development)
Economics (NIE) 148, 152, 160,
276
New Labour 119
new structural economics 278–80
Newly Industrialised Countries (NICs)
48, 248–9, 265, 277
NGOs (non-governmental
organisations) 38, 225, 260
and agriculture 148, 153, 162, 165,
168, 172, 175
and HIV/AIDS projects 130, 141
and violent conflict research 225,
226

NORAD (Norwegian aid agency) 217

OECD (Organisation for Economic
Cooperation and Development)
169, 177, 243
Official Development Assistance
(ODA) 53, 91
Olson, M. 218
opium industry 228–35
functions of policy narratives 234–5
impact of counter-narcotics (CN)
228, 231, 233–4
link with insurgency 228, 230, 231–2
link with poverty 228, 230–1,
232–3
policy and research 47, 234
resilience of policy narratives 234
ownership 56, 60, 65, 66
and agriculture 151, 167
of banks 190, 210
China 242, 251–2
and water sector 78, 81, 87
Oya, C. 166

Pain, A. 233
Pennington, M. 119
Peters, G. 230
Philippines, and foreign banks 193, 199
Philipson, T. 130
Pincus, J. 175
Poland, and foreign bank entry 200,
201
Policy Research Working Papers
(PRWP) 29, 158
Popov, A. 82, 86
Posner, R. 130
post-Washington Consensus (PWC)
1–2, 3, 7, 11, 14, 43, 109, 280
and agriculture 53, 148, 150, 162,
174
and aid allocation 47, 59, 62, 68
and social capital 18
state and market 265
and water privatisation 76
see also World Bank, shift from
Washington Consensus to PWC
poverty reduction 4, 5, 6, 11, 40, 54,
56, 60, 62–3
agriculture and 146, 152, 154, 158,
165, 166, 168